Meaning in Context

Meaning in Context

Strategies for Implementing Intelligent Applications
of Language Studies

Edited by Jonathan J. Webster

continuum

Continuum
The Tower Building
11 York Road
London SE1 7NX

80 Maiden Lane, Suite 704
New York
NY 10038

British Library Cataloguing-in-Publication Data
A catalogue record for this book is available from the British Library.

ISBN: 978–08264–9735–2 (hardback)

Library of Congress Cataloging-in-Publication Data
A catalog record for this book is available from the Library of Congress.

Typeset by Fakenham Photosetting Limited, Fakenham, Norfolk
Printed and bound in Great Britain by Biddles, Norfolk

Contents

Introduction: The Centre in Context

Jonathan J. Webster
City University of Hong Kong

Officially launched in March 2006, The Halliday Centre for Intelligent Applications of Language Studies (HCLS) bears the name of the world-renowned linguist, Professor M. A. K. Halliday. The Halliday Centre, located at City University of Hong Kong (CityU), has the distinct honour of being named after this distinguished scholar, who for over half a century has been enriching the discipline of linguistics with his keen insight into this social semiotic phenomenon we call language. His scholarship has advanced our understanding of language as an activity which is rational and relational, systemic and semantic, dynamic and diverse.

In his opening address, given on the occasion of the Centre's launch, and entitled 'Working with Meaning: Towards an Appliable Linguistics', Professor Halliday notes the Centre's full name highlights 'Intelligent Applications of Language Studies'. An 'intelligent' application, he argues, is one which rests on 'a theoretical understanding of the nature, the functions and the space–time organization of human language'. In line with Professor Halliday's theoretical approach, the Centre's research strategy is defined by a focus on the theoretical and computational modelling of meaning, and its commitment to the application of this linguistic insight in such areas as education, computer science and policy-making. Meaning and its theoretical and computational modelling is crucial for developing intelligent applications of language studies, since without meaning there is no intelligence.

The Centre aims to expand opportunities for collaboration with global partners in China, Australia, Europe, Japan and North America, concentrating on research related to corpus linguistics, computational linguistics, and comparative language studies. In March 2006, a number of internationally renowned scholars were invited to attend the official launch of The Halliday Centre, and participate in a Symposium on 'Meaning in Context: Implementing Intelligent Applications of Language Studies' at City University of Hong Kong. The list of participating scholars reads like a who's who of systemic functional linguistics, coming from Germany, Australia, Canada, and, of course, China. The purpose of the symposium was to provide a meaningful context for these scholars, to engage in discussion on potential areas for collaborative research in the development of intelligent applications of language studies.

Those speaking at the symposium whose papers appear in this volume include:

- **Prof. John Bateman *(University of Bremen, Germany)***
John Bateman's paper on 'Systemic Functional Linguistics and the Notion of Linguistic Structure: Unanswered Questions, New Possibilities' argues for greater attention to be given to the syntagmatic axis of linguistic description, which he feels has been neglected in most systemic functional accounts in favour of the paradigmatic axis. Instead, as Bateman notes, if automatic SFL analysis of texts is to succeed, then greater attention must be given to balancing efforts at dealing with both the syntagmatic and paradigmatic axes.

- **Dr. David Butt *(Macquarie University, Australia)***
In his discussion of 'The Robustness of Realizational Systems', David Butt illustrates the application of realizational systems in investigations of institutional problems with reference to research presently being carried out at the Centre for Language in Social Life at Macquarie University in the domains of health, finance and media.

- **Prof. Fang Yan *(Tsinghua University, China)***
In 'A Study of Topical Theme in Chinese', Fang Yan adopts a systemic functional approach in her analysis of clause structure in Chinese, focusing on Theme–Rheme structure, and, in particular, on the various features of Topical Theme. Noting the different views held by linguists on such basic grammatical concepts as Subject, Theme and Topic in the Chinese language, Fang stresses the need for a large corpus to facilitate the systematic study of Chinese.

- **Prof. Hu Zhuanglin *(Peking University, China)***
Hu Zhuanglin and Dong Jia, co-authors of 'How is Meaning Construed Multimodally? A Case Study of a PowerPoint Presentation Contest', discuss the findings from their study of PowerPoint presentations, which they regard as a genre whose instances are multimodal texts which draw on various semiotic resources to make meaning.

- **Prof. Huang Guowen *(Sun Yat-sen University, China)***
Employing register analysis in their study of examples of Chinese–English code-switching found in Chinese newspapers, Huang Guowen and Wang Jin, in 'A Systemic Functional Approach to Code-switching Studies: Some Chinese–English Examples', report on patterns occurring in their code-switching data. As they note, unless attention is paid to functional variation across different situation types, described in terms of field, tenor and mode, such patterns of occurrence will be likely to go undetected.

- *Prof. Christian Matthiessen (Macquarie University, Australia)*
  In their paper 'Multilingual Studies as a Multi-dimensional Space of Interconnected Language Studies', Christian Matthiessen and co-authors, Kazuhiro Teruya and Wu Cangzhong, explore the notion of a unified field of multilingual studies, grounded in systemic functional theory, whose coverage extends to such areas as language description, language typology, translation and interpreting, translator education, foreign/ second language teaching, multilingual lexicography and multilingualism/ bilingualism.

- *Prof. Jon Patrick (University of Sydney, Australia)*
  Jon Patrick's paper on 'The Scamseek Project – Using Systemic Functional Grammar for Text Categorization' illustrates the contribution of Systemic Functional Grammar in developing 'an industrially viable system' for detecting scam texts on the internet. In particular, SFG was used to model the semantics of scam classes.

- *Prof. Erich Steiner (Saarland University, Germany)*
  In his paper 'Explicitation: Towards an Empirical and Corpus-based Methodology', Erich Steiner suggests how the relationship of 'explicitation' between a translation and the original text might be operationalized in more empirical terms which may then serve as the basis for an annotation scheme for a corpus of translated texts between English and German.

- *Prof. Edwin Thumboo (National University of Singapore)*
  Drawing on his own experience as a poet, Edwin Thumboo, in 'Creativity in English Globalized: Signifiers and Their Signifieds', relates some of the cross-cultural challenges he faced when creating his poem, 'Uncle Never Knew'. Thumboo describes poetry as the 'signified' at its richest: 'where the denotative, the arithmetic of meaning, the simplest, the plainest of the signified, becomes the connotative, a calculus, and therefore the most complex of the signified'.

- *Prof. Zhu Yongsheng (Fudan University, China)*
  To better understand grammatical metaphor, Zhu Yongsheng proposes looking at it from the epistemic, systemic and lexicogrammatic perspectives. In his paper on 'Nominalization, Verbalization and Grammatical Metaphor', Zhu argues against taking nominalization as the primary means of grammatical metaphor, urging greater attention be given to the metaphoric role of verbalization.

Also on hand for the launch and participating in the symposium were:

- Prof. Ruqaiya Hasan (Macquarie University, Australia)
- Prof. Braj Kachru (University of Illinois, Urbana-Champaign, USA)

– Prof. Michio Sugeno (Doshisha University, Japan)
– Prof. Geoff Williams (University of British Columbia, Canada).

Among the funded research projects presently being undertaken by researchers connected with The Halliday Centre for Intelligent Applications of Language Studies are the following:

1. Modelling Meaning in the E-learning Context
   Principal Investigator:
   Jonathan J. Webster (City University of Hong Kong)
   Co-Investigators:
   David Butt (Macquarie University), Annabelle Lukin (Macquarie University), Christian Matthiessen (Macquarie University), Alison Moore (Macquarie University), Eva Wong (City University of Hong Kong), Douglas Vogel (City University of Hong Kong)
   Summary:
   The first step of the project is to produce an account of the interacting systems which occur in a Blackboard-mediated environment with the goal of (1) making the systems more explicit, and therefore more accessible to evaluation in terms of learning outcomes, as well as (2) improving our knowledge of how changes in the tenor of discourse (i.e., organizational structure and interpersonal relations), and mode of discourse (including technological factors such as the use of mobile technology) impact on the successful achievement of intended learning outcomes. In line with efforts for achieving outcome-based teaching and learning through constructive alignment, our methods of inquiry focus on meaning and meaning-bearing behaviour (i.e., performance), not just the acquisition of declarative knowledge/information; on relations of mutual determination, not simply causation within a system. Researchers aim to develop realizational models of context-based communication, in which human participation in complex systems (whether institutional or technological) is represented as 'meaning' transactions. In terms of practical outcomes, as the systems of inter-action and exchange in the e-learning context are made more explicit, they become more accessible to evaluation in terms of success in achieving learning outcomes. The insight gained from our analysis and description of the e-learning system will contribute to efforts aimed at achieving a qualitative assessment of both usability and performance.

2. Multi-document Automatic Summarization for Chinese-language Web-based Texts
   Principal Investigator:
   Jonathan J. Webster (City University of Hong Kong)
   Co-Investigators:
   Chunyu Kit (City University of Hong Kong)

Summary:

Information overload is becoming a serious problem as the Web continues to expand rapidly. Automatic text summarization is one of the most effective approaches to deal with the problem of information overload. It is proposed to carry out research into multi-document summarization. The following key issues will be tackled in the project: (1) a graph representation for a given multi-document set beyond the text structure tree commonly used for single-document summarization, to allow information fusion and other operations for summary generation; (2) theme identification, to transfer the multi-document set to an events flow, in which each event is considered a sub-theme of the multi-document set; (3) key information extraction, to select a certain amount of critical text information for generating a summary according to some given parameters such as summary length or compression rate, and (4) summary generation, to produce a concise, coherent and highly readable summary for the extracted information.

3. A Remote-Access Multilingual Corpus-Based System for Linguistic Applications (RAMCORP)
   Principal Investigator:
     Jonathan J. Webster (City University of Hong Kong)
   Co-Investigators:
     Alex Chengyu Fang, Chunyu Kit, Olivia Kwong, Tom Lai, Caesar Lun, Haihua Pan, King-kui Sin, Eric Zee, Chunshen Zhu (City University of Hong Kong)

Summary:

The primary objective of the proposed project is to enhance one of the three strategic areas of the Faculty, namely, Applications of Linguistics and Language Technology and Communications. Specifically, it is proposed to develop a remote-access multilingual, corpus-based (RAMCORP) system to serve as a platform for not only providing sophisticated automatic translation services via the latest mobile and internet technologies, but also for carrying out corpus-based linguistic investigations as part of translation and multilingual studies. The RAMCORP system will enable access to annotated parallel corpora, provide research tools to retrieve texts, generate empirical statistics and perform detailed functional-semantic analysis of texts. Of particular interest to industry, the RAMCORP system will also offer translation services at casual, sophisticated and professional levels. Modes of access will include desktop computers, mobile phones and landlines. The user base will cover Hong Kong and mainland China and eventually extend to other eastern Asian countries such as Japan, Korea and Singapore.

Also, at the suggestion of Christian Matthiessen, plans are under way at The Halliday Centre to make the following resources available to the wider academic community:

- A **virtual library** with electronic versions of documents that have appeared in print, and also other materials, such as PowerPoint presentations and multilingual glossaries.
- A **virtual resource centre** with a multilingual text archive (from which corpora can be extracted according to search criteria specified by users). The archive might contain 'raw' text – monolingual, parallel and comparable, and tagged texts annotated in terms of different kinds of analysis.

Further information about The Halliday Centre for Intelligent Applications of Language Studies is available at www.hallidaycentre.cityu.edu.hk.

Working with Meaning: Towards an Appliable Linguistics

M. A. K. Halliday
University of Sydney

1 My job here tonight is to launch. But I'm a grammarian; so I can't help observing that the verb *launch* represents a material process, one that is 'effective' (that is, having two participants, an Actor and a Goal), and in which the Actor is human and the Goal is an artefact, one designed to move across water (in other words, a boat). The process of launching consists in shifting the boat from where it has been built to where it is going to work: from land to water – unlike amphibians, which are born in the water and then move on to the land, boats are born on the land and then move into the water; and they have to be launched. But if we say that the Queen of England launched a new luxury liner, she may have performed some material act, like hurtling a bottle of champagne against the boat; but she didn't actually push it. Or rather, she didn't push it materially; she pushed it semiotically. She said something – she performed some act of meaning – which inaugurated the movement of the boat. So even with boats, launching may be a semiotic process rather than a material one; and in that case it is not such a distant step to launching a Centre, which is what I am doing now. And if I have launched my own discourse in this somewhat roundabout way, it is because the power of meaning, this potential for a significant outcome of a semiotic act, is in a sense what this whole enterprise is about.

The Centre has my name attached to it, for which I feel keenly embarrassed, because I don't think I have merited any such distinction – but also very gratified, because its aims as set out by Dr. Jonathan Webster, who initiated the whole project, correspond closely to what I have tried to follow as a guiding principle: the search for what I have called an 'appliable' linguistics – a comprehensive and theoretically powerful model of language which, precisely because it was comprehensive and powerful, would be capable of being applied to the problems, both research problems and practical problems, that are being faced all the time by the many groups of people in our modern society who are in some way or other having to engage with language.

The colleagues that Dr. Webster has brought together for this opening of the Centre share a common commitment to taking language seriously, to recognizing the crucial role that is played by language in all the domains of human life. The occasion, as you will have noticed, is not being referred to as a conference; it is a symposium. At a conference, one typically brings together people who may not – often do not – know each other, to talk and exchange ideas on a particular common topic. At a symposium, on the other hand, one brings together people who do know each other, to talk and exchange ideas on anything they like – which means on a variety of very different topics. It takes much more time to exchange ideas with people you don't know; a lot of effort is spent, by each participant, on establishing their own identity and their own credentials. We don't need to do that; most of us already know one another, and we can get down to business right away. We come from very diverse backgrounds: different linguistic and cultural backgrounds, different intellectual and disciplinary backgrounds, different ideological backgrounds – belief systems and modes of thought, and even different ways of moving between the two. But we respect each other; and we share a respect for language, as a key element in addressing our tasks and our problems; and, further than that, a conviction that we have to theorize language in order to be able to engage with it and take it seriously. Perhaps I should add to that, in the words of one of my favourite writers J. B. Priestley: seriously, but not solemnly – but then we have a poet among us, Edwin Thumboo, and we can rely on him to make very sure of that.

So rather than bringing different approaches to a common goal, those who have come together here are bringing a common approach to a variety of different goals. The focus is thematic, rather than disciplinary. How would I characterize the common theme? I might say: we think about things grammatically – because grammar is the mathematics of meaning. But if that seems obscure, then 'engaging with language' means that when you're facing up to some particular task – it might be managing and passing on information, or preparing courses in science and technology, or diagnosing a medical disorder, or examing the foundations of conflicting beliefs – you say 'this is a matter of language; if I want to understand it, and perhaps to intervene in it, I need to work with language as my terrain'. It means treating language not as a secondary channel for something else, but as our primary meaning-making resource: for cultural, aesthetic and religious experience, for knowledge and learning, for personal and social identity and interaction, and for material health and wellbeing. Underlying all of these is the principle that language is the essential condition for the evolution of the human species and for the development of every individual human being – because language is the defining property of the human brain.

I think that we would also, as part of the same general concern, want to make others aware of the importance of working with language. But there is a problem here. You learn a great deal of language, and maybe several languages, as you work your way through school; but you don't learn *about* language – you don't get to study linguistics. So most adult citizens – and I mean educated citizens, including our own colleagues who may be masters and intellectual powerhouses in their own disciplines – retain an image of language that is round about what they learned from their teachers in primary three. It happens that one of our group, Geoff Williams, has himself taught in the classroom, and worked with teachers, in the early years of primary education; and they have taught the children some linguistics (why not? after all, they are already being taught mathematics), and seen what a high level of understanding of grammar they can achieve, beginning at the ages of six or seven – interestingly, it seems to get harder to learn grammatics as you get older, just as it may get harder to learn language itself. But most people have never been exposed to serious discussion of language; so while our colleagues in maths or physics can talk about 'the localized gravitational attraction exerted by rapidly oscillating and extremely massive cloud loops of cosmic string', and accountants can set up seminars in 'evidence of the abnormal accrual anomaly incremental to operating cash flows', if we mention anything as forbiddingly complex as 'hypotaxis' or a 'non-finite clause' we are sent away and told to cut out the jargon.

Now scientists have to learn how to simplify: to describe in lay people's terms what they themselves, and their discipline, are on about. But there are limits to how far you can simplify without distorting. Language is not simple; its complexity is the complexity of the human brain, and it is of no help to anyone to pretend it is simpler than it really is. And theory is not simple: it means shifting your depth of focus away from the immediate and using virtual entities as the tools to think with. And any 'intelligent application of language studies' has to rest on a theoretical understanding of the nature, the functions and the space–time organization of human language.

2 So I shall need to say a few things about some of the properties of language, looking at language from the standpoint of linguistics as an applied science. I have already brought in one unfamiliar term, 'grammatics'; but that is a device for avoiding ambiguity. We distinguish, quite consistently, between 'language' and 'the study of language', and we refer to the study of language as 'linguistics'. But we use the same term, 'grammar', for both the object 'grammar' and 'the study of grammar', which causes a great amount of confusion. Chinese distinguishes *yuyan* and *yuyanxue*; and it also distinguishes – or it can do – between *yufa* and *yufaxue*; so 'grammatics' equals *yufaxue*, the study of grammar. Everyone learns grammar; it's the central processing unit of a language. Linguists also learn grammatics; and that's what these small children proved capable of doing. And they were not just capable of it; they enjoyed it, and they were able to think with it – an excellent example of outcome-based education.

But I shall mix together my observations about language with discussion of concerns of the Centre, with particular reference to those who are taking part in this symposium. To start with a note about language. A language is a semiotic system: a system of *meanings*; and more than that, it is a system which *creates* meaning: a meaning-*making*, or 'semogenic', system. Meanings are not stored and lined up somewhere else, either inside us in the mind or outside us in the real world, waiting to be meant; they are brought into being in the shape of language. (They may have to wait to be *said*; but they are already formed out of language.) All our applications are likely to be concerned in some way or other with the meaning-making power of language.

There are many spheres of action where there is work to be done and where language takes a prominent place. Some of these have been the province of applied linguistics for decades; so let me start by referring to two of these, language education and translation; and since we are here in China, but in a corner of China that was a British crown colony for 150 years, I will locate the discussion in contexts where the two languages concerned, Chinese and English, continue to impinge on one another.

Chinese and English are the world's two biggest languages, though with different manifestations of their bigness. Chinese has by far the greatest number of native speakers: if we count just Mandarin, then about 900 million, whereas English and Spanish, the next two in line, each has not much more than one third of this total. But English has the highest number of *users*, native and non-native; you can't really count these, but say between one and two billion. English is a world-wide language; it is not only *international*, as second language of countries throughout the Commonwealth, the former British Empire, but also *global*, in business and finance, in trade and tourism, in diplomacy, and in electronic modes of communication at every level. We shall have here at our symposium the leading authority on 'World Englishes', to use the term he introduced himself: Braj Kachru, who has provided the theoretical foundations for understanding the processes whereby a language expands its scope, and with it its semiotic force, in the social and political conditions of the modern world.

As an *international* language, English is just one among many: we can count Arabic, Malay–Indonesian, Hindi–Urdu, Swahili, Russian, German, French, Spanish, Portuguese – and of course Mandarin, since it is also a national language of Singapore. But as a *global* language, at present at least, English is unique: it is the only one. Though it may not be the only one for long, because unlike the Japanese, who despite their earlier predominance in technology and world trade took no steps towards internationalizing their language – if anything, they actively discouraged it – the Chinese are deliberately moving in this direction: I am told that the government has recently announced a plan for a hundred new institutes – Confucian Institutes, I think they will be called – for teaching Chinese to foreigners. And the authorities at different levels have also begun to pay attention to the critical domains of linguistic contact where Chinese interfaces with English. The second of these is perhaps less familiar; so let me look at it first.

China produces a huge quantity of material written in English, at every level from official documents and public notices to labels on packaging and tourist brochures; and almost all of it is translated from Chinese – even where there was no original Chinese text, it was written by Chinese and has Chinese meanings behind it. And much of the English is extremely bad; it is either unintelligible, or funny, and sometimes both. It is often assumed that this is because of mistakes in the lexicogrammar (the syntax and/or the vocabulary); such mistakes do occur, of course, as well as low-level errors in the printing. But the real problem arises in the wording as a whole, and even at the level of semantics. Here are two examples from a local tourist brochure:

> Temple of Sunshine Stone, originally named 'Lotus Temple', is one of four famous temples in Xiamen. As a matter of fact, this temple is a rock cave. Its ceiling is made of rock and, therefor, it is also called 'one piece of tile'.
> Gulang Island Concert Hall was built in 1984. The design of the hall is so good that at every seat music can be heard.

I wrote a piece of bad Chinese to try to give an idea of the effect.

It is usually believed that languages differ in their grammar and vocabulary but that the meanings they express are all the same. But in a way this puts it the wrong way round. Of course the words are different; but the grammar, the syntactic structures of Chinese and English, are actually fairly similar. The two languages differ, rather, in the way they construct their meanings. A language, as I said, is a meaning-making system; and different languages can mean in different ways. This will make little difference in a technical or scientific text, because meanings in science and technology tend to be universal; but the language of cultural monuments and tourist guides is much more variable. Whatever the source of the errors, the effect is disastrous: the language sabotages all the value of the culture it is intended to display. We have at the symposium Erich Steiner, a leading specialist in translation theory; and one of his areas of expertise is register-specific translation: that is to say, the problem of matching genres as a whole – say, monumental English with monumental Chinese. Very often the English used in such contexts in China is simply in the wrong register. A great deal of research is needed in this area, into generic variation in Chinese, the limits of acceptability in different contexts of translation, types of equivalence and their priorities, and the like, all of which could be addressed by the Centre.

Now to the other topic mentioned earlier, the teaching of Chinese to foreigners. For many customers over the past few decades, 'applied linguistics' has meant TESOL, Teaching English to Speakers of Other Languages; now I read in my *Guardian Weekly* that Americans are saying they are in 'critical need' of Mandarin, with the same consuming fervour (and the same 'critical' terminology) as I recall being used after the Russians launched their *Sputnik* in 1958; we will need Chinese for Speakers of Other Languages, or ChiSOL. I fear that this too might become a disaster area. Some time ago my son studied Chinese for two years in his secondary school in Australia, and it was a great waste of time; not because the teacher was bad, but because the syllabus was bad, a guarantee of failure for all except the students of Chinese origin, those who were already familiar with ways of meaning in Chinese. Now, I myself used to teach Chinese to speakers of English; this was my first profession, and I would say that many of the problems arise when students are expected to learn characters from the beginning. Before you tackle the script, you need to know the language, the way a child does: by the time they start on characters Chinese children are fluent in Chinese, and so it should be with the foreign learner. As I. A. Richards said, more than half a century ago, most language learners cannot cope with sight, sound and sense all being new to them at the same time.

From my own experience, first as a learner and then as a teacher, I gained the strong impression that the longer you delayed the characters the better the learners performed. Suppose you had a class for three years: if you didn't introduce any characters until halfway through, then at the end of the three years not only would they know more of the *language* but they would also know more *characters* than others who had been made to learn characters right from the start. Once you are reasonably fluent in the language, the charactery is not a formidable problem; but when you're not, then not only are the characters hard to learn but, more seriously, they inhibit the process of learning the language as well.

Of course, adult beginners need writing; so you give them a transcription. Pinyin will serve, provided the accents are included; modified Pinyin might be better, though I never taught it myself; best of all was Y. R. Chao's '*GR*' (*Gwoyeu Romatzyh*), which had just the degree of redundancy that a script really needs to have. Pinyin is excellent for the purposes for which it was designed: as a notation system for use by Chinese in China. But it lacks redundancy, especially if it is used without the tone marks: the distinctions are too minimal to be of help to the foreign learner. Sadly, I doubt whether *GR* can now be resurrected; but if I was starting a Chinese language school that's the script I would use.

For the adolescent or adult beginner, whatever the language being studied, the teacher they will find most difficult is the half-trained native speaker, who has little idea of the difficulties faced by a foreign learner and is also likely to be encumbered by all the mythology that attaches to any language. Myths about a language always get in the way of effective teaching of the language. A Chinese teaching his or her own language has two such problems to overcome: learning to detach the language from the script, and discarding the idea that Chinese is somehow unique. Of course, Chinese is unique because every language is unique; but Chinese is no more unique than any other – Mandarin is a rather typical specimen of a language of eastern Asia, just as English is a typical specimen of a language of Western Europe. And Chinese remains Chinese whether it is written in characters or not; characters happen to suit Chinese because its morphemes don't much vary – but by the same token they also suited Vietnamese, which gave them up, whereas they're not so well suited to Japanese (other than its Chinese loanwords), yet the Japanese quite happily continue to use them. There is no intrinsic connection between a language and its system of writing; most scripts around the world were borrowed and modified many times over before they arrived at the form and the location where they are now.

As a teacher of Chinese today I would want at least the following resources: one, a corpus of spoken Chinese, edited and annotated; two, a multiple transcription facility; three, an annotated corpus of texts in different genres; four, a dictionary and thesaurus arranged for foreign learners; five, a reference grammar of Chinese for teachers and for students; six, audio recordings of Mandarin spoken with different regional accents; seven, a game for learning the characters (such as one I devised myself many years ago, based on the old English card game of *Happy Families*). If Chinese is going to be taught on a world-wide scale, this would not be an unreasonable demand.

3 Both the fields of activity I have been talking about, translation and language teaching between English and Chinese, require comparative studies in which the two languages are brought into relation with each other. My own work as a grammarian began with descriptive studies of Chinese; more importantly, systemic functional linguistics has been widely disseminated in China, and applied in the description of many aspects of the grammar of modern Chinese. Four of the leading scholars concerned are here with us at the symposium: Hu Zhuanglin, of Peking University, who first showed the way with his own researches on Chinese, and founded the Chinese Association of Functional Linguistics; Fang Yan, who will be convening the 35th International Systemic Functional Congress at her own university, Tsinghua, in 2008 (informally known as the Systemic Olympics; please consult Professor Fang for the details!); Zhu Yongsheng of Fudan University, co-author with Professor Hu of the first Chinese introduction to the theory; and Huang Guowen, of Sun Yat-sen University, whose Functional Linguistics Institute is associated with our Centre for possible joint ventures in applications and research. Both Fang Yan and Zhu Yongsheng in their papers at the symposium are presenting aspects of Chinese from a systemic functional point of view, while Huang Guowen, co-authoring with Wang Jin, investigates Chinese–English code-switching in relation to functional varieties and their socio-linguistic contexts.

Behind many potential applications of linguistics lie key areas of linguistic research, in particular descriptive, comparative, typological and translation studies; and these now increasingly depend on access to large quantities of data in computable form – that is, a computerized corpus; and to computational linguistic methodology in general. Both English and Chinese are well-described languages for which corpus data are, or are becoming, readily available – although more is always needed, especially in natural spoken language where so much of the creativity, the creation of new meaning potential in language, tends to take place. At the same time there is still much more to be done in making the corpus friendly to the grammarian. Although the earliest corpora were thought of as sources for the study of grammar, it is much easier to access words than grammatical structures; so they evolved as tools for the lexicologist, and the grammarian had to formulate questions in terms of particular words that it might be hoped would lead to relevant sources of information. Grammarians need the corpus for numerous purposes: for study of quantitative patterns in the grammar, of genre-based grammatical variation, of systems that lie on the border of syntax and vocabulary, and so on. I hope the Centre will be able to nudge the computer further on its way to becoming a meaning machine.

I will come back to this towards the end. But let me note here that a number of our colleagues have been using computational methods in working with meaning for quite some time in a variety of different endeavours. Jonathan Webster, Acting Director of the Centre, has carried out a research project in example-based translation between English and Chinese, using parallel texts from the Hong Kong legal code. John Bateman worked for several years in a computational linguistic project at the Imperial University in Kyoto, Japan. Christian Matthiessen, together with his colleague Wu Canzhong at Macquarie University, has developed methods for multilingual comparison and text generation in English and Chinese, and collaborated with Kazuhiro Teruya, of the University of New South Wales, to include Japanese within the same research framework. Christian Matthiessen has also developed a 'text profiling' system which presents a picture of selected grammatical features within a text, so that it becomes possible to characterize different functional varieties of a language in terms of grammatical frequencies. It was from about 1980 onwards, with the 'fifth generation' of computers, that the computer became significant as a research tool for finding out more about language; two very large systemic functional grammars in computable form date from around that time, the PENMAN project at the University of Southern California directed by William Mann, on which Christian Matthiessen worked as consultant linguist, and Robin Fawcett's COMMUNAL project at the University of Cardiff in Wales. It was these experiences which gave systemic functional linguistics a place in the subsequent development of language technology.

4 These activities that I have been talking about – language teaching, translation, and natural language processing – are familiar today as domains of applied linguistics; and are some of the contexts in which our systemic functional linguistics has evolved. To say that the Centre will be concerned with 'intelligent' applications does not mean that all these preceding efforts have been unintelligent. To me what it means is that what has been learned from these experiences is that if you want to apply something, you have to have a theory to apply; there has to be a coherent body of knowledge behind the applications – but, by the same token, that body of knowledge will be shaped, modified, extended by what results from the effort to apply it.

So what is systemic? What is functional? What is linguistics? To do linguistics means to describe languages and to theorize language: that is, to explain language in theoretical terms. If you do functional linguistics, this means that your explanations are functional; but this itself is a complex notion. At the most abstract level, the nature and organization of language – its 'architecture', or (more dynamically) its town planning and traffic flow – are explained by reference to the most general functions that language evolved to serve in human lives; more concretely, the detailed internal workings of the grammar are explained in terms of their functional inter-dependence and mutual impact. If you do systemic functional linguistics, it implies perhaps three other things besides: one, that these general functions are theorized as 'metafunctions', as distinct modes of meaning, each making a specific contribution to the overall structure of language, like the different types of musical instrument in the orchestra; two, that the underlying model of a language is 'systemic', a network of interrelated systems that collectively define the meaning-making potential of a language (language seen as a resource, not as a set of rules); three, that language has a stratified, step-wise form of organization, in which the ordering relation is the semiotic one of realization, not the material, physical one of causality: the 'strata' of language are related as value-&-token, not as cause-&-effect. I shall come back to this last point later on.

As in any other field, a theory of language like this does not emerge ready-made; it evolves gradually, and many voices contribute to it. And of course it goes on evolving. It is a scientific theory, in the sense of a system of abstract concepts which helps us to understand what language is and how it works; and it is always under pressure as new challenges appear: new languages being described, new corpus data from languages already described, and findings from new applications, particularly in language technology. To me a theory has always meant a strategic tool, a problem-solving device, a guide to action; and this notion, of what I call an 'appliable' theory, implies a theory that learns from the experience of being applied (or **we** learn; we can't yet implement it as an automated learning device). In language technology, for example, systemic grammar has been being used in text generation for a long time, since Winograd's adaptation of it in the early 1970s, and much has been learned from the systems developed by Mann and Matthiessen, by John Bateman and by Robin Fawcett. Recently Jon Patrick, also one of our speakers at the symposium, has used it in the field of document classification, in a project designed to identify fake money-making schemes, or 'scams', put out in webpages on the internet. Positive results in Jon Patrick's project suggest ways of extending this kind of application, perhaps taking in more complex systems in the grammar, including interpersonal systems of 'appraisal' as theorized by Jim Martin and Peter White. John Bateman draws attention to a defect in the methodology – itself a theoretical issue – whereby the syntag-matic representations, the analyses of linguistic structure, simply cannot be automated to do the job required; it is, he says, 'beyond the capabilities of the linguistic resources provided'. He may be right – John usually is, though I do recall two earlier occasions in my life when I have been told that my grammar could not be computed and so must be wrong. One was in 1956, when I analysed a text in English, Chinese and Italian for a machine translation project at Cambridge, and another in the late 1960s when I wrote a network for generating the forms of the English verb. In each case, when the next generation of computers came along, the problem seemed to have disappeared. However, it would be unwise to hope that this might happen again.

In Erich Steiner's project, the grammar is being put into service for tackling a problem in translation theory. There is a perception that translators, at least in some registers, tend to make their translated text more explicit than the original: they fill in certain gaps and implications in the argument. What are the criteria for saying the translation is more explicit, and what linguistic moves take place in the process of explicitation? In this sort of computational study, as with those of Jon Patrick and John Bateman, we move between the lexicogrammar and the semantics. In fact we are always doing this when we are working with meaning; but, although these are recognized in the theory as different strata, in using the theory we don't seem to keep them apart.

It has always been an issue how, how far, and where – or even whether – semantics and lexicogrammar are to be represented as distinct. Lexicogrammar is the internal organization of meaning as a self-regulating categorial system; semantics is the organization of meaning as interface between the lexicogrammar and the outside world – the eco-social environment of human experience and human social relationships. Robin Fawcett, always a leading thinker in systemic functional theory, does not treat the two as different strata but maps the distinction into that between system and structure, reducing semantics to the more abstract facet of grammar. But his perspective is predominantly a syntactic one; whereas I need to separate the two in face of the complexity of language overall. You have to 'thicken' the description for various reasons: first, to explain that meanings are organized in different systemic spaces, called 'typological' and 'topological' by Martin and Matthiessen, at these two levels; secondly, to account for the two different kinds of structure, of different magnitudes, that are involved; and thirdly, most critically perhaps, to handle metaphor, which is one of the most pervasive of all meaning-making strategies (being addressed by Zhu Yongsheng in his paper at the symposium). Metaphor is a cross-coupling (decoupling, and recoupling in a different alignment) between the semantics and the lexicogrammar; it is a basic feature built in to the architecture of language, a concomitant of what Jim Martin calls 'stratal tension'.

The central problem of working with meaning is that being highlighted by Ruqaiya Hasan. She herself, both in earlier researches into language and verbal art (how language comes to be highly valued, as literature) and in a major research project into conversation between mothers and pre-school-age children, to find out what kind of learning goes on in ordinary everyday interaction, had to focus particularly on the construction of meaning in context, either where the context had to be constructed within the text, as in a literary work, or where it was 'given' by the situation of language use, as in the development and deployment of language in early childhood. When people are using language – including children, talking and listening without reflecting on what they are doing – they operate with a sophisticated model of meaning, such as Ruqaiya Hasan represents in her semantic networks; whereas their received notions of meaning at the conscious level are simplistic and impoverished (so 'semantic' comes to mean exactly the opposite of what it signifies to a functional linguist).

Hasan stresses that intelligent applications of language studies always demand the modelling of meaning. Christian Matthiessen explains how this requirement led to the evolution of the 'meaning base' in place of the 'knowledge base' of artificial intelligence research. This move was an essential step in the advance from highly specific, dedicated expert systems, for which a new inventory of concepts, and a new grammatical description, had to be provided every time, to a large-scale exportable system which could be adapted to a variety of tasks where language technology was involved.

Such systems, as Matthiessen makes clear, depend on a consistent 'metatheory', a theory of the metalanguage that is being used in modelling language. This cannot be a 'collection code', a patchwork of bits and pieces of knowledge assembled under the banner of eclecticism – often claimed to be theory-free 'common sense' but usually reflecting a level of understanding well below what is inscribed in our commonsense knowledge. The metatheory will offer – will demand – a comprehensive vision of language: one that, like language itself, will always be able to change its perspective and its focal length; and that also, like language itself, is constantly renewing its connection with life and updating its meaning potential.

5 A scientific theory is a system of related meanings – a 'semiotic system' – whose arguments are virtual phenomena, virtual processes and entities, that exist only on the semiotic plane. They owe their existence to the resource of grammatical metaphor; such as we find in

> the conducting capacity depends on the width of the channel

where all the doings and happenings are turned into or made dependent on nouns, like 'conducting' and 'capacity' and 'width', while all the logical relations between the happenings are turned into verbs, like 'depends on'. The thing called 'capacity' is a virtual thing; it doesn't exist in the material world, but it is robust and dependable in the virtual universe of theory.

A language likewise is a semiotic system: it is not made of matter, like a physical system; it is made of meaning. It is an evolved system: it was not designed, though people often try to interfere in it by design. Language evolved in the human species along with the human brain, as the form taken by higher-order consciousness. It is a highly complex system, involving social, biological and physical forms of organization: it is learned and used in contexts of social life, processed biologically in the brain via the organs of speech and hearing, and manifested in the physical process of sound waves moving through the air. And much of the time it hides below the level of our conscious attention.

A language is also a theory. The lexicogrammar of every language is a theory of human experience: a way of ordering and interpreting the natural world and the inner world of our own consciousness. It is also, and at the same time, an enactment of our interpersonal relationships. The complexity of the human brain came along with – as an aspect of – the increasing complexity of our relations with our material environment and with each other; and, as part of the evolution of the brain, there came language.

In the course of doing its job, or rather its jobs, that of construing the human experience and enacting the social process, language evolved a number of characteristics. It is indeterminate – its categories are fuzzy, not clearly defined. It is probabilistic – it works with tendencies, rather than with certainties. It is unquantifiable – some features of language can be measured, in the form of 'information', but most can't. It abounds in complementarities – pairs of contradictory codings both of which must be adopted to get an in-depth understanding of what is meant. And it is stratified, into a series of levels of organization or 'strata'; these are, in technical terms, semantic, lexicogram-matical, phonological and phonetic – meaning, wording and the two facets of expression in sound. Some languages also have a graphological mode of expression – in writing; but writing is secondary; it evolved only two or three times in the course of history, and, as I said, there is no inherent bonding between a language and its script – most scripts are the result of numerous cycles of borrowing and adaptation.

The relations among the various strata are complex; but there is one continuous thread, that of realization. While physical processes, those instan-tiating physical systems, take place in time, and so can be explained in terms of the relations of cause and effect, semiotic processes are different. Their manifestations are of course physical, and so located in time or space: speech unfolds in time, writing progresses through space. But their internal order is not based on space–time; it is based on realization. Meanings are realized as wordings; wordings are realized as sounds or writing. Each step is a pairing of value and token, or 'signified' and 'signifier' in the terminology of theory of signs.

Since human beings are programmed to find meaning in nearly everything that happens (or else doesn't happen), any phenomenon can be treated as semiotic, the way a doctor interprets your high fever as a token, or symptom, of influenza. Influenza doesn't *cause* the fever; influenza is a virtual condition that is manifested, or *realized*, as a fever. In linguistic terms, influenza is a meaning; it is a term in a theory, a theory of the human bodily condition.

With this conceptual fit the Centre could collaborate readily with medical specialists – especially where the pathology is manifested in disorders of language, like aphasia or Alzheimer's syndrome.

There are other semiotic systems that are closely related to language, those that function together as 'multiple modalities' in the formation of text: visual images of all kinds, which we could also see as forms of visual art. These are sometimes thought of as being independent of language; but most of the time they are parasitic on language, like the PowerPoint presentations analysed by Hu Zhuanglin. All those who produce and receive such images are also users of language. So although visual aids such as maps, plans, charts, diagrams, figures, tables and graphs may present information that is not verbalized, that is complementary to the information in the wording, the textual fusion always takes place in the semantics – that is, in the meaning system of language, not outside it. Hence the whole text is accessible to a linguistic theory – a critical factor if the Centre becomes involved in monumental discourses such as those of tourist guides and cultural displays.

The issue of realizational systems is in fact central to the intelligent application of language studies. David Butt has taken this up in his paper for the symposium, pointing up the robustness of such systems and stressing that along with our 'systems thinking', a key term in the theory and management of complexity, we need to be aware that many of the systems we are dealing with are in fact realizational systems. David Butt and Christian Matthiessen, at the Centre for Language in Social Life at Macquarie University, have been working in the field of 'systems safety', examining breakdowns in health care services and aircraft safety procedures, and showing that systems are liable to fail at a point of high semiotic risk, where the key factor is the management and transmission of 'information' – of meaning, in our systemic functional perspective.

6 In other words, failure in a system is often language failure – a failure in the flow and return of meaning. So can we say that success is also often language success? Meanings have been construed, exchanged and interpreted, transformed into appropriate action. We ought to be able to think this way about learning. Where learning has been successful, the learner's meaning potential has been extended, the new meanings integrated with the rest (which may have necessitated some shaking up of meanings that were already there); the new resources perhaps questioned, or even challenged, and the outcomes judged by some criterion of success. In learning in daily life – commonsense learning, let us say – learners typically manage their own search for meaning, and judge the success of the outcome for themselves; but where this could be problematic – something might blow us all apart if they fail – we train them: we manage the meanings for them, and set ourselves up as judges of their success. Unlike commonsense knowledge, educational knowledge has to be able to be assessed.

So any assessment of 'learning outcomes' in education, whether of the pedagogy that goes with them or of the effectiveness of the results, will depend on analytical awareness of the meanings that are involved. To be able to process the knowledge that has been gained, to pick it up and run with it, use it to think with, the student must be capable of extracting meaning from a text. To do this, the student has to extend the chain of realization outside language, to take into account the context, the domain at the other side of the semantic interface. Moreover the student has to be able to look from either end, to control both perspectives: the text as realization of the context, but also the text construing the context – in other words, using language to learn. Geoff Williams considers the question of making the whole design, or architecture, of language explicit to the learner as part of the 'abstract toolkit' for learning with. Geoff is thinking of the primary school; but perhaps we might raise the same question at the tertiary level as well!

It has always been a concern of systemic functional theory to extend our realizational vista outside the core levels of language itself, to include within the scope of the theory what my own teacher, J. R. Firth, called the 'exterior relations' of language. To understand instances of language, language as text, we bring in the context of situation, the frame within which the text is playing a part. To understand the potential of language, language as system, we bring in the context of culture, which means not just the traditional culture within which each language has evolved but the interlocking spheres which typically define the culture of a modern community. In computing with meaning, beyond the meaning base there has to be some representation of the context.

Michio Sugeno, formerly of the Tokyo Institute of Technology, has been a pioneer of fuzzy computing, and also of 'intelligent computing' which is his own contribution to, and extension of, computing with words. His work over a number of years had many applications in the material realm, from fuzzy washing machines to automated public transport systems. He recently spent five years at the Brain Science Institute in Tokyo, directing a project in the Laboratory for Language-Based Intelligent Systems, called a 'language-based approach to creating the brain'. He used the systemic functional model to construct a wording base, a meaning base and also a 'context base' in computable form, as a way in to investigating the nature and functioning of the human brain. It seemed to me that Sugeno's interpretation of computing with words was really computing with meanings. He considers that, if computers are to advance now any further, they will have to be taught to think like human beings. I have referred to this as 'thinking grammatically', but that was meant in contrast to thinking logically; in fact people don't remember, store and reason with wordings, they remember, store and reason with the meanings. Meanings are construed in the form of wording, and it is as wordings that they are exchanged in social life.

So working with meaning takes us inside the human brain; it also takes us outside, to human societies, and to the restlessness, the constant upheavals, of meaning in the modern world. Edwin Thumboo, who has studied the diffusion of English in Kachru's 'outer circle' of countries where it has domesticated itself in the regional and local cultures, heads his talk 'signifiers without the signified', as the language 'becomes neutral . . . without the energy and the identity of a strong cultural backing' (and I would add: without being flushed out by a continuing tide of toddlers). I do feel I want to distinguish here between the international and the global: between 'international English' and 'global English'. As a speaker, originally, of a northern variety of British English, I feel very aware that I have lost my context base; but that is mainly because I am an old man and my childhood world no longer exists. But English has put on new meanings in its own original home; and, by another process of cross-coupling, akin to metaphor, it has created new meanings out of the impact between its own native semiotic and those of India, Africa, south-east Asia and elsewhere. Becoming international does expand the meaning potential – though very few speakers control as much of it as Edwin does himself.

But globalization seems different. Here on the one hand the language finds itself hijacked, by the community of big players – bankers, business executives, their managers and lobbyists and advertisers – managers of meaning in a virtual world where there are no people doing things but only abstractions like visions and targets and outcomes and cash flow and maximizing shareholder value and winning the war on terror. At the other end are the large community of small players who use English to text each other via their computers and mobile phones; this is a different language, highly volatile and interpersonal – though always open to being invaded by the dominant meanings of the first. Where English is now, Chinese may be next. Chinese has no problem in taking on all the new meanings, and has already incorporated enough of them to be able to participate – though the discourses are not yet as wholly naturalized in Chinese as they are in English. There has already been the experience of Mandarin spreading around the multilingual and multidialectal regions of China; but that hardly at all perturbed its ways of meaning, whereas as it starts to get globalized it will also get resemanticized. And the Chinese will have to get accustomed to their language being performed by foreigners – badly.

7 The CTL Department is a healthy birthplace for the Centre, combining as it does teaching and research programmes in Chinese, in translation and in linguistics, and having as its next door neighbour the Department of English. Our overseas visitors may not appreciate what an unusual environment this is. Throughout China, while there are of course numerous departments of Chinese, and also of English, and not a few departments of translation studies, there are almost no departments in the critical field of linguistics. Languages are taught without reference to any general theory of language or overview of the world's languages. Even here in Hong Kong there is as far as I know only one other than this one, the Department of Linguistics at the University of Hong Kong. 'Chinese linguistics' is taught in Chinese departments, 'English linguistics' is taught in English departments; each language is presented *sui generis*, as if no other languages existed; and the description

is 'flattened' as a result. We might contrast this situation with that of India, where almost all major universities have linguistics departments in which languages, and language itself, find a place in the structure of knowledge.

So it has been a pleasure and a privilege to me to be working in this environment of C, T & L, all contributing to the nurturing of the Centre. I feel I have been very fortunate to be able to spend my working life working with meaning – working with all the different meanings of meaning, and engaging in a constant struggle to construe the wordings with which to understand them, and to discourse about them with other people. Many years ago I wrote a book about very young children's language; I called the book 'Learning How to Mean'. It then got translated into one or two other languages; but the translators always complained that they couldn't translate the title, because in their language you couldn't say the equivalent of 'learning to mean'. I pointed out that you couldn't say it in English either; but I meant it, so I said it, and why couldn't they do the same? Translators may explicitate, as Erich Steiner has demonstrated; but they seem to think they're not allowed to innovate, even to catch up with the original.

It can often become a problem: how to make your meanings explicit first to yourself, which you do by wording them; and then, even more, how to make them intelligible to others. I have usually been concerned with other people's questions about language rather more than those formulated by linguists; such questions never have easy answers – if they had, they wouldn't need to be asked; but at least the questions themselves are reasonably clear, because they are problem-oriented, and there are criteria for evaluating the answers, which either help to solve the problems or they don't. If they don't, you simply have to drop them, or at least send them back to the workshop for improving the design. I had thought that my 'translation at ranks' was a sensible working model for machine translation; but no-one else ever did, so – regretfully – I dropped it. It obviously wasn't such a bright idea after all. It wasn't explicit enough to test or to argue about.

Thinking about what makes such endeavours worthwhile, I came up with three factors, and then realized that they could all be brought together under the one guiding principle, that of being inclusive. And again I can't help thinking about them grammatically, because one is ideational, one interpersonal and one is textual. The ideational aspect is what I call comprehensiveness: we try to keep in focus the whole of language – meaning and expression, system and text, child and adult, local and global, reflection and action, and so on; which means that when you are struggling with a problem you can go and look at it from round the back, like an infant who has just learned how to crawl: you vary your angle of vision, and see if your ideas still make sense. The interpersonal aspect is just that: recognizing the importance of bringing people into the discourse, at all levels, and making them feel at home within the meaning group – this is something I always ask of organizers of conferences, where newcomers can very easily feel lost. The textual aspect is that of sharing information: organizing the discourse so that individuals and groups can keep in touch, can see its thematic source and its information focus, and so can participate rewardingly in the ongoing exchange of ideas.

Does this mean we all have to talk to each other in English, to accept it as the global language of intellectual activity? I hope not. I have always encouraged our colleagues to speak and write in their own language, especially where they are speaking or writing *about* that language, so that the protocol version of a lexicogrammatical study of Chinese, for example, is the version that is written in Chinese. Our colleagues in China often do write in Chinese, which is good for the development of the field because they can then be easily read by other Chinese scholars who are not specialists in English. But by the same token, the work doesn't get read by foreigners who don't know the Chinese language. This problem does need to be addressed: perhaps by some kind of English or multilingual digest of functional linguistic studies in China; and likewise for works written in other languages. Some of this, such as the writing of abstracts, is surely now something that could be automated.

Meanwhile I welcome a gathering such as the present one, where those of us working with meaning, in different directions but from a common point of departure, can convene to exchange our own meanings, with one another and with other interested parties. Many thanks to Jonathan Webster for setting the whole event in train and making it possible for this symposium to happen – and to the university and its representatives here for supporting it and taking part. I hope that many of those who have come to view the launch will take this chance, over the next two and a half days, to come and listen to the invited speakers and maybe talk to them about their initiatives for the Centre. Many thanks for your kind attention.

Systemic Functional Linguistics and the Notion of Linguistic Structure: Unanswered Questions, New Possibilities

John A. Bateman
University of Bremen

1.1 Introduction: setting the scene

> The paradigmatic representation frees the grammar from the constraints of structure; structure, obviously, is still to be accounted for ... (Halliday 1996: 21)

In this chapter, I revisit the much-debated area of the Systemic Functional Linguistics (SFL) approach to syntactic structure. I will argue that the currently prevailing descriptive mechanisms are insufficient. Very quickly and before the reader can reach for the remote to change channel I then also need to say that this will *not* be a further contribution to the long line of offshoots from SFL that have appeared over the years, such as Huddleston (1965), Hudson (1976), McCord (1977) and Hudson (1990); nor will it be a contribution to the equally long line of criticisms of central notions of SFL grammar, such as the attacks on rank or functional organization seen in Matthews (1966), Huddleston (1988) and others. The direction taken here is quite different in that I argue that we need all that has been proposed in SFL so far *and more*. It is the nature of this 'more' that is at issue.

Throughout its existence SFL has been primarily concerned with the paradigmatic axis of linguistic description. This emphasis has long been the main distinguishing feature of the approach. Accounts of the syntagmatic axis, i.e. linguistic structure, have been placed very much in the background. Since the initial characterizations of ranks, functional structure, classes and their interrelationships, extensions to the account have been restricted to some valuable but nevertheless rather programmatic proposals – such as those, for example, involving distinct 'kinds' of structures such as the particulate, prosodic and periodic modes of representation (Halliday 1979; Martin 1996; Halliday and Matthiessen 2004: 383). While this has led to insightful and quite distinctive accounts of how language is structured at all strata, the work left to do with respect to constituency has not gone away. Constituency as such has not been 'solved' within SFL accounts and this leaves a disturbing gap in what must be one of the central areas of any characterization of language. Many systemic grammars that are explicitly specified make statements about, among other things, constituency. But the mechanisms provided for making these statements by the theoretical framework itself appear to be, as I will argue below, insufficiently developed.

This may strike some readers as surprising: in daily practice it is clear that the syntagmatic axis is always present alongside other aspects of systemic description: examples of analysis are predominantly syntagmatic. It is, for example, only in the latest edition of Michael Halliday's *Introduction to Functional Grammar* (Halliday and Matthiessen 2004) that system networks have really made it into the picture at all; and a rallying cry of Robin Fawcett for several decades has been: 'no system networks without realisation statements' (Fawcett 1988: 9). So where is this gap? I will begin the chapter by addressing precisely this issue, establishing in what sense there is an imbalance between the axes of chain and choice and why it has now become particularly damaging.

To do this, the principal locus of the discussion will draw on the interaction between linguistic description and computational instantiations of theory – for it is here that the problem is most strongly felt. This orientation to a computational perspective will not involve any ideological battle between different positions on language – it simply sets out particularly clearly some of the tasks for which we might want to use linguistic theory and description. One may well then come to the conclusion that it is the task and the methods that are at fault – but it would be best if such a position were reached knowingly so that appropriate consequences can be drawn. At present these issues are rarely made sufficiently explicit.

The basic point of departure for my discussion is very simple. The automatic natural language *generation* of texts by computational systems using systemic-functional resources has had a long and successful history. But, in stark contrast to this, the automatic *analysis* of texts using systemic resources has suffered a very different fate: in short, automatic SFL analysis does not work. There are *no automatic computational tools* for producing even shallow systemic lexicogrammatical or semantic analyses of texts. If this were a technical accident, a question of lack of research, or of lack of interest, then the situation might be noted and passed over – indicative of nothing more than curious tastes in the problems that are selected for solution within the computational community. But the main point of this chapter will be to suggest that this could not be further from the truth. The problem is that the current conception of systemic-functional grammars alone *will never support effective automatic analysis components*. The difficulty faced is then very much more than a temporary technical problem of resources, investment or practical implementation and highlights issues of fundamental *theoretical* concern. Uncovering precisely *why* there is still no usable automatic systemic analysis system despite some very concentrated efforts to produce one will lead us to some foundational theoretical issues and open questions that call for detailed discussion. This chapter is intended to start that discussion and to make some proposals for paths to investigate.

The lack of automatic analysis capabilities drawing on SFL accounts also has broader consequences for the research and application contexts available for SFL. Ten years ago, the lack of successful automatic analysis capabilities would not necessarily have been seen as a critical deficit because other linguistic accounts could not provide this service either. Nowadays the situation is very different. Largely due to the very great progress that has been made precisely in the understanding of the syntagmatic axis of linguistic organization, we can now find large-scale linguistic descriptions that *are* supportive of the automatic analysis of large bodies of natural data. Automatic analysis is accordingly taking on increasing importance for linguistic research in general, and particularly in those areas that place weight on corpus evidence.

In order to support such work, approaches need methods for pursuing analyses automatically. The utility of basic corpora annotations, such as parts of speech and other simply derived information, is quite limited. Annotating large-scale corpora with detailed syntactic, semantic, textual information is currently in full swing: but not with systemically motivated features. The practical consequences of this are substantial. When all available linguistic corpora have been richly annotated with grammatical analyses allowing sophisticated searching for complex patterns, and those annotations rely on other linguistic accounts because it is those accounts that were capable of doing automatic annotation of large bodies of naturally occurring text, using a systemic description will quickly come to be seen as an unnecessary distraction.

Automatic analysis methods are also now used to test the adequacy and correctness of linguistic descriptions: if a grammatical description does not provide a reasonable analysis for some naturally occurring examples, then the account needs extension. Systematically testing a linguistic description 'against' a corpus now belongs to the standard tools of the trade of the computationally empowered linguist and marks a radical change in the state of the art and practice when compared with computational approaches of a decade or so ago. In essence, computational approaches now do what the SFL approach has always stated to be its goal – i.e., drawing on corpora – but has only been able to do in a relatively limited fashion because, unfortunately, SFL resources are demonstrably *not* working for automatic analysis.

This opens up an increasing gulf between SFL and the very detailed linguistic descriptions that are being formulated in computationally aware approaches. These descriptions, largely due to their applicability for automatic analysis, are receiving substantial financial support and interest, and are being pursued for an extremely broad range of languages. The lack of dialogue and re-use of results and perspectives between these and SFL approaches is then particularly unfortunate. On the one hand, it deprives SFL of access to a wealth of well-structured data; on the other, it also deprives computational accounts of an extremely rich source of information and theorizing about language since it is clear that in many areas there is considerably more detail to be drawn from systemic accounts than that available in other linguistic accounts. It would therefore be a sad waste if potentially valuable exchanges are blocked at the starting post.

1.2 So, what's the problem?

SFL has had an active and mutually productive relationship with computational approaches to language theorizing, description and processing for as long as there has been an SFL approach (for a detailed historical overview of this relationship, see O'Donnell and Bateman 2005). Often new approaches to linguistic phenomena have been proposed within SFL and subsequently taken up to good effect in computational accounts. This transfer between SFL and computation has typically involved a 'delay' or 'lag' between theoretical linguistic formulation and a principled (non-arbitrarily related) computational instantiation of that formulation (see Matthiessen 1988: 139 and Matthiessen and Bateman 1991: 19): ideas sketched theoretically usually involve a host of hidden issues that are only revealed when the more explicit formulations required in computation are addressed. The corresponding *linguistic* value of these exchanges is that our understanding of the technical details of certain aspects of a systemic description has been made increasingly explicit.

It is, however, by no means an accident that this productive interchange has been limited almost exclusively to the area of automatic *natural language generation*.[1] In this area, systems are built by which abstract semantic specifications and communicative goals are used to trigger the automatic production of connected texts achieving those goals. We can observe a striking congruence between natural language generation and systemic theory. Treating language as a resource decomposed along the paradigmatic dimension of functionally motivated choices between functionally relevant alternatives offers a succinct description of precisely what a computational generation system needs to achieve. Very early on in natural language generation we accordingly find explicit reliance on exactly the notion of *abstract choice* that underlies the paradigmatic organization of the SFL system network (see McDonald 1980).

Formalizing further the success of systemic-functional work in automatic generation, it is useful to consider the notion of 'search'. Many processes can be seen computationally in terms of search: solutions to a problem are found by navigating the problem's *search space*. Well defined problems allow the specification of well structured search spaces, which then help navigation to proceed effectively to find solutions. The paradigmatic organization of the lexicogrammar assumed within SFL turns out to organize the search space for possible grammatical units appropriate for specified communicative goals in an almost ideal manner. Halliday's emphasis on paradigmatic organization, already present in the work on machine translation in the mid-1950s (Halliday 1956, 1962) and carried on throughout the growth of systemic functional linguistics proper, therefore proved central in establishing the foundations of a strong connection between computational application and systemic theory.

Automatic analysis can also be seen as a problem of finding an appropriate analysis within a search space of possible solutions. Here it is again our linguistic resources, in the present case a systemic-functional grammar, that must be used to provide structure for that search space and to allow us to access it in various ways. But whereas the paradigmatic organization of a systemic lexicogrammar is effective for the task of generation, it turns out to be very much less supportive of analysis. The basic issue turns out to be simply one of size – in particular, the size of the search space. This returns us with a slightly different slant to Halliday's (1996: 9) question of 'how big is a grammar?' and the problem that answering the question raises:

> Given any system network it should in principle be possible to count the number of alternatives shown to be available. In practice, it is quite difficult to calculate the number of different selection expressions that are generated by a network of any considerable complexity. (Halliday 1996: 10)

The difficulty is caused by the fact that the size of a grammar depends very much on the kind of connectivity and *cross-classification* exhibited by its system network. If we have a network consisting of 40 systems, 'the size of the grammar it generates lies somewhere between 41 and 2^{40} (which is somewhere around 10^{12}). We do not know how to predict whereabouts it will fall in between these two figures' (Halliday 1996: 10).

The fact that relatively small networks can produce rather large numbers of distinct selection expressions was not, however, seen as problematic. This is because:

> the number of choice points encountered in generating or parsing a text is actually rather small – in the network of the verbal group it took only 28 systems to produce some 70,000 selection expressions, and in any one pass the maximum number of systems encountered would be even less, probably half the total, in a representative network. In other words, in selecting one out of half a billion clause types the speaker/listener would be traversing at the most about forty choice points ... [T]here is nothing impossible about a grammar of this complexity. (Halliday 1996: 12–13)

It is interesting that the phrase 'or parsing' appears here as an apparently unproblematic extension. Actually the claim being made holds *only* for generation – there it is indeed the case that very few of the actual possibilities produced by a network need to be explored when generating a clause. Possible feature selections become relevant only when they are revealed to be relevant by prior paradigmatic choices and it is only those alternatives that need to be considered.

During analysis, the situation is different. As we shall see in the next section in more detail, precisely what helps us navigate the search space effectively during generation – the paradigmatic context of choice – is no longer accessible during analysis. We do not know which features from a systemic network are relevant and which not. This gives rise to the radical asymmetry of the generation and analysis tasks: in generation, the simple traversal of the network *can* only find compatible combinations of features because that is what the network leads it to. In analysis, we do not know which path to follow through the network in advance: our task is to *discover* which features apply for the utterances heard or read. We have then to consider *any* of the features that utterances or context suggest might be relevant; the paradigmatic context is not automatically available. This means that we cannot reverse the generation argument in order to quickly and simply find a solution. We have to be able to jump into the grammar network as a whole to see what solutions it supports given any evidence that becomes available. And this means that we cannot restrict access to the search space along familiar paradigmatic lines.

1.3 Failing to analyse: more than a temporary technical difficulty

In this section, I set out the problem sketched in the previous section with respect to a concrete grammar and a concrete analysis task. The grammar used is the currently available version of the Nigel grammar originally developed within William Mann's Penman text generation project (Mann 1983). The Nigel grammar was developed primarily by Christian Matthiessen around a core set of networks provided by Halliday (Halliday 2005b); this grammar was the computationally instantiated version of the linguistic description subsequently taken considerably further non-computationally in Matthiessen (1995). Although the discussion will draw centrally on Nigel and the Penman-style definition of a systemic-functional grammar, it is important to realize that all variants of systemic-functional grammars currently existing for computational specification of such grammars (e.g., most significantly, Fawcett et al. 1993) face the same problems.

The computational form of the Nigel grammar has now grown from its original 81 systems to 767 grammatical systems defined over 1381 grammatical features; it is still a very large computational grammar by current standards, although nowadays by no means the broadest when considered in terms of raw grammatical coverage. The figures and listings of concrete components of the grammar used in this chapter have been made using the version of the grammar currently available for use with the KPML text generation system (Bateman 1997), which also provides many ways of exploring systemic-functional resources statically and during generation.[2]

The overall task will be to take a string of words as input and to produce a 'systemic parse' – i.e., a functional description of that string of words that shows its constituency structure and corresponding collections of features selected from the grammatical system network. The discussion here is in many respects similar to that followed in O'Donnell (1993) and precisely the *reverse* of the 'walk throughs' of systemic generation given by Mann and Matthiessen (1985) for Penman/Nigel and Fawcett *et al.* (1993) for his Cardiff Grammar. In addition, O'Donnell's description follows an analysis example with respect to a somewhat smaller grammar, enabling him to focus on possible methods for making the analysis work that will, unfortunately, largely elude us here. To show the scale of the general problem I consider, on the one hand, the full version of the current Nigel grammar and, on the other hand, an extremely simple input string: 'The cat sat' – a more artificial and over-simplified example would be difficult to imagine.

It is also important for the concreteness of the discussion that we commit entirely to what is permissible within the computational formalism employed for defining Nigel. This forces us to be explicit. We cannot 'magically' solve problems that arise by drawing on other sources that have not been spelled out. By making this strong commitment we can show clearly where extensions are required.[3] This version of systemic grammar allows the construction of arbitrarily complex system networks where systems have entry conditions (the paradigmatic conditions for their applicability) expressed in terms of conjunctions and disjunctions over features from other systems. Systems capture choices between one or more features. Each feature may have an arbitrary number of realization statements attached that define the syntagmatic consequences of selecting that feature. Realization statements consist of realization operators that are applied to either grammatical functions (functionally labelled units making up the unit), grammatical features (terms of systems), or lexical features (i.e., additional features associated with particular lexical items). The realization operators available are set out in Table 1.1. Most of these have been standardly assumed in versions of systemic-functional grammar for over 30 years and so will not be further motivated or discussed here (see Matthiessen 1988; Matthiessen and Bateman 1991). It is important to be clear about the fact that this description is *exhaustive*: we allow no other mechanisms for the purposes of the present discussion. Any further mechanisms would constitute an addition to the framework studied and so would need detailed re-evaluation of their consequences for the complexity of the analysis task. However, I note in passing that it cannot in general be assumed that additions necessarily make things easier! – often they do not.

In order to see what we are trying to produce as a result of our analysis, the grammatical structure that Nigel currently *generates* for our adopted

Table 1.1 The Penman-style realization operators of the Nigel grammar

Immediate dominance	Insert	$+F$	a constituent labelled as F is present in the structure at the current rank
	Expand	$F_1 (F_2)$	an intermediate (non-ranking) labelled level of structure is present in the structure at the current rank, decomposing the first function to include at least the second
	Conflate	F_1/F_2	two functionally labelled constituents are combined to co-describe a single constituent
Linear precedence	Order	$F_1 \char94 F_2$	immediate ordering of one functionally labelled constituent adjacent to another
	Partition	$F_1 .. F_2$	relative ordering of one functionally labelled constituent with respect to another
Inter-rank, inter-axis	Inflectify	$F_1 :: :1_1$	a constituent is constrained to have the specified features from morphological ranks
	Classify	$F_1 : :1_1$	a constituent is constrained to have the specified features from word ranks
	Preselect	$F_1 : f_1$	a functionally labelled constituent is constrained to require the presence of a specified feature in its selection expression
	Lexify	$F!1$	the specified constituent is specified to receive the specified lexicalization

example sentence is shown in Figure 1.1. This presentation is the default 'grammar engineer's' style produced by the KPML system; visualizations in a variety of more traditional systemic views are also possible. Here, conflation (co-labelling) of functional constituents is indicated by forward slashes; expansion of functional constituents, e.g. Mood into Subject and Finite, is indicated by added labels in square brackets. The features in curly brackets *above* a constituent, e.g. 'nominative' above Topical, indicate features pre-selected from the rank above; the features in curly brackets *immediately* below a constituent, e.g. 'do-verb' under Voice, indicate classifications of word rank features to be passed down; the features in curly brackets below these show inflectifies of morphologically relevant properties, e.g. 'thirdperson-form'. If the realization of a constituent is selected directly by the grammar via lexicalization, then this is also indicated, e.g. for Deictic 'the', in the current example.

As usual for a systemic grammar, this structure is the result of traversing the system network defining the grammar and collecting the constraints imposed by the realization statements of the features selected. The selection expression, i.e., the features selected from the overall grammar during a single traversal, positions its grammatical unit uniquely within the entire space of potential grammatical units provided by the grammar. The selection expression for the Topical/Medium/Subject constituent 'the cat' includes

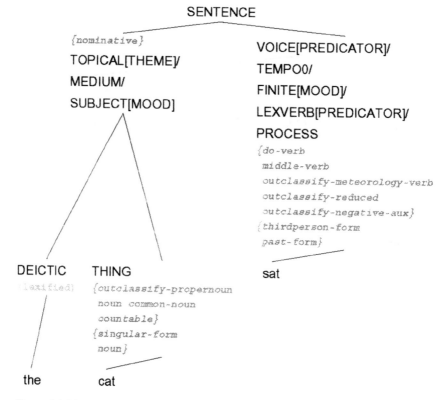

Figure 1.1 The structure produced by Nigel for the utterance 'the cat sat'

48 grammatical features; that for the clause as a whole 60 grammatical features. This shows us that for generation, as suggested in our quotation from Halliday concerning the size of grammars above, there is indeed no great complexity involved. 60 choice points from clause rank were sufficient to home in on precisely the clause structure given and to differentiate this clause from all other possible clauses. The search space has therefore been navigated with considerable efficiency.

When we come to analysis, however, the first difficulty the grammar faces is to discover from the sequence of three words, 'the', 'cat' and 'sat', what possible groupings of these words are potentially combinable into groups and phrases. Our question and problem is: how can it do this *using only the information that is directly available or derivable from the grammar?*

1.3.1 From words to groups

The first task we face is bridging the divide from instantial syntagmatic organization in the form of a known sequence of words presented as input[4] to, on the one hand, a richer instantial syntagmatic organization involving configurations of grammatical functions and, on the other, instantial paradigmatic organization – i.e., selections from a system network. And here we immediately find some gaps in the information that is *explicitly available* for organizing our search: for example, we know as systemic linguists that if we are starting from words it is probably going to be beneficial to start our search for applicable parts of the grammar network working up the rank scale. That is, we should already be confining our search for syntagmatic options to groups and phrases. Within the Nigel grammar, however, there is no formal reflection of this principle (and, indeed, as we will see when we come to 'sat', it is not even an accurate description of how the Nigel grammar is organized).

Since there is no explicitly specified difference between those features associated with clauses and those associated with groups – all are possibly relevant – we need to see what information we can obtain from the words themselves. Anchoring the words we find in the input utterance to places in the grammar network can be achieved in Nigel in two ways. First, we may assume that we can access morphological features directly from the words we find in an input utterance; this is possible within the Nigel approach because there is a lexicon component where such information is maintained. Such features may then be employed in the grammar network in either *classify* or *inflectify* realization statements: we can therefore search for such occurrences and locate potentially relevant grammatical features. Second, we may find places in the grammar network where some functionally labelled grammatical constituent is directly *lexified* to be realized by the specified word; this latter option corresponds to statements of lexical delicacy, which are found in Nigel for closed class items of several kinds.

The features found in the lexicon for the words of our example sentence are the following:

> 'the' : *none*
> 'cat' : noun common-noun countable
> 'sat' : verb do-verb middle-verb

The definite article has no relevant features because it is specified directly in the grammar by lexify statements. There are in fact three grammatical systems where this is done. The grammatical features involved are: 'ordinal-determined', 'nonselective', and 'determined'. These all involve lexify realization statements of the form:

> (lexify Deictic THE)

This gives us the strong hypothesis concerning the syntagmatic configuration at hand that it contains the function 'Deictic' realizing 'the'. There would appear to be no other way for 'the' to find its way into an utterance. If we make an assumption of 'once lexified, always lexified', then we raise the hypothesis to a certainty.

For 'cat' and 'sat', however, we do not find any such systems since the grammar is not lexically delicate for open class items. We can therefore ask the grammar if there are realization statements involving any of the *lexical features* required. For 'cat' we find eight features where its lexical features are classified for: 'otherindividual', 'lexical-thing', 'determined', 'tertiary-classification', 'secondary-classification', 'quaternary-classification', 'primary-classification', and 'countable-noun'. The realization statements specified for these features involve five grammatical functions; that is, each feature has at least one realization statement of the form:

(classify F f)

where 'f' is one of the three lexical features given for 'cat' and F is one of Classifier1, Classifier2, Classifier3, Classifier4 or Thing. Similarly for 'sat', we find four features where its lexical features are classified for: 'ascriptive', 'declarative-tagged', 'material' and 'middle', involving two grammatical functions: Process and Tagfinite.

Working from the names of the features, we might well guess that those features resulting from 'cat' are drawn from the portion of the network responsible for nominal-groups and those from 'sat' from the portion for clauses. But actually this information is not readily available in the grammar: there is no explicit record that these features belong to one rank rather than another apart from the connectivity of the paradigmatic network. The only *general* way of discovering this is then to ask whether, for example, 'determined' is *compatible* with the rank feature 'clause', 'nominal-group', 'prepositional-phrase', etc. to see what the result is. For two features to be compatible means that there is at least one selection expression allowed by the grammar network where both features occur.

And it is here that the particular structure of the problem space hits us with full force for the first time: *we do not know on which possible selection expressions the features being compared might lie.* Since we did not arrive at these features by following the paradigmatic organization, we do not now know which paradigmatic contexts might be relevant. Then, because we do not know in advance which selection expressions those might be, we are faced with *the full search space.*

This takes us back to the issue of the size of a grammar introduced above. Moreover, we can now follow through Halliday's calculations for the Nigel grammar as we are using it here. For some ranks in this grammar, the number of selection expressions produced remains relatively constrained. There are, for example, only 744 distinct selection expressions produced for the prepositional phrase. For the nominal group, however, I do not at present know how many selection expressions are covered by the Nigel system network: it is certainly over 2 billion (2×10^9) because when I recently attempted to enumerate all the possibilities this is as far as my computer got before giving up. When we turn to the larger network associated with the clause grammar, the situation is markedly worse. However, since the clause grammar network allows a cleaner decomposition according to metafunctions than has been attempted so far in the Nigel grammar for nominal groups, it was possible to try and estimate how many selection expressions are covered by factoring the network into subnetworks that are assumed to be largely independent: we can then take the network to be cross-classifying across the experiential and interpersonal metafunctions.

Taking the experiential part of the network alone and decomposing this into subnetworks in a similar way gives a figure of at least 8,265,022,920 experiential selection expression contributions. Doing the same for the mood part of the network gives at least 371,945,952 different interpersonal selection expression contributions. Under the assumption that these are largely independent, this gives a total of

$$3,074,141,818,281,219,840 \text{ (i.e., } 3 \times 10^{18})$$

selection expressions. For a further approximation we would need to multiply this by the full range of textual variations supported; this is made difficult in Nigel because the textual systems are interwoven with the non-textual systems and we cannot apply the same technique of decomposing a network into independent subnetworks and cross-multiplying the resulting selection expressions to get an overall estimate.

To put these figures into some kind of perspective, we can note for comparison that the number of neurons in the human brain is currently estimated to be around 10^{12} and these support around 10^{15} interconnections. This means that even if an entire selection expression, which for the clause in Nigel often contains around 60 features, could be encoded by a single connection between neurons (which is rather unlikely), we would need 1000 brains just to represent the possible selection expressions of the current Nigel grammar of the clause. Table 1.2 lists the 'sizes' of all the individual ranks of the Nigel grammar as far as I have been able to approximate them to date.

Table 1.2 Size of major components of the Nigel grammar expressed in terms of the number of selection expressions generated (estimates as of September 2006)

rank or primary class	size
adverbial-group	18
words	253
quantity-group	356
prepositional-phrase	744
adjectival-group	1045
nominal-group	$> 2 \times 10^9$
clause	$> 3 \times 10^{18}$

Given these figures, and returning to the example that we are trying to analyse, we can see that even to check whether the word 'cat' belongs to a different grammatical unit than 'sat', we are faced with checking compatibility with respect to 3×10^{18} possibilities. If this seems implausible in that it raises what is surely a trivial linguistic observation to a gargantuan task, I agree. The point that this makes, and it is one that reoccurs at many points in the present discussion, is that *although this information should be more accessible, with the specification form provided by the systemic-functional resource directly it is not*. Speakers obviously do not need to 'unfold' all of the possibilities that a systemic network resource expresses when producing or analysing utterances, but they must still in some sense *have access* to those possibilities in order to position any utterance with respect to the functionally differentiated space of possibilities available. Just how they might achieve this access is not provided by the lexicogrammatical specification as given.

In this case, it is relatively straightforward to imagine extensions that would help out. For example, if we were to add information that assigns particular grammatical functions to particular grammatical ranks, we would immediately be able to see which features are potentially compatible and which not even though we do not know their paradigmatic context. This must be an additional piece of linguistic specification – it cannot be determined automatically by looking at the existing network because this would involve exhaustive search (again, going through 3×10^{18} possibilities and recording for each rank which grammatical functions are inserted). There are in the current Nigel grammar over 200 distinct grammatical functions and it is possible to associate each of these with a unique grammatical rank or primary class. This would provide a fast link from words to ranks that, in some cases at least, would reduce the search space somewhat. Such 'inventories' of grammatical functions were already suggested in, for example, the early accounts of Halliday (1961); perhaps they were not considered further because from the *generation perspective* the inventory appears to do little work – functions are inserted into structure as required. It is in fact likely that several useful pieces of *structural* information of this kind are no longer maintained in any form in our computational accounts precisely because the generation task has been our measure of formalization requirements – for analysis this is not adequate.

Restoring the information relating grammatical functions to ranks would then let us assume that we can discover that 'the' and 'cat' are potentially compatible (thereby shortcutting the need to find relevant features on at least one of the 2 billion plus selection expressions for nominal groups) and those of 'sat' are not since they are associated with clauses (thereby shortcutting a search through 10^{18} possibilities). But we are still being relatively lucky with our three-word utterance in that two of those words involve features that share a rank and a third does not. For longer sentences we still might not have a good idea just which words should be grouped together for further exploration, and which not, and no clear sense of where the boundaries between them might be. For a longer utterance, such as 'the cat that chased the mouse sat on the mat', we would simply have the sequence of rank-assignments:

ng ng ng clause ng ng clause pp ng ng

This might also involve ambiguous assignments in cases of grammatical metaphor, nominalizations and the like. Each additional possible combination that we need to check multiplies the overall cost of checking for compatibility.

In order to ascertain reliably that 'the' and 'cat' belong to a single nominal group we also need to see if the grammar allows them to be combined in that order. Clearly, if the grammar supports 'the' as a realization of some function F_1, and 'cat' as a realization of some function F_2 and these both are functions of the same rank and have an allowable ordering such that F_1 immediately precedes F_2, then we have a candidate analysis. This information must be in the grammar somewhere, otherwise we would not have been able to generate the sentence, but can we find it?

When we try to identify the potential grammatical functions that might be involved, the grammar is not very forthcoming. Whereas the allocation of 'the' to Deictic is unique, we have seen that 'cat' can be associated with at least 5 grammatical functions. Therefore, if the grammar supports a grammatical unit that allows any of the following structures

Deictic ˆ Thing
Deictic ˆ Classifierl
Deictic ˆ Classifier2
Deictic ˆ Classifier3
Deictic ˆ Classifier4

then we have successfully found a *potential* analysis. To check this, we need to recover the ordering information that is expressed in the grammar. Ordering information is expressed both directly, in terms of *immediate ordering*, and indirectly by both relative ordering without adjacency (*partition*: cf. Table 1.1) and default orders.[5] So if we can find such ordering statements somewhere then we may be on the way to a possible analysis.

Unfortunately, the elements that may actually be referenced in the ordering statements found in the grammar may be elements that turn out to have been *conflated* with the required function rather than that function directly. To illustrate this, consider the following grammatical system. This system involves one of the features mentioning that Deictic is to be realized as 'the'; it has the following set of realization statements:

ORDINATIVE-DETERMINATION:
  ordinal-determined
    (insert Deictic)   or
    (lexify Deictic THE)
    (order Deictic Ordinal)

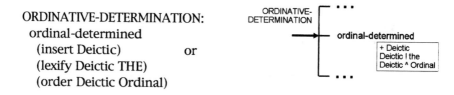

The ordering statement looks potentially useful in that it mentions Deictic and tells us that one of the grammatical functions that can directly follow Deictic is Ordinal. This means that if Ordinal *were conflated with* one of the five grammatical functions we are looking for to anchor 'cat', then, under these circumstances, this feature would be a candidate feature for our analysis. We can check this explicitly if we know that this is what we need to do and we would find, in this case, that in fact Ordinal does not conflate with anything and so is not a candidate. This feature should therefore be *ruled out* as a potential analysis.

This is again a relatively fortunate case. In general, we need to find out not single possible conflations for our grammatical functions but the complete *transitive closure* of possibly conflated grammatical functions.[6] This is necessary in order to know that we have definitely got hold of all the real candidates where ordering information may be hiding. But this transitive closure of possibly conflated functions also grows quickly and in ways that are often unhelpful. For the current Nigel grammar, the transitive closure along conflation for both the grammatical functions Deictic and Thing is the same, namely:

{ Actor Addressee Agent Attribute Auxstem Beneficiary Carrier Cause Circumstance Comparator Deictic Directcomplement Finite Goal Identified Identifier Lexverb Manner Means Medium Nonfinitive Obliquecomplement Phase Phasedependent Phenomenon Possession Process Quality Range Reality Realitydependent Reason Report Sayer Senser Spacelocative Subject Tempo0 Tempo1 Tempo1dependent Tempo2 Tempo3dependent Thing Timelocative Token Topical Value Voice Voicedependent Wh }

At first, this may look simply like a mistake: how can Thing be conflated with Voice or Agent, for example? The problem is partially that we have simply followed pairs of grammatical functions related by conflation without checking whether the realization statements involved could ever occur together – that is, we have not checked the *compatibility* of the grammatical features involved. Factoring this by rank improves the situation in this case in that the clause functions, which form the huge majority, disappear. For the nominal group this bring us considerably further; but for the clause, as we shall see, it still leaves us with a major problem.

However, the situation is, even for the nominal group, worse that than described because the question we actually need an answer to is not whether the concrete features associated with lexical items contain potentially relevant ordering information, but rather whether those concrete features *entail any other features in the grammar* that contain relevant ordering information. That is, although our ORDINATIVE-DETERMINATION system above did not contain useful ordering information, perhaps a less delicate feature leading to that system did – we would also need to check this. Which again leads to very expensive questions of compatibility between collections of features: for any features *f*, we need to check for useful ordering statements for *any* feature *g* with which *f* is compatible. This information is not available without accessing the expanded search space including all selection expressions. The organization of the grammar therefore does not provide a convenient way of predicting just what sequences of grammatical functions may occur. Reliable hypotheses concerning ordering in *any specific case* are not then available.

But to continue, let us assume that we have managed to find a constituent that is at least internally consistent. Can we do anything with it? – that is, can the grammar as specified locate a grammatical function at the rank above that can carry the constructed constituent?

1.3.2 Looking for a clause

We have already seen that the lexical features associated with the word 'sat' would lead us directly to clause rank – or would if we could check compatibility between the rank feature 'clause' and the features 'ascriptive', 'declarative-tagged', 'material', and 'middle'. The explicit association of grammatical functions and ranks proposed above would also support this decision: so we need to find ways of bringing a constituent $_{ng}$[the cat] together with $_{word}$[sat] within a single clause. When we try and link in not a word, but a subconstituent to a higher ranked structure, the situation becomes more complex in that we are dealing not with relations between lexical items and classify/inflectify realizations but with *preselections*. For the current example, any feature from a rank above 'nominal-group' that includes realization statements that *preselect* some grammatical function for one of the features in one of the selection expressions produced for 'the cat' could be relevant and useful to follow up.

With the Nigel grammar, there are essentially three candidate selection expressions for 'the cat' relevant. Given the problems described above, we would not have been able to find these automatically, but let us assume for the current discussion that we have, somehow, isolated these for consideration. Each of these contributes 48 grammatical features (the full selection expression for 'the cat' produced during generation) that are potentially relevant. That is, for each feature *fi* from one of these selection expressions, there *may* be features from clause rank that have realization statements of the form:

$$(\text{preselect } F_? \, fi)$$

These are then potentially appropriate for bringing the nominal group into the clause. Carrying this out gives us a set of clause rank features where, yet again, we have no indication of paradigmatic preference or constraint: all we know is that each member of this set may (but need not) be relevant for the nominal group at issue. The result is an ordering of hypotheses to try in the search space that is no doubt somewhat better than a blind search, but how much better is unclear.

The constraints actually delivered by these selection expressions of the nominal group are, in a grammar like Nigel, less restricting than may have been thought. Many of the actual decisions made are motivated semantically directly at nominal group rank and there are no corresponding restrictions to be found at clause rank. As a consequence, not many of the 48 features on offer in the present case are found in realization statements at clause rank (or anywhere else in the grammar). Beginning with the least delicate feature on the selection expression, the primary class 'nominal-group', and examining the grammar for any features where a grammatical function is preselected to be a nominal-group, we find 42 features involving 29 possible grammatical functions. The next feature on the selection expression, 'nominative', is preselected in four places (involving the grammatical functions Initiating, Continuing and Subject), and 'nonwh-nominal' also in four places (also involving Initiating and Continuing). The remaining 45 features are not used for preselection. This is also a reflection of the different role being played by these features with respect to determining classes and subtypes of classes, although this distinction is also not given in the grammar in any explicit way: the grammar writer can in general choose to preselect on *any* feature. We then have, on the basis of the information available in Nigel, no less than 31 grammatical functions that could be being filled by our nominal group 'the cat'. One might expect a lexically more delicate grammar to be of help in that finer nominal group features (e.g., 'non-conscious'?) might restrict the likely grammatical functions: just how much this can constrain the process remains an open question at this time.

For current purposes, and staying with the possibilities of the Nigel grammar, we need to consider the entire clause configuration in order to find which of these grammatical functions might be actually applicable for the case at hand. Therefore we need to consider the other potential constituents of the prospective clause grammatical unit; note that for a less artificial utterance this would already be a considerable hurdle: we have only managed with several unlikely and charitable assumptions to get to a selection expression for our initial two words at all. For a longer sentence we would already be faced with the combinatorial problem of deciding which of the subsequences of words represent single units and which not. We would need to be repeating all of the operations described so far *for each potential constituent.*

Whereas the search space within the nominal group was relatively constrained (10^9), that within the clause is not (10^{18}). With this order of magnitude, there is no way in which the connectivity of the network is going to help us further in establishing which features should be combined in a selection expression for a hypothesized clause. Precisely the strength of the paradigmatic description, that it allows a very concise representation of a large number of possibilities, trips us up when we attempt paradigmatically based analysis. We will need to fit our hypothesized constituency structures and associated selection expressions for 'the cat' into filling a functional role at a higher rank by some other means and, for this, we need to explore other sources of guidance.

1.4 Succeeding to analyse

In this section I turn to some linguistic accounts currently under development where the difficulties of grammatical analysis have been addressed very differently. A prime concern in these approaches has been to combine broad coverage grammatical resources with theoretical models that are provably 'well behaved' computationally. Whether or not an account is 'well behaved' is measured by applying *computational complexity theory* (see Barton et al. 1987), an area of computer science that addresses the abstract properties of problems *without* reference to any concrete algorithms or computational implementations. This abstractness is very important for understanding that complexity theory is not a restriction of views of problems to vagaries of computer hardware, which may in any case change dramatically over any given time period. Complexity theory is concerned with the inherent 'difficulty' of problems as such. Abstract search, and the complexity of performing that abstract search, relies *on the structure of the problem*, on how the problem space is itself organized so that it supports finding solutions (or not). The independence of the results of complexity theory from details of algorithm and hardware also makes it relevant for addressing issues of natural language – the difficulty of a *problem* does not change when we shift from using a PC to a brain: complexity theory issues concern any possible instantiation of the abstract search involved in a problem, of whatever make-up, e.g. highly parallel, neuronal, quantum, etc. and even regardless of whether this is computationally instantiated or brought about by some dynamic system seeking equilibrium.

The two main frameworks I will draw on are Tree Adjoining Grammars (TAG: Joshi 1987; Kroch and Joshi 1985) and Combinatory Categorial Grammar (CCG: Steedman 1993, 2000). These are examples of approaches that have taken computational complexity very seriously. Although they were developed independently of one another, they have since been shown to have some deep theoretical properties in common. In particular, they belong to the same 'complexity class' – one which is significantly lower than anything that we can find for current systemic grammars. It is precisely in this deeper foundation that we can now see a considerable advance in the current understanding of syntagmatic organization.

1.4.1 Formal computational complexity theory and its relevance

Complexity theory describes complexity in terms of known *complexity classes*. Complexity classes group problems according to their known complexity behaviour. There are now many distinct classes, with sometimes as yet unknown relations holding between them. The most commonly used complexity classes are called *P*, standing for *polynomial*, and *NP*, standing for *non-deterministic polynomial*.

Problems in *P* are considered to be 'computationally tractable' problems: solutions can be found on an ordinary computer in a time given by a polynomial expression involving a specification of the problem size. In linguistic work on computational complexity concerned with analysis, it is common to take the length of the input utterance in words as an indication of the problem size. An analysis problem that lies in *P* would then be soluble within a time bound given by n^k where n is the length of the input and k is some constant value arising from the inherent complexity structure of the problem. One describes this in complexity theory by saying that the time-complexity of the problem is of the order of n^k, written as $O(n^k)$. One of the standard results from complexity theory is that recognition using a context-free phrase structure grammar can be carried out in a time that is proportional to n^3. One could write very bad algorithms that might take even longer, but the inherent complexity structure of the problem means that no algorithm can be found that performs better than n^3. Assuming that each step in an implemented algorithm might take 1 microsecond, even 'sentences' consisting of 100 'words' (i.e., $n = 100$) would be analysable with a context-free grammar *in the worst case* in one second.[7]

In contrast, problems in *NP* can present more difficulties and are considered technically to be 'hard'. In particular, those that have neither efficient deterministic nor nondeterministic (parallel) solution algorithms and which take not polynomial but *exponential* time are considered to be computationally intractable. Exponential time-complexity means that a solution can be found at best in a time proportional to that given by an expression such as k^n, where k is determined by the type of problem and n is the length of the input string as before. If we take n to be 100, k to be 2, and each step to take 1 microsecond as above, then a solution can only be guaranteed in 10^{15} *centuries*.

For the linguistic system, the question is how a solution can be found using the linguistic resources defined – do the resources help us (and any instantiation of a system) to a solution or do they not. If we define the problem as uncovering a lexicogrammatical analysis from a systemic network as definable within the framework used in Nigel in the previous sections, for example, we obtain results that are fully independent of the processing substrate: the inherent complexity of the problem in this case, shown by the search space, is extremely high.

A similar negative result was achieved relatively early in the development of the Chomskyan approach to syntax. By the late 1960s, it had become clear that the mechanisms being proposed within that approach were extremely powerful in terms of just what structures could be produced. As the transformational paradigm unfolded and ever more varied kinds of transformational mechanisms were suggested, it was increasingly unclear what the model was capable of describing and what not. Since Chomsky's position was that his theoretical model should closely constrain just what should count as a 'learnable human language' and what not, this was an issue of some concern. The question of the model's formal computational complexity was then taken up by Peters and Ritchie (1973), who proved formally that the account of transformations pursued was not capable of restricting the notion of 'human language' in any sensible way. In fact, they demonstrated that a transformational-generative account was able to produce descriptions of *any* language (perceived as a set of strings) that an arbitrary computer program could process. This includes a considerable number of 'languages' that would never plausibly bear any claim to belonging to the set of 'natural' languages.

As a consequence of this result, most formal theories of syntax derived since that time have at least attempted to restrict the power of their adopted mechanisms; this can only be done effectively if the account is itself sufficiently well formalized as to provide complexity results. This is to take the complexity lesson to heart and to design proposed approaches to syntax so that they appear to approximate more appropriately the kind of organizations found within natural language lexicogrammar and are formally provable as well behaved with respect to complexity. Both the non-systemic accounts I discuss in this chapter have taken this path.

There is a natural relationship between the different complexity classes and the standard formal language classes, sometimes referred to as the Chomsky hierarchy as shown in Figure 1.2. The simplest kinds of grammars, those of the regular languages, can be analysed very quickly indeed; context-

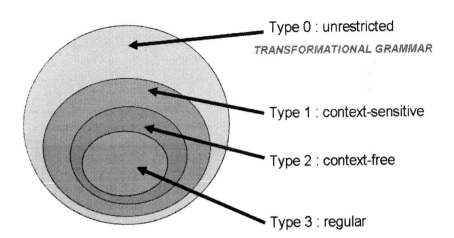

Type 0 : unrestricted

TRANSFORMATIONAL GRAMMAR

Type 1 : context-sensitive

Type 2 : context-free

Type 3 : regular

Figure 1.2 The Chomsky complexity hierarchy for formal languages

free grammars, as mentioned above, can be analysed in $O(n^3)$. From then on, the situation gets increasingly worse. Recognizing whether an input is covered by some specific context-sensitive grammar lies in a strictly harder complexity class called PSPACE ('polynomial space and unlimited time'); such grammars are already too powerful to provide efficient processing because in the general case recognition algorithms may exhibit exponential time complexity. Finally, the original transformational-generative grammars, falling under Chomsky's Type 0, are shown by Peters and Ritchie's results to be equivalent to arbitrary computer programs and go even beyond PSPACE to include both exponential time and exponential space requirements.

The poor computational properties even of context-sensitive grammars may come as a surprise. Surely, the argument long went, natural human languages are at least this complex? Taking computational complexity results seriously has supported the development of several approaches to syntax that are interesting precisely because they are less complex than context-sensitive languages while still being more complex than context-free languages. Both TAGs and CCGs described below are of this kind and both accounts make strong, although differing, claims about what can be expressed in a grammar. Interestingly, it is now known that both of these forms of grammar, although superficially very different, lie within the same complexity class; technical proofs of this are given in, for example, Joshi et al. (1991). Crucially for us here, that complexity class is simply P. In fact, both TAGs and CCGs are able to analyse sentences with a time-complexity of $O(n^6)$. Therefore, while somewhat slower than context-free grammars, the exponential explosion of more complex grammars does not occur.

To suggest the consequences of this graphically, Figure 1.3 contrasts the complexity curves according to the size of input for (i) an exponentially complex problem, such as early transformational grammar and systemic functional grammars expressed within the Nigel framework, assuming a modest problem constant of 6, and (ii) a polynomially complex problem with k=6, such as TAGs and CCGs. We can see again that even for relatively short inputs, the exponentially complex problem quickly disappears off the graph, even though the selected problem constant is probably very much higher than 6 in the Nigel case.

It is a direct consequence of the explicit management of the syntagmatic axis within the TAG and CCG frameworks that it is not only possible to produce complex and semantically motivated grammatical analyses of long, naturally occurring utterances relatively quickly, it is also possible to *prove* that they will deliver results quickly regardless of the complexity of the input. The performance shown in the graphs of Figure 1.3 is then not only a theoretical prediction: the speed of results with large grammars is already being observed in running systems. In addition, the complexity profiles of approaches to syntax falling within this complexity class appear to match far more closely the observed performance of humans and much of the apparent mystery of how utterances can be analysed so quickly disappears. This is the

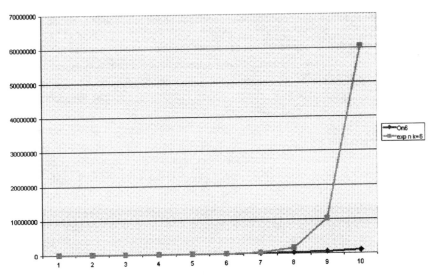

Figure 1.3 Complexity curves for $O(k^n)$ and $O(n^k)$ with k=6

opposite side of the coin to the discussion of systemic grammars presented in 1.3, where I suggested that it is possible to prove that no matter how simple the input, a result will *not* be forthcoming in any reasonable time. It is for this reason, therefore, that I propose that we now pay far more attention, even as systemicists, to the kinds of statements being made concerning lexicogrammatical syntagmatic organization being developed in such approaches.

1.4.2 TAG

In this section, I briefly and informally characterize Tree Adjoining Grammars in order to bring out precisely what it is that leads to their improved ability to analyse (and produce) the grammatical units that they describe. Whereas traditional phrase structure grammars work with rules, typically re-write rules or 'well-formedness' rules that state, for example, that a well-formed sentence is a sentence that consists of two constituents, a noun phrase and a verb phrase, TAGs work only with syntactic trees. Rather than having an $S{\rightarrow}NP\ VP$ rule, a corresponding TAG would simply list the tree fragment corresponding to such a rule as one of its supported structures. These basic tree fragments provided by a grammar are called *elementary trees*. A slightly more complex example is shown to the left of Figure 1.4: this tree corresponds to clauses of the form 'someone [like] something'. Within TAGs it is customary to refer to elementary trees with a label built on α, this tree then might be labelled: $\alpha_{like.}$

The effect of expanding this structure by a further rule – e.g., a rule of the form $NP{\rightarrow}Det\ N$ – is achieved by the operation of *substitution* which combines two tree fragments. Thus we would in this case take one tree fragment consisting of the partial structure involving S and another tree fragment consisting of the partial structure involving NP and by means of substitution join these together to form a single larger tree fragment with the NP node filled out as given by its contributing tree. So far this simply reproduces a context-free phrase structure grammar.

TAGs then go further by allowing one further operation for combining tree fragments, the operation of *adjunction*, and it is here that the formalism achieves a very different kind of linguistic generalization. Adjunction allows tree fragments to be placed *internally* within other tree fragments, thereby achieving a kind of 'mixing' of structures that is, at the same time, very tightly regulated. Tree fragments that can be combined into other fragments by adjunction are called *auxiliary trees* and have the following crucial property: each secondary tree has a root node and *at least one node on its periphery that is identical to that root node.* An example is shown in the centre of Figure 1.4. It is customary to designate auxiliary trees with a label built on β and so this tree is labelled $\beta_{\text{yesterday}}$. In this tree, the repeated node is S.

The operation of adjunction then operates by allowing a complete auxiliary tree to 'take the place' of any matching node in an elementary tree. In the present case, we can adjoin tree $\beta_{\text{yesterday}}$ into tree α_{like} in only one way: by replacing the S of the latter tree by the tree fragment of the former tree. The result of this is shown on the right of Figure 1.4, corresponding to clauses of the form 'yesterday someone [like] something'. Adjoining and substitution can then also be applied to any 'derived' trees resulting from combinations of elementary and auxiliary trees; a TAG then consists of just these two latter types of tree fragments. In general, auxiliary trees can be as complex as required, as long as the condition above is satisfied, and the node that is 'matched' can be anywhere in the tree being adjoined into. The adjunction operation is therefore the most distinctive contribution of TAGs; its operation in general can be illustrated graphically as shown in Figure 1.5.

The consequences of the addition of adjunction to the capabilities of the grammatical formalism are rather more far-reaching than might have been thought. First, the ability to insert structural fragments anywhere they might be required supports a clean separation of semantics and grammar analogous to that attempted within frameworks such as the Nigel grammar. The relation between the systemic network of the grammar and the semantic

Figure 1.4 An elementary tree, an auxiliary tree and the result of adjoining from a Tree Adjoining Grammar

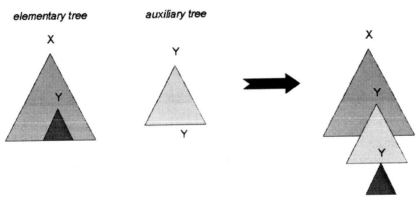

Figure 1.5 An abstract graphical view of adjunction

specifications used to drive the grammar in generation are maintained sufficiently far apart as to allow quite diverse lexicogrammatical realizations of particular semantic configurations. This is, as usual, readily applicable in generation but leads to problems of interpretation during analysis. We can suggest something of this benefit within TAGs by considering the semantics of the tree fragments that we have seen so far. The first tree, α_{like}, might correspond to an experiential semantic configuration of the form like (*a*, *b*, *t*), i.e., 'a likes b at time t'. The second tree, $\beta_{yesterday}$, might correspond to a semantic configuration such as yesterday(t), i.e., there is some time t and that is characterized as yesterday. We can then combine the two experiential semantic configurations simply by logically conjoining them: i.e.,

$$like(a, b, t) \wedge yesterday(t)$$

Now this simple semantic combination can also be matched syntactically; we just take the corresponding trees and adjoin them. The details of the grammatical integration are taken care of by the appropriate details in the syntactic fragments and the mechanics of adjoining.

Expressed somewhat more abstractly, the main design feature of TAGs is that they *localize* information around small chunks of syntactic constituency structure. Technically, TAGs factor out recursion and the domain of syntactic dependencies and so achieve a strict localization of dependencies. The grammatical mechanisms provided can then scatter this information around quite complex structures but the statements of locality are maintained throughout. That is, once we have specified, for example, a basic transitivity structure relating process and participants, very diverse changes can be made

$$\frac{NP \quad S \backslash NP}{S} \qquad \frac{S/VP \quad VP}{S}$$

Figure 1.6 Simple equivalent CCG derivations

to the syntactic form without losing this information. It nevertheless remains guaranteed that analysis will be achieved within $O(n^6)$.

1.4.3 CCG

We see a very different perspective being taken on syntactic description in CCG. The main feature of a CCG is that grammatical units are associated with complex categories which simultaneously serve as instructions for how grammatical derivation can proceed. Categories consist of two components: a grammatical unit category that is being 'looked for' in order to complete the current unit and the grammatical category that results when that unit is found. Thus, returning to the prototypical linguistic example rule $S \rightarrow NP$ VP, in the CCG framework this could be expressed by replacing the VP label with the category:

$$S \backslash NP$$

This category means that if this unit finds an NP to its left, then that unit can combine with the current one, resulting in a unit with the category S. This is generally written as shown on the left of Figure 1.6. It is also possible to construct categories that look for their completing elements on the right. Thus a formally equivalent, but linguistically perhaps less likely, way of capturing the same rule would be as shown on the right of the figure: here we have a category S/VP, which is a unit that is looking for a VP on its right for completion. Since this latter treatment would suggest that NPs always look for VPs on their right, it is not a particularly convincing analysis, but does show the principle of leftward-looking and rightward-looking categories.

The starting point for a CCG description is, similarly to TAGs, the lexical items in the description. Each lexical item is associated with a complex category description. This means that there is no further need for any additional grammatical mechanisms: the lexical item categories specify how they can be combined and combination proceeds until the largest category possible for the sequence of words being analysed is found. Two more complex examples are shown in Figure 1.7.

We can see how this dramatically improves the ability to analyse utterances

Keats	eats	apples	Keats	cooked	and	ate	apples
NP	*(S \ NP) / NP*	*NP*	*NP*	*(S \ NP) / NP*	*CONJ*	*(S \ NP) / NP*	*NP*

Figure 1.7 CCG derivation examples: taken from Steedman (2000: 10 and 31)

the	cat	that	chased	the	mouse	sat	on	the	mat
ng	ng	ng	clause	ng	ng	clause	PP	ng	ng
NPN	N	(NP\NP)/(S\NP)	(S\NP)/NP	NPN	N	(S\NP)/PP	PP/NP	NPN	N

Figure 1.8 CCG categories for an example sentence

by considering again the sequence of rank-allocations from our extended example 'the cat that chased the mouse sat on the mat' above: i.e., 'ng ng ng clause ng ng clause pp ng ng'. We saw that this was problematic because we could not get access to information about combinability of these elements. Representing these words not in terms of their ranks but in terms of their categorial grammar assignments would give a sequence of categories similar to that shown in Figure 1.8.[8] As we can see, some of the categories are quite complex: the most complex being the relative pronoun. However, this is actually what one would expect in that the function of this item is to link both what went before and what comes after. This is reflected in the composite nature of both the constituent that the item is looking for and the constituent produced. The former, an S\NP, is itself a category looking for an NP on its left to become an S, i.e., something similar to a traditional VP; the latter, an NP\NP, is a category looking for an NP on its left to become another NP – i.e., a category that acts like a relative clause, modifying an existing NP to become another NP.

This complexity pays off when we come to analysis. We can scan the sequence from left to right and see if there are any elements that are combinable. We immediately find that 'the' and 'cat' may be combined, yielding an NP; we can do this for all the noun phrases in the sentence. We can also then see that both 'chased', (S\NP) /NP, and 'on', PP/NP, are looking for NPs on their right and in fact find them. This enables 'sat', (S\NP) /PP, to find the PP that it is looking for on its right, combining 'sat on the mat' into a S\NP. Note at this point that we have the first potential local structural ambiguity because 'sat on the mat' is looking for an NP on its left and there is one, i.e., 'the mouse'. Locally, therefore, these might be combined to produce a sentence: 'the mouse sat on the mat'. This local alternative is quickly ruled out by the fact that there is no constituent with a category looking for S on its right and so no complete analysis would be found if we were to take this path. 'The mouse' has also been claimed by 'chased', however, and this path can be followed further.

The combined constituent 'chased the mouse' has the category (S\NP) and now the complex category of the relative pronoun comes into play: this category is looking for precisely what is on offer, i.e., an (S\NP) on its right. This can therefore be combined producing 'that chased the mouse' as an (NP\NP). Then, as we saw above, this can be simply added to 'the cat' to produce the complete NP 'the cat that chased the mouse'. This provides the NP on the left that 'sat on the mat' is waiting for and the analysis is done. The complete parse tree for the clause is therefore as shown in Figure 1.9. If this account creates the impression that the structure more or less 'builds

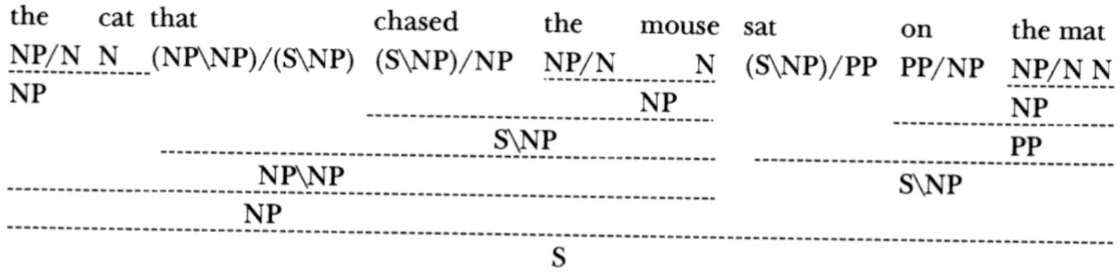

```
the     cat   that            chased     the    mouse  sat        on     the mat
NP/N  N  (NP\NP)/(S\NP)  (S\NP)/NP  NP/N      N  (S\NP)/PP  PP/NP  NP/N N
NP                                      NP                          NP
                                     ---------------                    ------
                                           S\NP                          PP
                                                                     ----------
        NP\NP                                                          S\NP
        NP
                              S
```

Figure 1.9 CCG analysis of an example 'cat' sentence

itself', this is not far wrong. It is indeed the case that the precise categorial information associated with each lexical item defines exactly which of its neighbours it can combine with. As a consequence, the automatic production of an analysis given a CCG is extremely fast – in practice as well as in theory. The process is indeed so fast that even adding in multiple lexical categories to handle words that may occur in a variety of syntactic contexts scarcely slows things down. In addition, just as with TAGs, there is no need for the analysis to wait until a complete unit is present: combination begins as soon as there is something to combine and the categories match. This also appears to be more reminiscent of how humans process their incoming language and, as with TAGs, the entire process remains guaranteedly within $O(n^6)$.

1.5 Discussion: where next?

We have seen in the previous sections that the approach to grammatical description taken in our systemic accounts and those in the TAG-and CCG-based accounts are almost exact opposites. Within Nigel, for example, the lexical item is as simple as possible: some items, e.g. 'the', have no information attached apart from their spelling. Within CCG, the 'simpler' the lexical item, the more complex the category. This is because within Nigel all information concerning what a word can be used for has been moved into the system network. Unfortunately, it is not then possible to get that information out of the network again if all we are given is the lexical item itself. This is what makes it so difficult during analysis to go from the input, the stream of words, to hypotheses concerning which features from the system network apply.

In the CCG and TAG approach, each word contains encapsulated within it, so to speak, its entire collection of possible usages. Within a TAG, lexical items act as lexical anchors for elementary trees that can undergo substitution and adjoining; within a CCG, lexical items are given complex combinatorial categories that function as explicit instructions for how they are to combine with their neighbours. In both cases, the path from string of words to candidate structures that can be checked for feature compatibility is maximally short. Systemically we can see this as making explicit a record of syntagmatic instantiations. It is, however, more than this, because these records are themselves stated to have quite specific formal features of their own. In the case of TAGs, they obey locality principles and may only be composed by substitution and adjunction; in the case of CCGs, they must obey the composition rules by which categories combine. This contrasts with the situation within a systemic functional grammar such as Nigel, where the grammars have to build up structure each time as if there were no *syntagmatic* generalizations to be made. This is somewhat unlikely: if the complexity of syntactic analysis really can be kept within the bounds of mild context sensitivity, this will not happen by chance in a description. It instead requires descriptions that follow very specific formal constraints.

Whereas this chapter has followed the problem faced by a paradigmatically organized grammatical resource when attempting to describe syntagmatic configurations, there is in fact a parallel story to be told concerning the increasing need that heavily syntagmatic accounts, such as TAG and CCG, face when constructing larger-scale resources: they too are forced to devise notions of *paradigmatic* organization. One of the broadest grammatical descriptions of English currently available is being developed within the TAG framework and is called the XTAG system. This system has a coverage of English well beyond that of Nigel's *and* works equally (in fact better) for analysis (see Doran *et al.* 1994, XTAG Research Group 2001 and www.cis. upenn.edu/~xtag/).

As described in the introduction to TAG above, TAG grammars essentially consist of very large collections of tree fragments. These tree fragments must also be organized sensibly in order to be developed and maintained and also to capture linguistic generalizations. For this purpose, such TAG resources now work with the important notion of *tree families*.

Tree families group together trees that describe a similar 'subcategorization frame', or basic transitivity pattern, and which undergo a common set of syntactic 'transformations' – although there are no actual transformations, of course. Moreover, since the tree fragments identified as tree families are strongly driven by corpus work, there is a close resemblance to the kinds of patterns uncovered in work such as the COBUILD project (Sinclair 1987). Tree families are then grouped into inheritance networks which capture generalizations across the syntagmatic configurations they describe. There are also now increasingly large-scale accounts of English within the CCG framework (see Doran and Srinivas 1997, Clark *et al.* 2002), some of which build directly on the formal relationship noted above between CCG and TAG to derive automatically broad-coverage CCG resources from the already very large TAG grammars. Within this work, there is also a need being felt for an organization similar to the tree families of XTAG.

In essence, a description in terms of tree families is similar to the state reached at any point in a system network where the alternative choices describe a set of ways in which the syntagmatic structure entailed by that point undergoes a specified set of further 'refinements'; one can equally look (metaphorically) at these refinements as a collection of 'transformationally

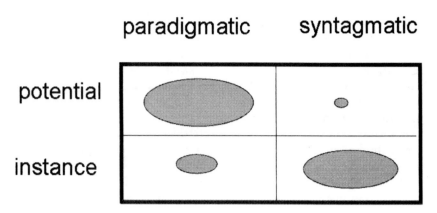

Figure 1.10 Characterization of the current state of systemic functional grammar

related' structures. This suggests a specific course of investigation for developing systemic accounts further. Whereas TAGs and CCGs are looking toward sensible organizations for their tree families, systemic-functional grammars require, given the arguments I have set out here, a tighter specification of what constitutes syntagmatic constituency structure. A logical path of investigation would be to see to what extent the systemic functional paradigmatic organization can fill the need for tree family organizations within TAGs and CCGs and, conversely, to what extent the syntagmatic accounts of TAGs or CCGs can fill the need for syntagmatic precision within systemic-functional accounts.

This issue has, in fact, already been posed and an exploratory hybrid approach of this kind was first introduced in the early 1990s by McCoy *et al.* (1990) and set out in more detail in Yang *et al.* (1991). This was an explicit attempt to combine aspects of TAG and systemic-functional grammars – albeit for generation. The approach taken was exactly that suggested as natural here: i.e., since TAGs appear to cater for the properties of the syntagmatic axis so well, it appeared worthwhile exploring to what extent they might augment a systemic network. This work came to a premature end due to the vagaries of research – researchers leaving, funding priorities changing, etc. – and it is particularly unfortunate that it has still not been taken further. The value of the experiment at that time may perhaps have been unclear: given the discussion I have given here, however, a continuation of this line of research should be seen as a matter of some priority.

1.6 Conclusions

I have set out some of the reasons why computational complexity is relevant for considering the problem of providing systemic-functional lexicogrammatical analyses. It brings with it some strong claims. For example, the reason *why* we cannot have a functioning analysis component using the resources of the Nigel grammar lies deeper than any technical issues of how well one can write an algorithm: it is not just that a computer could not do the analysis, *no system*, be it a computer or a brain, could do the analysis if it were restricted to the mechanisms defined within a system network of this kind. We can imagine a superfast neuron-based connectionist machine running everything massively in parallel (as presumably our brains do), or new experiments in quantum computation, or whatever, and the problem will still not go away.

It is sometimes suggested that one reason for the apparent failure to achieve automatic analysis systems based on systemic-functional lexico-grammatical descriptions might be found in the sophistication of systemic functional accounts – they are in some way 'too complex' for computational treatment and so, if they are to work, will have to be simplified in some way and so will not be truly 'systemic'. I have suggested in this chapter that the situation is actually rather different. In one particular area, that lying along the syntagmatic axis, systemic functional grammars are *too simple* and need to be made more complex. It turns out to be precisely their relative simplicity along the syntagmatic axis that is causing many of the problems.

We can characterize the situation graphically as suggested in Figure 1.10. Systemic theorizing has focused overwhelmingly on the 'potential x paradigmatic' and the 'instance x syntagmatic' cells of the matrix – and within these probably more on the paradigmatic. The cell 'potential x syntagmatic' has remained undeveloped and yet it is precisely this area of the account that is needed to make analysis work. Within systemic theorizing the asymmetry in the treatments of the paradigmatic and syntagmatic axes has no doubt been invaluable in providing a counterweight to the syntagmatic domination found in most other schools of linguistics that have emerged over the last 50 years. By allowing descriptions to focus on functionally motivated alternations, systemic-functional linguistic accounts have succeeded in providing deep and revealing analyses of a host of phenomena that have scarcely made it onto the research agenda in other accounts.

This success has come at a cost, however, and, in the current discussion, I have pursued the idea that it is time to readdress the syntagmatic axis of linguistic description. I have argued that the syntagmatic resources available to the systemic linguist are far too weak and this disempowers us in many current circles of discussion. In particular, the ideological counterweight function served by attention to the paradigmatic has led to a delay in theorizing the syntagmatic axis. While syntagmatic descriptions are commonly given, the work that they can do is limited precisely because the properties of such descriptions are too weakly defined. The extent to which syntagmatic descriptions can be used to reason about analyses is accordingly restricted. The question remains, therefore, whether the asymmetry is still functional. In order to balance the account to cover equally strongly

all of the cells of the semiotic matrix of Figure 1.10, we need researchers
who are at home in both systemic-functional paradigmatic descriptions and
non-systemic-functional syntagmatic descriptions. But systemic-functional
training has now established a tradition whereby such syntagmatic accounts
receive little attention. This may need to change.

Notes

1   For the purposes of the current discussion, I will not be considering other
    areas of computational language processing which are now attempting,
    sometimes quite successfully, to bring systemic-functional insights to bear
    by deliberately (and very sensibly, given the arguments that I make in
    this chapter) 'avoiding' the particular problem that I describe (see, e.g.,
    Honnibal 2004, Whitelaw and Patrick 2004, Patrick 2006). My main focus
    will remain on fine-grained lexicogrammatical description and its direct
    use in computational contexts.
2   It is also possible, therefore, for the interested reader to follow through
    precisely the kinds of questions that will be asked of the grammar below:
    the generation system KPML and respective grammars, including Nigel,
    are freely available from the website www.purl.org/net/kpml and this
    section is made up simply of the results obtained when addressing the
    questions relevant for analysis to that grammar.
3   Another reason for working with the Nigel grammar and its formalization
    is that we have a very good understanding of just what that formalization
    permits and what it does not. The most extensive formal characterization
    of systemic grammars to date is given in Henschel (1997).
4   I will ignore for the present discussion ranks below word and all other
    complex issues of form – these make the problem harder not easier and
    we will soon see that the problem is hard enough even with these unreal-
    istic simplifying assumptions.
5   Default orders are similar to the 'potential structures' used in the Cardiff
    Grammar of Fawcett *et al.* (1993).
6   That is, we need to repeat looking for possible conflations of grammatical
    functions until we find no new possibilities. This means finding all
    functions that conflate with, for example, Thing, then finding all
    functions which conflate with those, and so on until we reach a stable
    set.
7   This account is very much simplified for the purposes of the current
    exposition: clearly, problems that are in P with very high exponents, such
    as $O(n^{10000})$ are not going to be easy to solve despite their polynomial
    nature. None of the points made in this chapter depend on such extreme
    cases, however.
8   This description is selected to cover the example and should not be taken
    as a complete CCG analysis according to the current state of the theory.

References

Note: The articles from Michael Halliday cited here as Halliday (1961), Halliday (1966), Halliday (1979), and Halliday (1996) are also now available reprinted in the *Collected Works of M. A. K. Halliday*, Vol. 1: *On Grammar* Halliday (2002); the articles Halliday (1956), Halliday (1962) and Halliday and James (1993) are available in Vol. 6, Halliday (2005a).

Barton, G. E., Berwick, R. C. and Ristad, E. S. (1987), *Computational Complexity and Natural Language*. Cambridge, MA and London: MIT Press.

Bateman, J. A. (1997), 'Enabling technology for multilingual natural language generation: the KPML development environment'. *Journal of Natural Language Engineering*, 3(1), 15–55.

Clark, S., Hockenmaier, J. and Steedman, M. (2002), 'Building deep dependency structures using a wide-coverage CCG parser', in *'Proceedings of the 40th Annual Meeting of the Association for Computational Linguistics (ACL)'*, pp. 327–34. www.citeseer.ist.psu.edu/article/clark02building.html.

Doran, C., Egedi, D., Hockey, B. A., Srinivas, B. and Zaidel, M. (1994), 'XTAG system – a wide coverage grammar for English', in *Proceedings of the 15th. International Conference on Computational Linguistics (COLING 94)*, Vol. II, Kyoto, Japan, pp. 922–8.

Doran, C. and Srinivas, B. (1997), 'Developing a wide-coverage CCG system'. Technical report, IRCS, University of Pennsylvania. www.citeseer.ist.psu. edu/doran97developing.html.

Fawcett, R. P. (1988), 'What makes a "good" system network good?', in J. D. Benson and W. S. Greaves (eds), *Systemic Functional Approaches to Discourse*. Norwood, NJ: Ablex, pp. 1–28.

Fawcett, R. P., Tucker, G. and Yuen, L. (1993), 'How a systemic-functional grammar works', in H. Horacek and M. Zock (eds), *New Concepts in Natural Language: Planning Realization and Systems*. London: Pinter, pp. 114–86.

Halliday, M. A. K. (1956), 'The linguistic basis of a mechanical thesaurus, and its application to English preposition classification'. *Mechanical Translation*, 3(3), 81–8.

Halliday, M. A. K. (1961), 'Categories of the theory of grammar'. *Word*, 17(3), 241–92.

Halliday, M. A. K. (1962), 'Linguistics and machine translation'. *Zeitschrift für Phonetik, Sprachwissenschaft und Kommunikationsforschung*, 15(1–2), 145–58.

Halliday, M. A. K. (1966), 'Some notes on "deep" grammar'. *Journal of Linguistics*, 2(1), 57–67.

Halliday, M. A. K. (1979), 'Modes of meaning and modes of expression: types of grammatical structure and their determination by different semantic functions', in D. J. Allerton, E. Carney and D. Holdcroft (eds), *Function and Context in Linguistic Analysis. A Festschrift for William Haas*. Cambridge: Cambridge University Press, pp. 57–79.

Halliday, M. A. K. (1996), 'On grammar and grammatics', in R. Hasan, C. Cloran and D. Butt (eds), *Functional Descriptions – Theory in Practice, Current Issues in Linguistic Theory*. Amsterdam: Benjamins, pp. 1–38.

Halliday, M. A. K. (2002), *On Grammar*, Vol. 1 of *Collected Works of M. A. K. Halliday*. London: Continuum.

Halliday, M. A. K. (2005a), *Computational and Quantitative Studies*, Vol. 6 of *Collected Works of M. A . K. Halliday*. London: Continuum.

Halliday, M. A. K. (2005b), 'Systems of the English clause: A trial grammar for the PENMAN text generation project [Information Sciences Institute, University of Southern California]', in J. J. Webster (ed), *Computational and Quantitative Studies*, Vol. 6 of *Collected Works of M. A. K. Halliday*. London: Continuum, pp. 265–84. Published version of an internal Penman project note from 1980.

Halliday, M. A. K. and James, Z. L. (1993), 'A quantitative study of polarity and primary tense in the English finite clause', in M. Hoey, J. M.Sinclair and G. Fox (eds), *Techniques of Description: Spoken and Written Discourse (A Festschrift for Malcolm Coulthard)*. London and New York: Routledge.

Halliday, M. A. K. and Matthiessen, C. M. (2004), *An Introduction to Functional Grammar* (3rd edn). London: Edward Arnold.

Henschel, R. (1997), 'Compiling systemic grammar into feature logic systems', in S. Manandhar, W. Nutt and G. P. Lopez (eds), *CLNLP/NLULP Proceedings*. www.citeseer.ist.psu.edu/136797.html.

Honnibal, M. (2004), 'Converting the Penn Treebank to systemic functional grammar', in *Proceedings of the Australasian Language Technology Workshop (ALTW04)*. www.alta.asn.au/events/altw2004/publication/04-27.pdf.

Huddleston, R. (1965), 'Rank and depth.' *Language*, 41, 574–86.

Huddleston, R. (1988), 'Constituency, multi-functionality and grammaticalization in Halliday's functional grammar.' *Journal of Linguistics*, 24, 137–74.

Hudson, R. A. (1976), *Arguments for a Non-Transformational grammar*. Chicago: Chicago University Press.

Hudson, R. A. (1990), *English Word Grammar*. Oxford: Basil Blackwell.

Joshi, A. K. (1987), 'An introduction to Tree Adjoining Grammar', in A. Manaster-Ramer (ed.), *Mathematics of Language*. Philadelphia: John Benjamins Company, pp. 87–114.

Joshi, A. K., Vijay-Shanker, K. and Weir, D. (1991), 'The convergence of mildly context-sensitive grammar formalisms', in P. Sells, S. Shieber and T. Wasow (eds), *Foundational Issues in Natural Language Processing*. Cambridge, MA: The MIT Press, pp. 31–81.

Kroch, A. S. and Joshi, A. K. (1985), 'The linguistic relevance of Tree Adjoining Grammar'. Technical report, University of Pennsylvania, Department of Computer Science, Philadelphia, Pennsylvania.

McCord, M. C. (1977), 'Procedural systemic grammars'. *International Journal of Man-Machine Studies*, 9, 255–86.

McCoy, K. F., Vijay-Shanker, K. and Yang, G. (1990), 'Using tree adjoining grammars in the systemic framework', in *5th International Workshop on*

Natural Language Generation, 3–6 June 1990', Pittsburgh, PA. pp. 1–8. Organized by Kathleen R. McKeown (Columbia University), Johanna D. Moore (University of Pittsburgh) and Sergei Nirenburg (Carnegie Mellon University).

McDonald, D. D. (1980), 'Natural Language Production as a Process of Decision Making under Constraint'. PhD thesis, MIT, Cambridge, MA.

Mann, W. C. (1983), 'An overview of the PENMAN text generation system', in *Proceedings of the National Conference on Artificial Intelligence*, AAAI, pp. 261–5. Also appears as USC/Information Sciences Institute, RR-83-114.

Mann, W. C. and Matthiessen, C. M. I. M. (1985), 'Demonstration of the Nigel text generation computer program', in J. D. Benson and W. S. Greaves (eds), *Systemic Perspectives on Discourse, Volume 1*. Norwood, NJ: Ablex, pp. 50–83.

Martin, J. R. (1996), 'Types of structure: deconstructing notions of constituency', in E. H. Hovy and D. R. Scott (eds), 'Computational and Conversational Discourse: Burning Issues – an interdisciplinary account', number 151 in *NATO Advanced Science Institute Series F – Computer and Systems Sciences*. Berlin: Springer, pp. 39–66.

Matthews, P. H. (1966), 'The concept of rank in neo-Firthian linguistics'. *Journal of Linguistics*, 2(1), 101–18.

Matthiessen, C. M. I. M. (1988), 'Representational issues in systemic-functional grammar', in J. D. Benson and W. S. Greaves (eds), *Systemic-functional Approaches to Discourse*. Norwood, NJ: Ablex, pp. 136–75. Also available as USC/Information Sciences Institute Reprint Series Report ISI/RS-87-179.

Matthiessen, C. M. I. M. (1995), *Lexicogrammatical Cartography: English Systems*. Tokyo, Taipei and Dallas: International Language Science Publishers.

Matthiessen, C. M. I. M. and Bateman, J. A. (1991), *Text Generation and Systemic-functional Linguistics: Experiences from English and Japanese*. London and New York: Frances Pinter Publishers and St. Martin's Press.

O'Donnell, M. (1993), 'Reducing complexity in a systemic parser', in *Proceedings of the Third International Workshop on Parsing Technologies*. Tilburg, Netherlands, pp. 203–17. www.wagsoft.com/PapersHtml/IWPT93/IWPT93.html.

O'Donnell, M. and Bateman, J. A. (2005), 'SFL in computational contexts: a contemporary history', in J. Webster, R. Hasan and C. Matthiessen (eds), *Continuing Discourse on Language: A Functional Perspective*. London: Equinox, pp. 343–82.

Patrick, J. (2006), 'The Scamseek project – text mining for financial scams on the internet', in G. J. Williams and S. J. Simoff (eds), 'Data Mining – Theory, Methodology, Techniques, and Applications: Selected Papers from AusDM', Vol. 3755 of *Lecture Notes in Computer Science*. Berlin: Springer, pp. 295–302. www.dx.doi.org/10.1007/11677437_23.

Peters, S. P. and Ritchie, R. W. (1973), 'On the generative power of transformational grammars.' *Information Sciences*, 6, 49–83.

Sinclair, J. M. (ed.) (1987), *Looking Up: An Account of the COBUILD Project in Lexical Computing*. London and Glasgow: Collins.

Steedman, M. J. (1993), 'Categorial grammar.' *Lingua*, 90, 221–58.

Steedman, M. J. (2000), *The Syntactic Process*. Cambridge, MA: MIT Press.

Whitelaw, C. and Patrick, J. (2004), 'Selecting systemic features for text classification', in *Proceedings of the Australasian Language Technology Workshop (ALTW04)*. ALTA. www.citeseer.ist.psu.edu/whitelaw04 selecting.html.

XTAG Research Group (2001), 'A lexicalized tree adjoining grammar for English.' Technical Report IRCS-01-03, IRCS, University of Pennsylvania. www.cis.upenn.edu/~xtag/tech-report/tech-report.html.

Yang, G., McCoy, K. F. and Vijay-Shanker, K. (1991), 'From functional specification to syntactic structures: systemic grammar and tree adjoining grammar.' *Computational Intelligence*, 7(4), 207–19.

2

The Robustness of Realizational Systems

David G. Butt
Macquarie University

'Nature does not come as clean as you can think it.' – A. N. Whitehead
'Empirical knowledge is no longer a topic for academic discussion but an issue of public concern.' – Ervin Laszlo
'Theory is the most practical thing in the world.' – Oliver Wendell Holmes

A crucial first step in the maintenance of society's most valued services – including medical care, education, workplace safety, transport infrastructure, and financial services – is the accurate depiction of relevant aspects of the human experience of those institutions. Furthermore, the safe and effective management of such institutions requires the interpretation of more and more information, and from more diverse, and sometimes unpredictable, sources. This demand to process disparate and unpredictable information represents an intensification of complexity in our world. One of the ways in which this intensification of complexity has been addressed is through systems thinking. However, systems views of human experience typically omit certain defining characteristics of the most successful adaptive systems in our biological, cultural and institutional histories. These characteristics are the basis for what is encompassed here under the classifier 'realizational' – hence realizational systems.

Realizational systems have been the object of careful and powerful investigation (e.g. Laszlo 1972; Dietrich and Jochum 2004; Helmreich and Merritt 1998; Strauch 2002). Nevertheless, the legacy of beliefs and assumptions concerning systems still reflects a 'non-realizational' approach to these systems. Essentially, systemic perspectives continue to be dominated by metaphors of cause and effect, mechanism, seriation/linearity (even if in parallel lines of development), individual modules, and components. All these concepts are themselves of fundamental importance to intellectual analysis and to technological enterprise in general (including in the construal of realizational systems!), but such metaphors do not capture the defining characteristics of realizational systems even when the term 'realization' is invoked in the accounts or theories of particular systems. The problem here is what these metaphors miss in the complex interaction of materiality, organic growth and social/semiotic invention.

Of particular concern in both characterizing and tracking realizational systems is the way technologies are created in such interactions and, then, the way these technologies come to direct how those levels of material, organic, and semiotic organizations further interact. By 'technologies', I am not referring only to the overt tools of preceding revolutions in moving matter, or even in moving information, but also to the conventions of meaning-making which structure our inner life and guide us through our strategies for dealing with change – the personal change of moments and days, as well as the transpersonal change of community institutions. These are, then, mental tools, after the characterizations of Vygotsky (1978) and Richard Gregory (1981).

2.1 Definitions of realization

Hjelmslev:

> ... we call a class *realized* if it can be taken as the object of a *particular analysis,* and virtual if this is not the case. We believe that we have thus attained a formal definition that guards us against metaphysical obligations, the necessary and sufficient fixing of what we mean by the word *realization.* (1953: 25)
>
> A process is unimaginable – because it would be in an absolute and irrevocable sense inexplicable – without a system lying behind it. On the other hand, a system is not unimaginable without a process; the existence of a system does not presuppose the existence of a process. The system does not come into existence by virtue of a process's being found. (*ibid.*: 24)
>
> But even a purely virtual text presupposes a realized linguistic system ... (*ibid.*: 25)

Halliday (2002 [1992]: 352):

> Realization ... is prototypically an interstratal relationship; meanings are realized as wordings, wordings realized as sound (or soundings). We often use the term to refer to any move which constitutes a link in the realizational chain, even one that does not by itself cross a stratal boundary (for example, features realized as structures); but the phenomenon of realization only exists as a property of a stratified system ... realization may be formalized as metaredundancy, as this is defined by Lemke (1985).

Halliday (1974: 86):

> ... the key concept is that of *realization,* language as multiple coding. Just as there is a relation of realization between the semantic system and the

lexicogrammatical system, so that *can say* is the *realization* of *can mean*, so also there is a relation of realization between the semantic system and some higher-level semiotic which we can represent if you like as a behavioural system. It would be better to say that *can mean* is a realization of *can do*, or rather is one form of the realization of *can do*.

Hasan (1996: 105–06):

... the relation of realization between context, semantics and lexico-grammar is a dialectical one. The claim is, then, that the warrant for analysing a linguistic meaning and such and so resides in the perceived relations of semantics to context on the one hand, and to lexicogrammar, on the other. Context is implicated as the activator of a speaker's choices in meaning; lexicogrammar enters into the picture as the resource for construing those semantic choices in that specific language. Conversely, it is also the case that contexts – the relevant aspects of extra-linguistic situation – are unknowable without reference to meaning: it is the semantic choices which construe much of the context for the listener; and a similar dialectic obtains between semantics and lexicogrammar ...

2.2 Functions of realization in a linguistic model

Realization is a particularly hard-working concept in systemic functional linguistic models. Beside the cross-stratal role, it also describes the relation on one stratum between a system and its exponents – it is the 'mechanism mediating between networks and structures' (Hasan (1996 [1987]: 74) and, as such, is crucial to the systemic conceptualization of language as a network. The interstratal role of realization has been foregrounded in this discussion as the fundamental relation in realizational systems.

2.3 Differences between realization, exponence and instantiation

My recommendation is to define realization interstratally in linguistic theory and to reintroduce the term 'exponence' for the relationship between a system of contrasts (say, in the grammar – hence in mood, transitivity, modality, etc.) and the structures and functions which correspond to the specific contrastive features of the system under investigation. Exponents of a system are the 'output' of the process that the system contributes to the wider domain (although the term 'output' has the engineering implications of sequence and cause which a relational theory needs to relinquish).

If one can accept a reintroduction of the term 'exponence' to cover the intra-stratal realization of the linguistic literature, then we can similarly narrow down the work that has to be encompassed by the third term, 'instantiation'. This latter term can be confined to actualized and manifested choice – hence, the 'phase portrait' which has been taken up from the parametric space, i.e., the 'phase space' (as described by Cohen and Stewart 1994: 199ff). If the instantial choices are always the manifested choice, one can still manage the relation between the concept of register (a variety of meaning-making specific to the situation) and the notion of instance. A register is a probabilistic account of which domains of the background system, or space, are actualized. Such an account 'sits' halfway along a cline of instantiation, that is, mid-way between a manifest instance and the potentiality of the system (when regarded in the abstract).

2.4 Towards a characterization of realizational systems

Three preliminary questions to a characterization of realizational systems are:

1. What are examples of realizational systems?
   Realizational systems are ubiquitous, being the typical formation of any clustering or integration of community actions. Examples of realizational systems include (setting off from our own current work at the Centre for Language in Social Life at Macquarie University) the various governmental services in Australia concerning general health care and (more specifically) the systems for mental health care, as well as systems (in individual States of Australia) for the delivery of residential support for the aged, for those with disabilities, or for families experiencing forms of crisis. Other broad domains which involve clusters of realizational systems are finance, media, security, and education. All these domains depend upon structures of mediation, professional advice, and continuous monitoring (with responsibilities variously divided between public and private organizations).

   As the emergent formations of cultural evolution, any arrangement in one social environment will not correspond to, let alone equate with, arrangements in other societies or earlier periods of the same society – they will all display variable relational profiles – specific 'valeurs', to use Saussure's term (de Saussure 1974 [1915]: 99–126); but so too they will involve similarities in the substantial transactions by which they derive their denomination and defining business – Saussure's 'signification' (de Saussure 1974 [1915]: 99–126).

2. What role do realizational systems play in current social and academic priorities?
   Taken individually as systemic domains – health, finance, media – or when sometimes taken in cognate sets or clusters, public investigations and academic research into these systems absorb enormous resources

and involve continuous ferment, albeit controversy. And so they should! These systems are the parametric architectures within which we make our day-by-day, little, but consequential decisions about the conditions of living.

3. What promise does an alternative metaphor hold in relation to (those) urgent issues of social and academic concern?

It is not controversial to claim that our models of change and complexity in human affairs should reflect those dimensions of the social processes which make a difference. Models are built on metaphors, often unconsciously (and this is the most dangerous), but sometimes with conscious human design. Evolved systems – in particular those expressing human purposes but which incorporate material and biological levels as instruments of those purposes – rarely appear elegant or minimal (from the perspective of 'design'). Yet these 'messy' accretions of levels, layers and redundancies persist, while the 'elegant' interventions of social engineers and ideologues often have only spluttering passages of success and then disappear.

This chapter will discuss in detail the defining characteristics of realizational systems, and presents research with my current colleagues in the Centre for Language in Social Life at Macquarie University that draws on realizational models to investigate institutional problems in the domain of health (see Appendix 2.1).

Much of this chapter is motivated by the theoretical clarifications I derive from the work of M. A. K. Halliday, and from others working in the Firthian tradition in linguistics – for example, Ruqaiya Hasan, Christian Matthiessen and Jim Martin. The best summary of the general semiotic issues discussed here, from the point of view of each of a number of distinct sciences, can be found in the work of the physicist-semiotician, Jay Lemke (e.g. Lemke 1995: 106–29). Lemke's account of ecosocial systems and dynamics highlights many of the conceptual difficulties pertaining to systems in which a semiotic system is dependent on a material manifestation, which then shapes the future of both the semiotic and the material within a single 'unified dynamics' (Lemke 1995: 107). The project at RIKEN, Tokyo, on the modelling of a semiotic base for brain science – an initiative of Michio Sugeno – was important as a focus and a forum for building realizational theory. Also influential for my thinking here is the realizational theory of stratificationists, especially that of Sydney Lamb (see section 2.12 below).

2.5 Characteristics of realizational systems

How then is a realizational system unlike the more typical conception of system with which we work when addressing problems in government, artificial intelligence, computing, engineering, health sciences, prisons, and the wider delivery of care and services?

Factors to be considered with respect to realizational systems include the following:

1. Causation must be reconceptualized. While realizational systems are among the most consequential configurations in human experience, their internal relations cannot be understood in terms of a simple functional sequencing of processes or inputs. At both ends of its stratal organization, a realizational system constructs and is responsive to the wider patterns of community behaviour; and this naturally involves the organization and interpretation of material, biological, and social regularities. Such realizational systems, then, are open to the world in that they are each a vortex of changes that constitute our worlds. But this is not a situation in which one can take an individual system within the larger ensembles of interacting systems and regard it as a link in the chain, or a component in which input will be transformed in order to be passed on to another component which will add its transformation towards a goal, in the way we expect of strong sequencing rules: viz. even Chomsky's models in the 1960s and 1970s (see Macleay 1971). See also the use of arrows in the various schematic versions of Chomskyan models to date.

2. Stratification separates out different orders of abstraction at which regularities of patterning must occur together, simultaneously, OR NOT AT ALL. The patterns do not cause each other (see point 1 above), but they do depend on one another (see point 3 below).

    ... the phenomenon of realization only exists as a property of a stratified system. (Halliday 2002 [1992]: 352)

    The linguist must be clearly aware of the levels at which he is making his abstractions and statements and must finally prove his theory by renewal of connection with the processes and patterns of life. Without this constant reapplication to the flux of experience, abstract linguistics has no justification. (Firth 1968: 19)

3. The dependency (as noted in point 2 above) is the source of the values by which all the choices (paradigms) within the totality of the system work or function. Such values, though themselves in change, provide the bases for the stability of the field of action, in part because they generate units and structures, which are themselves conflations of functional roles/responsibilities. Structures are motivated by functions, which are themselves undergoing constant pressure from the relative efficacy of the institution to which they contribute as well as from the intra-stratal and cross-stratal co-dependencies themselves.

4. Change can come from anywhere because changes of various scales are going on everywhere all the time.

5. Adaptation can be functional or dysfunctional because change is managed through non-conscious, unconscious, and conscious strategies of action. These strategies, or types of strategy (with varying degrees of conscious human design or intervention), also move about in the overall field of action – at particular historical moments a whole community can become sensitive to even highly abstract terms of meta-description (see the current idiom of 'systemic' issues discussed widely in relation to hospital care in Australia). In other instances, one can see groups who are trained into a particular meta-theoretical perspective misconstruing a problem – for example, the grammarian who claims English has a two-tense system (consisting of past and present) rather than a three-tense system (consisting of past, present and future), on the basis that the new 'valeurs' (of futureness) involve the recruitment of the modal resources of earlier versions of English to a new allocation of responsibilities and functions in modern English. Human institutions – from language to medical care – challenge us to clarify a cline of behaviour – i.e., the range of possible behaviours. The 'verbal space' of humans is a non-conscious, evolved set of relationships, and the grammar is typically employed unconsciously; on the other hand, many semantic strategies may be not just conscious but pre-meditated. Training and habituation involve us taking on 'second natures'. Realizational systems are one of the domains in which we see the gift of these second natures – our transpersonal, cultural tools – most at work.

6. An artificial teleological impression derives from the combination of:
   a) The retrospective evaluation of the overall functionality or relative success of the system through time.
   b) The quantum of goal-directed behaviour inherent in every choice of institutional meaning – in each of the 'innumerable small momenta' (Whorf 1956: 151) of daily action.
   c) The trans-historical development of the institution overall by comparison with any interventions by individuals or groups (even when the latter appear relatively well-informed).
   d) The inability of monitors to produce reliable predictions as to how the system will be construed from decade to decade.

The next section develops further the last of these points – the effect of this artificial teleological impression in the modelling of complex phenomena.

2.6 The teleological illusion

In the light of a number of significant examples – including warnings on climate change; demographic studies of ageing (e.g. in Australia and Japan); the destruction of species; and a number of predictions concerning mental health and so on – the points made under 6c) and 6d) above require lengthy qualification. But, the force of a general impression of impersonal vectors of change over human design remains relevant. Current work on complexity and non-linear dynamics has provided some clarification for the wider public as to how systematic sciences are catching up with the basis for the public's mistrust of claims, statistical or theoretical, about the future.

Linguists have long had explicit views on these matters (e.g. Sapir (1970 [1921]) on 'Drift', Jespersen (1924) on 'progress', and Jakobson (1961) on the 'teleological principle'). The narratology of Russian Formalism also drew out an analogue or homologue of those generalizations on drift, namely that there is the artifice of goal-directness or design across a large number of similar but separate events, a kind of statistical order amidst the 'indeterminacy' of myriad cases. Following Tynjanov and Jakobson (1978), the Formalists described the language of verbal art as 'teleological' by contrast with the 'causal' character of language as it is driven by circumstances in day-by-day transactions.

The teleological impression conveyed by, say, a novel derives from the craft of the storyteller. The details that construct the unfolding plot can exist in themselves as incidental (although motivated by the inner context of plot). They can also be retrieved by the denouement – that is, as the plot extends, more of the details generated earlier provide a motivation for some twist or turn in the resolution of the narrative (thereby giving the impression, retrospectively, of crafted intention when the detail was first introduced). The storyteller or novelist may not have been in the least aware, however, that this or that detail would furnish the opportunity for a later resolving move in the denouement. This integrating, even organic effect (much responsible for the description of 'craft' in a work) is part of the evaluation we make of modern narratives. It lies behind the Formalist use of the term 'teleological', because a work can seem to have generated nothing but steps towards its emergent, eventual theme, as if the writer had had no doubt about the final form of all the semantic decisions in relation to the text.

This teleological illusion – truly an epiphenomenon or 'after image' of the writer/community interaction – recapitulates the long-range illusion produced by retrospections in biological evolution. The accumulation of adaptive change is, apparently, the result of utilizing units and structures under the conditions of slightly modified contextual values (when contextual here is thought of as 'under external pressures' and in terms of 'functional roles'). While it is misleading to animate evolutionary process by saying that it recruits its own latent past in a messy opportunistic way, nevertheless, we need some new idiom to encompass the causally driven increment of non-directed changes, which, upon retrospection, appear to have followed a pattern of reciprocation with a recognizable niche in nature. This matrix of physical and biological conditions becomes even more complex as social and semiotic organizations become both dimensions of, and directors of, evolutionary process. Darwin's revolution has little relevance to religion (because only an ingenuous adoption of religion could currently be at odds with Darwin). On the other hand, the revolution of talking and thinking demanded by Darwin's work may be beyond the textual potential of human languages, since even middle voice selections in transitivity (e.g. 'the sun is rising') do not suspend misleading semantic assumptions of entity-ness and agency/volition.

Added to this, there is a class of system that involves a new order of human control within the non-directed, non-goal-oriented patterns of biological continuity. These goal-directed systems produce a myriad of moment-by-moment choices, each with a quantum of social purpose expressed through polyphony of functional resources (i.e., the semiotic paradigms of the culture, and most especially those of the grammar). These systems are held in 'commonwealth' (across social groups) at the same time as they become individually inscribed through the practices of persons in specific social networks. To generalize abstractly about the totality of such a system is dangerous, and needs the corrective of constant grounding in particular instance(s). Similarly, at the other pole, to take the individual as the unit of relevance is to miss completely the cognitive and evolutionary significance, the scale, the range, and the social consequences of the regularities of behaviour under description. Conventional wisdom publicizes the fact that conventions and institutional structures cannot be reduced to molecular behaviour; but a 'fashion of speaking' which accounts for the relational ensembles of socio-semiotic, biological, and physical regularities may be beyond the scope of current semantic systems.

In place of a genuine discourse of relational complexity, we see the rise of new tribes of the 'simplicimi' – evolutionary psychologists and their inferences on universals, on the one side; and the post-modern 'instantialists' (i.e., those who believe that every instance of language is so absolutely unique that it is uninterpretable by reference to any system) on the other, who claim to have freed themselves by being free of theory.

Between system and instance, and between description and prediction, we can adopt Boltzmann's methods – his method of taking relevant dimensions and quantifying values along each dimension (see Boltzmann 1974). We will discuss this more below. Values and meanings, when systemicized under paradigms of 'choice', can be examined for predictive general patterns much after the manner of atoms/molecules. This is not to treat values and meanings as if they were merely molecular, but rather to examine the figure of meaning selections against the ground of behavioural potential that, in each cultural setting, is what we can imagine as human experience.

2.7 A multi-dimensional model of value – the case of linguistic semantics

If realizational systems do not only involve matter or information coded as bits, how are the higher order semantic values quantified? The first move is to construe value through the notion of choice, following Saussure's discussion of associative/paradigmatic relations (de Saussure 1974 [1915]: 122–7). Such choices, typically unconscious, have to be allocated to the different levels of abstract patterning by which an enormous behavioural potential (the culture) can be expressed by a relatively small range of contrastive combinations. A recognizable social transaction draws in its self-constructing meanings (context realized in semantics). The semantic patterns are themselves a construct of specific coding 'choices' in the grammar and lexis (semantics realized in lexicogrammar). Every variant in the lexicogrammar has consequences for the semantics because only all strata taken together construct meaning. If one adopts, for the purposes of analysis, a perspective in which strata are described as if they were isolated patterns of order, the levels become useful fictions in the 'management' of language events (echoing Firth's instrumentalism, e.g. Firth 1957 [1935]). But there is always a cost in such 'hypostatization' (Firth 1957 [1948]: 125–6): your method too easily becomes your interpretation, with each stratum taking on an autonomous status and with its own academic specialists who attest to the bewildering one-to-many and many-to-one relations at each of the stratal boundaries (given that there is typically only ever specialized work being coordinated on two strata in any given phase of research). The semantics and the lexicogrammar are different ways of addressing the content of language – its power to direct and define a social transaction.

Semantics and lexicogrammar **in context** actually whittle down the realizational complexity because parametric information from a third stratum excludes possibilities from the other two. The coding (realization) of the lexicogrammar in complex articulations completes a four-stratal realizational 'ensemble' (see Janik and Toulmin (1973) for the way this term was used in the statistical approach to multiple dimensions introduced by Boltzmann, as part of work generally regarded more fundamental to the conduct of sciences than the formulations of Einstein). Every cross-stratal ensemble constitutes a cultural and mental tool, an element in a repertoire of behaviour, in the 'meaning potential' (Halliday 1973).

The stratal organization, with its critical codings of codings of codings, appears unlimited in its capacity for extension and renewal. This is to say the systemic potential, as a confederation of paradigms or systems, is both renewing and extending itself as system at all times. Note, this is not the mechanical increment of recursion (which received a celebrated status as a sign of creativity in the Chomskyan theories of 1957 and following). The renewal can be illustrated by the re-alignment of units and patterns on different strata with every utterance of the system. For example, a context may motivate a crucial meaning (or the meaning construct the context). These patterns may be aligned with a given unit in the lexicogrammar (say a clause). But this clause can be expressed in a 1:1 relation to the unit of intonation (i.e., a tone group/information unit/prosodic tone) or, for reasons of functional and stylistic variation (in order to 'construct' the grammar – semantics – context to a slightly different purpose), the single alignment of units from context to semantics to lexicogrammar may be uttered in two (or more) tone groups (Halliday began his lectures in Cardiff, 1998, by making this point and drawing out its 'systemic' significance). The whole alignment can then be revisited by the same relevant group of interactants so that the patterning across strata is varied in another distinctive or 'marked' alignment – for instance, two semantic arguments or figures could be packaged in one grammatical clause which is uttered in two tone groups, and so on. Every cross-stratal patterning (or realization) can modify the cultural values of the whole performance (thereby constructing a variant form of the context). These realizations are a continuous resource for marked or contrastive managements of social behaviour. The social process is 'tossing up' an incessantly changing array of possibilities which can be usefully regarded as 'systematic' in that the dynamics of actual social behaviour can only be utilized and expressed by people who share in the palpable, but fast receding, paradigm. The semantic universe is expanding away from us, dramatically, like the dynamic physical universe.

Our statements about the universe must be set according to the relativities of the observer; and the evanescence of personal and group needs ensures that the meaning system that we set out metalinguistically will be, of epistemological necessity, an after image of specific transactions by particular persons, not a snapshot of what all people do. But, given that limiting principle on what can be established in the ongoing complementarities between process (instance) and system, the responsibility for systemic modelling of realizational relations takes on greater significance (i.e., greater than if the description of relations were resolvable in unequivocal terms). The stability of the cultural practices and of their semantic functions depends on constant change. And this change can only happen because there is some point to emulation and variation, namely, a socialized person can align with any number of points of view or groups of interest according to unmarked and variously marked constructions. A useful case in point from the linguistics of social networks comes from speakers of a West Indian form of English (as studied by Le Page, and cited in Milroy 1987 [1980]) in which five different choices of English present tense align a speaker with five different, influential community sub-groups. Even such minima of selection are constructing social reality by the complementarity of process and paradigm.

The variability is the guarantee of continuity, of what is sometimes called 'metastability' (see for instance Lemke (1995); although Saussure (1974 [1915]) pointed out that because values change, the system avoids being thrown out despite the changing environments of use). The accumulating choices create a web of possibilities that defies quantification – there are all the co-dependencies of selection on any one stratum; and then all the possibilities of alignment across the four strata (context, semantics, lexico-grammar, phonology). These are numerically extended by the fact that they – the potential arrangements of options – are constantly re-valued and repeated with the events along three different vectors of semiotic change, i.e., the logogenetic, ontogenetic and phylogenetic vectors. These vectors are illustrated in Figures 2.1 and 2.2, and explained further below.

The change in the moment-to-moment unfolding of text is the first vector of change; this is known, following Halliday and Matthiessen (1999), as 'logogenesis'. As one moves through the arc of interaction, certain options at certain levels of meaning-making – for example, opening gambits in the rhetorical structure (hence, in the semantics) – may be closed off. More typically, however, systems remain 'open' to participant selection, but with shifted probabilities of take-up in the text. The size of the available potential may even undergo creative extension: a speaker can create humour or tightness of rhetorical structure by re-using a formulation which was unremarkable on its first expression, but which becomes a leitmotif when invoked under a slightly modified 'topos' (viz. Robert Frost's use of 'on a percentage basis' in his 1956 speech at the University of California, Berkeley). The process cannot help but shift the system, at the very least in confirming or modifying its probabilistic 'spin'.

Clearly, each creative deployment of language is simultaneously a logogenetic process, an ontogenetic event, and a phylogenetic instance. The terms process, event and instance, however, all apply equally and interchangeably

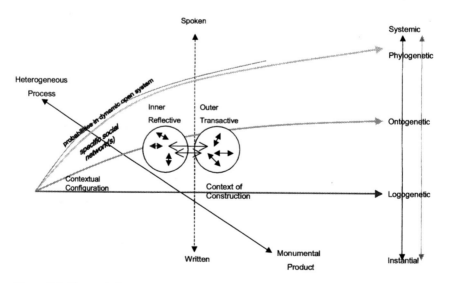

Figure 2.1 Change in language

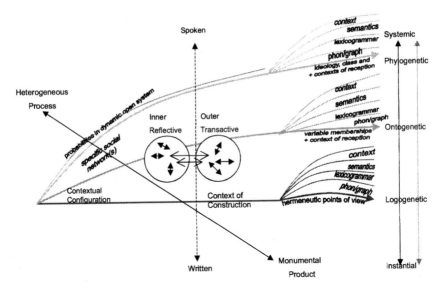

Figure 2.2 Change in language within strata

to each vector of change, though they orient to the observer somewhat differently and hence justify the use of more than a single term. A text instantiates the changing ontogenetic character of each of its interactants; so too, it is an instantiation of the culture (note, not merely a reflection of the culture). One's personal 'character' is an abstraction from the co-ordinate system of contexts available to you and what you make of them, through meaningful behaviour, at least, what you contribute by way of construction according to the 'theory' of those, including yourself, who may be evaluating your character. That co-ordinate system of contexts – variously a network, a patchwork, a palimpsest, a 'rhizome' – is the culture, when on those few occasions it is productive (rather than over-productive) to use a definite article on a loose assemblage of participatory structures (momentarily defined against often artificial collections for the purposes of voting, warfare, or economic expedience).

As with logogenesis, the passage of living (ontogenesis) and the cycles or arcs of cultural exchange (phylogenesis) provide ways of understanding the functional drift of a realizational system (when we continue to use language as a case from which to exemplify the properties of realizational patterns more generally). Each child is open to the possibilities of the culture through varying forms of access and to different degrees, since these forms of access create differences of 'coding orientation' or 'habitus'. Vygotsky's (1978: 86) findings on 'zone of proximal development' are an ideational aspect of a many-faceted phenomenon in which different coding orientations are recruited to latent discriminations for the maintenance of class (see Hasan and Cloran (1990) on a range of investigatory projects in this area). The inherent variability of the resulting behaviours in any given social process ensures that change is a constant of the system, not a deviation away from some idealized expectation.

Although certain analogies between cultural and biological processes are misleading, it is worth noting that the 'system' of genetic recombination of parental DNA actually guarantees the uniqueness of the product at the same time that it sustains the biological processes of development and change. The 'system' – with the context built in as the third strand of the helix just as social context and personal embodiment are both 'sine qua non' of semiotic process – is not inimical to representing variation and 'hybridity'. It is of the essence. Without the 'systemness' of realizational institutions in culture, there is no basis for experiencing variation, let alone describing variation (through some meta-theory). All could only be classified as 'noise', since the basis for regularity has not been established; and all that falls outside of the theory of regularity becomes 'random', or unmotivated variation.

This analogy is worth emphasizing because there has been a strong movement in humanities to eschew any claims of order and system-ness in the description of human behaviour. This prejudice has been based on the defence of the instance and on an impoverished notion of system. The majority of systems that are fundamental to humans are open, dynamic systems, namely, systems of life and of social practice. Closed systems tend to be exclusive to the earlier stages of human design (mechanical, logical, and computational systems). Now it is unequivocal that even human designed systems can produce novelty and 'solutions' that were in no way envisaged by the human designers (viz. neural networks; distributed, parallel processing). I conclude from these developments that structuralisms of the past did not claim too much, but rather proclaimed too early. In an era of complexity tropes, the dynamic, non-linear modelling of social process is not an interesting option but a moral and democratic responsibility. To be without the data which underpins such non-linear modelling is to leave one's community open to all manner of distortions from the top.

2.8 Dimensions of semantic space

In Halliday's concept of 'meaning potential' (e.g. Halliday 1973, 1978), we have a theoretical proposal that is isomorphic with the idea of 'phase space' (Cohen and Stewart 1994: 198ff). A specific cultural context involves certain forms of possible meaningful behaviour: what we can do is what we can mean. Specific instances of behaviour can be tracked across the parameters of the phase space – they become 'phase portraits' in a probabilistic account of the range of our experience.

Our chief concern is with stating the ensembles of choices in concrete interactions. Our phase space is calibrated, then, to a register (or, in terms of social units, to a social network). This calibration is addressing the specific demands of research questions in medical projects, pertaining to cancer care, surgical teams and operating theatre management, and to mental health, focused on psychotherapy. If we can bring out the 'differences' of relation that have semantic consequences for those working in these contexts – or, at least, if we can address the dimensions of the interaction most relevant to the meaning-making – then we will have assisted both in the understanding of the register (of the social context) and in the modelling of semantic behaviour for future professional planning.

The following questions, using English as the language under investigation, offer an informal way of understanding what is meant by dimension in this view of a science of text. The most significant dimensions, at least for the purposes cited, are brought together in the three-dimensional diagram in Figure 2.3 (taken from Halliday 1978).

1. How does the text under discussion look against the expectation you have of the English 'system'?
   [*As an instance of English, how does it appear? remarkable/unremarkable, marked/unmarked? How are your own habits of English automatized or*

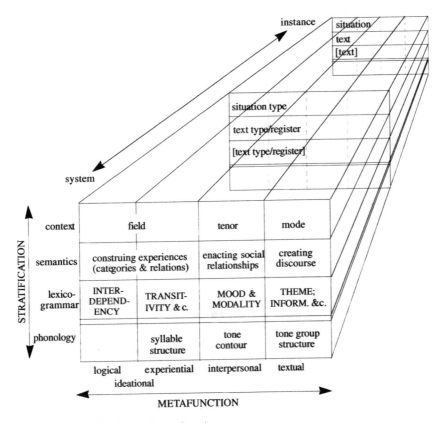

Figure 2.3 Stratification and metafunction

'de-automatized' by the reading? Are your own habits of English usefully specified here?]

{*Technical term:* **Instantiation**}

2. How might we allocate responsibilities for the patterns, consistencies or 'ordinariness' that we find?

   [*Are the noteworthy, attention-grabbing aspects of the text tied up with, say, complexities in the lexicogrammar? Do these have semantic consequences for complexity and indeterminacy? Or, perhaps, the lexicogrammar appears 'natural' while still having disturbing consequences in the semantics? Is the phonology the 'dominant' as in a lyric, or other verse?*]

   {*Technical term:* **Stratification**}

3. Across a spectrum of kinds of meaning, can we find tendencies which characterize, say, a generic element or a pattern across the whole text? Can we separate the meaning into 'strands' in order to track similar choices and mutually dependent choices for the separate tasks they fulfil?

   [*Here one might be seeking separate perspective on:*

   − *the reflection of the world as processes and events through the representational functions of the clause; so a 'world building' function;*
   − *the enactment and securing of social relations: hence 'interpersonal meaning; so an 'intervening in the world' function.*
   − *the enabling function by which language has to act on, and integrate, the choices of ideational and interpersonal meanings; so a 'textual' function.*]

   {*Technical term:* **Metafunction**}

4. What is revealed about the text as we analyse it, i.e., as we regard it word by word, group by group, clause by clause, clause complex by clause complex (in the lexicogrammar); or by syllable, foot, tone group (in the phonology); or by message, trope, and rhetorical move (in the semantics)?

   [*By decomposing the text, which 'ranks' provide the most interesting information for the task at hand?*]

   {*Technical terms:* **Constituency, Composition,** *and* **Rank**}

5. What is the degree of detail (in the contrasts of meaning or grammar) that the project requires?

   {*Technical term:* **Delicacy**}

6. What are the consequences of the choices under focus for other choices in the text? Do associated words, for instance, pile up in clusters? Or are there structures which require completion by other structures in the way that a question requires an answer, or a narrative moves to a climax?

   [*What resources seem open-ended and suggestive of a loose structure in the text? and which contribute to closure, regularity, and a tight form?*]

   {*Technical terms:* **Axial Orientation: Paradigmatic** *vs.* **Syntagmatic Organizations**}

7. What emerges when a system view is adopted and the results are compared across different temporal and cultural distances?

{*Technical term:* **Temporal Seriation**}
8. Can we check our findings and our inferences against outside information, i.e., information outside our own project?
   [*e.g., check against concordances, Cobuild, and computer corpora*]
   {*Technical term:* **Corpus Validation**}

2.9 Realizational systems invite quantification

Characteristics of dynamic behavioural systems are *not* difficult to quantify. This follows from the fact that semantic behaviour – whether symbolic or indexical in its sign function – is *not* subjective. Even when turned inwards to our private experiences, meaning is a public business, or it is nothing. It can, of course, involve idiosyncratic values; but they become 'marked' selections which are integral to the meaning. The selections one makes in making an interaction can be given values on scales on a categorial basis. From these values one is able to position any instance under discussion against any other instance or emergent group of instances. In this way, the comparative way, quantification against a number of values provides a basis for operating with meanings and meaning potential much as one uses map coordinates to know where one is in a physical space. Like a reading on the surface of the globe of earth or, even more, a topographic specification (with four dimensions), semantic dimensions are both arbitrary (conventional) and natural (motivated). They are arbitrary because the same task could be tackled by numerous alternative conventional arrangements. They are natural in that they must work (function) within uncompromising conditions of biological, neurological, and social experience. For purposes of grammatical quantification, I offer below a scalar method for comparative measures of 'instantial weight': the semantic prominence of a grammatical structure and of its specific contributing roles and relations. The scales are the overlay of options for allocating prominence or weight to a clausal element. Each scale is a strand in a rope of strands, or in an ensemble of polyphonic routines.

2.10 From instantial to systemic

Every element of a text can be regarded in relation to its **instantial weight**: the overall measure of the prominence bestowed upon that element by the profile of choices which have gone into the development of the particular text – its logogenetic 'history'. As a concept, instantial weight can be applied to the structures of each stratum individually. Below, I will illustrate the notion in detail with respect to grammar, showing also that there are many possibilities for quantifying the weight of elements by clause/clause complex.

2.11 Dimensions of textural visibility and semantic/grammatical 'weight'

By tracing *choice*, and *non-choice*, across the instantial deployment of the grammatical system, we can achieve an overall picture of motivated selection across a text. This is the core activity of stylistics – the study which always took variation as the 'norm'. It is economically achieved by network representation (see Butt and Matthiessen 2000). The issue of semantic complexity, however, is multi-dimensional in ways that suggest that linguists need to combine many different perspectives and a variety of tools of analysis. For instance, every element or semantic motif can be tracked for its 'instantial weight' (see Figure 2.4), according to both the features of the grammatical environment (clause) to which it contributes (those features numbered 1 to 4 in Figure 2.4) as well as by its role within that clause (the features numbered 5 to 9 in Figure 2.4).

Instantial weight (at the level of grammar) can be thought of, provisionally, as the sum of the values that apply to an *Element* (a semantic motif realized in a lexicogrammatical group) when interpreted clause by clause across a given span of text. There is no mystery to this concept; it is merely an aid in tracking how grammatical roles are related to each other, at least in terms of visibility, or foregrounding, within the texture.

Instantial Weight, as a tool of analysis, can be expanded:

1. by multiplying the number of relevant dimensions, depending on the semantic motivation of research and the potential for choices to be interpreted as a scale or cline.
2. by taking the scale to greater degrees of delicacy, again depending on the degree of difference demanded by the research questions.

These two kinds of expansion are illustrated together in Figure 2.5.

Tense and modality were further unpacked as dimensions of *Finiteness* and as subdivided scales in their own right. The technique can be straightforward in many analytical situations in that, as can be seen with tables, even a modicum of systematic tracking across a few dimensions has a significant bearing upon evidence and inference in discourse analysis. But not in all cases. A discourse tool is an aid to interpretation, not a substitute for it.

By further combining selections, or by 'seeing' them against one another, other semantic consequences of texture can be given rudimentary correlates, especially along clines. For instance, the traditional concepts of actualized/unactualized events – **realis/irrealis** – can be built up by mapping **finite/non-finite** (x/x-1 etc.) against **process** type (x,y,z,m,n). The result needs to be further interpreted against the **clause status** above (with conditional clauses typically expressed by βx clauses), and so on.

But these dimensions are activated themselves by a specific cultural task. The grammar is the **realization** of a specific social configuration and,

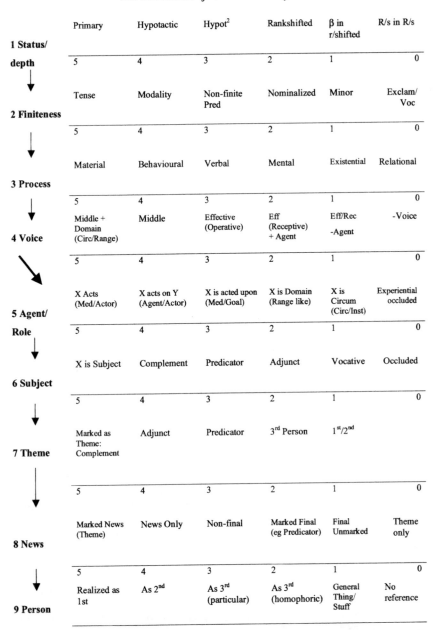

Figure 2.4 Instantial weight

reciprocally, the form of that specific social process is '**configured**' by what is possible, and habitual, in the grammar. The social order makes specific demands on the meaning potential of the grammar, while the generalizing patterns of the grammar present the social process back to us as phenomena

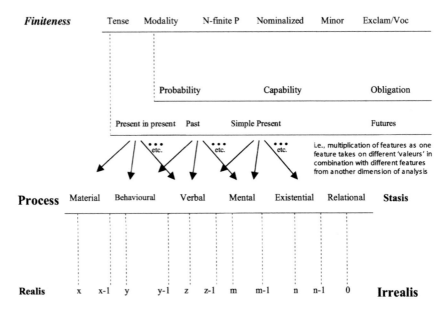

Finiteness   Tense   Modality   N-finite P   Nominalized   Minor   Exclam/Voc

Probability   Capability   Obligation

Present in present   Past   Simple Present   Futures

i.e., multiplication of features as one feature takes on different 'valeurs' in combination with different features from another dimension of analysis

Process   Material   Behavioural   Verbal   Mental   Existential   Relational   **Stasis**

Realis   x   x-1   y   y-1   z   z-1   m   m-1   n   n-1   0   **Irrealis**

Figure 2.5 The expansion of features of instantial weight

of the types, classes, and consistencies that we have seen and sanctioned through the habitual use of our grammar.

2.12 Quantification at other strata: contextual/semantic weight

We can see the above review of the grammatical choices as an attempt to bring out the semantic force, the consequences for meaning, of the structural relations of the message. It is important, however, to address the rhetorical 'unit' in its own terms, namely as a phenomenon that has to be accounted for in any semantic theory that purports to describe the structure of meaning-making – the discriminations that speakers observe in ordering English for persuasion or explanation, for construing experience. Correspondingly, it needs to be said that, while there are a number of productive proposals for managing the semantic strategies on display – in particular, as we combine the traditional coverage of classical theories with the realization statements of current work – there is as yet no standardized account in the toolbox of linguists. The theory required would have to be linked in a principled way to the stratum of context above (so demonstrating the significance of changing generic elements) and to the stratum of lexicogrammar below (with some specification, by probabilities, of realizations). Important contributions to this area have come from Halliday and Matthiessen (1999: 50ff) on semantic *elements, figures,* and *sequences* and from proposals for a rank scale in semantics developing out of the work of Hasan and Cloran (1990).

Some sense of a practical rapprochement between the classical and contemporary can be gleaned from Figure 2.6. In essence, its practical coverage of contextual matters, its proto-metafunctions, and the subtlety of the concept of trope, all make the classical legacy an invaluable foundation to contemporary thinking – unfortunately one taken up more assiduously outside linguistics than within; see, for example, Johnstone (1996). A diagram of the traditional concepts and subdivisions of rhetoric is set out in Figure 2.6, with key terms from systemic functional theory added to suggest some affinities of metalinguistic approach.

Proposals must encompass the range of actual units over which we exercise our modicum of choice and our deep habits of unconscious textual design. This is no more than to say that the first requirement of a rhetorical theory is its being able to accord with the *relevant* phenomena – the resources upon which we draw in our habitual practices, and over which we discriminate the success or otherwise of human interactions. Semantics has been limited by narrow conceptions of what could be formalized when the focus of analysis should not have been switched from what can be meant (for example, large claims were made for the atomism of componentialist approaches – compare Leech (1974) with Leech (1983)). We could not persist in denying the differences between a symphony and plainchant, nor between either of these and a raga. While most of the discriminations we make are going to be latent or unconscious, as is the case on any level of analysis in linguistics, the goal of description is to bring such implicate orders into an 'explicate' theory.

The quantification I discussed in the previous section begins at the stratum of lexicogrammar because this stratum has:

- a smaller numerical field;
- an elaborated systemic map; and
- a defensible rank scale (of constituency).

But other strata are not resistant to parametric representations which are relational and which may be quantified. Let us consider a longstanding conundrum on the semantic stratum: namely, how to represent semantic relations which span grammatical units in such a way that higher order inferences or deductions must be invoked in order to recognize that a progression, and a discovery, have taken place in the discourse. In Sydney Lamb's networks, a syllogism (e.g., 'All men are mortal. Socrates is a man. Therefore Socrates is mortal') can be consistently represented as in Figure 2.7 (after Lamb 1970).

Read from the top down (just for purposes of explanation), the network represents 'mortal' as one of the many unordered attributes of 'men'. 'Socrates' is one of the instances of 'men' (again unordered). We can immediately recognize that Socrates must be 'mortal'. The wiring and the 'and' and

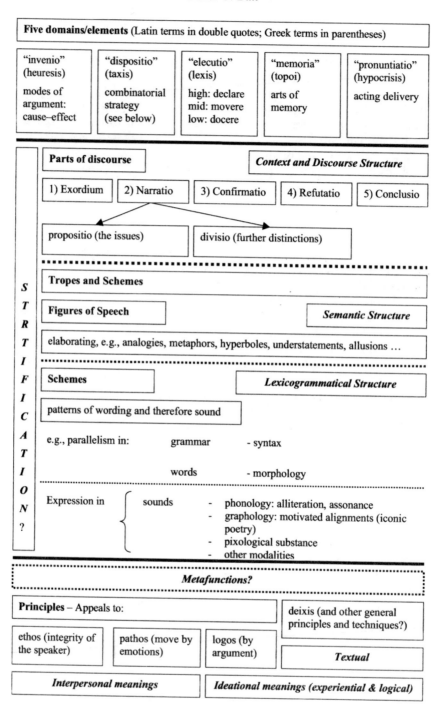

Figure 2.6 Rhetorical traditions in the West

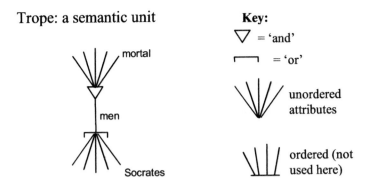

Figure 2.7 Concepts and the contextual/semantic strata

'or' symbols (as well as those indicating ordered and unordered attributes/ instances) permit us to 'see' the meaning through both conventions and a high order of iconicity. What is crucial, however, is that the representation maintains the necessary relations in a semantic structure. Ingeniously, it can hold a 'place' in a cultural phase space that we are seeking to map.

Realizational relationships are not beyond our human powers of depiction and construal. It is merely that, as in other sciences, we need to 'regionalize' (i.e., focus on a specific registerial locale) and we need to seek useful scales on relevant parameters.

Appendix 2.1

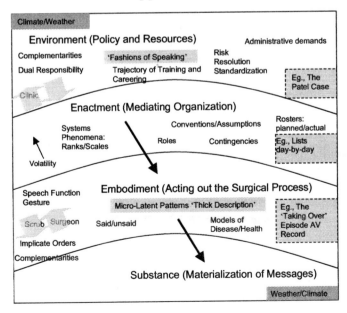

Appendix 2.1 Stratification of surgical care

The diagram is a response to an initial aim of analysing team work in the operating theatre – in surgery. In order to track the interdependent relations, three strata of organization needed to be proposed – Environment (of Policy); Enactment (by Management); and Embodiment (of the Actions of medical expertise). The relevant pressures on the contexts of surgery could not be construed without these three levels of mapping, these three levels of systemic relations. Our presentations of this project have set out numerous networks of semantic choice, organized around typicality of meaning for each Role in the Context. (Schema drawn from Australian Research Council funded project: Systemic Safety in Surgical Care: D. G.Butt, A. R. Moore, and J. Cartmill).

References

Boltzmann, L. (1974), *Theoretical Physics and Philosophical Problems: Selected Writings.* Dordrecht and Boston: Reidel Publishing Co.

Butt, D. G. and Matthiessen, C. M. I. M. (2000), *The Meaning Potential of Language: Mapping Meaning Systemically.* Sydney: Department of Linguistics, Macquarie University.

Cohen, J. and Stewart, I. (1994), *The Collapse of Chaos: Discovering Simplicity in a Complex World.* London: Penguin.

de Saussure, F. (1974 [1915]), *Course in General Linguistics.* Trans. W. Baskin. London: Fontana/Collins.

Dietrich, R. and Jochum, K. (2004), *Teaming Up: Components of Safety under High Risk.* Aldershot: Ashgate.

Firth, J. R. (1957 [1935]), 'The technique of semantics', in *Papers in Linguistics, 1934–1951.* London: Oxford University Press, pp. 7–33

Firth, J. R. (1957 [1948])., 'Sounds and prosodies', in *Papers in Linguistics 1934–1951.* London: Oxford University Press, pp. 121–8.

Firth, J. R. (1968), 'Linguistic analysis as a study of meaning', in F. R. Palmer (ed.), *Selected Papers of J. R. Firth 1952–59.* London: Longman, pp. 12–26.

Gregory, R. L. (1981), *Mind in Science: A History of Explanations in Psychology and Physics.* Harmondsworth: Penguin Books.

Halliday, M. A. K. (1973), *Explorations in the Functions of Language.* London: Edward Arnold.

Halliday, M. A. K. (1974), 'Discussion', in H. Parret (ed.), *Discussing Language.* The Hague: Mouton, pp. 81–120.

Halliday, M. A. K. (1978), *Language as Social Semiotic: The Social Interpretation of Language and Meaning.* London: Edward Arnold.

Halliday, M. A. K. (2002 [1992]), 'How do you mean?', in J. J. Webster (ed.), *On Grammar. Collected Works of M. A. K. Halliday* (Vol. 1). London: Continuum, pp. 352–68.

Halliday, M. A. K., and Matthiessen, C. M. I. M. (1999), *Construing Experience through Meaning: A Language-based Approach to Cognition.* London: Cassell.

Hasan, R. (1996), 'Semantic networks: a tool for the analysis of meaning', in

C. Cloran, D. G. Butt and G. Williams (eds), *Ways of Saying, Ways of Meaning: Selected Papers of Ruqaiya Hasan*. London: Cassell.

Hasan, R. (1996 [1987]), 'The grammarian's dream: lexis as most delicate grammar', in C. Cloran, D. G. Butt and G. Williams (eds), *Ways of Saying, Ways of Meaning: Selected Papers of Ruqaiya Hasan*. London: Cassell.

Hasan, R. and Cloran, C. (1990), 'A sociolinguistic interpretation of everyday talk between mothers and children', in M. A. K. Halliday, J. Gibbons and H. Nicholas (eds), *Learning, Keeping and Using Language: Selected Papers from the 8th World Congress of Applied Linguistics, Sydney, 16-21 August 1987*. Amsterdam: Benjamins, pp. 67–99.

Helmreich, R. L. and Merritt, A. (1998), *Culture at Work in Aviation and Medicine*. Aldershot: Ashgate.

Hjelmslev, L. (1953), *Prolegomena to a Theory of Language*. Trans. F. J. Whitfield. Bloomington, IN: Indiana University Publications in Anthropology and Linguistics.

Jakobson, R. (1961), 'The concept of sound law and the teleological criterion', in *Selected Writings* (Vol. 1). The Hague: Mouton.

Janik, A. and Toulmin, S. (1973), *Wittgenstein's Vienna*. New York: Simon and Schuster.

Jespersen, O. (1924), *The Philosophy of Grammar*. New York: Holt.

Johnstone, C. L. (ed.) (1996), *Theory, Text, Context: Issues in Greek Rhetoric and Oratory*. Albany: State University of New York Press.

Lamb, S. M. (1970), 'Linguistic and cognitive networks', in P. Garvin (ed.), *Cognition: A Multiple View*. New York: Spartan.

Laszlo, E. (1972), *The Systems View of the World: The Natural Philosophy of the New Developments in the Sciences*. New York: George Braziller.

Leech, G. (1974), *Semantics*. Harmondsworth: Penguin.

Leech, G. (1983), *Principles of Pragmatics*. London and New York: Longman.

Lemke, J. (1995), *Textual Politics: Discourse and Social Dynamics*. London: Taylor and Francis.

Macleay, H. (1971), 'Overview', in D. Steinberg and L. Jakobovits (eds), *Semantics: An Interdisciplinary Reader in Philosophy, Linguistics and Psychology*. London: Cambridge University Press.

Milroy, L. (1987 [1980]), *Language and Social Networks* (2nd edn). Oxford: Basil Blackwell.

Sapir, E. (1970 [1921]), *Language. An Introduction to the Study of Speech*. London: Rupert Hart-Davis.

Strauch, B. (2002), *Investigating Human Error: Incidents, Accidents and Complex Systems*. Aldershot: Ashgate.

Tynjanov, J. and Jakobson, R. (1978), 'Problems in the study of literature and language', in L. Matejka and K. Pomorska (eds), *Readings in Russian Poetics: Formalist and Structuralist Views*. Cambridge, MA: MIT Press.

Vygotsky, L. S. (1978), *Mind in Society: The Development of Higher Psychological Processes*. Cambridge, MA: Harvard University Press.

Whorf, B. (1956), *Language, Thought, and Reality: Selected Writings*. Cambridge, MA: MIT Press.

A Study of Topical Theme in Chinese: An SFL Perspective

Fang Yan
Tsinghua University

3.1 Introduction

In 2004 systemic functional linguists gathered in Kyoto for the 31st ISFC, discussing the directions and strategies of globalizing SFL. Today we are faced with the same issue – finding ways to propel Hallidayan linguistics in the world. Undoubtedly the official launching of The Halliday Centre in City University, Hong Kong, is a noteworthy symbol of this endeavour. The Centre will certainly provide a platform for SF linguists coming from various countries to exchange views and to develop collaborations on 'implementing intelligent applications of language studies'.

In the past century since the publication of *Ma's Grammar* in 1898 (1983), many researchers have been involved in the study of Chinese on the mainland of China. However, the mainstream has been influenced by the formal approach, whether structuralism or generative-transformational grammar, which focuses on the study of form rather than meaning. In the last decade, however, more and more Chinese linguists have realized that the formal approach does not fit the Chinese language, which has 'few formal signals' (Li and Thompson 1981), and that meaning should be taken as the basis for linguistic studies. This view is shared by the SF linguists who take meaning as the point of departure and form as the way to realize meaning. Articles taking this approach on various themes have appeared in great numbers in the leading linguistics journals and magazines on the mainland in the past decade. For example, there are over fifty articles on Topic and a dozen on Theme. Those on Topic either adopt the cognitive approach (Shi 2001) or the various functional approaches including SF linguistics (Fang 1989, 1990; Zhang and Fang 1994; Fang and Ai 1995). The dozen on Theme use the SFL framework in their discussions, among which, however, only a few are on Topical Theme. These few articles define Topical Theme in different ways and thus make it a controversial issue. I have chosen this topic in order to arouse interest in a more systematic study of Topical Theme and also to draw more SF linguists on the mainland of China and elsewhere to the study of Chinese grammar.

This chapter will address several issues. It will first discuss briefly clause structure, from both the traditional Chinese linguistics perspective and the functional perspective, which will provide a basis for exploring Theme as part of the clause. Then it will deal with the concept of Theme in general but the focus will be on Topical Theme. Finally it will arrive at some conclusions.

3.2 Views on clause structure – from the Chinese linguistics perspective

Shi Yuzhi (2001: 82) states that there are mainly three views on clause structure in Chinese: the Subject only view, the Subject and Topic view and the Topic only view. However, Fang *et al.* (1995) believe that the second and the third views are similar in nature, and are able to be combined into one, as shown below.

3.2.1 Subject only view

This view is represented by Zhu Dexi and Lv Shuxiang. Subject is defined structurally: Subject precedes Predicate or 'is the starting point of the clause' (Lv 1984), and is separated by an optional pause and/or particles; Subject may be omitted if understood semantically from the context. Yet, Subject and Predicate relation needs to be interpreted semantically and expressively. Semantically, Subject may be agent, patient, recipient, time, etc.; expressively, this relation can be explained as 'Topic – Comment', and Predicate may be a 'Subject Predicate construction', or there are two levels of Subject and Predicate (Zhu 1981: 95–6). For example, in (1)

(1)	那	块	田	稻子	长	得	很	大。
	Na	kuai	tian	daozi	zhang	de	hen	da
	that	piece	field	rice	grow	VADV	ADV	big
	Subject1			Predicate1				
				Subject2		Predicate2		

(In that piece of field, rice grows big in size.)

both '那块田' (Nei kuai tian or that piece of field) and '稻子' (daozi or rice) are defined as Subject in accordance with this view. However, two questions arise: do the two Subjects perform the same function? And if Subject is regarded as an element preceding Predicate, how should we analyse the following clause?

(2)   主席台上   坐着   个   老人。
      Zhuxitaishang   zuozhe ge   laoren
      Platform upon   sit PROG MEAS old man.
      (On the platform sits an old man.)

Where the circumstantial: location '主席台上' (zhuxitaishang or on the platform) appears initially and precedes the Predicate, is it Subject? If it is, then it implies that there is no constraint put on the grammatical unit next below to realize the function of Subject. If it is not, then which element in the clause performs the function of subject?

Actually, this type of analysis of clause structure and the confusion derived from the concept of Subject gave rise to heated nation-wide discussions on the classification of word classes and Subject/Object distinction during two linguistics conferences in the 1950s on the mainland of China. Subject has been regarded as 'a headache' by some linguists (Fang and Shen 1997).

3.2.2 The Subject and Topic view

This view is maintained by Li and Thompson (1981), Shen Jiaxuan (1999) and Shi Yuzhi (2001), etc. Subject is defined as a 'noun phrase that has a "doing" relationship with the verb' while Topic 'sets a spatial, temporal or individual framework within which the main prediction holds'. Further, Topic contrasts with Subject, which appears after Topic and does not overlap with Topic (Li and Thompson 1981). This view is shared by Chao Yuanren (1968) and Xu Tongqiang (1990) although there is a slight difference between them, which will not be discussed here. Therefore, (1) would be analysed as

(1)   那 块   田   稻子   长   得   很   大。
      Na kuai tian   daozi zhang   de   hen   da
      that MEAS   field   rice   grow   VADV   ADV   big
         Topic   Subject   Predicate
      (In that piece of field, rice grows big in size.)

where the first nominal group is Topic and the second Subject. In this clause both Topic and Subject are present, in which Topic '那块田' (Na kuai tian or that piece of field) 'sets a spatial framework' for the 'main predication', and Subject '稻子' (daozi or rice) has a 'doing' relationship with the verb '长' (zhang or grow).

We can arrive at the following features relevant to Chinese clause structure from these views:

1. 'the clause is commonly defined in "message" terms'; in other words, 'the clause ... has some form of organization giving it the status of a communication event' (Halliday 1994 [1985] 38);
2. structurally, the clause divides into two parts: the first part, the

beginning of the message; the second part, the continuation of the message; and

3. 'the first part is significant in the creation of discourse' (Fang *et al.* 1995).

There exists a problem, however, in the two views: there are other elements than Topic or Subject appearing initially in a Chinese clause in a certain context, such as (3)

(3) 好,   我们   就   这样   决定   了。
    Hao   women   jiu   zheyang jueding   le
    Text   we   ADV   VADV   decide   VPART
    (All right, let's decide in this way.)

in which only '我们' (women or we) is Subject or Topic (referring to the above two views) while '好' (hao or all right) is not. Then what is it? The answer can be found in the SFL framework, which provides a multifunctional view of clause structure. We believe that approaching Chinese grammar from this view can help us solve the problem and 'understand better the types of grammatical patterning present in Chinese' (Fang *et al.* 1995).

3.3 Clause structure in Chinese – an SF perspective

Mathesius (1939, see Fries 1981: 1) divides a sentence into two parts: Theme and Rheme from the functional perspective, which has had an impact on Halliday's functional approach in mapping out one of his meta-functions – Textual Function – in organizing the constituents in a clause in a given context (1994 [1985]). In what follows we will summarize in brief the multi-functional view represented by Halliday, and then elaborate on two models of clause structure.

3.3.1   A multifunctional view

Systemic functional theory incorporates three types of meaning relation into a framework that explicitly recognizes the multifunctional nature of the clause as a 'combination of three different structures deriving from distinct functional components' (Halliday 1994 [1985]: 158): the experiential structure, representing patterns of our objective and subjective experience in the world; the interpersonal structure, enacting interpersonal relationships in the social world, and textual structure, which is concerned with the organization of a message in a clause or a discourse. This multifunctional view is the basis for the study of clause structure in Chinese in this chapter.

3.3.2 Two models of clause structure

Fang *et al.* (1995) state 'A clause in Chinese is the combination of a single experiential structure and a single thematic structure' as shown:

Clause
$$\begin{cases} \text{Theme + Rheme} \\ \\ \text{Actor + Process + Goal} \end{cases}$$

This definition is made on the ground that the form, concept and function of Subject differ in Chinese from those in English. First, Subject is hard to recognize as it has no morphological inflections (Lv Shuxiang 1984); second, the concepts of Subject given by different linguists differ a great deal, as mentioned in 3.2 – therefore the status of Subject is indefinite; and third, Subject does not perform the function of realizing Mood as in English, in which the sequential positions of the finite verb and Subject are decisive in the making of Mood in a clause (Halliday 1994 [1985]). In Chinese, Mood is very differently realized – by the intonation and the mood particles. Compare:

In English:

The sequence of a clause in the Declarative Mood

(4)   I finished my homework yesterday evening.

in which Subject precedes the Finite 'finished' fused with the Predicator. The sequence of a clause in the Interrogative Mood:

(4')   Did you finish your homework yesterday evening?

in which the Finite verb 'did' precedes Subject 'you'.
However, in Chinese:
The sequence of a clause in the Declarative Mood:

(5)   我 昨天   晚上   做   完   作业   了。
      Wo zuotian   wanshang   zuo   wan   zuoye   le
      I yesterday   evening   finish ASP   homework. VPART
      (I finished my homework yesterday evening.)

The sequence of a clause in the Interrogative Mood

(5')   你 昨天   晚上   做 完   作业   了   吗?
      Ni zuotian   wanshang   zuowan   zuoye   le   *ma?*
      You yesterday evening   finish ASP homework   VPART   MPART
      (Did you finish your homework yesterday evening?)

in which there is no change of word order as Chinese has no finite verb. The Interrogative Mood is realized by the mood particle '吗' (*ma*) and the rising intonation in spoken Chinese or the question mark in the written form. The second reason for this definition is that we find that Halliday's experiential functional structure and textual structure correspond to Zhu's semantic structure and his expressive structure (Fang *et al.* 1995).

However, further studies on the nature of dialogues reveal that Subject does play a role in making an interaction possible. For example,

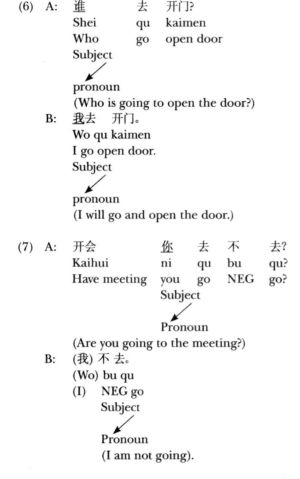

(6) A: 谁   去   开门?
          Shei   qu   kaimen
          Who   go   open door
          Subject

          pronoun
          (Who is going to open the door?)

     B: 我去   开门。
          Wo qu kaimen
          I go open door.
          Subject

          pronoun
          (I will go and open the door.)

(7) A: 开会   你   去   不   去?
          Kaihui   ni   qu   bu   qu?
          Have meeting   you   go   NEG   go?
                          Subject

                          Pronoun
          (Are you going to the meeting?)

     B: (我) 不 去。
          (Wo) bu qu
          (I)   NEG go
                Subject

                Pronoun
          (I am not going).

In A and B of (6), the dialogue argues about who should be the person going to open the door; it is this element which makes the interaction between the interrogators possible. This element is realized by the pronoun: '谁' in the interrogative clause, and '我' in the declarative clause. Different from (6) in structure, (7) has a verbal group taking the initial position, yet it is still the pronoun '你' (ni or you) or '(我)' (wo or I) being argued about between the two speakers. They are the elements which make the dialogue or interactive event valid or possible. All these pronouns function as Subject in the respective clauses. Semantically, Subject can be defined as the element performing the interactive function of making a proposition arguable (Halliday 1994 [1985]; Matthiessen 1995) or as the element responsible for the clause as an interactive event, and structurally, it usually precedes Predicator and is realized by a noun/nominal group or a pronoun.

Therefore, a clause in Chinese is the combination of a single experiential structure, a single interpersonal structure and a single thematic structure as shown:

$$
\text{Clause} \begin{cases} \text{Theme + Rheme} \\ \text{Subject + (Adjunct) + Predicator + (Complement)} \\ \text{Actor + (Circumstance) + Process + (Goal)} \end{cases}
$$

From the point of view of its experiential function, the clause divides into a process, one or more participants, and associated circumstances – an Experiential Structure. From the point of view of its interpersonal function, the clause divides into a Predicator, Subject, Complement and Adjuncts – an Interpersonal Structure. From the point of view of its textual function, the clause is made up of Theme and Rheme – a Thematic Structure, the concept of which will be discussed in the next section.

3.4 The concept of Theme

As mentioned above, systemic functional theory recognizes the clause as a combination of three different structures (Halliday 1994 [1985]: 158): the experiential, interpersonal, and textual structures. The textual clause grammar provides resources to realize the experiential and interpersonal meanings as text organized in a succession of peaks of prominence followed by non-prominence elements, thus forming two different types of wave, namely thematic and information waves. The peaks represent two types of prominence – thematic prominence and news prominence, which are realized by Theme and New respectively (Halliday 1994 [1985]; Matthiessen 1992). This chapter will only concentrate on the study of Theme, the realization of thematic prominence.

3.4.1 Definition of Theme

Mathesius (1939, see Fries 1981: 1) defines Theme as 'that which is known or at least obvious in the given situation and from which the speaker proceeds'.

In his earlier writings, Halliday gives the following definitions: Theme is 'the point of departure of a message' (1967, 1994 [1985]), or 'the starting-point for the message' (1994 [1985]: 39) or 'the peg on which the message is hung' (1970), and also 'what is being talked about' (1967: 212), or 'that with which the clause is concerned' (1994 [1985]). The two aspects of definition imply 'whatever is chosen as Theme is put first', and Theme is 'what the message is about' (Fang *et al.* 1995).

There are some differences between Mathesius and Halliday: the former holding the combining approach (Theme = Given) and ignoring the contribution of word order; the latter holding the separating approach (Theme may not be Given) and using the term Theme to indicate the meaning of initial position in the clause (Fang *et al.* 1995).

Halliday's definition has given rise to some criticisms. The major criticism comes from the argument that a point of departure may not be what the clause is about. While the experiential meaning may be what the clause is about, neither the textual nor the interpersonal has this connotation (Fries 1981; Wu Weizhong 2001). For instance, in (8)

(8)	可是	说不准	明天	会	更	热。
	Keshi	shobuzhun	mingtian	hui	geng	re
	But say	NEG sure	tomorrow	MADV	ADV	warm
	Text	Inter	Topic			

--------- Theme ------------------   Rheme -------

(But I am not sure whether it will be warmer tomorrow.)

'明天' (mingtian or tomorrow) is Topical Theme (see section 3.4.2) realizing the experiential meaning of the clause; however neither '可是' (keshi or but) nor '说不准' (shuobuzhun or not sure) has anything to do with expressing the experiential meaning or is concerned with the 'aboutness' of the clause. In fact, the former, being a coordinate conjunction linking this clause with the previous one, performs Textual Function whereas the latter, being a modal element expressing the assessment of the speaker, performs Interpersonal Function.

Matthiessen (1995) describes Theme as 'the resource for manipulating the contextualization of the clause ... for setting up a local context for each clause in a text'. Halliday and Matthiessen redefine Theme later as 'the point of departure of the message; it is that which locates and orients the clause within its context' (2004). There are two points noticeable in these two definitions: (i) they no longer mention the 'aboutness' of a message; and (ii) they highlight the role of context in defining this textual function, thus pushing the Hallidayan grammar a step further towards a 'discourse grammar' (Halliday 1994 [1985]).

Chinese scholars provide various definitions of Theme in Chinese: some adopt Mathesius' view (Zhang and Fang 1994); some only take the first part of Halliday's 1994 [1985] definition (Wu Weizhong 2001); some follow Halliday's 1994 [1985] concept literally in their earlier articles (Fang Yan 1990).

Fang *et al.* in 1995 claimed: 'Theme normally comes first in the clause, and may be marked off from the Rheme by a pause and/or a textual particle such as a, ba, me, ne'. The reason why they stated that 'Theme normally comes first in the clause' is because they believed that in spoken Chinese the position of Theme and Rheme may be reversible. The second half of the definition comes from their consideration of recognizing Theme formally. However, it seems now that the reversibility of Theme and Rheme needs to be further verified.

Referring to Fang *et al.* (1995) and Halliday and Matthiessen (2004), this chapter has revised the definition of Theme in Chinese: Theme is the point of departure of a message; it provides the context for the clause and may be marked off from Rheme by a pause and/or a textual particle such as 啊 (a), 吧 (ba), 嚜 (me) or 呢 (ne). Again take (8) as an example, in which '可是' '说不准' and '明天' are the point of departure of the message; these three elements provide respectively the ideational, interpersonal and textual context for the clause, and they may be separated by the textual particle 啊 (a) from the Rheme of the clause.

(8)	可是	说不准	明天	(啊)	会	更	热。
	Keshi	shobuzhun	mingtian	(a)	hui	geng	re
	But	say NEG sure	tomorrow	(Text P)	MADV	ADV	warm
	Text	Inter	Topic				

-------- Theme -----------------------   Rheme -------

(But I am not sure whether it will be warmer tomorrow.)

Halliday (1994 [1985]) argues that the Theme of a major clause extends up to the first element that has an experiential meaning. This gives rise to two major types of Theme: simple and multiple, which will be discussed in the following section.

3.4.2 Simple Theme and multiple Theme

When we discussed (3) '好, 我们就这样决定' (hao, women jiu zheyang jueding, or All right, let's decide in this way), we pointed out that '我们' (women or we) is the Topic but '好' (hao or all right) is not. Then what is it? We can find the answer from the concept of Multiple Theme. Halliday (1994 [1985]) claims that if there is only an element of the experiential mode of the ideational metafunction or Topical element in a clause, it is called Simple Theme. The Themes in the clauses of (1), (2), (5), (6) and (7) are Simple Themes. However, in (3), '好' and '我们' function differently though both appear at the beginning of the clause: '好' performs the function of 'continuative' (Halliday 1994 [1985]: 53), thus labelled as 'Textual Theme' as it connects this clause with the previous one in this context while '我们' is expressing its Topical meaning. To avoid confusion arising from the term Topic, which is associated with 'only one particular type of Theme' (Halliday 1994 [1985]: 39), this chapter labels this function as 'Topical Theme'. Therefore this clause can be analysed as:

(3)

好,		我们	(啊)	就	这样	决定。
Hao		women	(a)	jiu	zheyang	jueding
Continuative		we	(Text P)	ADV	VADV	decide
Text Theme		Topical theme				

---------- Theme ----------------   ---------------- Rheme -----------

(All right, let's decide in this way.)

In the previous section, we pointed out that in Clause (8), there are three thematic elements simultaneously existing in the clause. More examples can be found in (9), (10) and (11). The vocative elements '昌林哥, 玉翠嫂子' (changlin ge, yucui saozi or Changlin brother, Yucui sister) in (9) are used to bring closer the interpersonal relation between the speaker and the hearer; the exclamatory elements '啊呀, 天' (a ya tian or oh, heaven) in (10) to express the feeling of surprise of the speaker; and '不用说' (buyongshuo or needless say) in (11) to render the speaker's comment. Since all of them appear initially, they are all elements of Interpersonal Theme.

(9)

昌林哥,		玉翠 嫂子,	你们 两位	(啊)	同意 不?
Changlin ge		yucui saozi	nimen liangwei	(a)	tongyi bu
Changlin brother		Yucui sister	you two MEAS	(Text P)	agree NEG.
	Vocative				

--- Interpersonal Theme -----   Topical Theme
------------------------Theme--------   ----------Rheme-------------

(Brother Changlin, Sister Yucui, don't you two agree?)

(10)

啊呀,	天,	你	(啊)	长得	多	结实	啊!
A ya	tian	ni	(a)	zhangde	duo	jieshi	a
Oh,	heaven	you	(Text P)	grow	ADV	sturdy	MPART
Exclamatory							
Inter Theme		Topical Theme					

-----------Theme --------- -----   -------------Rheme --------------------

(Oh, my God, how sturdy you have grown)

(11)

不用说, 两个人 的 劲头 (啊) 都 绷得 像
Buyongshuo lianggeren de jintou (a) dou bengde xiang
梆子戏 上 的 琴弦。
　　bangzixi shang de qinxian
Needless say two MEAS people POSS look (Text P) ADV stretch
　　like opera upon fiddle
Modal
Inter Theme Topical Theme
------------- Theme ------------------   Rheme ----------------------------------

(Needless to say, the two people are intensely stretched mentally like the fiddles being played in an opera.)

To sum up, in Chinese, a Simple Theme is made up only of Topical Theme while a Multiple Theme can comprise Textual Theme, and/or Interpersonal Theme and Topical Theme. A Textual Theme may consist of (i) continuative, which is 'one of a small set of discourse signalers' (Halliday 1994 [1985]: 53), such as 好 (hao or all right), 是的 (shide or yes), 不是 (bushi or no), which 'signals that a new move is beginning' (*ibid.*) or indicates the speaker is ready to continue the interaction (Li, forthcoming); (ii) structural, including conjunctions and conjunctives (Halliday 1994 [1985]: 53), such as 虽然 … 但是 (suiran … danshi or although …), 可是 (keshi or but), 其实 (qishi or in fact), 换句话说 (huanjuhuashuo or in other words), etc. Types (i) and (ii) are two types of Textual Theme functioning as a cohesive tie in the text, denoting a certain logico-semantic relationship between the neighbouring clauses. Interpersonal Theme may include (i) an exclamatory element such as啊呀 (aya or oh), 天 (tian or heaven), as in (10); (ii) a vocative, usually a personal name as in (9), which is used to identify the addressee in the interaction; (iii) a modal element, such as, 可能 (keneng or possible), 肯定 (kending or certain), 会 (hui or tend to), 应该 (yinggai or must), or 说不准 (shuobuzhun or not sure) as in (8) or, 不用说 as in (11), etc. These modal elements are used to show the speaker's attitude towards the proposition or proposal expressed in the clause, either by means of modalization or of modulation (Halliday 1994 [1985]). Topical Theme is an ideational element, which is rather complex and will be elaborated in the next section. In other words, a Multiple Theme can contain all the three Themes or either Textual Theme and/or Interpersonal Theme plus Topical Theme. It follows, therefore, that there must be a Topical Theme in a clause although it can be omitted if the context is made clear, but a clause can go without one of the other two, as illustrated in examples (3), where there are Textual Theme and Topical Theme but without Interpersonal Theme, and (9), (10) and (11), where there are Interpersonal Theme and Topical Theme but without Textual Theme. Similar to English, the sequence of the three elements when they all appear initially would usually be: Textual Theme ∧ Interpersonal Theme ∧ Topical Theme, which is well illustrated in (8). However, a few conjunctions such as '虽然' can come before or after Topical Theme. For example, it is possible to choose either (12a) or (12b) to express similar meanings (hereafter we will omit the possible textual particle, due to limitations of space):

(12a) <u>虽然</u> 我 不 知道 这事 是 谁 干 的, <u>但是 我</u> 敢
      Suiran wo bu zhidao zheshi shi shui gan de danshi wo gan
      肯定 与他有关。
        kending yu ta youguan
      CONJ I NEG know this matter be who do VADV CONJ I MADV
      PREP he concern
      Text Theme Topical Theme,   Text Theme Topical Theme
      (Although I don't know who did this, I am sure it has to do with
        him.)

(12b) 我 虽然 不知道 这事 是谁 干的， 但是 我 敢 肯定 与他 有关。
Wo suiran bu zhidao zheshi shi shui gande danshi wo gan kending
  yu ta youguan
I CONJ NEG know this matter be who do VADV CONJ I MADV
  PREP he concern
Topical Theme   Text Theme Topical Theme
(Although I don't know who did this, I am sure it has to do with
  him.)

Therefore, there are two positions for 虽然 (suiran, or although) in
Chinese, either before or after Topical Theme. Some linguists (Li, 2007)
argue that usually this kind of conjunction appears at the second initial
position, and therefore, when it takes the initial position, it is in its marked
position.

3.5 Topical Theme

This section will address several subtopics: 1) definitions of Topic given by
various linguists; 2) types of Topical Theme, namely, Contextual Topical
Theme and Experiential Topical Theme, Unmarked Theme and Marked
Theme, Preposed Theme, and Thematic Equative; 3) functions of Topical
Theme; and finally 4) realization of Topical Theme.

3.5.1 Definition of Topic

We mentioned in section 3.4 that Topical Theme originates from the term
Topic but it has replaced the latter on the ground that it is only one type of
Theme in the SFL framework. Apart from this, the two terms share the basic
concept.

The earliest definition of Topic comes from Hocket (1958), the linguist
who initiates the concept of 'discourse'. He defines Topic: 'The speaker
brings up something and goes on to talk about it', which is obviously a view
based on the function performed by this element, i.e. providing the basis
for the verbal act to continue. Different from Hocket, Chomsky gives a
definition from the formal perspective (1965): Topic refers to the most left
NP in a sentence in the surface structure, which defines this concept from
the position it takes without giving attention to its function(s). Chao Yuanren
(1968) combines the two approaches by stating that Topic is the most left
NP, which provides Comment, and that the Subject and Predication relation
is one as 'topic and comment rather than actor and action'. For example, in
(13), '我' is a pronoun and takes the most left position of the sentence, and
it is the element which provides the ground for the comment. Hence it is the
Topic of the clause.

(13) 我   头   疼。
      Wo   tou   teng
      I   head   ache
      Topic   Comment
      (My head aches.)

Li and Thompson (1981) propose a definition which is frequently quoted: Topic 'sets a spatial, temporal, or individual framework within which the main predication holds'. Accordingly in (13), '我' (wo or I) provides a setting for the main predication '头疼' (touteng or headache). Hence it is the Topic of the clause. Similarly, '那场火' (na chang huo or that fire) in (14) sets a framework for the rest of the clause. It is regarded as the Topic of the clause.

(14) 那 场 火, 幸亏   消防员   来   的   快。
      Na chang huo, xingkui   xiaofangyuan   lai   de   kuai
      That MEAS fire, fortunately fire-fighters come   VAVD   quickly
      Topic
      (As for that fire, it was fortunate that (as) the fire-fighters came
          quickly (it was put out.)

Note that this Chinese clause is a simple one as there is only one verb process '来' (lai or come), yet the underlying meaning conveyed by the commentary adjunct '幸亏' (xingkui or fortunately) implies that logically there could be a hypotactic relation between '幸亏消防员来的快' (xingkui xiaofangyuan lai de kuai or fortunately fire-fighters came quickly) and an omitted clause such as 'it was put out', which is understood in the context. Chafe (1976) regards this type of Topic as 'Chinese Topic'.

Shen Jiaxuan (1999) maintains that Topic should have the following features:

1) It always appears at the beginning;
2) There is a pause or a mood particle after it;
3) It expresses given information;
4) It is a concept of discourse, which can govern the following clause(s) as well.

There are three characteristics in the four features: 1) and 2) take the formal features of Topic into consideration: its initial position and how it is parsed from the rest of the clause (as far as we are concerned, 'is' should be replaced by 'may be' and 'a mood particle' changed into a textual particle as mood is not involved); 3) points out that it overlaps with given information (in an unmarked case); and 4) states that it is a concept derived from discourse; therefore Topic is also a discourse feature. Similarly, Shi Yuzhi (2001) claims that Topic is Given and appears initially; but he emphasizes that the topicalized elements are not only nouns, but also time, location, tool and beneficiary; however, these concepts are not on the same level: nouns are a notion of word class and the others notions of functions. Qu Chengxi (1997) defines Topic as a noun phrase or a pronoun or a zero anaphora appearing at the beginning of a clause and having the meaning of 'aboutness'. His definition restricts Topic as being realized by NP only; and having noticed the feature of zero anaphora appearing in a string of clauses in Chinese, he points out that it can also function as Topic in a discourse. Fang (1990) regards (in reference to Halliday 1994 [1985]) Topic as 'what the clause is about', and terms it as Topical Theme.

Referring to the above, this chapter defines Topical Theme as follows:

Topical Theme is the point of departure of a message; it expresses the experiential meaning and/or provides a setting for the clause and may be marked off from Rheme by a pause and/or a textual particle.

There are three features in the definition:

1) It starts with the positioning of Topical Theme – as a point of departure of a message; therefore, it should usually appear initially;
2) It stresses the semantic meaning or function of this element – expressing the experiential meaning and/or providing a setting for the clause;
3) It formalizes Theme by stating how it may be parsed from Rheme – by a pause and/or a textual particle.

3.5.2 Types of Topical Theme

In 3.5.1 Topical Theme is defined as expressing the experiential meaning and/or providing a setting for the clause, which, accordingly, gives rise to two types of Topical Theme: Experiential Topical Theme and Contextual Topical Theme.

3.5.2.1 *Experiential Topical Theme and Contextual Topical Theme*

(i) *Experiential Topical Theme*: As mentioned above, when there is only one element in the Theme, we term it as Simple Theme, which performs the experiential function as Actor '我' (wo or I) as in (15) or as Location '学校里' (xuexiao li or in school) as in (16). This type of Topical Theme is termed as Experiential Topical Theme, or for short, Experiential Theme; in the case of a Multiple Theme, the last thematic element is usually Experiential Theme as '明天' (mingtian or tomorrow) in (8), which expresses the experiential meaning of the clause as Carrier.

(15)　我　　打算　　去北京。
　　　　Wo　dasuan　qu beijing
　　　　I　　plan　　go beijing.
　　　　Experiential Theme/Actor
　　　　(I plan to go to Beijing.)

(16) 学校里   我 见 过   他。
      Xuexiao li   wo jianguo ta
      School in   I   see ASP he
      Experiential Theme/Circumstance: Location
      (In school I saw him.)

(8)   可是   说不准   明天   会   更   热。
      Keshi   shuobuzhun   mingtian   hui   geng   re
      But   say NEG sure   tomorrow   MADV   ADV   warm.
      Text   Inter   Experiential Theme/Carrier
      --------- Theme ----------------------   --- Rheme -----------------
      (But I am not sure whether it will be warmer tomorrow.)

ii) *Contextual Topical Theme*: When two nouns or two nominal groups appear
initially, both may be regarded as Topical Themes. The first provides the
setting for the clause, thus termed as Contextual Topical Theme or, for short,
Contextual Theme. Since the second noun usually performs the experiential
and interactive functions, it may be regarded as Experiential Theme – the
analysis is based on the consideration of Thematic patternings in a text, as
shown in (1) and (14) below:

(1)   那 块 田   稻子   长   得   很   大。
      Na kuai tian   daozi   zhang   de   hen   da
      that MEAS field rice   grow   VADV   ADV   big
      Contextual Theme Experiential Theme -----Rheme ----------
                          Actor/Subject
      (In that piece of field, rice grows big in size.)

Note that '那块田' (na kuai tian or that piece of field) is a nominal group,
which should not be regarded as a circumstantial element or as following
an omitted coverb or preposition '在……里' (zai……li or in) structurally,
although when rendered in English, it may be thought of as '在那块田里' (zai
na kuai tian li or in that piece of field).

(14) 那 场   火,   幸亏   消防员   来的快。
      Na chang huo, xingkui xiaofangyuan   laide kuai
      That fire,   fortunately fire-fighters   come VADV quickly.
      Contextual Theme   Experiential Theme   Rheme
                                      Actor/Subject
      (As for that fire, it was fortunate that (as) the fire-fighters came
          quickly (it was put out).)

Note that the concept of Contextual Theme resembles Topic as given by Li
and Thompson (1981) in two aspects: 1) both stress its function of providing
a setting for the clause; 2) both regard the first initial noun/nominal group

as Topic or its equivalent Contextual Theme, which could be a 'peripheral element' in front of the clause proper (Lv 1990: 120).

Matthiessen (1995) holds a similar view although he uses the term Absolute Theme. He argues that this Theme provides the textual 'subject matter', and serves no role in the ideational and interpersonal metafunctions.

Similarly, some Chinese scholars also claim that there could be two Themes in Chinese (Wu 2001). Li Yunxin (2002) labels them as Subject Theme and Topic Theme. Therefore, (1) and (14) can be analysed as

(1) 那块田　　　　　稻子　　　　　　长　　　得　　　很 大。
     Na kuai tian   daozi   zhang   de   hen da
     That MEAS field rice   grow   VADV   ADV big
     Topic Theme   Subject Theme   ------ Rheme --------------------
     (In that piece of field, rice grows big in size.)

(14) 那　　场　　　火，辛亏　　　消防员　　　　来的快。
     Na   chang huo, xingkui   xiaofangyuan   laide kuai
     That fire,   fortunately fire-fighters come VADV quickly.
     Topic Theme   Subject Theme
     (As for that fire, it was fortunate that (as) the fire-fighters came
        quickly (it was put out).)

Next the chapter will elaborate on the sub-categories of Experiential Theme: Marked Theme, Preposed Theme and Thematic Equative. The primary contrast is between 'Unmarked' Theme and 'Marked' Theme.

3.5.2.2 Unmarked Theme and Marked Theme

In Chinese, 'almost every functional component in the experiential metafunction can take the clause-initial position and can therefore be given thematic prominence'. 'Theme may conflate with any participant' (Li, forthcoming). However, the frequency of the appearance in the initial position of these elements is different, which results in what is known as the distinction between Unmarked and Marked Theme. For example, Shi Yuzhi (2001) finds that the structure Actor ^ Verb ^ Patient, which is equivalent to the experiential structure Actor ^ Process ^ Goal in the SFL terminology, is the most important structure in Chinese. This implies that in most cases it is Actor which is given Thematic prominence. Li (forthcoming) discovers from his data that 'about 90% of thematic prominence is assigned to the "participant" which is conflated with the Subject of the clause, a pattern which constitutes the "unmarked" case'. In classifying Unmarked Theme and Marked Theme, we may refer to either the Experiential Structure or the Interpersonal Structure or both. In the following, the chapter will discuss the two concepts in clauses of different types of mood.

(i) In an indicative: declarative clause, the typical structure is Subject ^ (Adjunct) ^ Predicator ^ (Complement) or Actor ^ (Circumstance) ^ Process ^ (Goal), which gives the ground for Shi (2001) and Li (2007) to state that Unmarked Topical Theme is usually conflated with Subject/Actor in the clause as in (17a)

(17a)	我		已经	知道	这	件	事。
	Wo		yijing	zhidao	zhe	jian	shi
	I		ASP	know	DET	MEAS	matter.
	Theme (Unmarked)/		-----	Rheme ------------------------			
	Subject/Actor			Predicator/Process			
				Complement/Goal			

(I already know this matter.)

in which '我' (wo or I) is Theme which is conflated with its role as Subject/Actor in the Interpersonal Structure and Experiential Structure. Hence it is Unmarked. When the Complement/Goal is given the thematic status, it becomes Marked Theme as in (17b):

(17b)	这	件	事	我 已经	知道。
	Zhe	jian	shi	wo yijing	zhidao
	DET	MEAS	matter	I ASP	know
	Theme	(Marked)/			
	Complement/Goal				

(This matter I already know.)

However, the structure Complement ^ Subject ^ Predicator (or the OSV structure in traditional linguistics) is not infrequent in novels and spoken Chinese (Fang 1989). The markedness of Theme may have to do with genre. More research needs to be done on whether text types or genre would impose constraints on the markedness of a component in a clause. However, one thing is clear, that Context contributes a great deal to thematization of a component of a clause, which will be discussed later.

In Chinese, an Adjunct denoting time or location typically appears at the second initial position (Shi 2001), which is its unmarked position. Its marked position would be at the beginning or at the end of a clause. Compare (18a), (18b) and (18 c).

Unmarked position: as in (18a), the time adjunct '现在' (xianzai or now) takes the second initial position.

(18a)	我	现在	不	想	结婚。
	Wo	xianzai	buxiang	想	jiehun
	I	now	NEG	want	marry
	Unmarked Position				

(I don't want to get married now.)

Marked position: as in (18b), the same element appears initially, giving prominence to the time of the happening event, thus functioning as Marked Theme whereas in (18c) it takes the final position, functioning as Marked New.

(18b) <u>现在</u>　　我　　不　　　　想　　结婚。
        Xianzai　wo　buxiang　　　　jiehun
        Now　　I　　NEG　　want　marry
        Marked Theme
        (Now I don't want to get married.)

(18c) 我 不　　　想　　结婚　　<u>现在</u>。
        Wo buxiang　　jiehun　xianzai
        I NEG　want　marry　now
                      Marked New
        (I don't want to get married now.)

However, there is another clause structure in Chinese: Adjunct ^ Predicator ^ Subject or Circumstance ^ Process ^ Actor or the AVS (Adverbial ^ Verb ^ Subject) structure. Some Chinese linguists take it as a structure in the inverted order (Fang 1989), yet Lv Shuxiang (1984) disagrees by stating that it is common in this type of structure for Subject to take the final position, which is in the normal word order. Hence the Adjunct Theme in this structure is Unmarked as in (2) and (19):

(2) <u>主席台上</u>　　　　坐着　　个　老人。
    Zhuxitaishang　　zuozhe　ge　laoren
    Platform upon　　sit PROG MEAS old man.
    Adjunct (location)　Predicator　　Subject
    Theme (Unmarked)
    (On the platform sits an old man.)

(19) <u>羊　群　　里</u>　跑 出 骆驼 来　了。
    Yang qun　li　pao chu luotuo lai　le
    Goat MEAS　in　run out　camel　come ASP
    Adjunct (location)　Predi-　Subject　-cator
    Theme (Unmarked)
    (Among the herds of goats ran out a camel.)

Note that verbs used in this structure are limited to a small group, such as '坐' (zuo or sit), '立' (li or stand), '来' (lai or come), '到' (dao or arrive), '出 (来)' (chu lai or come out) '进 (来)' (jin lai or enter), '下 (来)' (xia lai or descend), etc. (Fang 1989). Li (forthcoming) terms this type of clause as 'Existential'. This paper regards it as a sub-category of Material Process.

'Predicator is rarely thematized, thus "extremely marked" (Li, forth-coming). However, it is not impossible. For example, in a given context, we may have a clause such as (20):

(20) ...... 失败　　　　　他们　　　将　　　肯定　　　会。
Shibai　　　　　　tamen　　jiang　　kengding　hui
Fail　　　　　　　they　　　ADV　　ADV　　　MADV
Predicator　　　　Subject
Theme (Marked)
(... fail they certainly would.)

However, Fang (1989) finds that in the Chinese Experiential Structure, there exists the Predicator ^ Subject structure or the VS structure, where the verbs, usually '来' (lai or come) or '去' (qu or go) plus '了' (le, a particle denoting the completion of the verb process) have the connotation of 'disappearance' or 'emergence'. Lv argues (1984: 457–8) that in this type of clause 'the speaker would take the element denoting "disappearance" as the starting point of the clause'. Therefore, when a verb denotes either 'disappearance' or 'emergence', it would become the point of departure in this type of clause; hence Unmarked Theme as in (21):

(21) 冒　　出　　了　　　你 这 个　　　　小　　　兔崽子。
Mao chu　le　　　ni zhe ge　　　xiao　　tuzaizi
Emerge　　PART　you DET MEAS　little　　rabbit son
Predicator　　　　Subject
Unmarked Theme
(Emerge you, the son of rabbit.)

To sum up, the Circumstantial Adjunct or Predicator may be Unmarked Theme when taking initial position in some particular experiential struc-tures. However, Circumstantial Adjunct is the most frequent Marked Theme in Chinese 'followed by Complement and Predicator/Process' (Li, 2007), as shown below:

Theme ⎰ Unmarked: Theme = Subject
　　　　⎱ Marked: Theme = Adjunct / Complement / Predicator

The primary means for a component to become Marked Theme is the change of word order as mentioned above. In Chinese there are two other ways to thematize an element: by putting the preposition '对于' (duiyu), '关于' (guanyu), '至于' (zhiyu) ('as for' or 'as to') or the copula '是' (shi or be) in front of the element as in (22) and (23). We follow Halliday's terminology (1994 [1985]) and take this construction as a Predicated Theme, that is, the

Predicator '是' (shi or be) and its Complement are given thematic prominence, with '是' (shi or be) functioning as a marker of affirmation on the part of the speaker in a dialogue in which the hearer is doubtful about what has been said.

(22) 对于波斯湾战争,   我们   都 很   关心。
      Duiyu bosiwan zhanzheng,   women   dou hen   guanxin.
      PREP Gulf War,   we   ADV   VADV concern
      Marked Theme   Subject/Carrier
      (As for the Gulf War, we are all very concerned about it.)

(23) 是 小王   看   完   了   信。
      Shi Xiao Wang   kan   wan   le   xin.
      Be Xiao Wang   see   finish ASP   letter
      Marked Theme (Predicated)
      Pre- Subject   -dicator
      (It is Xiao Wang who has read the letter.)

(ii) In the indicative: interrogative clause, the structure generally is the same as that in the declarative. Yet there are two types of interrogative clauses: the polar- interrogative and that with WH type question words such as '为什么' (weishime or why) or '怎么' (zeme or how), etc. In both types of clause, the element being queried would occupy the second initial position in the corresponding declarative clause. However, this element may be 'assigned thematic prominence' when taking the initial position. 'In this case, it is the element carrying both thematic and news prominence' (Li, 2007) as in (24a):

(24a) 为什么   他   还   没   来?
       Weishime   ta   hai   mei   lai
       Why   he   ADV   NEG   come
       WH word
       Marked Theme Subject/Actor
       (Why has he not come yet?)

However, if there is an Adjunct, it will be the Marked Theme of the clause as in (24b):

(24b) 昨天晚上   为什么   他   没   来?
       Zuotian wanshang   weishime   ta   mei   lai
       Yesterday evening   why   he   NEG   come
                            WH word
       Marked Theme   Subject/Actor
       (Yesterday evening why didn't he come?)

The system of Unmarked Theme and Marked Theme in an interrogative clause is summarized as follows:

Theme
{
Unmarked: Theme = Subject

Marked: Theme = Interrogative Element/Adjunct
}

(iii) The sequence in the exclamatory and the imperative clause is the same as in the declarative. The principles for thematization in the declarative clause can be applied to both types of clause, except that Theme may be omitted in the imperative.

(25) is an exclamatory clause, in which '你' (ni or you) is Theme/Subject/Actor; in a particular context, the Adjunct '多结实' (duo jieshi or how sturdy) can be switched to the front functioning as Marked Theme. Compare (25a) and (25b):

(25a)
你	长得	多	结实	啊!
Ni	zhangde	duo	jieshi	a
You	grow	ADV	sturdy	MPART

Unmarked Theme/Subject/Actor

(How sturdy you have grown)

(25b)
多		结实	啊	你	长得!
Duo		jieshi	a	ni	zhangde
ADV		sturdy	MPART	you	grow

Marked Theme/ Subject
Exclamatory Element

(How sturdy you have grown)

When there is an Adjunct appearing initially, it functions as Marked Theme as shown in (25c):

(25c)
那时候	你	长得	多	结实	啊!
Na shihou	ni	zhangde	duo	jieshi	a
DET that time	you	grow	ADV	sturdy	MPART

Marked Theme

(How sturdy you grew at that time!)

The system of Unmarked Theme and Marked Theme in an exclamatory clause is summarized as follows:

Theme
{
Unmarked: Theme = Subject

Marked: Theme = Exclamatory Element/Adjunct
}

(26) is an imperative clause, in which Theme is omitted and there is only Rheme.

(26)   (你)   走   吧!
       (Ni)   zou   ba.
       (You)   go   MPART
       (Theme) Rheme
       [You'd] better leave!

An Adjunct may become Marked Theme in an imperative clause as in a declarative one when it appears initially.

(27)   现在   你   走   吧!
       Xianzai   ni   zou   ba.
       Now   you   go   MPART
       Marked Theme --------- Rheme -----
       (Now you'd better leave!)

The system of Unmarked Theme and Marked Theme in an imperative clause is summarized as follows:

Theme   { Unmarked: Theme = (Subject)
         { Marked: Theme = Adjunct

3.5.2.3 *Preposed Theme*

In Chinese, there is another way to thematize a noun or pronoun or a set phrase denoting a characteristic of a person or object: by preposing it so that it becomes a prominent element and this element is referred to again later in the clause. A noun is usually referred to by a pronoun; a pronoun or a set phrase by a noun. For example in (28a), '这个人' (zhe ge ren or this person), a nominal group, is preposed as compared with that in its normal position in (28b) and is referred to as the pronoun '他' (ta or him) later in the clause (Shi Yuzhi 2001):

(28a)   这   个   人   我 跟   他 通   过   信。
        Zhe   ge   ren   wo gen   ta tong   guo   xin
        This MEAS person   I   PREP *he* correspond ASP   letter
        Preposed Theme
        (This person I exchanged letters with him.)

(28b) 我   跟   这   个   人   通   过   信。
      Wo   gen   zhe   ge   ren   tong   guo   xin
      I   PREP   this   MEAS   person   correspond   ASP   letter
      Theme
      (I exchanged letters with this person.)

(29) 他   这   个   人   就   知道   吃。
      Ta   zhe   ge   ren   jiu   zhidao   chi
      He   *this* MEAS   *person* VAVD   know   eat.
      Preposed Theme
      (He is such a kind of person that all he knows is to eat.)

In (29), the Preposed Theme '他' (ta or he), which is a pronoun, is referred to as the nominal group '这个人' (zhe ge ren or this person) later.

(30) 通情达理, 有求必应,   大家   都   喜欢   这   种   人。
      Tongqingdali, youqiubiying, dajia   dou   xihuan   zhe zhong   ren
      Reasonable ready to help   everybody VADV like   this CLASSIFIER
                                                                       person
           Preposed Theme
      [A person is] reasonable and ready to help; everybody likes such a
      person.

'通情达理, 有求必应' (tongqingdali, youqiubiying or reasonable and ready to help) are two set phrases used to describe the characteristics of the nominal group '这种人' (zhe zhong ren or this type of person). They are fronted from their original positions before this nominal group. They are preposed because the speaker intends to impress the hearer first with the characteristic features of this person.

The system of Non-Preposed Theme and Preposed Theme is summarized as follows:

                        ⌈ Non - Preposed: Theme = Subject
      Theme   ⎨
                        ⌊ Preposed: Theme: ◄— Pronoun/Noun/Set Phrase

Some linguists argue that this type of clause may be 'analysed as having two layers of thematic structure' (Li, forthcoming). For example, (28a) may be analysed as:

(28)

这	个	人	我	跟	他	通	过	信。
Zhe	ge	ren	wo	gen	ta	tong	guo	xin
This	MEAS	person	I	PREP	*he*	correspond	ASP	letter
Theme1			Rheme1					
			Theme2/Subject	Rheme2				

(This person I exchanged letters with him.)

3.5.2.4 *Thematic Equative*

In Chinese, there is an A ^ 是 (shi or be) ^ B construction, in which A is a nominal group or a nominalized verbal group ended with the particle 的 (de), while B is also a nominalized construction. A and B are linked by the copula 是 (shi or be) or 就是 (jiu shi with jiu as an intensifier), resulting in an identifying clause; the two parts are equative with the first thematized. This construction is thus labelled as Thematic Equative (Halliday 1994 [1985]) as in (31):

(31)

我	说	的	就	是	这	件	事。
Wo	shuo	de	jiu	shi	zhe	jian	shi
I	say	PART	INTEN	be	DET	MEAS	matter
Token				Predicator		Value	
Subject			(Identifying)			Complement	
Theme			Rheme				

(What I said is this matter.)

Such clauses are usually reversible; however, in such a case the clause is possibly rendered in another wording as in (31'):

(31')

这 件 事	就 是 我 说 的	(那 件 事)。
Zhe jian shi	jiu shi wo shuo de	(na jian shi)
DET MEAS matter	INTEN be I say PART	(DET MEAS matter)
Value	Predicatior	Token
Subject	(Identifying)	Complement
Marked Theme		

(This matter is what I said.)

The system of Unmarked Theme and Marked Theme in a Thematic Equative clause is summarized as follows:

Theme
{
Unmarked: Theme = Subject/Token (de construction)

Marked: Theme = Subject/Value
}

In summary, we can arrive at the following system of Topical Theme:

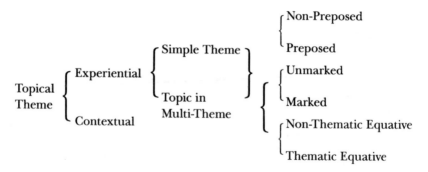

3.5.3 Functions of Topical Theme

Topical Theme may perform several functions: 1) aboutness function (Shi 2001); 2) clause-linking function (Chu 1997) or as a cohesive tie; 3) providing a setting of time or location; and 4) restricting a domain (Wu 2001), which will be illustrated below.

1) *Aboutness function*
'对于波斯湾战争' (duiyu bosiwan zhanzheng or as for the Gulf War) in Clause (22) is what the speaker is concerned with or performs the aboutness function. More examples are as follows:

(32) 这盆盆景,   叶子很大,   花太小,   不好看。
      Zhepeng pengjing, yezi henda,   hau taixiao,   bu hao kan.
      This bonsai,   leaves ADV big, flowers ADV small, not good-
                                                          looking.
      Carrier 1   Car21 Attr21   Car 22 Attr22   Attribute 1
      Theme1   Rheme1
                      Theme21 Rheme21 Theme 22 Rheme22
      (As for this bonsai, the leaves are big but the flowers are small so it
        is not good-looking.)

This is a clause complex. The main clause is '这盆盆景不好看' (Zhepeng pengjing bu hao kan or This bonsai is not good - looking.). Structurally, there are two layers: on the first layer, it is in paratactic relation with the two clauses '叶子很大' (yezi henda or leaves are too big) and '花太小' (hau taixiao or flowers are too small); at the second layer, these two clauses are also in paratactic relation; however, semantically these two clauses could be regarded as giving the reason why the bonsai does not look good. '这盆盆景' (zhepeng pengjing or this bonsai) serves as the Experiential Theme; it is this element that the whole clause complex is about.

(33) 我   打算   去   北京。
      Wo   dasuan   qu   beijing
      I   plan   go   Beijing.
      Theme/Actor   Rheme
      (I plan to go to Beijing.)

In (33), the Experiential Theme '我' (wo or I) is the element the speaker is concerned with.

2) *Clause-linking function in a Theme–Rheme Chain*

We notice that in Chinese, there exists the structure: Topical Theme + Rheme ^ comma ^ (01 Topical Theme) + Rheme ^ comma ^ (02 Topical Theme) + Rheme ^ comma ^ (0n Topical Theme) + Rheme ^ full stop, or Topical Theme ^ Rheme ^ [(Topical Theme) ^ Rheme) n], which is termed as a Theme – Rheme Chain. In a T–R Chain, the first Thematic element is an Experiential Theme with the rest of the Themes realized by zero anaphora referring to the first. This chain of Topical Themes contributes to building up the cohesion among the clauses in a discourse as in (34):

(34) 老吴   欠 了 我   两百块 钱,   0一直说   0没有 钱 还。
      Lao Wu qian le wo erbaikuai qian yizhishuo meiyou qian huan
      Lao Wu owe ASP I 200 MEAS yuan, always say NEG money repay
      Theme1   Rheme1   Theme2 Rheme2 Theme3 Rheme3
(Old Wu owes me 200 yuan, but he always says that he has no money to repay me.)

3) *Providing a frame of time or location*

(35) 明天   我   打算   去   北京。
      Mingtian   wo   dasuan   qu   beijing
      Tomorrow   I   plan   go   beijing.
      Topical Theme (Contextual)
      (I plan to go to Beijing tomorrow.)

The Topical Theme in (35) provides the frame of the time when the actor will take the action.

4) *Restricting a domain or range*

(36) 水果   我   只   吃一个。
      Shuiguo   wo   zhi   chi yige
      Fruit   I   VADV   eat MEAS.
      Topical Theme
      (As for fruit, I only eat one.)

In (36), the Topical Theme '水果' (shuiguo or fruit) functions as the domain

for the action to take place. In (37) it is '物价' (wujia or price) that provides
the range for the comparison of prices.

(37) <u>物价</u>   纽约   最   贵。
      Wujia   niuyue   zui   gui
      Price   New York   CADV   expensive.
      Topical Theme
      (As for prices, the most expensive will be in New York.)

3.5.4   Realization of Topical Theme

Halliday holds a multi-strata theory of language, in which the higher level is
realized by the level next below (Halliday 1994 [1985]), as shown:

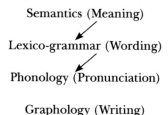

Semantics (Meaning)

Lexico-grammar (Wording)

Phonology (Pronunciation)

Graphology (Writing)

Therefore, Topical Theme as a function at the semantic level may be realized
by the choices made at the lexical–grammatical level. Concretely, it may
be realized by a noun/nominal group, a verbal group/nominalized verbal
group/clause, a prepositional phrase (or a 'coverbal phrase') or a circumstantial element, which will be illustrated in this section.

1) *Theme is realized by a noun, a pronoun or a nominal group as in (6)*:
   (6) 我   去 开门。
        Wo   qu kaimen
        Theme   Rheme

        pronoun
        I   go open door.
        (I will go and open the door.)

2) *Theme is realized by a verbal group as in (7)*:
   (7) <u>开会</u>   你去不去?
        Kaihui   ni qu bu qu?
        Theme (contextual) Rheme

        verbal group
        have meeting   you go or not go?
        (Are you going to the meeting?)

3) *Theme is realized by a nominalized verbal group as in (38):*

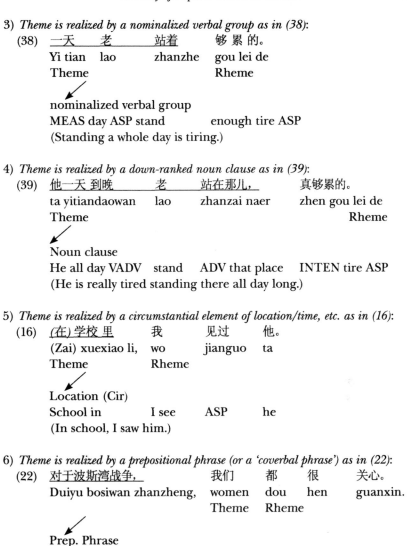

(38)　一天　　老　　　　站着　　　够 累 的。

Yi tian　lao　　zhanzhe　gou lei de

Theme　　　　　　　　　　Rheme

nominalized verbal group

MEAS day ASP stand　　　enough tire ASP

(Standing a whole day is tiring.)

4) *Theme is realized by a down-ranked noun clause as in (39):*

(39)　他一天 到晚　　　老　　站在那儿，　　　真够累的。

ta yitiandaowan　lao　　zhanzai naer　　zhen gou lei de

Theme　　　　　　　　　　　　　　　　　　　　　Rheme

Noun clause

He all day VADV　stand　ADV that place　INTEN tire ASP

(He is really tired standing there all day long.)

5) *Theme is realized by a circumstantial element of location/time, etc. as in (16):*

(16)　*(在)* 学校 里　　　我　　　见过　　　他。

(Zai) xuexiao li,　wo　　jianguo　ta

Theme　　　　　　Rheme

Location (Cir)

School in　　　I see　ASP　　　he

(In school, I saw him.)

6) *Theme is realized by a prepositional phrase (or a 'coverbal phrase') as in (22):*

(22)　对于波斯湾战争，　　　　我们　　都　　很　　　关心。

Duiyu bosiwan zhanzheng,　women　dou　hen　　guanxin.

　　　　　　　　　　　　　　　Theme　Rheme

Prep. Phrase

PREP Gulf War,　　　　　　　we　　ADV　VADV　concern

(As for the Gulf War, we are all concerned about it.)

3.5.5 Theme and context

The SFL model takes the concept of Context as indispensable in the study of clause structure (Halliday and Hasan 1985); Context puts constraints on which element should be Theme in a clause of a discourse and could be a decisive variable for the patterning of Thematic Progression (Fries 1981). We have mentioned that Matthiessen (1995) and Halliday and Matthiessen (2004) give a great deal of weight to the role of Context in defining Theme. Any of the clauses cited above would only occur within a given context. We mentioned that in example (3), '好' performs the function of 'continuative' and is a Textual Theme as it connects this clause with the previous one in the given context. One more example would suffice. Compare (36) and (40). The Context would be a dialogue between two people talking about the habit of having fruit. A says:

(40)	A:	我	每天	吃	两种	不同	的	水果。
		Wo	meitian	chi	liangzhong	butong	de	shuiguo
		I	everyday	eat	two MEAS	different	POSS	fruit

Theme1/Actor ------------------Rheme1----------------------------
(I have two kinds of fruit everyday.)

B, who has a different dietary habit in having fruit, takes part of the Rheme of (40) as the starting point for his part in the dialogue and says:

(36)	B:	<u>水果</u>	我	只	吃一个。
		Shuiguo	wo	zhi	chi yige
		Fruit	I	VADV	eat MEAS.

Topical Theme2   Rheme2
(As for fruit, I only eat one.)

The patterning of Thematic Progression in this dialogue is Theme1–Rheme1, part of which (水果, shuiguo or fruit) becomes Theme2 followed by Rheme2. Due to the limitation of space, this chapter will not give a more detailed discussion on the relation between Theme and Context, and on how Context imposes constraints on the choice of Theme in a longer discourse, or on how the patterning of Thematic Progression is folded in an extensive discourse. For the patternings of Thematic Progression, refer to Fang and Ai (1995).

3.6 Conclusions

This chapter has attempted to apply the systemic-functional model to dealing with clause structure in Chinese, mainly from the textual point of view, or in terms of Theme–Rheme structure. It has focused on the discussions on the various features of Topical Theme.

However, this is only a tentative study of this topic, which is not able to cover every aspect of this concept. Chinese, as every other language, is a complex system, which has caused controversial views on some basic concepts such as clause structure, Subject, Theme and Topic or Topical Theme. Clarification and common ground can be reached only by conducting more research on a more extensive scope at both clause and discourse level. This, we believe, can only be achieved by building up a large corpus for a systematic study of Chinese and by establishing the collaboration of linguists from various institutions in different regions in the world, which, we are happy to see, is exactly the aim of founding the Halliday Centre of City University.

Note

I am grateful to Dr. Eden Li for reading the final draft and for giving critical comments.

References

Chafe, W. (1976), 'Givenness, contrastiveness, definiteness, subject, topics and point of view', in C. N. Li (ed.) *Subject and Topic*. New York: Academic Press.

Chao, Y. (1968), *A Grammar of Spoken Chinese*. Berkeley and Los Angeles: University of California Press.

Chomsky, N. (1965), *Aspects of the Theory of Syntax*. Cambridge, MA: MIT Press.

Chu, C. C. (1997), ' "Aboutness" and clause–linking: two separate functions of topic in Mandarin'. *Tsing Hua Journal of Chinese Studies*, New Series XXVII, 1:37–50.

Fang Yan (1989), 'A tentative study of theme and rheme in Chinese'. *Journal of Tsinghua Uinversity*, No. 2, 66–72.

Fang Yan (1990), 'On subject in Chinese – "subject", "actor" and "theme"', in Hu Zhuanglin (ed.), *Language, System and Function*. Peking: Peking University Press, pp. 53–62.

Fang Yan and Ai Xiaoxia (1995), 'Analysis of thematic progression in Chinese discourse'. *Journal of Foreign Language Research*, No. 2, 20–24.

Fang Yan, Edward McDonald and Cheng Musheng (1995), 'On theme in Chinese from clause to discourse', in R. P. Hasan and Fries (eds), *On Subject and Theme*. Amsterdam and Philedalphia: John Benjamins Publishing Company, pp. 235–73.

Fang Yan and Shen Mingbo (1997), 'A functional trend in the study of Chinese', in Hu Zhuangli and Fang Yan (eds), *Advances in Functional Linguistics in China*. Beijing: Tsinghua University Press, pp. 1–14.

Fries, P. H. (1981), 'On the status of Theme in English: Arguments from discourse'. *Forum Linguisticum*, pp. 6.I, 561–88.

Halliday, M. A. K. (1967), 'Notes on transitivity and theme in English'. *Journal of Linguistics*, V, 3.1, 3.2 and 4.2.

Halliday, M. A. K. (1970), 'Language structure and language function', in J. Lyons (ed.), *New Horizons in Linguistics*. Harmondsworth: Penguin Books.

Halliday, M. A. K. (1977), 'Text as semantic choice in social contexts', in T. van Dijk and J. Petofi (eds), *Grammars and Descriptions*. Berlin: Walter de Gruyter.

Halliday, M. A. K. (1994 [1985]), *An Introduction to Functional Grammar*. London: Edward Arnold.

Halliday, M. A. K. and Hasan, R. (1985), *Language, Context and Text: Aspects of Language in a Social-Semiotic Perspective*. Geelong, Australia: Deakin University Press.

Halliday, M. A. K. and Matthiessen, C. (2004), *An Introduction to Functional Grammar* (3rd revised edn). London: Edward Arnold.

Hocket, C. F. (1958), *A Course in Linguistics*. New York: MacMillan.

Ma Jianzhong (1983), *Ma's Grammar*. Beijing: Commercial Press.

Matthiessen, C. (1992), 'Interpreting the textual metafunction', 'in M. Davies and L. Ravelli (eds), *Advances in Systemic Linguistics*. London: Pinter.

Matthiessen, C. (1995), 'THEME as a resource in ideational "knowledge" construction', in M. Ghadessy (ed.), *Thematic Developments in English Texts*. London: Pinter.

Li, C. N. and S Thompson, (1981), *Mandarin Chinese: A Functional Reference Grammar*. Berkeley: University of California Press.

Li, E. (2007), *Systemic Functional Grammar of Chinese*. London: Continuum.

Li Yunxin (2002), 'The applications of "Theme" in translation studies'. *Foreign Languages and Their Teaching*, No. 7, 19–22.

Lv Shuxiang (1984), 'Issues on grammatical analysis in Chinese', in *Proceedings of Chinese Grammar*. Beijing: Commercial Press.

Lv Shuxiang (1990), *Selected Works of Lv Shuxiang*. Beijing: Commercial Press.

Qu Chengxi (1999), 'The Y-movement and its inverted order in English from the perspective of focus and topic in Chinese'. *Journal of Learning*, No, 4: 1–13.

Shen Jiaxuan (1999), *On Irregularity and Markedness*. Nanchang: Jiangxi Education Press.

Shi Yuzhi (2001), 'Subject and topic in Chinese'. *Journal of Language Research*, No. 2, 82–91.

Wu Zhongwei (2001), 'A tentative study on theme–rheme structure in Chinese clause'. *Journal of Language Teaching and Research*, No.3, 11–17.

Xu Tongqiang (1990), *On Language*. Changchun: Northeast Normal University Press.

Zhang Bojiang and Fang Mei (1994), 'On thematic structure in oral Chinese'. *Journal of Peking University*, No. 2, 66–71.

Zhu Dexi (1981), *A Grammar Course*. Beijing: Commercial Press.

How is Meaning Construed Multimodally?
A Case Study of a PowerPoint Presentation Contest[1]

Hu Zhuanglin
Peking University and Dong Jia
Renmin University of China

4.1 Meaning and mediated discourse analysis

4.1.1 Mediated discourse analysis

The tenet of systemic functional linguistics is the study of language from the perspective of choice, levels, function, context, text/discourse, register, etc. However, we can only 'give a semantic interpretation of a text, describe the semantic system of a fairly restricted register, and provide a general account of some of the semantic features of a language, but in one way or another semantic studies remain partial and specific' (Halliday 1994: xx). This suggests, in spite of natural language being the most important mode of expressing meaning (Halliday 1978a: 39), that it does not exhaust all the resources from which meanings are construed. To get the whole picture of meaning, implicit and explicit, internal and external, abstract and concrete, we have to go outside the language, which is only one of the semiotic modes. In this case, we should bring to the fore the study of Mediated Discourse Analysis (MDA).

Mediated discourse analysis examines the interrelationship between individuals, social practices or actions, and various forms of text – that is, discourse (Disler 2003).

There are two perspectives involved, discourse and social action (Scollon 2001). The role of social action in construing meaning was foreseen in Halliday's theoretical framework on social semiotics (Halliday 1978a), later summarized by Deborah Schiffrin (1994) as: (1) 'A social reality (or a "culture") is itself an edifice of meaning – a semiotic construct' created by language, which is just one semiotic system among others. (2) A meaning-making process is based on a process of coding and decoding with the same set of values, in which the associative potential is furthermore limited by the social context. (3) The prior semantic level and the lexicogrammatical level are closely internally related, since each kind of meaning tends to be realized as a particular kind of structure. (4) The semantic system is described by Halliday as having 'an internal organization in which the social functions of language are clearly reflected'. All these remarks can be boiled down to one basic notion: discourse is to be studied in relation to the social context, and on top of it, the social-cultural aspects of the human world.

There appears to be little difference between the systemic-functional approach and Scollon's approach, which bears the name 'mediated discourse analysis'. Scollon focuses on concrete, situated, real-time practices and their relationship to 'mediational means'. This enables concrete objects and actors in the world to become, through their integration in practice, classes or representations of objects. As recognized by Scollon (2001), MDA combines the close linguistic analysis of social interactions and practice theory and shares much common ground with critical discourse analysis (CDA), inter-actional sociolinguistics, and linguistic anthropology. Scollon claims, unlike interactional linguistics, that MDA invokes a social rather than an under-developed psychological theory; unlike CDA, conversational analysis, and interactional sociolinguistics, MDA does not privilege conversation as a genre and discursive practice more generally.

4.1.2 Multimodality

When people interact, sometimes they are co-present situationally, sometimes they communicate through information technology, that is to say, they can resort to multiple modes with which to communicate information and establish relationships. Meaning is construed and communicated. In this sense, discourse is by no means monomodal. It is inherently multimodal. For instance, the everyday experiences of every individual are multimodal: we see, we hear, we touch, we smell, and we taste. Our experience of the world comes to us through the multiple modes of communication to which each of our senses is attuned (Williamson 2003).

Multimodality, or 'a satellite view' in CDA's terminology, is a more prominent feature of mediated discourse analysis (Kress and van Leeuwen 2001: 8), that is, it investigates the complex relations existing between multiple modes of acting in the world. This shows natural language cannot realize all the meanings of a given culture. As a result, in addition to those semantic-functional categories that have been uncovered in systemic functional linguistics, we need more categories that were not studied in the past. Meaning potential cannot be separated from social semiotics, or semiotic potential, or modality potential, or however you wish to label it.

M. A. K. Halliday was a pioneer in the practice of multimodality. With the help of his colleague, Dr. Barbara Horvarth, Halliday made an analysis of a half-hour long film, which confined itself to a very few settings, such as the job interview, the school classroom and the department store (Halliday 1978b). Even within these limits, Halliday saw the extent of the different demands on language, the variety of things that people expect to achieve through talk. In his comment, he said, 'The "communication network" is not just a list of individuals; it is a network of relationships that get built up in the various settings in which we act out our lives. Each of the settings, and each of these relationships, makes its own demands on language' (Halliday 1978b: 24).

Halliday has maintained this stance in his later work (Halliday 1990). He notes that 'when new demands are made on language ... [and when] we are making language work for us in ways it never had to do before, it will have to become a different language in order to cope' (p. 82) (quoted from Biesenbach-Lucas and Weasenforth 2001).

On another occasion, Halliday said, 'Now a physical system is a physical system. But a physical theory is a semiotic system: a "system of related meanings"'. As he remarked, 'We gain our understanding of physical phenomena – of a semiotic system to transform them' (Lemke 1990).

This calls for multimodality and multisemiotics to theorize these multiple forms of communication, ascertaining how multiple modes such as words, sound, image and actions depend on each other to create whole meanings. To put it another way, regardless of its being an utterance of real-time speech or recording, a stretch of printed materials or handwriting, a diagram or a picture, a gesture or a movement, they all make sense, they all embody meaning. Each mode serves as a semiotic resource and contributes to the meaning being made (Williamson 2003).

With respect to the relation between multimodality and multisemiotics, van Leeuwen concludes that they are attempted (1) to merge linguistic theories of stratification with theories of social stratification in communication; (2) to show that meaning is made at every one of these levels, or strata; and (3) to argue that modern technology should become an integral part of semiotics (in Reutstaetter *et al.* 2005).

In answer to the question why we should study discourse and technology and multimodal discourse analysis, Deborah Tannen observes that (1) discourse is inherently multimodal, not monomodal; and (2) there are new forms of discourse in conjunction with new technology (Tannen 1982: ix–xiii). Similar views were voiced by Scollon and Levine (2004), who argued that: 'Discourse and technology live in a symbiotic relationship'. What concerns us is 'the impact on how we collect, transcribe, and analyse discourse data, and, possibly more important, the impact on social interactions and discourses themselves that these technologies are having'.

4.1.3 Computer-mediated discourse analysis

Thanks to the mass production of computers coupled with the advancement in digitalization, we are now in the era of hypertextualization. We are able to perceive the world, store the knowledge gained through various perceptive organs, and express meaning, explicitly and implicitly, directly and indirectly, through the use of new technology. This pushes the study of MDA forward to CMDA (computer-mediated discourse analysis). The fact that the medium of e-mail produces its own new register is a case in point (Halliday 1990: 44).

CMDA or CMD (computer-mediated discourse) is the communication produced when human beings interact with one another by transmitting messages via networked computers. The study of CMD is a specialization within the broader interdisciplinary study of computer-mediated communication (CMC), distinguished by its focus on language and language use in computer networked environments, and by its use of methods of discourse analysis to address that focus. Text-based CMC takes a variety of forms (e.g. e-mail, discussion groups, real-time chat, virtual reality, and role-playing games). Their linguistic properties vary depending on the kind of messaging system used and the social and cultural context embedding particular instances of use. Human-to-human communication via computer networks, or interactive networking, is a recent phenomenon (Herring 2001).

Several questions arise: Do the formal properties of the language used vary accordingly, as Halliday (1990) predicts? Do such variations in the formal properties of computer-mediated language constitute a distinct genre or register? How do humans make meaning of the information when it is generated, heard, or read? How would the discourse be impacted at various points along the way? How does that discourse result in specific human actions (Disler 2003)?

The aim of this study is to attempt to provide answers to these questions.

4.2 A CMDA study of a PowerPoint presentation contest

4.2.1 A PowerPoint presentation contest at Renmin University in Beijing

On 22 October 2005, we attended a PowerPoint presentation contest at Renmin University of China in Beijing. The contest was sponsored by Renmin University's Australian Studies Centre as one of the events for its 2005 Australian Culture Festival. The contestants were told to prepare a 3–6 minute deck of PowerPoint slides which should be aimed to present the people, the land and culture of Australia to the audience. There were 64 PowerPoint texts (PPTs) submitted. After a preliminary check, 24 texts were selected for the final contest.[2] The festival organizers also invited seven distinguished scholars to serve as judges. Since we had been working on CMDA for the national discourse analysis conference in 2006, this PPT contest caught our attention immediately and it struck us that we should save all the files for future analysis.

There were other reasons, also, behind our choice of PPT presentations to pursue the study of CMDA:

(1) When talking about different modes relevant to CMDA, people tend to talk about e-mails, net conferencing, online chat, googling, etc., but PowerPoint presentations have so far received little serious attention from language-focused scholars. As a matter of fact, over the past few years, PPT has become one of the most common presentation tools. For instance, by 2001, PowerPoint captured 95% of the market in presentation graphics, and Microsoft estimated that at least 30 million PowerPoint presentations were being made every day (Yates and Orlikowski, forthcoming).

(2) People used to see PowerPoint merely as a tool of communication, but today PowerPoint is accepted as a genre rather than a medium of communication if we see genre as recurrent types of communication (House *et al.* 2005).

(3) There are differing views among scholars with regard to the value of PowerPoint presentations. As reported by House *et al.* (2005), in Edward Tuffe's (2003) critique of PowerPoint presentations he remarked that a key slide was 'a Powerpoint festival of bureaucratic hyper-rationalism'. Also, Jamie McKenzie is quoted as saying that: 'It's done more damage to the culture'. In contrast, the Microsoft's chief product manager for the Office software, Dan Leach, argued that the Office package which includes PowerPoint had 400 million users around the world, and that his customers loved PowerPoint. The creator of HyperCard, Bill Atkinson, said 'It just helps you express yourself. The more tools people have to choose from the better off we are' (Schwartz 2003).

4.2.2 Data analysis

4.2.2.1 Theme

As mentioned earlier, the general theme of this contest is to describe the people, land and culture of Australia. With this in mind, the following topics were included in the PowerPoint texts:

History and Geography	14
Symbols	13
Aboriginals	9
Cities and Architecture	9
Resources	20
Culture and Sports	12

4.2.2.2 Participants

There were altogether 24 presenters (7 males and 17 females), with one presentation having two presenters (No. 3). They came from the English Department, School of Law, School of Economics, etc. Out of the 24 presenters, 22 were undergraduates, two were postgraduates.

4.2.2.3 The requirement of presenting

All the presenters had to make a short introduction (30 seconds) in English as a start. For example, No. 5 presenter (Qin Ting) started her presentation like this:

> Good evening everybody, I am a student from the school of foreign languages and my major is English. Today my topic is about the sheep culture in Australia. 今天我要给大家展示的就是关于澳大利亚的羊文化。How heavy is Australia? Just ask an Australian sheep, because Australia is a country riding on sheep's back! Hope you enjoy it.

When the show started, some presenters described the content of the slides orally one after another. Usually, they asked the staff to help change the slides. For instance, the first presenter, Shu Yu, described the first slide as follows:

Prelude
The Aboriginal people were the first inhabitants of the Australian continent. Most anthropologists currently believe they migrated to the continent at least 50,000 years ago and occupied most of the continent by 30,000 years ago. Subsequently, rising sea levels separated Tasmania and other immediate offshore islands from the rest of the continent. Although

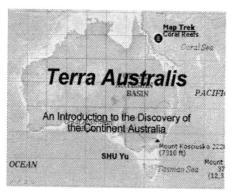

Chinese, Malaysian, Indonesian, and Arab seafarers may have landed in northern Australia well before 1500 AD, Australia was essentially unknown in the West until the 17th century.

Some presenters chose to step down from the platform and let the PowerPoint text run automatically; some sought the help of the staff to manually change the slides. The former can be exemplified by the third (Li Guomei and Li Ruifeng) presentation.

4.2.2.4 Deck of slides

There were two presenters who had the least number of slides, or just eight in total (Nos 1 and 9); those with the largest number of slides were No. 17 with 41, and Nos. 10 and 11 with 36.

The average was 22 slides for each presentation.

4.2.2.5 The visual mode of slide presentations

Though all the slides were visual in mode, still they differed with regard to the following:

(1) those with language only (No. 2, Li Yuan:, slide 2)
(2) those with both language and photos/pictures/cartoons (No. 2, slide 17)
(3) those with photos/pictures/cartoons only (No. 2, slide 12)

4.2.2.6 The audio mode of slide presentations

The audio mode can be divided into three categories:

(1) without music accompaniment (Nos 1, 4, 8, 9, 10, 12, 18, 19 and 22);
(2) with music/song by means of an additional file and operated by the staff (Nos 3, 7, 16, 21, 23);
(3) with in-built music playing synchronously (Nos 2, 5, 6, 11, 13, 14, 15, 17 and 20).

Songs played in the contest were *Advance Australia Fair, The Blue Coral, Here I Am, Two Beds, Delta Goddream, Serat Garden, Enigma* and *The Lonely Goatherd.*

4.2.2.7 Awards

After every four presentations the judges handed in their scores, eventually giving the following results:

(1) Extraordinary Prize: No. 14 (Yang Xiaoqin)
(2) First Prize: No. 15 (Fei Yinyin); No. 17 (Huang Bijun)
(3) Second Prize: No. 19 (Zhang Liyun); No. 22 (Ma Yangchen); No. 5 (Qin Ting)
(4) Third Prize: No. 1 (Shu Yu); No. 13 (Liu Shumin); No. 3 (Li Guomei and Li Ruifeng); No. 6 (He Dan)

4.3 Discussion

In this section, we will report the findings of our analysis.

4.3.1 The function of language

Natural language remains the chief mode of expressing meaning. What we want to focus on is how people are actually using language in combination with this technology. As partially touched upon in section 4.2.2.3, natural language (English and Chinese) occurs as follows:

(1) Before the slide show started, all the presenters would give a short introduction, mainly in English.

(2) After the slide show started, some presenters gave their descriptions synchronously.

(3) Text appeared on the slides, some written in complete sentences (slide 10, No. 3), some given in single words or short expressions (Slide 8, No. 4).

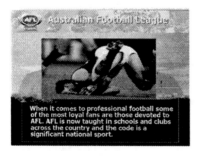

(4) Language also occurred in connection with the accompanying songs (No. 14, Yang Xiaoqin).

Since the general theme of this event was Australia, it was natural that most vocabulary was Australia-related. Moreover, our findings agreed with Baron's observation that in computer mediated discourse people use 'fewer subordinate clauses' and 'a narrower range of vocabulary' (Baron 1984: 131).

This confirms Kramsch *et al.*'s claim (2000) that a familiarity with new kinds of electronic multimodal texts is an aspect of electronic literacy. As language teachers, we should be aware that it would be anachronistic to merely encourage learners to concentrate on written text in an age where text is no longer exclusively 'written'.

4.3.2 Images, colour and function

On this point, we referred to van Leeuwen's inspiring work on semiotic resources in general, and colour schemes in particular (in Reutstaetter *et al.* 2005).

The magic of PowerPoint lies in its use of images or pictures. A PowerPoint presentation without images or pictures would be dull and uninteresting. With regard to Renmin University's PPT presentations we noted the following:

(1) Many slides showed the images in a dynamic manner (No. 11, Hu Yu).
(2) The slides were colourful and bright. For instance, No. 19 (Zhang Liyun)'s text dealt with the theme: 'The 7-colour country in my heart', in which the presenter assigned 7 capital cities or areas to 7 different colours respectively:

Canberra	red
The Gold Coast	gold
Melbourne	green
Brisbane	orange
Adelaide	pink
Cairns	violet
Sydney	blue

In this case, the presenter imparted meaning to colour, with each colour representing the features of a particular place in Australia. Another example was the description of the Aboriginal Flag in terms of its three colours:

Black	the complexion of aborigines
Red	the colour of the Australian soil
Yellow	the sun which represents Hope (No. 5, Qian)

4.3.3 Sound and function

When dealing with the function of sound (or music) in multimodality, van Leeuwen (in Reutstaetter *et al.* 2005) holds the view that the interpersonal function is more fully developed than the ideational function, and that the ideational has to ride on the back of the interpersonal. However, in the case of the visual, it is the other way around, the ideational is dominant, and the interpersonal is dependent on the ideational.

In the case of these PowerPoint presentations from the Renmin University contest, it seems that the music and text complemented each other such that both cooperated to present a coherent presentation. For instance, No. 3 presentation, which included the song *Here I Am*, the melody of which fits so well with the spirit of Australia's football fans, illustrates perfectly how certain meanings find more complete expression in music than in words.

4.3.4 Illustrating mediated action

Mediated action is the basic unit of analysis. It is the moment when an individual, as a social being, engages in an action in a 'dialectic between [the] action and the material means' which mediate it (Scollon 2001).

All the presenters first had to think about what they knew about the social and cultural aspects of Australia: the land, the history, the aboriginals, the early settlers, the sports, the food, etc. Next the presenters had to collect their resources from the internet, and then consider how best to present their materials.

The mediated action occurs in a site of engagement (Scollon 2001). As a result, the action becomes 'the focal point of attention of the relevant participants' at a 'unique moment in history'. In the Renmin University's contest, the actor, or more specifically, the presenter, had to be able to co-ordinate his action synchronously with the screen on the one hand, and to pass on information to the audience in the hall on the other hand. Thus, intertextuality and interdiscursivity/dialogicality, as mentioned by Scollon, are inherent in the mediational means. It goes without saying that even a single mediated action is complex and highly involved, even in a controlled and reliable environment (Disler 2003).

4.3.5 The nature of text and discourse in CMD

Disler (2003) states: '[T]he basic question a discourse analyst asks is "Why is this text the way it is? Why is it no other way?"' He went on to group the questions that need to be asked about a text into six broad categories. Each aspect of text-building is both a source of constraint and a resource for creativity. The six categories are: (1) Discourse is shaped by the world, and discourse shapes the world. (2) Discourse is shaped by language, and discourse shapes language. (3) Discourse is shaped by participants, and discourse shapes participants. (4) Discourse is shaped by prior discourse, and discourse shapes the possibilities for future discourse. (5) Discourse is shaped by its medium, and discourse shapes the possibilities of its medium. (6) Discourse is shaped by purpose, and discourse shapes possible purpose.

The PowerPoint presentations which we witnessed in Renmin University's contest have fully shown that there is something unique for each of the six categories:

(1) Our expected discourse is confined to the description of the people, the land and the culture in Australia.
(2) The expected discourse calls for the use of both spoken language and the written language.
(3) The presenters in the contest stood on the platform, sometimes facing the audience, sometimes facing the screen. Being a contestant in this case, the presenter also had to be mindful of the judges.
(4) All the presenters had to resort to some reference materials either

from the library or the internet and to do some editing before presentation.

(5) The PowerPoint presentation in the contest was shaped by multimodal means.

(6) The RUC's PowerPoint presentation was shaped by the aim and requirements of the sponser/organizer.

The PowerPoint texts were not ordinary texts, but rather were multimodal, integrating language, image and sound, to say nothing of the other factors contributing to the outcome, including the roles played by the presenter and the technology itself.

4.3.6 The PowerPoint presentation as a genre

The PowerPoint tool is the software used to create the presentation visuals. It enables the users to communicate, but by itself it does not express meaning.

A PowerPoint text includes the various visual, graphic, audio and video elements that may be integrated together using the PowerPoint software application. In our data, the 23 decks of slides can be seen as 23 texts. Or, we might specify that the notion of text here is not merely a linguistic text, but a multimodal text. Also, the term 'language' here does not refer simply to verbal activity, but also to the contribution made by art, music and technology.

When we talk about PowerPoint presentations as a genre, we see it as a whole. It is something which is different from a letter, a memo, a diary, a story, a talk, a novel, a speech, a play, etc.

Over the past several years, people have thought of PowerPoint presentations as merely a tool of communication, but today more accept the fact that it needs to be considered as a genre, if 'we think of genre as recurrent types of communication' (House *et al.* 2005). As House argued, 'If we are starting to say that we're assigning a "PowerPoint presentation" rather than, say, "a research paper", or a "progress report", that might be a sign that we're beginning to think of "the PowerPoint Presentation" as a genre with certain conventions which need to be followed within the communities that use it.'

In the course of our analysis, we observed the following:

(1) The sub-theme for each text (say, aboriginals, Australian football, Australian women writers, etc.) should be relevant to the general theme of the contest. As a rule, the sub-theme of each presentation text is indicated at the very beginning of the deck of slides.

(2) The ubiquity of bullet points makes it easier for the audience to catch the main points. See the slide on the right (No. 12, slide 8, Liu Lin).

(3) All the words and images/pictures have to appear on the slides, which can either be hand-operated or coded in the software.

(4) The structure of context is dominated by lines of hierarchies. See the slide on the left (No. 23, slide 4, Guan Genliang).

(5) Quantitative information is likely to be presented with only a few key numbers highlighted (whether in bullet points or tables). See the slide about 'The Construction' (No. 18, slide 3, Zhang Yan).

(6) The presenter can either talk about the content of each slide, or simply let the slides move by themselves.

4.3.7 Towards a better understanding of socio-semiotics

In discussing the notion of 'socio' in 'socio-semiotics', van Leeuwen makes several points. The first is that semiotic resources are created by humans in social contexts, as a response, at a given historical moment, to certain social and cultural (and economic) needs, and that they have to be studied as such. The second concerns the regulation of semiotic resources in different ways and to different degrees in the context of various kinds of 'semiotic regimes'. Finally, because every instance of using semiotic resources takes place within a particular social setting, it needs to be explained on the basis of the interests prevailing in that setting.

The PowerPoint presentation contest can serve as a good illustration of what we mean by socio-semiotics. First, these texts were created by presenters in a specific social context as a response to the call of a contest sponsor. Second, semiotic resources are integrated in such a way as to meet the requirements of the contest, and the expectations of the judges.

4.4 Epilogue

Meaning in PowerPoint presentations can be construed multimodally and described systemically as shown in Figure 4.1. On the leftmost side, MEANING comes from various sources, such as purpose, participant, content, context, etc., which in fact are the semiotic resources. In the middle, there are different MODES to help communicate the meaning. Speech, writing, action

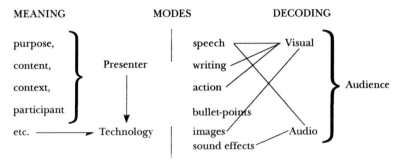

Figure 4.1

are the three modes employed by the Presenter directly, whereas bullet-points, images, and sound effects belong to the employment of Technology. However, the execution of Technology is determined by the Presenter. If the Presenter has no knowledge about the PowerPoint software, he is not able to use technology to help communicate meaning. In systemic literature, we use a square bracket to mark the 'either ... or' relation, and a curved bracket to mark the 'both ... and' relation, but in our data, we find the option of modes is neither 'either ... or' nor 'both ... and', so we try to use straight lines to mark this feature. When it comes to the rightmost side, things become simpler, the Audience only makes use of the Visual mode and the Audio mode to decode MEANING.

We have to admit that our analysis is preliminary, and there is room for improvement in our future work. For instance, we did not do any real-time recording of the presenters' speaking, which actually is very important to show the interaction between the presenter and the slides, and between the presenter and the audience as well. Likely there would also be differences in the style of presentation depending on whether the context is academic or commercial, and other aspects of the physical environment.

Human communication is developing, from orality to literacy to hypertextualization (or multimodality, multiliteracy, multimedia ...). This suggests we are learning how to employ all our perceptive power to know the world, to tell people what we know about the world, to understand what other people have communicated to us.

One of my friends once entitled one of his books 'Language: the last garden of mankind'. I would rather change this title to 'Sign: the eternal garden of mankind'.

Notes

1   We are grateful to all the presenters for their wonderful presentations at the PowerPoint presentation contest held on 22 October 2005 at Renmin University of China in Beijing.

2   The final figure was 23, as one presenter did not turn up that night, but there were two presenters for one of the items, so there were still 24 presenters.

References

Baron, N. (1984), 'Computer-mediated communication as a form in language change'. *Visible Language*, 18(2), 118–41.

Biesenbach-Lucas, S. and D. Weasenforth (2001), 'E-mail and word processing in the ESL classroom: How the medium affects the message.' *Language Learning and Technology*, Vol.5, No.1, January 2001, pp. 135–65.

Disler, E. A. (2003), 'Words and weapons: the power of discourse.' *Air & Space Power Journal*, Fall 2003.

Halliday, M. A. K. (1978a), *Language as Social Semiotic*. London: Edward Arnold.

Halliday, M. A. K. (1978b), *Talking Shop: Demands on Language*. Film Australia.

Halliday, M. A. K. (1990), *Spoken and Written Language*. Oxford, UK: Oxford University Press.

Halliday, M. A. K. (1994), *An Introduction to Functional Grammar*. Edward Arnold.

Halliday, M. A. K. and Hasan, R. (1990), *Language, Context and Text: Aspects of Language in a Social-semiotic Perspective*. Oxford, UK: Oxford University Press.

Herring, S. C. (1996), 'Computer-Mediated Discourse Analysis.' *The Electronic Journal of Communication*, Volume 6, No. 3.

Herring, S. C. (2001), 'Computer-Mediated Discourse,' in D. Tannen, D. Schiffrin and H. Hamilton (eds), *Handbook of Discourse Analysis*. Oxford: Blackwell.

House, R., Watt, A. and Willams, J (2005), 'Work in Progress – What is Power Point? Educating Engineering Students in Its Use and Abuse.' A paper presented at the 35th ASEE/IEEE Frontiers in Education Conference.

Kramsch, C., A'Ness, F. and Lam, W. S. E. (2000), 'Authenticity and authorship in the compter-mediated acquisition of L2 literacy'. *Language Learning and Technology'*, Volume 4, No. 2, September, 78–164.

Kress, G. and van Leeuwen, T. (2001), *Multimodal Discourse: The Modes and Media of Contemporary Communication*. London: Edward Arnold.

Lemke, J. L. (1990), 'Technical discourse and technocratic ideology', in M. A. K. Halliday, J. Gibbons, and H. Nicholas (eds), *Learning, Keeping, and Using Language: Selected Papers from the 8th AILA World Congress of Applied Linguistics*, Vol. II. Amsterdam: John Benjamins, pp. 435–60.

Reutstaetter, J., Rheindorf, M. and van Leeuwen T. (2005), 'Media discourse: social semiotics and the study of multimodal discourse. An interview with Theo van Leeuwen.' *Reconstruction*, Volume 5, No. 2 (Spring 2005).

Schiffrin, D. (1994), *Approaches to Discourse.* Chicago: University of Chicago Press.

Schiffrin, D., Tannen, D. and Hamilton, H. E. (eds) (2001), *The Handbook of Discourse Analysis.* Malden, MA and Oxford, UK: Blackwell.

Schwartz, J. (2003), *The Level of Discourse Continues to Slide.* The New York Times Company. Online.

Scollon, R. (1998), *Mediated Discourse as Social Interaction: A Study of News Discourse.* New York: Longman Group, p. 10.

Scollon, R. (2001), *Mediated Discourse: The Nexus of Practice.* New York: Routledge.

Scollon, R. and Levine P. (2004), *Multimodal Discourse Analysis as the Confluence of Discourse and Technology.* Washington, DC: Georgetown University Press.

Tannen, D. (ed.) (1982), 'Introduction', in *Analyzing Discourse: Text and Talk. Georgetown University Round Table on Languages and Linguistics 1981.* Washington, DC: Georgetown University. Press.

Thibault, P. J. (1993), 'Social Semiotics'. Editorial in Volume 4 (3) of *The Semiotic Review of Books.*

Tuffe, E. R. (2003), 'The Cognitive Style of PowerPoint'. *The New Yorker.* May 28, 76–87.

Williamson, B. (2003), 'What are multimodality, multisemiotics and multiliteraies?' *NESTA.* Futurelab

Yates, J. and Orlikowski, W. (forthcoming), 'The PowerPoint presentation and its corollaries: how genres shape communicative action in organizations', in M. Zachry and C. Thrall (eds), *The Cultural Turn: Communicative Practices in Workplaces and the Professions.* Amityville, NY: Baywood Publishing.

A Systemic Functional Approach to Code-switching Studies: Some Chinese–English Examples

Huang Guowen
Sun Yat-sen University and
Wang Jin
Shenzhen University

5.1 Introduction

According to estimations, about half of the earth's population speaks at least two languages (Auer 1984: 1), and bilingualism is considered to be the norm rather than the exception (Thomason 2001: 10). In the last half-century, the enhancive mobility and globalization of modern society have resulted in many language contact situations which are nowhere as obvious as in the case of code-switching. Aspects and dimensions of this interesting phenomenon have been attracting the attention of researchers from different perspectives such as linguistics, sociology, psychology, anthropology and ethnography. It is no exaggeration to say that code-switching is now a research area of human sciences that has come into its own.

This chapter attempts to approach this area of studies with Halliday's systemic functional theory of language, more specifically, the register analysis within the Hallidayan framework of functional linguistics. The motivation behind the present research is that, although, in the literature to date, there are numerous studies of code-switching from different theoretical perspectives, few scholars have attempted to investigate this phenomenon within the systemic functional framework. Our attempt is encouraged by what Halliday (1994: xv) says about his aim in *An Introduction to Functional Grammar*: 'In deciding how much ground to try to cover, I have had certain guiding principles in mind. The aim has been to construct a grammar for purposes of text analysis: one that would make it possible to say sensible and useful things about any text, spoken or written, in modern English.' As our studies will show, the Hallidayan linguistics is also appliable to the analysis of code-switched text.

According to Benson (2001), some scholars were identifying and discussing code-switching as early as the 1930s although the term did not come into use until 1954 when it was coined by Vogt in his review of Weinreich's pioneering work *Languages in Contact* (1953). Since then, different types of code-switching have been studied and a number of approaches have been proposed. In the present research, we limit the term 'code-switching' to the definition that two or more languages are used in one and the same utterance or discourse, shelving the phenomenon of using different languages or codes in different situations, as in Fishman's (1965) sense. Despite the plethora of publications on code-switching, the literature, however, is limited in several aspects and here we wish to identify two gaps which are relevant here. First, few studies have been undertaken with special focus on the dimension of functional variation across different situation types. Usually researchers look into individual cases and interactions without referring to the genre, text type or register[1] a specific interaction instantiates. Second, describing code-switching is one thing and trying to explain it is quite another. Although there are a few studies where functional variation is treated as one dimension (e.g. Li 1996), to date, however, no coherent theory has been proposed to address this problem.

At least in one language contact situation, we feel that code-switching needs to be described and explained by reference to the notion of functional variation and that the register analysis within systemic functional linguistics provides us with the most useful and satisfactory framework. More specifically, we shall investigate Chinese–English code-switching in several Chinese newspapers published in Guangzhou, China.

In the last two decades, with increasing economic development and global mobility, the frequent contacts between Chinese and English have resulted in a large number of Chinese–English bilinguals[2] in China (also see McArthur 2000, Jiang 2003). Guangzhou is the capital of the South China Guangdong Province and is considered a window to connect China and the outside world. Like Beijing and Shanghai, there are more Chinese–English bilinguals here than in other places in China. Furthermore, the local dialect in Guangzhou is Cantonese, which has made Guangzhou more easily influenced by the nearby Cantonese–English bilingual Hong Kong and more compatible with the alternative use of the two languages. Consequently it is little wonder to see that English elements have found their way into both oral and written discourse in Guangzhou. To avoid too many foci, we shall confine ourselves to the analysis of the code-switching examples[3] in several Chinese newspapers published in Guangzhou since written code-switching is much less explored than its spoken counterpart. For the present study, we have collected three Chinese newspapers in Guangzhou, i.e., *Guangzhou Daily* (Guangzhou Ribao,《广州日报》), *Yangcheng Evening News* (Yangcheng Wanbao,《羊城晚报》), and *Nanfang Metropolitan News* (Nanfang Dushibao,《南方都市报》) over a week, i.e. from 28 October to 3 November 2002.

In the rest of the chapter, we shall first give a very brief introduction to the register analysis and set down two questions which the study will investigate. This will be followed by two sections that describe and explain the code-switching in the newspaper discourse by using register analysis. Our conclusion and discussions of the register approach to the studies of code-switching in general will be presented in the last section.

5.2 The register analysis

Given the rapid developments that have been made in systemic functional linguistics during the past several decades, it is surprising that few attempts have been made to address questions of bilingual texts, although as early as the 1960s, Mackey (1962) proposed that register analysis can be used to investigate bilingual issues. It becomes even more surprising when we recall that systemic functional linguistics, developed from the Malinowski–Firth tradition, has obvious ethnographic intellectual roots as it encourages the study of language in its social and cultural context (see Halliday 1978; Halliday and Hasan 1985) and therefore is a natural schema to frame our analyses concerning bilingualism and code-switching.

According to Halliday (Halliday, *et al.* 1964; Halliday 1978; Halliday and Hasan 1985), register is the name given to a variety of language distinguished according to use. In other words, we do not use language in the same way in every activity we are involved in. Rather, to achieve different communicative purposes in various types of situations, we are supposed to select from the language system those patterns that are appropriate and correspond to the situation types. This is one important aspect of describing our language since it best reveals the nature and function of language. These patterned language choices, far from free variation, are functional in certain situation types and can be discussed with reference to the context. In doing so, systemic functional linguists have found the tripartite register analysis most useful. The situation type of a register can be described by three variables (i.e., field, tenor and mode), each corresponding to one aspect of the context. As Halliday (Halliday and Hasan 1985) points out, the notion of register is a very simple but at the same time a very powerful idea. The relationship between the contextual configuration and the language choices of a register is a dialectical and constructive one. On the one hand, the contextual factors contribute to demarcate the meaning potential of a register and help to predict some language choices rather than others; on the other hand, the language choices serve to construe the context.

Before we embark on a register analysis of our data, there is one prior question: What registers do we have in the collected newspapers? In the present study, we shall regard hard news, IT reports, automobile reports, financial reports, arts and show business, fashion and advertisements as the most frequent registers in our data, with weather forecasts, sports, travel features, real estate reports and so on also identified as registers. These registers are established on two grounds. First, as we understand it, register is a notion which permits different degrees of delicacy. For example, while media discourse might be counted as a register, sharing many common language features, it is still possible to find more registers along the delicacy if we decide to look into the media discourse in more detail. In the same way, it is possible for us to establish several registers in our collected newspapers. Second, Bell (1991: 12) holds that genres are the particular kind of media content in which readers are interested, such as news, classified advertising, game shows, weather forecasts, and so forth. Similarly, Scollon (2000) classifies newspaper genres as official meets, official statements, press conferences, sports, and China develops with sections like editorials, financial reports, travel features, extended essays, arts and entertainments features also called genres. Guided by these media language studies and also taking the convenience of analysis into consideration, we take the newspaper sections basically as a convenient candidate in register establishment. However, exceptions are found with two types of registers. Hard news discourse in different sections like national news, international news, local news and so on is classified as one register. Advertisements and weather forecasts, on the other hand, usually should be picked out from different sections.

Although our approach is a systemic-functional one and the focus of the chapter is a register analysis of code-switched examples of Chinese–English, the questions that we wish to address here are more specific:

(1) In what way does the code-switching in our data display a patterned occurrence across the newspaper registers?
(2) How can these patterns be related as functional variations to the context?

In the following two sections, we shall try to answer these two questions respectively and we hope to have adequate answers to the questions.

5.3 Code-switching patterns across registers

In this section, we shall look into the Chinese–English code-switching examples in our data and try to show how the code-switching patterns vary from register to register.

In our study, hard news is the register where fewest code-switching instances can be found. When code-switches do occur, Chinese translations or explanations are usually provided. For example,

(1) 'Woman   Power'   (女人强权)已成为我们时代的特征之一。(*Nanfang Metropolitan News* 2/11/2002 A02)
'*Woman Power*' (woman power) has become one of the features of our times.

Most of the code-switched items are acronyms, more likely influenced by the 'least effort' principle. Sometimes the use of English items in the hard news discourse is out of the consideration for consistency and accuracy, especially when a foreign item is newly introduced into the Chinese context and has not yet been given an established translation. In this case, the English items are usually offered in brackets, resulting in what Newmark (1981: 75–7) calls 'translation couplets'.

(2) 这个神奇的小型机械臂被称作'幻影'（Phantom），可以模拟出人类手臂的各种动作。（*Yangcheng Evening News* 31/10/2002 A12）This amazing small size mechanical arm is called 'Phantom' (*Phantom*), it can imitate the movements of human arms.

In example (2), while 'huàn yǐng' (幻影) can be considered as a Chinese equivalence of the English word *Phantom*, *Phantom* here refers to a specific newly invented device. In other words, *Phantom* here is more of a proper noun than a common noun and it might not be clearly identified if only the Chinese 'huàn yǐng' （幻影） was provided. In order to keep a clear link between the signifier and the signified, the original *Phantom* is offered and at the same time the Chinese characters are modified with translation labels (Newmark 1981: 75-77), viz. the quotation marks, in order to remind the readers that this 'huàn yǐng' （幻影）is, however, not a phantom as commonly understood.

Similar to the hard news register, code-switching hardly occurs in the registers of sports, real estate reports, travel features and weather forecasts. On the contrary, IT reports and automobile reports are registers where a large quantity of code-switches can be found. Code-switching instances such as those in the following example (3) can be found here and there in these registers.

(3) Awave Audio可将MP3、WMA和WAV、CD Audio等转成RA。（*Yangcheng Evening News* 29/10/2002 C2）
Awave Audio can transform *MP3, WMA, WAV, CD Audio* and so on into *RA*.

In these registers, the switched items as in example (3) usually stand alone without any Chinese translations or explanations in the embedded texts. As can be seen from the above example, most of the switched items are technical terms and jargons. English acronyms are very common in these two registers. It is revealed by one of the texts in the automobile register that there are more and more spare parts for modern automobiles and for the sake of convenience, English acronyms are usually used to replace these spare parts' long names (*Nanfang Metropolitan News* 28/10/2002 C54). Also switched into English in these registers are some proper nouns such as company names and brand names. This parallels the code-switching pattern in financial reports.

While non-Chinese names are usually switched into English in the register of arts and show-business, an interesting phenomenon is that superstars and VIPs are usually referred to by using the Chinese translations of their names, while 'small potatoes' are, on the contrary, coded directly in English, without winning for themselves set Chinese translations of names. For example,

(4) 皮尔斯布鲁斯南的30岁女儿Charlotte，……Charlotte并非皮尔斯亲生女，
是前妻Cassandra与前夫Dermot所生…… (*Guangzhou Daily* 30/10/2002 B4)
Pierce Brosnan's 30-year-old daughter *Charlotte*, … *Charlotte* is Pierce's stepdaughter, she is the daughter of his ex-wife *Cassandra* and her ex-husband *Dermot* …

In this example, Pierce Brosnan is coded in Chinese as 'pí ěr sī bù lǔ sī nán' (皮尔斯布鲁斯南) which is a household name in China, while *Charlotte*, *Cassandra* and *Dermot*, with whom the Chinese audience may be much less familiar, are in English.

Items such as *Hip-Hop, rap, pop, fans* appear at least in two texts without Chinese explanatary elements in the art and show-business register. They are in a way similar to the technical terms in the IT reports and automobile reports registers. These code-switching instances are associated with the topic of the register, which we shall return to later.

Other English items associated with Hong Kong stars can be discussed by reference to the Hong Kong Cantonese–English bilingualism (Li 1996; Chan 2003). For instance, Hong-Kong-based actors and actresses are sometimes referred to by their English names such as *Kelly, Jay, Gi Gi, Elva*, just to mention a few, which is one feature of the Hong Kong naming system (Li 1997). From time to time, these actors' discourse is embedded with English items as those shown in the following two examples:

(5) 这是最后一次扮孙悟空，Never Again，因为真是太辛苦。(*Nanfang Metropolitan News* 1/11/2002 B41)
This is the last time I act Sun Wukong, *Never Again*, because it's so back-breaking.
(6) 他其实就是个很down-to-earth（实际）的男人。(*Nanfang   Metropolitan News* 29/10/2002 B40)
He is actually a man who is really *down-to-earth*.

Some other code-switches are manipulated to create a casual and humorous flavour. This is in accordance with the entertaining function of the arts and show-business register. For instance,

(7) 至hot影视碟指引 (*Guangzhou Daily* 2/11/2002 B5)
Introducing the *hot*test movies, TV programmes and CDs.

(8) 2002年，两位名嘴齐齐出道10年，又齐齐30岁，于是十年之养酿出了这
    个'10th·30th Party!'。(*Nanfang Metropolitan News* 29/10/2002 B44)
    In the year 2002, it has been 10 years since the two famous emcees
    commenced their career and they are both 30 years old, hence it takes
    ten years to bring out this '*10th·30th Party!*'.

In this aspect, code-switching instances in the art and show-business register
parallel those in the fashion register. For example,

(9) 民族风由春夏一直吹到秋冬，设计师已将民族Look玩得不亦乐
    乎。(*Yangcheng Evening News* 2/11/2002 C4)
    The fashion trend of China style has been in from Spring and
    Summer to Autumn and Winter, the designers have been playing a
    great deal with the China *look*.

(10) 9样发生在农林下路最HIT最CURRENT的事情，以流行榜的形式披露于
     各位面前，……(*Nanfang Metropolitan News* 1/11/2002 D70)
     9 most *hit* and most *current* things in Nonglinxia Rd, presented before
     you as Top 9...

In this dimension, the motif of fashion is doubly coded both by the topic and
by the style of language use.

Advertising is another domain of frequent code-switching. However,
the code-switches display quite different patterns in the recruitment and
non-recruitment advertisements. In the latter, embedded are some English
lexical items while in the former, some whole mini-texts may be totally coded
in English as textual code-switching embedded in a cluster of Chinese texts
(see Huang 2001: 281–3). Elsewhere, we (Huang 2001: 291–2) argue that
in the non-recruitment commercial advertisements, the embedded English
items serve to create some fashionable and 'foreignizing' flavour while in
the recruitment advertisements, English is used to exclude Chinese monolinguals from becoming potential employees, serving a discriminatory function.
In Bell's (1991) terms, code-switching in the recruitment advertisements is
used as a kind of audience design and in the non-recruitment commercial
advertisement, referee design.

Now it seems quite clear that code-switching displays a patterned occurrence in different newspaper registers rather than a homogeneous or random
one. It is plausible for us to argue that these code-switching patterns are one
way of encoding the semantics within the meaning potentials defined by the
register. In other words, these code-switching patterns serve as candidates
of indexical features (Halliday and Hasan 1985: 39) or realization patterns
(Eggins 1994: 41–2) of specific registers. In this sense, the choices of code-
switching patterns are not so different from the lexicogrammatical choices in
the monolingual situation. These indexical features of registers contribute to
a better understanding of the newspaper discourse. Below is an extract from
a text from the IT reports section:

(11)   …… 镶嵌闪片和烤印着ET图案的T-Shirt都是他的最爱。……我轻松地翻
动滑板kick-flip，接着冲上U型板的顶端，…… 我们爱闪，因为我们热衷最
FUN的运动，崇尚最IN的理念，…… (*Nanfang Metropolitan News* 29/10/
2002 C55)

T-Shirt(s) with flashing pieces and *ET* pictures are his favourites … I
kicked my skateboard with ease to make a *kick-flip*, and jump to the
top of the *U* board … We love flash, because we love the most interesting (*FUN*)[4] sports, we love the most *in* ideas.

Although the frequent occurrence of English items in example (11) is one
of the characteristics of the code-switching pattern in the IT reports, also
clear enough is that the inserted English items in the example are far from
technical terms as happened in the IT register. Here comes the question of
whether this text belongs to the IT register. If the reader goes through the
whole text, he will find that this is a mobile phone advertisement rather than
an IT report.

5.4 Code-switching patterns and register variables

In the previous section, we have shown that the code-switching patterns help
to index different registers. These code-switching patterns, however, do not
happen to be the register realizational patterns; rather, as functional variations, they have a continuous bearing on the context. In this section, we
shall try to see how the context influences the code-switching patterns thus
arrested. It would be more convenient and more explicit for us to do so if we
relate the code-switching patterns to the three register variables (i.e., field,
tenor and mode) of the context configurations respectively. We hope this
will not be understood to mean that the three variables influence the code-
switching patterns independently; rather, on the contrary, the three combine
to bring out the whole picture interactively and interwovenly.

5.4.1 *Field*

Field refers to the activities in which we are involved with language. Topic
is an important dimension of field. In the present study, topic also has an
important role to play in the register establishment. Several registers can be
distinguished by the topics, which are indicated by the section titles such as
IT, finance, fashion, travelling, and so forth.

Some topics tend to have more code-switched items than others. The more
frequent occurrence of English items in the IT and automobile reports is
closely associated with the topics. Since we cannot talk about something
without referring to it, it is obvious that the technical terms coded in English
combine to form lexical sets of these registers. Recall example (3), which is
represented below for convenience.

(3) Awave Audio可将MP3、WMA和WAV、CD Audio等转成RA。（*Yangcheng Evening News* 29/10/2002 C2）
  Awave Audio can transform *MP3, WMA, WAV, CD Audio* and so on into *RA*.

Example (3) is extracted from a text discussing the transformation between different music formats. If we single out the switched items (i.e., *Awave Audio, MP3, WMA, WAV, CD Audio, RA*), they will give us a general impression of what the text is about.

As Hasan (1994: 139) points out, topic in the sense of subject matter refers to some domain of human experience, and so bears a close relationship to field of discourse. The fact that some topics are more associated with certain languages is because some areas of human knowledge are originally conceived or usually discussed in a certain language in our daily life. The use of English items reflects that this embedded language has some advantages in the areas concerned, IT development and automobile production in the present case, and has contributed more notions and concepts to our understanding of these areas of the experiential world. The following example vividly reveals the status of the English language in the IT area.

(12) 问：我的计算机启动时出现了这么的一句话：SMART failure predicted on primary master quantum fireball 1ct10 Immediately back-up your data and replace your hard disk drive A failure may be 'imminent' (should be 'imminent', noted by the present authors）。我得按F1才可进入windows,不然就进不去。究竟怎么解决呢？（*Yangcheng Evening News* 29/10/2002 C1）
  Question: This sentence appears when my computer starts up: *SMART failure predicted on primary master quantum fireball 1ct10 Immediately back-up your data and replace your hard disk drive A failure may be imminent.* I have to press F1 to enter *Windows*. Otherwise, I cannot get in. How can I solve this problem?

Although we can use the Chinese operating system, it seems that English, if not other computer languages, is the only choice when we need to communicate with the computer outside the Windows system. This helps to explain why field is treated as projection of experiential meanings on the context, which is in line with Appel and Muysken (1987: 118) who have argued that all code-switches related to the topic tend to express referential meaning.

5.4.2 *Tenor*

Tenor is the variable which deals with the relationships between the participants involved in the interactions. It is the projected contextual parameter of Interpersonal metafunction. We shall be trying to show how some finer distinctions of this variable contribute to the code-switching patterns. The following analysis takes the research on the tenor variable by Hasan (Hasan 1977; Halliday and Hasan 1985), Poynton (1985), Martin (1992) and Eggins (1994) as our starting point, and the code-switching patterns will be discussed under the sub-headings of agent role, power, and social distance.

Participants always interact with certain agent roles. Generally speaking, the two parties involved in the newspaper discourse are writers/editors on the one hand and readers on the other. According to Kronrod and Engel (2001), different sections are meant for different populations. Hence we believe that a finer distinction of the target readers of different registers is highly relevant here. For example, hard news needs to use explicit language and try to use as few English items as possible since the register is targeted at the whole reader population, part of which might be Chinese monolinguals; the register of IT reports, on the other hand, uses embedded English jargon to target IT technicians or IT amateurs, and laymen can be shut off by the overloaded English jargon. Sometimes, the same embedded item appears in different registers with and without the Chinese translation. The following examples are cases.

(13) 现时广州，到美容院做facial（脸部护理），到健身房keep fit（瘦身），是都市女性的主流选择，……（*Yangcheng Evening News* 1/11/2002 A5）
Nowadays in Guangzhou, to receive *facial* treatments (facial treatments) in beauty salons and to *keep fit* in gyms are the main choices of city women ...

(14) '……我用了95%的精神、时间去做健身、按摩、做facial、整头发……'
（*Nanfang Metropolitan News* 29/10/2002 B40）
'... I used 95 per cent of my energy and time to keep fit, to do massage, to get *facial* treatments, to get hair service ... '

Example (13) appears in the hard news register while example (14) in the arts and show-business. It seems that when the register switches, the role of the readers also switches, contributing to the switch of the code-switching patterns.

Once the agent roles of the participants are established, we can describe the power distribution between the two parties. Since newspapers need to fight for the readers' attention and win more newspaper buyers, readers in a way obtain more power. Accordingly, newspapers have to take their target readers' language preference into consideration. As we showed in the previous section, if people in their daily life use English acronyms to refer to some automobile spare parts, editors or authors of the newspaper discourse will follow suit. Recruitment advertisements, however, seem to be an exception. In this case, one party is the employer, and the other is the potential employee. Usually, the former obtains more power. We can see that the power has been utilized to reserve the positions to those who have a good command of English and to block the access of Chinese monolingual readers to the advertisements by using embedded English texts. Gregory and Carroll's (1978: 61) remark is highly relevant here that tenor-roles have the inclusive and exclusive social functions and they 'mark the boundaries of relationships, of group formations'. The present analysis shows that the inclusive and exclusive social functions can be more coherently viewed as the two sides of the same coin. To include the bilinguals at the same time indicates the exclusion of the monolinguals.

Social distance here is used to refer to the psychological distance between the participants. Hasan (1977) and Martin (1992) have shown that contact frequency and range are important factors in deciding social distance.[5] We depart here from what Hasan and Martin have postulated and instead suggest that the degree of social distance is also associated with the degree of similarities of different aspects between the participants on a more abstract level, which might be called ideological or psychological contact. More specifically, same origin, common hobbies, or even similar opinions on specific issues are possible candidates for connector serving to reduce the social distance between the two participants.

We may, then, argue that in such registers as IT reports, financial reports or automobile reports, the social distances between the editors/authors and the readers are less than those in registers such as hard news. The logic is that the former has a more finely targeted readership and the same interest in IT, finance or automobiles serves to connect the two parties. These are the registers where more embedded English items can be found, which seems to be one way of understanding Martin's (1992: 531) conceptions of proliferation and contraction concerning social distance. Martin (*ibid.*) holds that from the perspective of system, the more contact, the more choices available and vice versa; from the perspective of process, less contact means that the expressions need to be more explicit, while more contact means that implicity can be more the case. Hence in the shorter distance type of registers, the interactants have one more code at their proposal and at the same time code-switched items are considered to be more implicit than their Chinese counterparts. The present analysis also indicates that the more technical the register is, the more evident will be this tendency. According to their technicality, the established newspaper registers can be located on different points of a continuum, with IT reports and automobile reports at the one end and hard news at the other (see Figure 5.1).

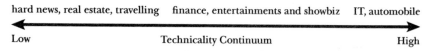

Figure 5.1 The technicality continuum

More to the left end, there will be lower technicality, more social distance, and consequently less code-switching; more to the right end, on the contrary, higher technicality, less social distance, and consequently more code-switching. Note that the discussion of technicality has strayed into the variable of field. However, technicality simply serves as the connector to reduce the social distance in the present analysis.

5.4.3 *Mode*

The variable of mode refers to the function that language plays in the inter-action, for example, spoken or written. It is now generally accepted that as a feature of discourse, 'spoken' and 'written' are better understood as the two poles of a continuum rather than a sharp dichotomy. Hasan (Halliday and Hasan 1985: 58) proposes two terms, viz. 'medium' and 'channel' as two dimensions of mode to solve the problem. The former refers to the continuum between spoken and written while the latter describes the physical nature of the text, either graphic or phonic.

Obviously, although all the newspaper registers are of graphic channel, they locate on different points of the medium continuum. Hard news, especially political news, is closer to the written end of the continuum. Usually such registers require the use of formal language and it is the monolingual norms that tend to prevail (Li 1996: 42). On the other hand, registers of fashion, arts and show-business and so on are closer to the spoken end which permits informal use of language (including the alternative use of two codes). Hence the code-switching patterns show close association with the medium rather than the channel of the registers.

The incongruence between medium and channel has been discussed with special attention to the case of 'written to be spoken'. However, it is useful to suggest that there are other cases where we find interaction between medium and channel, which is made possible by projection. Projection has been one important mechanism that enables language to cope with different levels of experience. Halliday (1994: 250–52) distinguishes between two basic categories of projection, i.e., quote and report. The former enables the medium features of the projected speeches to be preserved while in the latter, authors will be in a better position to adjust the medium properties of the projected speeches to make them more in line with that of the texts into which the speeches are introduced. It is found in our data that more code-switching instances are detected in quoted projections. This may be explained by that, together with the projected speeches, their spoken and informal medium is also projected in the somewhat more written and formal medium of the newspaper texts.

5.5 Concluding remarks

In this chapter we have attempted to show that code-switching in the collected Chinese newspapers published in Guangzhou does not occur homogene-ously or randomly across registers; rather, different patterns across different registers are detected. These patterns are closely related to the context and can be explained as functional variations by reference to the contextual configurations, which can be pinned down to field, tenor and mode.

Although the present research is simply a case study with which we have found register analysis of systemic functional linguistics to be most useful and satisfactory, we believe that register analysis as an underlying principle in explaining language use is by no means marginal in addressing issues of bilingualism and code-switching. Here we wish to end this chapter by trying to locate the proposed approach in a larger context of code-switching studies.

In the early stage of code-switching studies, special attention was given to those situations where speakers switched from one language to another language and then probably did not switch back or only switched back after a long stretch of language (e.g. Blom and Gumperz 1972). There are, however, situations where frequent switches between two languages can be found and most of the switches are intra-sentential code-switching. This type of code-switching is first and mostly explored by scholars who are interested in the structural and grammatical dimensions of code-switching (e.g. Poplack 1980; Di Sciullo, *et al.* 1986; Myers-Scotton 1993a). More recently, researchers have also tried to examine the social and functional dimensions of this type of code-switching. According to Myers-Scotton (1993a: 13), as unmarked code-switching (Myers-Scotton 1993b), each individual switch is not intended to convey a special social message and it is the overall pattern which is intended to index simultaneous identities. Some other researchers (e.g. Alvarez-Cáccamo 1998; Meeuwis and Blommaert 1998; Gafaranga and Torras 2001), in implicit or explicit ways, suggest that speakers who are involved in this type of code-switching may believe that they are not using two languages at the same time, but simply allowing alternation within one code. We refer to this argument as 'one code argument' for the present. Gafaranga and Torras (2001) even claim that the concept of code-switching should be narrowed to exclude this type of code-switching, i.e., medium as they term it. The one code argument, as we view it, has very important implications but we beg to differ from Gafaranga and Torras' claim, whose problem arises from two sources. First, this type of code-switching on the one hand has provided researchers of the structural and grammatical dimensions of code-switching with a very important testing ground and consequently should not be deleted from the code-switching arena. Second and more importantly, what the researchers seem to attempt to do is to arrive at a more accurate definition of code-switching or code. As is usually the case, this kind of effort should be deemed as a starting point for further studies rather than as an end. On the contrary, we argue that the one code argument has very important implications for how we can take it as a starting point to further explore this type of code-switching. Following the one code argument, we shall be able to see the conjunction between the notion of code thus arrested and Halliday's (Halliday *et al.* 1964) conception of variety according to user. To avoid terminological ambiguity, we use 'variety' to replace 'code' in the one code argument.[6] This kind of variety is similar to dialect in nature and will be subject to functional variations. This is another way of saying that it is plausible for code-switching to display different patterns across different registers. In this dimension, it does not take the type of very frequent code-switching to be counted as a variety; the type of code-switching in the Guangzhou case may as well be defined as a variety, and we have shown in this chapter that this variety displays functional variations across registers. Hence register analysis is proposed as a natural and necessary approach if the one code argument is to be accepted as valid.

Notes

1. The terms 'register', 'genre' and 'text type' may mean different categories of abstraction from a cluster of texts according to different researchers, but the demarcation is far from clear and unanimous. For the present, we look at them as having the same referent.

2. The definition of bilingualism has been a notorious one. Some researchers such as Bloomfield describe bilingualism as 'native-like control of two or more languages' while others might on the other hand have very low demands (see Appel and Muysken 1987: 2; Romaine 1989: 11). We otherwise follow Auer (1984: 7) in viewing bilingualism as a displayed feature of participants, i.e., language behaviour rather than competence since our study is basically an inter-organic one rather than an intra-organic one.

3. Items like WTO, GDP, APEC, etc. are treated here as borrowings since they appear in *A Dictionary of Contemporary Chinese* (*Xiandai Hanyu Cidian* 《現代漢語詞典》) and thus are ruled out as instances of code-switching.

4. The word 'FUN' is used as an adjective and a synonym of 'interesting' in some cases when it comes into the Chinese language.

5. It seems that 'social distance' is equivalent to Martin's (1992: 528–30) notion of contact, which, according to Martin, is decided by how much contact participants involve in and the nature of the fields they are participating in. These two factors, as we understand, are similar to Hasan's notions of frequency and range.

6. We do so for two reasons. First, 'code' in systemic functional linguistics is more usually used in Bernstein's sense. Second, we wish to keep the term 'code-switching' so that all types of the alternative use of two languages can be included in this area of studies. Alvarez-Cáccamo's deconstruction of 'code' might lead to a deconstruction of the term 'code-switching'.

References

Alvarez-Cáccamo, C. (1998). 'From "switching code" to "code-switching": towards a reconceptualisation of communicative codes', in P. Auer (ed.), *Code-switching in Conversation: Language, Interaction and Identity*. London and New York: Routledge, pp. 29–48.

Appel, R. and Muysken, P. (1987), *Language Contact and Bilingualism*. London: Edward Arnold.

Auer, P. (1984), *Bilingual Conversation*. Amsterdam: Benjamins.

Bell, A. (1991), *The Language of News Media*. Oxford: Blackwell.

Benson, E. J. (2001), 'The neglected early history of codeswitching research in the United States'. *Language and Communication*, 21: 23–36.

Blom, J. P. and Gumperz, J. J. (1972), 'Social meaning in linguistic structure: code-switching in Norway', in J. J. Gumperz and D. Hymes (eds). *Directions in Sociolinguistics*. New York: Holt, Rinehart & Winston, pp. 407–34.

Chan, B. H. S. (2003), *Aspects of the Syntax, the Pragmatics, and the Production of Code-switching: Cantonese and English*. New York: Lang.

Di Sciullo, A., Muysken, P. and Singh, R. (1986), 'Government and code-mixing'. *Linguistics*, 22: 1–24.

Eggins, S. (1994), *An Introduction to Systemic Functional Linguistics*. London: Pinter.

Fishman. J. A. (1965), 'Who speaks what language to whom and when?' *La Linguistique*, 2: 67–88.

Gafaranga, J. and Torras, M. C. (2001), 'Language versus medium in the study of bilingual conversation'. *The International Journal of Bilingualism*, 5: 195–219.

Gregory, M. and Carroll, S. (1978), *Language and Situation: Language Varieties and their Social Contexts*. London: Routledge & Kegan Paul.

Halliday, M. A. K. (1978), *Language as Social Semiotic*. London: Edward Arnold.

Halliday, M. A. K. (1994), *An Introduction to Functional Grammar*. London: Edward Arnold.

Halliday, M. A. K. and Hasan, R. (1985), *Language, Context and Text: Aspects of Language in a Social-semiotic Perspective*. Geelong, Vic.: Deakin University Press.

Halliday, M. A. K., McIntosh, A. and Strevens, P. (1964), *The Linguistic Sciences and Language Teaching*. London: Longman.

Hasan, R. (1977), 'Text in the Systemic-Functional model', in W. Dressler (ed.), *Current Trends in Textlinguistics*. New York: Walter de Gruyter, pp. 228–46.

Hasan, R. (1994), 'Situation and the definition of genres', in A. D. Grimshaw (ed.), *What's Going On Here: Complementary Studies of Professional Talk*. Norwood, NJ: Ablex, pp. 127–72.

Huang, G. W. (2001), *Yupian Fenxi de Lilun yu Shijian* (*Theory and Practice of Discourse Analysis*). Shanghai: Shanghai Foreign Language Education Press.

Jiang, Y. J. (2003), 'English as a Chinese language'. *English Today*, 19 (2): 3–8.

Kronrod, A. and Engel, O. (2001), 'Accessibility theory and referring expressions in newspaper headlines'. *Journal of Pragmatics*, 33: 683–99.

Li, D. C. S. (1996), *Issues in Bilingualism and Biculturalism: A Hong Kong Case Study*. New York: Lang.

Li, D. C. S. (1997), 'Borrowed identity: signaling involvement with a western name'. *Journal of Pragmatics*, 28: 489–513.

McArthur, T. (2002), Editor's note to 'Reading, writing, listening and thinking in English'. *English Today*, 18 (2): 46.

Mackey, W. F. (1962), 'The description of bilingualism'. *Canadian Journal of Linguistics*, 7: 51–85.

Martin, J. R. (1992), *English Text: System and Structure*. Amsterdam: Benjamins.

Meeuwis, M. and Blommaert, J. (1998), 'A monolectual view of code-switching: layered code-switching among Zairians in Belgium', in P. Auer (ed.), *Code-switching in Conversation: Language, Interaction and Identity*. London and New York: Routledge, pp. 76–98.

Myers-Scotton, C. (1993a), *Duelling Languages: Grammatical Structure in Codeswitching*. Oxford: Clarendon Press.

Myers-Scotton, C. (1993b), *Social Motivations for Code-switching*. Oxford: Oxford University Press.

Newmark, P. (1981), *Approaches to Translation*. Oxford: Pergamon Press.

Poplack, S. (1980), 'Sometimes I'll start a sentence in Spanish Y TERMINO EN ESPAÑOL: toward a typology of code-switching'. *Linguistics*, 18: 581–618.

Poynton, C. (1985), *Language and Gender: Making the Difference*. Geelong, Vic.: Deakin University Press.

Romaine, S. (1989), *Bilingualism*. Oxford: Blackwell.

Scollon, R. (2000), 'Generic variability in news stories in Chinese and English: a contrastive discourse study of five days' newspapers'. *Journal of Pragmatics*, 32: 761–91.

Thomason, S. G. (2001), *Language Contact*. Edinburgh: Edinburgh University Press.

Weinreich, U. (1953), *Languages in Contact*. The Hague: Mouton.

Multilingual Studies as a Multi-dimensional Space of Interconnected Language Studies

Christian M. I. M. Matthiessen
Macquarie University,
Kazuhiro Teruya
University of New South Wales and
Wu Canzhong
Macquarie University

6.1 Introduction

In this chapter, we will be concerned with *multilingual studies* as a possible new field of investigation and application where areas such as *language typology, language description, translation* (including interpreting), *translator education, translation studies, foreign/second language teaching, multilingual lexicography* (including multilingual term banks for translation) and *multilingualism* (with bilingualism as a special case) can be brought into mutual relevance even though they have tended to remain fairly insulated from one another as these areas have been developed over the last half century or so. In a sense, a number of these areas used to be closer. For example, the 'translation method' used to be part of language teaching before it fell out of fashion as part of the traditional grammar-based approach; and contrastive analysis provided a link between comparative linguistics and language teaching for about a decade from the late 1950s to the late 1960s before attention focused on error analysis and inter-lingua of second language learners. Similarly, there was a period in the 1960s when a number of researchers drew attention to the links between comparative linguistics and translation studies (e.g. Catford 1965 and Halliday [1959]). At the same time, the conditions for bringing these areas into closer contact with one another are now better than ever before because the engagement with *text in context* has become increasingly central to many of them. For example, while translation and translation studies are inherently text-based, comparative linguistics and typological linguistics have not been; but researchers have shown how translation studies and comparison interpenetrate (see in particular Teich 1999, 2003) and at least since the early 1980s a number of linguists working in the area of language typology have demonstrated the value of text-based investigations (for some early important and influential studies providing models for later work, see, e.g., Grimes 1978; Longacre 1990; Hopper and Thompson 1980; Hopper 1982; Givón 1983).

Our central goal in this chapter will be to suggest how these different areas of activity can be related to one another – more specifically, how they can be related to one another in terms of (i) the dimensions of systemic functional theory of language in context, and to indicate how activities within these different areas support and reinforce one another; and (ii) the dimensions of systemic functional meta-theory of systemic functional theory. In other words, to bring out the *coherence of multilingual studies* as a domain of activity, we will need to explore both the nature of the phenomenal realm of multilinguality using systemic functional theory and the nature of our scientific engagement with this realm using systemic functional meta-theory. Briefly, we will need systemic functional theory to show how multilingual studies are in fact concerned with one and the same phenomenal realm, and that although different branches of multilingual studies have focused on different areas within this realm, these areas are – and need to be conceived as being – intimately interrelated; and we need systemic functional meta-theory to show how different modes of theoretical and practical engagement with this realm complement one another.

We will organize our discussion as follows:

- We will begin by using systemic functional theory to theorize the phenomenal realm of multilinguality in its broadest sense in order to identify the dimensions in terms of which different areas of multilingual studies can be located.
- We will then explore the possibility of developing a unified field of multilingual studies by taking interpersonal systems as a case study.
- Finally, we will turn to systemic functional meta-theory in order to characterize the activities of multilingual studies and to show how they complement one another.

Let us begin by elucidating the notion of systemic functional meta-theory as a theory of systemic functional theory.

6.2 Multilingual studies: theorizing the phenomenal realm

The phenomenal realm of multilingual studies is a sample of languages – and a single language taken from such a sample to be described against the background of other languages is the limiting case. How the sample is constituted and how large it is are issues relating to our meta-theoretical engagement with multiple languages, so we will return to these issues below. However, specifying what aspects of a language are in focus in different areas of multilingual studies is a task for our theory of the phenomenal realm. We can characterize this realm in terms of two of the *semiotic dimensions* of the 'architecture' of language according to systemic functional theory (see, e.g., Halliday 2002, 2003; Halliday and Matthiessen 2004: Ch. 1; Matthiessen in press a) – the *cline of instantiation* and the *hierarchy of stratification*.

6.2.1 The cline of instantiation

Let us consider the cline of instantiation first (references as above; see also Halliday 1992; Matthiessen 1993). The cline of instantiation is the continuum from language as *instance* to language as *potential*. At the instance pole of the cline, we can observe language unfolding as texts in their context of situation. At the potential pole of the cline, we can make generalizations based on instances we have observed about languages 'distilled' as systems evolving in their contexts of culture. Between these two outer poles, there are intermediate patterns, which we can characterize either as instance types by approaching them from the instance poles (text types operating in situation types) or as subpotentials by approaching them from the potential pole (registers operating in institutional domains). Recalling Halliday's (1992) meteorological analogy, we can say that language extends from weather – observable instances of texts unfolding over short periods of time – to climate – the meaning potential we infer from instances, the system evolving over extended periods of time.

Turning now to the phenomenal realm that multilingual studies are concerned with, we can explore it in terms of the cline of instantiation: see Figure 6.1. Two or more languages can be brought into relation with one another at any point along the cline of instantiation. Drawing on Saussure's distinction between *langue* (the potential pole) and *parole* (the instance pole), Koller (1979) suggested that *correspondence* between features of linguistic systems can be studied in contrastive linguistics, and *equivalence* between segments of texts can be studied in translation studies (see Munday 2001: 46-9). This is an important point in relation to the cline of instantiation. However, correspondence and equivalence are not actually distinct phenomena; they are simply manifestations of the same phenomenon seen from different observer standpoints. As instance observers, we can see equivalences between pairs (or *n*-tuples) of (segments of) texts in different languages; and as system observers, we can postulate correspondences between pairs (or *n*-tuples) of features of different linguistic systems. And we can approach the region along the cline of instantiation between potential and instance from either of these poles, exploring registers (text types) in terms of either correspondence (moving in from the potential pole) or equivalence (moving in from the instance pole).

At the instance pole of the cline, we can observe multilinguality instantiated in texts unfolding in their contexts. This includes speakers producing texts successively first in one language, then in another; and it includes speakers

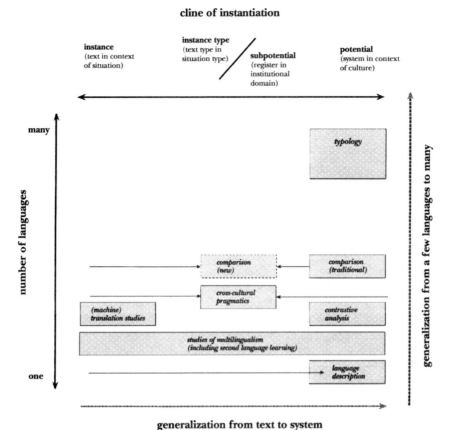

Figure 6.1 Phenomenal realm explored in multilingual studies differentiated in terms of the number of languages in focus and in terms of the cline of instantiation

engaged in 'code switching' and 'code mixing' (e.g. Marasigan 1983), where they instantiate the meaning potential of two (or more) languages in the same text, in the same context of situation. It also includes translators and interpreters 're-instantiating' a text in one language as a text in another language, keeping the meaning potentials of these two languages distinct in textual instantiation. These instances of multilinguality are precisely that – instances of multilingual systems of the type explored in, e.g., Bateman *et al.* (1991) and Bateman *et al.* (1999) and implemented in the framework of KPML[1] (see also Ellis's, 1987, notion of dia-categories in the service of comparative linguistics).

Translation and interpreting are investigated in *translation and interpreting studies*; Steiner (2005) provides a recent overview of the interaction between systemic functional linguistics and translation theory, taking note of important precursors in the work by Malinowski and by Firth. Recent important developments include the deployment of corpora and corpus-based techniques, often with a clear registerial focus (e.g. Teich 2003; Steiner 2004; Hansen-Schirra and Neumann 2005; Pagano *et al.* 2004; Pagano and Vasconcellos 2005), the bridging from detailed text analysis to investigations of ideological considerations (e.g. Mason 2003, 2007; Calzada Pérez 2007), and the development of register-focused and text-based comparisons of languages (see further below).

One of the challenges faced in translation and interpreting studies is that while the focus is naturally on instances, there is a need to develop general theories of translation. The question is what the domain of this general theory should be. For example, how far up the cline of instantiation should this domain be extended? We believe part of the answer lies in relating translation to other areas of multilinguality. (Another question is whether a general theory of translation should be concerned with reflection or with action; see below.) Translation scholars have produced a range of different approaches to issues in translation and interpreting (see, e.g., Gentzler 1993; Munday 2001). These approaches address questions relating to *translation equivalence* and *units of translation*. Such questions are concerned with locating translation in relation to the text as a semantic unit, and the different answers that have been proposed can be characterized in terms of the strata of language and contexts and in terms of ranks within these strata. Some approaches, such as Even-Zohar's polysystem theory and Bassnett and Lefevere's 'cultural turn', are also concerned with broader questions relating to the significance of translation within a given context of culture – questions that are concerned with the potential pole of the cline of instantiation.

At the potential pole of the cline of instantiation, we can hypothesize that dialects of languages gradually drift apart, becoming more distantly related systems, as their communities of speakers migrate in different directions; and we can also hypothesize that linguistic systems impact one another in areas where contact situations between speakers of different languages are common – multilingual communities, areas of trade. Such impact may be anything from small-scale borrowing to the more large-scale effects of pidginization and creolization.

We can investigate such multilingual conditions systemically, describing multilingual systems along the lines explored by Bateman *et al.* (1991) and Bateman *et al.* (1999). However, we can also take descriptions of the linguistic systems of any sample of languages, and compare and contrast them to identify similarities and differences. If the sample is fairly small, this is the domain of *comparative linguistics*, developed originally as a technique designed to determine genetic relationships as part of historical linguistics in the nineteenth century – the 'comparative method', and updated in systemic-functional terms by Ellis (e.g., 1966, 1987). If the comparison of a small sample of languages, often just two, is undertaken to shed light on potential difficulties for language learners, then this is *contrastive linguistics* as it was practised in particular from the late 1950s to the late 1960s (see, e.g., Lado

1957). If the comparison involves a large sample of languages designed to be representative of some group of languages such as languages spoken in South-East Asia or of languages spoken around the world in general, then this is *typological linguistics* (see, e.g., Croft 1990; Shibatani and Bynon 1995). Here different linguistic subsystems (see Halliday 1960 [1959]) such as vowel systems, case systems and tense/aspect systems are compared and contrasted in order to establish the range of variation within the group of languages under investigation, and to identify different recurrent types.

Comparative linguistics, contrastive linguistics and typological linguistics differ in terms of their *time frames*. In contrastive linguistics, the time frame is that of the 'semiotic growth' of the individual learner; the focus is on *ontogenesis* – as it is more generally in second/foreign language education research, where the value of longitudinal case studies is now being emphasized (see, e.g., Ortega and Byrnes forthcoming.). In comparative and typological linguistics, the time frame is that of the evolution of languages and populations; the focus is on *phylogenesis*. In typological linguistics, phylogenesis has increasingly come into focus in studies of *grammaticalization* and typology (see, e.g., Heine *et al.* 1991; Heine and Kuteva 2004; Hopper and Traugott 1993) and in investigations of the distribution of linguistics features around the world in relation to the migrations of populations (see, e.g., Nichols 1992; Nettle 1999).

Comparative linguistics, contrastive linguistics and typological linguistics are, as already noted, focused on the potential pole of the cline of instantiation; they are concerned with comparing and contrasting aspects of linguistic systems. One challenge to these kinds of multilingual study is thus the source of *data* – the evidential base upon which comparative and typological generalizations are based. Traditionally, such generalizations tended to be based on secondary sources, more specifically on descriptions of individual languages such as reference grammars. However, more recently, starting in the later 1970s and early 1980s, a number of functional typologists have supplemented this traditional method with studies based on *texts* in different languages; early contributions include Hopper (1982), Givón (1983), Mithun (1987) and Longacre (1990), and they are often focused on narrative texts, but more recent contributions have emphasized spontaneous dialogue (e.g. Ochs *et al.* 1996).

Such contributions make it possible to explore and explain typological patterns by reference to language in use, and they also make it possible to introduce quantitative information based on counts in texts (see Halliday 1960 [1959]) in the specification of similarities and differences among languages. Quantitative information gives us a much clearer picture of variation across languages. It brings out covert differences not revealed by purely qualitative accounts, e.g. differences in the relative frequency of the terms in voice systems of different languages (a point made many years ago by Mathesius, e.g., 1975, in his comparison of English with languages spoken on the European continent with respect to the frequency of the passive voice); but it also brings out covert similarities not revealed by purely qualitative accounts, as shown early on by Givón (1979) with respect to Subjects and 'definiteness': Subjects tend to be definite rather than indefinite in many languages, and the limiting case in some languages is that they are definite with a probability of one – i.e., they are required to be definite.

Evidence from the analysis of text thus enriches comparative and typological studies. However, this enrichment comes at a price: serious text analysis is labour-intensive and time-consuming, so it is virtually impossible at present to provide textual evidence for large samples of languages. There is thus a trade-off between the sample size and the richness of the typological information.

One approach to this situation is to focus the comparison and the typology not on the overall linguistic systems located at the potential pole of the cline of instantiation but rather on registerial subsystems located along the region intermediate between the potential pole and the instance pole – that is, on the region characterized by register variation. This is an important way of managing the complexity of the task of text-based linguistic typology. A recent systemic functional study of this kind is Rose's (2005) typological investigation of grammatical properties of narrative discourse in languages around the world. In fact, a good deal of text-based typological research has actually been based on narrative discourse, including, e.g., investigations of tense and aspect systems (e.g. Hopper 1982) and of factors influencing 'word order' (e.g. Longacre 1990).

In addition to being a strategy for managing the complexity of text-based typological research, linguistic typology with a registerial focus is of inherent interest in any case. On the one hand, it is important to know how registers vary around the world, and typological and comparative studies such as Abelen *et al.* (1993), Biber (1995), Downing and Lavid (1998), McCabe (1999), Murcia-Bielsa (1999) and Martinec (2003) are shedding light on variation in registers from one language to another, as are register-focused studies within *contrastive rhetoric* (see, e.g., Connor 1996: Chapter 8, on 'Genre-specific studies in contrastive rhetoric'). On the other hand, by focusing on registers, we can reveal subtle differences between languages that are not likely to be easy to see if the focus is on linguistic systems at the potential pole of the cline of instantiation. Teich (1999) makes this point: see further section 6.3.3.6 below.

As we have seen, the cline of instantiation extends from the potential pole via intermediate patterns of subpotentials/instance types to the instance pole; and these different regions of the cline of instantiation have all now received attention in multilingual studies, as shown in Figure 6.1. However, more connections are now being made along the cline of instantiation. Typology and comparison are making contact with the instance pole of the cline through the introduction of text-based evidence, and machine translation studies are making contact with more system-based comparative generalizations about pairs or *n*-tuples of languages (see, e.g., Dorr 1994 and discussion in Bateman *et al.* 1999).

In addition, one area of multilingual studies, *cross-cultural pragmatics* (see, e.g., Blum-Kulka *et al.* 1989) has a kind of natural registerial location mid-way along the cline since it makes sense to study requests, apologies, and other speech functions ('speech acts') situated within some situation type or institutional domain (in terms of which discourse completion tests tend to be formulated[2]), but it refers to general interpersonal systemic categories such as apologies and requests ('CCSARP': cross-cultural study of speech act realization) in relation to tenor considerations ('politeness') and is based on evidence from instances, although the examples that constitute the data are often elicited by means of questionnaires rather than taken from naturally occurring texts in context.[3]

Cross-cultural pragmatics is interesting in that its focus of investigation can be interpreted as extending along the cline of instantiation from potential to instance, thus being relevant to both comparison and typology on the one hand and translation and interpreting studies on the other. In this respect, it can be seen as symbolizing the inter-connectedness of multilingual studies, with different areas of investigation that are mutually relevant. We will explore this inter-connectedness further in reference to the cline of instantiation, but first we will briefly explore multilingual studies in relation to the other semiotic dimension we mentioned above – the hierarchy of stratification.

6.2.2 The hierarchy of stratification

There is no theoretical reason why the different areas of multilingual studies we have discussed above in relation to locations along the cline of instantiation should not be pursued equally across all the strata (levels) of the *hierarchy of stratification*. In practice, there are significant differences in terms of the stratal focus, as can be seen from Table 6.1.

Since *translation* is concerned with meaning in the first instance, its focus is on the *stratum of semantics*. Therefore *translation studies* have also tended to be concerned with different aspects of meaning – Nida's notion of 'dynamic equivalence', different kinds of meaning (e.g. 'denotative' and 'connotative'), meanings at risk in particular registers, and so on. While translation has traditionally been source-text oriented, target-oriented translation is concerned with 'communicating' in the target language-culture, so the central task is to produce a text in the relevant target-culture context, with the source text as one source of information rather than as the only one (for an early application to machine translation, see Anwyl *et al.* 1991).

Comparative and typological linguistics have tended not to venture above the stratum of lexicogrammar, thus focusing on the strata below semantics (see Croft 1990; Haspelmath *et al.* 2005) – *phonetics and phonology* (going back to Trubetzkoy 1939; e.g. Ladefoged and Maddieson 1996; Hirst and Di Cristo

Table 6.1 Areas of multilingual studies in relation to the cline of instantiation and the hierarchy of stratification

		potential (system)	subpotential/ instance type	instance (text in context of situation)
context				• translation studies (target-oriented)
language: content	**semantics**		• contrastive rhetoric with a register-focus; • cross-cultural pragmatics [speech functions and …	• translation studies (typical)
	lexicogrammar	• typology, comparison	… their grammatical realizations in different languages]	
language: expression	**phonology**	• typology, comparison		
	phonetics	• typology, comparison		

1998) and *lexicogrammar* (e.g. Greenberg *et al.* 1978; Comrie 1981; Mallinson and Blake 1981; Shopen 1985; Whaley 1997; Haspelmath *et al.* 2001; Shopen 2007). The focus on lexicogrammar includes studies of both grammaticalization (e.g., Hopper and Traugott 1993; Heine *et al.* 1991; Bybee *et al.* 1994; Heine and Kuteva 2004) and lexicalization (e.g. Talmy 1985, 2000, and many publications developing his seminal work).

Obviously, some researchers have made the stratal ascent to semantics and context in comparative and typological research – for example Anna Wierzbicka (e.g. 1996) Anvita Abbi. At the same time, the research conducted under the heading of *cross-cultural pragmatics* indicates that it would be possible to develop it to extend comparison and typology to the semantic subsystem. In systemic functional linguistics, Martin (1983) is a pioneering study showing the value – even the necessity – of basing comparison on considerations of semantic properties rather than on lexicogrammatical ones.

6.3 Multilingual studies: interpersonal systems as a case study

As far as the phenomenal realm is concerned, the challenge of demonstrating that multilingual studies constitute a coherent field of research consisting of areas that are mutually supportive and relevant is one of showing that the different foci identified above in terms of the cline of instantiation and of the hierarchy of stratification are interrelated rather than insulated from one another. To meet this challenge, we can choose any subsystem of language as a case study to explore the interconnectedness of multilingual studies. We have chosen to explore *interpersonal systems* as they are manifested in context (*tenor*) and across the strata of language.

Interpersonal systems operate in languages within the stratal subsystems of semantics, lexicogrammar and phonology; and they resonate with tenor parameters in context:

- Context – tenor: institutional roles, power (status) roles ['vertical' relations], familiarity (contact) roles ['horizontal' relations, 'solidarity'], sociometric roles (affect); speech roles, valuation (of domains within field);
- Language, content: semantics – interpersonal: NEGOTIATION (exchange, speech function, appraisal);
- Language, content: lexicogrammar – interpersonal: MOOD, MODAL ASSESSMENT, MODAL DISTANCE (HONORIFICATION & POLITENESS, or 'speech level');
- Language, expression: phonology – interpersonal: TONE.

There have been multilingual studies dealing with all strata, but the coverage varies from one stratum to another and it also varies along the cline of instantiation: see Table 6.2.

As Table 6.2 shows, the coverage of interpersonal systems is not evenly distributed in terms of stratification and instantiation. For example:

- In translation studies, a great deal of research based on the analysis of parallel texts (original and translation pairs) has been done within the textual metafunction – in particular with respect to thematic organization – but as far as we know, relatively little work based on comparable text analysis has been done within the interpersonal metafunction. There is thus an urgent need for interpersonal analysis of parallel texts to identify patterns in translation shifts between pairs of languages with respect to interpersonal systems such as MOOD, SUBJECT PERSON, POLARITY and MODAL ASSESSMENT (including MODALITY and EVIDENTIALITY, as well as attitudinal comments). At the same time, there is an important opportunity created for such research by the text-based contrastive studies of interpersonal systems undertaken by Teich (1999), Lavid (2000) and Murcia-Bielsa (2000), and by the typological studies of interpersonal systems referred to in the table.

Table 6.2 Multilingual studies of interpersonal systems

		potential (system)	subpotential/instance type	instance (text in context of situation)
context		• typology: politeness based on Goffman's notion of 'face' – Brown and Levinson (1978, 1987); power and solidarity – Brown and Gilman (1960)		
language: content	semantics		• contrastive linguistics and translation studies: SPEECH FUNCTION – Teich (1999), Lavid (2000), Murcia-Bielsa (2000) [speech functions in particular registers across languages] • cross-cultural pragmatics: Blum-Kulka *et al.* (1989) and studies building on this foundation, e.g. Aoyama (n.d.), Kasper (1995), Hong (1999); speech functions of requesting and apologizing …	

Table 6.2 *Continued*

		potential (system)	subpotential/instance type	instance (text in context of situation)
language: content	**lexicogrammar**	• typology: MOOD systems – Sadock and Zwicky (1985), Palmer (1986), Payne (1997: Section 10.3), König and Siemund (2007), Teruya *et al.* (in press) [see further below]; EVIDENTIALITY – Chafe and Nichols (1986), Ellis (1987), Willett (1988), Wierzbicka (1996: Ch. 15) [theorizing Chafe and Nichols, in terms of semantic primitives], de Haan (2005a,b); POLARITY – Payne (1985), Kahrel and van den Berg (1994), Payne (1997: Section 10.2), Dryer (2005a); PERSON – Siewierska (2004) • comparative studies: EVIDENTIALITY – Ellis (1987); modal structure of the clause – Haegeman (1997);[4] idioms from an interpersonal point of view – Chang (2004)	… their grammatical realizations in different languages Rodrigues *et al.* (2006) • interpersonal meaning in advertising: Liu and Fang (2007) • poetry: Huang (2006)	• translation studies – MODALITY: Wang (2004)
language: expression	**phonology**	• typology: intonation – Bolinger (1978), Hirst and Di Cristo (1998), cf. also Gussenhoven (2004)		

- In typological studies, there has been a fair amount of research dealing with interpersonal systems within lexicogrammar in particular, as indicated by the references in the table; but these have tended to be focused on systems without support from large-scale investigations of interpersonal choices in dialogic text. This means that while we know a fair amount (though by no means enough) about different mood types in mood systems, we know relatively little about their instantiation in text. For example, how does the 'imperative' mood vary across languages in terms of patterns of instantiation? There is enough evidence from text-based contrastive studies of particular registers (including those mentioned above – Teich 1999; Lavid 2000; Murcia-Bielsa 2000) to show that the 'imperative' mood does vary in usage from one language to another, and that division of labour between 'imperative' clauses and 'modulated' 'indicative' ones varies across languages, and there is further evidence for this variation coming from studies in cross-cultural pragmatics of the realization of requests.

- In typological studies, the main focus has been on lexicogrammar (as far as interpersonal systems within the content plane are concerned), as already indicated. Much more research is thus needed to investigate other strata. However, in addition, more research also needs to be done on inter-stratal patterns of realization, so that we will get a clearer picture of general tendencies of the realization of mood systems by intonation systems, and the realization of speech function systems by mood systems. The realization of speech functional categories by mood categories has been explored in cross-cultural pragmatics, with particular attention being given to requests and apologies; but this research needs to be scaled up to the level of typological coverage, and it needs to be based on evidence from naturally occurring (dialogic) texts.

Let us now discuss interpersonal systems stratum by stratum, starting with interpersonal translation shifts analysed in terms of lexicogrammatical systems.

6.3.1 Interpersonal translation shifts

At the instance pole of the cline of instantiation, we can observe translation shifts within interpersonal systems such as MOOD (the grammatical system of speech function: 'indicative' [giving or demanding information] vs. 'imperative' [giving or demanding (typically demanding) goods-&-services], and more delicate contrasts), SUBJECT PERSON (the grammatical system of personal deixis for the Subject of the clause: 'interactant' vs. 'non-interactant', and more delicate contrasts, typically 'interactant': 'speaker' vs. 'addressee'), DEICTICITY (the grammatical system of deixis for the Finite operator: 'temporal' vs. 'modal', and more delicate contrasts) and MODAL ASSESSMENT (the grammatical system of interpersonal assessment – giving or demanding assessments of some aspect of the move realized by the clause). Let us give some examples from different pairs of languages: see Table 6.3.

Table 6.3 Examples of interpersonal translation shifts

system	original			translation		
	language	selection	example	language	selection	example
DEICTICITY	French	temporal: present	– *Tu devines? dit Zumlauf.*[5]	English	modal: modulation: potentiality	*'Can you guess?' says Zumlauf.*
SUBJECT PERSON	French	interactant: addressee	*« Tu dois être vraiment trop mal, sur le carrelage », dit Antoine.*[6]	English	non-interactant	*'It must be very uncomfortable for you on the stone floor,' said Antoine.*
SUBJECT PERSON	French	non-interactant	*on s'accorde pas trop mal*	English	interactant: speaker+	we don't get on too badly
SUBJECT PERSON	French	non-interactant	*Il s'agit du sacristain de la cathédrale de Santiago-del-Chili ...*	English	speaker	*I'm talking about the sacristan of the cathedral of Santiago-de-Chile ...*
SUBJECT PERSON	English	interactant: addressee	*You are invited to a special event.*	Chinese	interactant: speaker	*Wǒ yào ǐng nǐ cānjiā yīge tèshū de huódòng.*
MOOD	French	exclamative [bound]	*« Ce que j'avais envie de t'embrasser aujourd'hui! »*[7]	English	declarative	*'I wanted so much to kiss you today!'*
MOOD	French	interrogative: polar [alternative]	– *En somme, vous êtes écuyer ou matelot?*[8]	English	interrogative: wh-	*'What are you then, a stableman or a sailor?'*

Table 6.3 *Continued*

system	original			translation		
	language	**selection**	**example**	**language**	**selection**	**example**
MOOD	French	bound: conditional	– Si j'essayais, dit Marcelin.[9]	English	imperative: oblative	'Let me try,' said Marcelin.
MOOD	English	imperative	Look for Flora pro-activ in your supermarket.	Chinese	declarative	Flora pro-activ zài chāoshì li kěyi zhǎodào.
POLARITY	English	positive	American people have risen to every test of our time.	Chinese	negative	Měiguó rénmín cónglái méiyǒu zài shídài de tiǎozhàn miànqián dī tóu.
SPEAKER IDENTITY	English	unmarked	Dad, knock it off, will you?	Japanese	marked: female	Toosan, moo yamete yo.
HONORIFICATION	English	unmarked	Welcome	Japanese	Marked: honorific	Yookoso oide kudasaimashita.
MODALITY, MOOD	English	declarative	Why should that be?	Japanese	explanative	Doo shite soo nan desu ka. 'why is [the explanation for] that so?'

From the examples in Table 6.3, it is clear – and not unexpected – that instantial differences in selections within interpersonal systems occur in the course of translation. One interesting issue that relates directly to the coherence of multilingual studies as a unified field of research is whether such differences are purely instantial or reflect more systemic differences. When we examine parallel texts, we will no doubt find a mixture of differences that range from purely instantial ones to systemic ones – including differences that are sub-systemic ones, i.e., confined to particular registers.

6.3.2 The system of (SUBJECT) PERSON

In some cases, it is clear that the instantial differences between the parallel texts are also systemic in nature; that is, the instantial differences reflect – and help create – differences between linguistic systems. For instance, the difference in selections in SUBJECT PERSON above between French *on* in *on s'accorde pas trop mal* and English *we* in *we don't get on too badly* is not only instantial but also systemic in the sense that it reflects a difference between the French SUBJECT PERSON system and the English one. French *on* is treated by the grammar as a non-interactant person as far as concord with the Finite element is concerned (third person singular). It can serve as a 'generalized' person, like English *one* (see Halliday and Matthiessen 2004: 325). However, on the one hand, English *one* is quite restricted as a generalized person pronoun compared with French *on* – and also for example with German *man* and Swedish *man*, English often preferring to use generalized versions of *we*, *you* or *they* instead; and, on the other hand, French *on* can be used also for particular persons (from an English point of view), including apparently increasingly 'speaker+' (see Siewierska 2004: 212). There are thus a number of English translation equivalents for French *on*, as exemplified in Table 6.4; and these are instances of fairly complex systemic correspondences. In the European context, English would appear to be the odd language out – both in comparison with its Germanic siblings (see, e.g., Johansson 2002/03) and in comparison with its Romance neighbour French.

The system of SUBJECT PERSON in French and English is an example of one area where translation shifts are not merely instantial but can be related to systemic differences between these systems in French and English – differences that would be brought out by a comparative study of the PERSON systems of these two languages (either the 'subject person' systems or the general 'person' systems). And sample of languages can be extended to the point where we can begin to make typological observations and generalizations, as Siewierska (2004) is able to do, drawing on over 700 languages. Here we should note that while it is likely that all languages have some kind of PERSON system (Siewierska 2004: 8–13), it is quite possible that the manifestation of this system in the clause as the system of SUBJECT PERSON – a system concerned with the personal deixis of the Subject as the element held

Table 6.4 French *on* ~ English *we/I/they*

system	original		original	translation		translation
	language	selection	example	language	selection	example
SUBJECT PERSON	French	non-interactant	– *On peut se voir?*[10]	English	interactant: speaker+	*'Can **we** see each other?'*
	French	non-interactant	– *On part!*[11]	English	interactant: speaker+	*'**We**'re off!'*
	French	non-interactant	*on s'accorde pas trop mal*	English	interactant: speaker+	***we** don't get on too badly*
	French	non-interactant	*On est arrivés ce matin et on n'a pas été bien reçus, ... On a sauté dans l'eau ...*[12]	English	interactant: speaker+	***We** arrived this morning and **we** weren't exactly given a welcome ... **We** jumped into the water ...*
	French	non-interactant	*On s'est mis derrière le tank.*[13]	English	interactant: speaker+	***We** got behind the tank.*
	French	non-interactant	*– Avec ce jus poisseux, on n'y voit pas grand-chose, fit-elle.*[14]	English	interactant: speaker+	*'I can't see much, with sticky juice like this,' she said.*
	French	non-interactant	*On ne peut pas prévoir comment ça va être.*[15]	English	addressee	***You** can't tell what it's going to be like.*
	French	non-interactant	*– Pour les orages, on sait jamais trop à quoi s'en tenir.*[16]	English	addressee	*'**You** never know where you are with storms.'*
	French	non-interactant	*– On l'a annoncé ...*[17]	English	non-interactant	*'**They** said it was coming ...*
	French	non-interactant	*On est en train d'équiper les autres bagnoles avec une lame d'acier ...*[18]	English	non-interactant	***They**'re just fitting steel blades on the front of the other jeeps ...*
	French	non-interactant	*On n'osait pas le toucher ;...*[19]	English	non-interactant	***They** didn't dare touch him, ...*
	French	non-interactant	*On était en train de fermer ; ...*[20]	English	non-interactant	***They** were just closing; ...*

modally responsible for the proposition or proposal realized by the clause – is more restricted around the world since it is not clear that all languages operate with a category of Subject. For example, Martin (1990, 2004) does not postulate a category of Subject in his account of the interpersonal grammar of the clause in Tagalog; he shows how Tagalog has evolved other strategies for dealing with modal responsibility.

The French and English approaches to the generalized person category can be located within a typology of strategies that languages have evolved. Thus Siewierska (2004: 210–13) shows that the generalized person category (her 'impersonalization') is more likely to occur with plural pronouns than with singular ones, and among plural pronouns with 'non-interactant' ones ('third person plural') – like *they* in English. The typological profiles of a set of languages will of course determine what kinds of issue are in the translation of generalized person references between these languages.

Generalized person categories are in some sense expansions of basic PERSON systems, having evolved out of an interactant or non-interactant person category, so in this respect they are somewhat peripheral to basic PERSON systems. But PERSON systems also vary in their basic properties in the languages of the world. They vary syntagmatically, of course, with respect to how terms in the person system are realized (e.g. Siewierska 2004: 16–40): as free items – ranging from more lexical (as in Japanese) to more grammatical, the latter being true closed system pronouns (as in English), or as bound pronominal affixes, or intermediate between the two types, as pronominal clitics (e.g. the 'weak' pronouns in French) – pronominal items on their way to becoming pronominal affixes.[21] But here we are more concerned with paradigmatic variation – variation in the organization of person systems themselves. Such systemic variation includes variation in the number and nature of the person categories within the system itself: the basic distinction between interactant persons (speech roles – traditionally, first and second person) and non-interactant persons (non-speech roles – traditionally, third person) is very wide-spread, and many languages have markers for both types, but there are languages that only have dedicated markers for interactant persons. Some languages have more delicate distinctions, e.g. languages distinguishing between 'inclusive' and 'exclusive' in the category of 'speaker+'. Systemic variation also includes variation in how the person system intersects with other systems – NUMBER, GENDER, CASE, the tenor-related system of POLITENESS, and (more rarely) other tenor-related systems such as kinship. Let's consider the interaction with systems of POLITENESS briefly because this type of interaction will also be relevant when we discuss mood systems below.

Whether or not the PERSON system of a given language interacts with a system of POLITENESS is itself a typological variable. In a study of politeness distinctions in addressee ('second person') pronouns in a sample of 207 languages, Helmbrecht (2005) found that the majority of these languages – around two thirds (136 languages) – make no such politeness distinction.

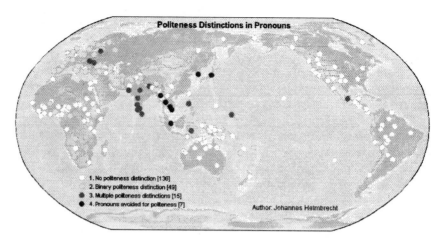

Figure 6.2 Politeness distinctions in addressee ('second person') pronouns (Helmbrecht 2005)

English thus belongs with the majority in this area, but it is exceptional among languages in the sample spoken in Europe, the only other one without such a distinction in the sample being Irish. The European distinction is a binary one – the *tu* vs. *vous* distinction of French; and it was illuminated by Brown and Gilman's (1960) classic study of 'pronouns of power and solidarity', which showed (in our terms) that these systems are sensitive to the tenor variables of power (status; also called 'vertical' relations in discussions of Japanese and Korean) and familiarity (solidarity, contact; also called 'horizontal' relations in discussions of Japanese and Korean). And this type of binary distinction is most widespread in Helmbrecht's sample, but there are two other types: 'multiple politeness distinctions' and pronoun avoidance, the latter involving some term other than a pronoun such as a title (plus name) or a kinship term. The geographic distribution is shown in Figure 6.2.

As can be inferred from the map, Chinese has a binary system, e.g., *nín* is often used in place of *nǐ (you)* to indicate politeness. In contrast, Japanese avoids the use of pronouns as a strategy to enact politeness; this same strategy is found in East Asia and in South-East Asia (see, e.g., Iwasaki and Ingkaphirom 2005: Ch. 3, on Thai).[22]

Let's return for a moment to French and English to explore another point. The systemic differences between French and English are located at the potential pole of the cline of instantiation. However, it is also likely that differences in particular registers are part of the picture. For example, the French and English parts of the manual for a machine translation software package, *PowerTranslator*, differ systematically at certain points in the selections within the system of SUBJECT PERSON, as illustrated by the aligned extracts in Table 6.5. Both start out with 'addressee' subject in [1.1] – *vous pouvez* . . .; *you can* . . .; but in the section of the text that provides an overview of the organization of the manual, English retains 'addressee' as the selection in SUBJECT PERSON, but French switches to 'non-interactant', with a nominal group denoting the relevant part of the manual as Subject and the addressee (*vous*) as Complement rather than as Subject (see also [6.2] *il vous est conseillé*). In this passage, the English text thus involves the addressee more centrally as that element which is held modally responsible – the nub of the argument, i.e., the Subject. It seems likely that this difference in the choice of SUBJECT PERSON is a registerial trait, but this is only a hypothesis. However, multilingual research on MOOD systems based on the analysis of texts belonging to particular registers has revealed similar register-based variation, as we shall see below.

Table 6.5 Parallel French and English software manual texts illustrating differences in selections within the system of SUBJECT PERSON

		French from manual	English from manual
0		Bienvenue au Power Translator	Welcome to Power Translator
1	[1.1]	Vous pouvez utiliser le Power Translator	You can use Power Translator
	[1.2]	pour traduire pratiquement n'importe quel texte de l'anglais vers le français ou du français vers l'anglais.	to translate almost any text – from English to French or from French to English.
2		Le Power Translator produit un premier jet [[que vous pouvez éditer]].	Power Translator produces draft translations [[that you edit into final form]].
3	[3.1]	Vous pouvez également utiliser la fonction Voice	In addition, you can use the Voice feature
	[3.2]	qui permet au Power Translator de vous lire n'importe quel texte en anglais.	to have Power Translator speak any English text.
4		**La partie I** *vous* guide pas à pas dans les travaux pratiques [[qui vous sont proposés]].	In part I, **you**'ll find a step-by-step tutorial.
5	[5.1]	**La partie II** *vous* indique	In part II, **you**'ll find out
	[5.2]	comment traduire des documents	how to translate documents
	[5.3]	et réviser le premier jet de votre traduction.	and review your draft translation.
6	[6.1]	Pour améliorer la qualité de vos traductions,	To improve the quality of your translation,
	[6.2]	**il** *vous* est conseillé	**you** may want to add terms to Power Translator's dictionaries.
	[6.3]	d'ajouter des mots aux dictionnaires du Power Translator.	
7		**La partie III** *vous* donne un panorama des fenêtres du dictionnaire.	In Part III, **you**'ll be given a tour of the dictionary windows and guidelines [[for updating the dictionaries]].

6.3.3 The system of mood

6.3.3.1 As grammaticalization of moves in dialogic exchanges

Let's now turn to the interpersonal system of MOOD.[23] While the interpersonal systems of SUBJECT PERSON and DEICTICITY are from 'universal', it seems very likely that all languages have grammaticalized the speech functions of moves in dialogic exchanges as a system of MOOD since exchange is so central to the human condition. In their study of the evolution of human societies, Johnson and Earle (2000) suggest that all human societies are based on the principle of reciprocity. The notion of reciprocity as a central organizing principle in human societies goes back to Bronislav Malinowski's (e.g. 1922) account of the Kula exchange system in his description of Trobriand society, and it was developed further in a now famous study by Mauss (1925), who examined gift-giving customs in a number of societies, arguing that gifts are never free

Table 6.6 The basic speech functions (based on Halliday and Matthiessen 2004: Table 4(1), with added Japanese examples)

		initiation [A/B]	response	
			expected [C]	discretionary [D]
give [M]	goods-&-services [X]	offer *shall I give you this teapot?* *Kono kyuusu o ageyoo ka?*	acceptance *yes, please do!* *Ee, onegai shimasu!*	rejection *no, thanks* *Iie, kekoo desu.*
demand [N]		command *give me that teapot!* *Ano kyuusu o kudasai!*	undertaking *here you are* *Hai, doozo.*	refusal *I won't* *Ie, sore wa chotto. [lit.] 'no, that is a little.'*
give [M]	information [Y]	statement *he's giving her the teapot* *Kare wa kanojo ni kyuusu o agete iru.*	acknowledgement *is he?* *Kare desu ka?*	contradiction *no, he isn't* *Iie, kare ja arimasen.*
demand [N]		question *what is he giving her?* *Kare wa kanojo ni nani o agete iru no ka?*	answer *a teapot* *Kyuusu desu.*	disclaimer *I don't know* *Wakarimasen*

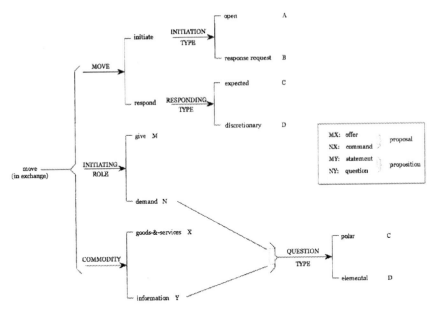

Figure 6.3 The basic system of SPEECH FUNCTION (from Halliday and Matthiessen 2004: Fig. 4.2)

and that gift-giving always involves reciprocity. (Since then scholars have suggested various counter-examples showing that gifts can be free, but these seem to be exceptions of the kind that prove the rule that the foundation is one of reciprocity.)

Reciprocity is manifested socially in many activities, including large-scale ones such as the Kula exchange system and the 'potlatch' system of the American North-West and small-scale ones such as the division of labour in a family; but it is also enacted semiotically through the semantic system of SPEECH FUNCTION in dialogic exchange. As described by Halliday (1984), exchange involves TURN ('initiating' vs. 'responding'), ORIENTATION ('giving' vs. 'demanding') and COMMODITY ('information' vs. 'goods-&-services'); together these subsystems define the primary types of speech function, as shown in Table 6.6 with examples from English and Japanese. The basic SPEECH FUNCTION network is set out in Figure 6.3.

The basic system of speech function set out in Figure 6.3 seems to be grammaticalized in similar ways in many – perhaps most, or even all – languages according to certain general principles (see Sadock and Zwicky 1985; König and Siemund 2007; Teruya *et al.* in press):

- Of the four basic initiating speech functions – statements ('give' & 'information'), question ('demand' & 'information'), offer ('give' & 'goods-&-services') and command ('demand' & 'goods-&-services'), statements, questions and commands are grammaticalized as 'declarative', 'interrogative' and 'imperative' clauses, but offers typically do not have a grammar of their own or are at least 'extremely rare' in the languages of the world (see, e.g., Halliday 1984; Portner 2004, who calls them 'promissives').

- Of the three basic initiating speech functions that are grammaticalized in languages – statements, questions and commands – those concerned with the exchange of information, i.e., statements and questions, tend to be more elaborated in the grammar, whereas the one concerned with the exchange of goods-&-services – commands – tends to be less elaborated in the grammar. That is, 'imperative' clauses typically have simpler paradigms, lacking or having more constrained versions of various systemic distinctions in the areas of tense/aspect, modality/evidentiality and other types of modal assessment (see, e.g., Sadock and Zwicky 1985; Mauck 2005; König and Siemund 2007). König and Siemund (2007) make the point that distinctions in evidentiality tend to be restricted to 'declarative' clauses: 'In languages with markers signalling the kind of evidence (hearsay, common knowledge, first-hand visual evidence, etc.) on which a claim is based or the degree of strength with which an assertion can be made, these so-called "evidential markers" can normally only be combined with declarative sentences.'

- Of the three basic initiating speech functions that are grammaticalized in languages – statements, questions and commands – those concerned with the giving of information, i.e., statements, are the unmarked type in the overall system, and since they are typically realized by 'declarative' clauses, the 'declarative' mood tends to be the unmarked type in the mood system of languages (see Halliday 1984; König and Siemund 2007: Section 2.1): they are the most common mood type in discourse, they are least constrained in their distribution, and they have the fullest range of systemic possibilities; and while some languages have a special segmental 'declarative' mood marker (i.e., a modal particle or a verbal affix), as Korean does (see, e.g., Sohn 1999), many languages mark the 'declarative' mood by the absence of a mood marker of the kind found in their interrogative or imperative clauses.

One generalization across languages is thus that the grammar of propositions is more highly elaborated than the grammar of proposals. Halliday (1984: 19–20) suggests why this should be the case:

> ... as a general feature, languages display a greater tendency to congruence in the exchange of information than in the exchange of goods-&-services. This is hardly surprising. Since information is a commodity that is defined and brought into being only by semiotic systems, with language leading the way, it is no surprise to find that there exist clearly defined categories of declarative and interrogative in the grammar, and that these are typically used as the mode of giving and demanding information. When it comes to exchanging goods-&-services, however, this is a process that takes

place independently of the existence of a semiotic in which to encode it; and languages do not display clear-cut categories in the grammar corresponding to offers and commands. The imperative is at best a fringe category, teetering between finite and non-finite (in languages which make the distinction), having either no distinct clause or verb form or else one that is only minimally distinguished; and even when a distinct imperative form does exist it may be rarely used, with other, non-congruent forms taking over the command function. The position is even clearer with offers: no language seems to have a clearly distinguished grammatical form for offers, the closest perhaps being special types of indicative like the English *shall I ... ?*

This is not to say that offers and commands are not ordinarily verbalized at all. On the contrary, they often are. The difference between information and goods-&-services is that, since information is a semiotic commodity, it is impossible to exchange it except by a semiotic process – in fact a semiotic process can be defined as one through which information is exchanged; so when we exchange information, there are explicit and regular grammatical patterns for doing so, the forms of declarative and interrogative mood, and these are the forms that are typically used. Goods-&-services on the other hand can be exchanged without the intervention of any symbolic act. Adults, being oriented towards the verbal mode, do typically verbalize offers and commands: for example, *here you are!*, *would you like a newspaper?*, *shall I hold the door open for you?*, *come on – follow me!* But the grammatical system of English does not display any clearly defined pattern of congruence in the realization of offers and commands; and this is true of many other languages, perhaps all. The exchange of goods-&-services, because of its lesser dependence on language, has not brought about the evolution of special modes of expression in the same way that these have evolved for the exchange of information.

6.3.3.2 'Free' and 'bound' clauses

The speech functional categories set out in Figure 6.3 are realized by 'free' clauses but, in the environment of project, they are also realized indirectly by 'bound' clauses. 'Free' clauses realize both the act of exchange – stating, questioning, commanding, or offering – and the commodity being exchanged – information or goods-&-services. Thus in the following exchange –

Jingfu: What's that?
Hesheng: Your medicine.

– we can interpret *What's that?* as 'I ask you: what is that?' and *Your medicine* as 'I tell you: it is your medicine', using verbal clauses to represent the act of exchange, in this case the acts of questioning and of stating. And this is of course how they get represented in dramatic dialogue, as in the original version of the exchange above, taken from Lu Xun's *Wandering* (English translation, p. 130):

> 'What's that?' asked Jingfu, opening his eyes.
> 'Your medicine,' he answered, roused from his stupefaction.

Here the clauses are quoted, and thus 'free' in terms of the choice of mood. In this sense, the mood of 'free' clauses is 'straight': it is an act of wording that enacts an act of meaning. In contrast, the mood of 'bound' is 'projected': it does not itself represent an act of meaning:

> Jingfu asked what that was.
> He answered that it was his medicine.

The 'bound' clauses *what that was* and *that it was his medicine* do not themselves serve as question and statement respectively; they do not demand and give information. The mood is projected through *Jingfu asked* and *he answered*. Other projecting clauses can give them quite different values; for example:

> Jingfu wasn't certain what that was.
> Jingfu guessed what that was.
> Jingfu knew what that was.
> He doubted that it was his medicine.

'Bound' clauses thus do not *enact* acts of exchange. They do not represent interactive moves in dialogue, and this is reflected in constraints on their grammar. For instance, in English, 'bound' clauses cannot normally be tagged because MOOD TAGGING is a system for positioning a move interactively in dialogue. In Japanese, 'bound' clauses cannot enact politeness because the system of POLITENESS is only open for selection at clause final as it positions a move relative to tenor relationship in dialogue.

While projected bound clauses do not represent the *act* of exchange ('I ask you', 'I tell you' and so on), they do represent the nature of the *commodity*. (i) On the one hand, they represent the contrast between information and goods-&-services:

> information – projected proposition: 'finite' bound clause, with 'declarative' structure (in English, Subject ^ Finite: *that/whether they had arrived*); goods-&-services – projected proposal: 'non-finite' bound clause, of the 'irrealis' type (i.e., non-actualized; in English, the infinitival form of the verb: *(for them) to arrive*), or 'modulated' 'finite' bound clause (in English, modulated by a modal auxiliary indicating obligation or readiness, with 'declarative' structure: *that they should arrive*; in languages such as German and Spanish with a subjunctive mode contrasting with an 'indicative' mode, this is one of the environments of the subjunctive).

Here the goods-&-services type is the same for projected commands and offers: he told his parents → to take care of the kids, he offered his parents → to take care of the kids.

(ii) On the other hand, they represent a distinction between two states of information:

open information – projected question: *whether they had arrived, who had arrived*
closed information – projected statement: *that they had arrived*

That is, they embody a distinction having to do with the 'epistemic' status of the information, which is why they are projected by different sets of 'mental' and 'verbal' clauses.

The realization of moves by 'free' clauses and by 'bound' clauses serving in logical nexuses of projection is represented diagrammatically in Figure 6.4.

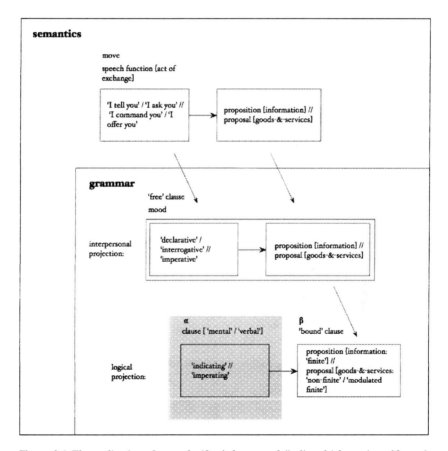

Figure 6.4 The realization of moves by 'free' clauses and (indirectly) by projected bound ones

In the case of 'free' clauses, the act of exchange is *enacted* interpersonally through the choice of mood. In contrast, in the case of 'bound' clauses, the act of exchange may be *construed* ideationally through the choice of 'mental' or 'verbal' process type in a projecting clause. However, logical nexuses of projection may be pressed into interpersonal service as explicitly subjective realizations of selections within speech function (see Blum-Kulka *et al.* 1989, categories of 'want statement', 'performative' and 'hedged performative' in the realization of requests) and different types of modal assessment; for example:

[command:]
Therefore, **I urge you** --> to vote against the Nuclear Freeze Initiative.
KANE (he has risen): Susan, **I want** --> you to stop this. And right now!
I would strongly advise you --> to pay a visit to your doctor in the very near future.
[offer:]
Do you want --> me to send her some copies of the journal or? – She probably doesn't need a copy.
[question:]
Would you say --> that a lot of fiction lacks this compassion or empathy? – You see a lot of stories that are clever, that use contemporary idiom, maybe they have a resounding paragraph or two, but the plot never points beyond itself.
And what, what, if **you were to describe more specifically** --> what, what does it mean to be a facilitator? What is it that you actually do?
Can you explain --> what that concept is and why the right wing and the Bush Republican Party use it so well?
[statement:]
I bet --> you've seen a lot of famous people come and go? Movie stars? – No. We live simply, Mr. Jimmy and I.
'When smokeless fuel is produced in abundance, and when it is a reasonable price, **I can assure you** --> that Leamington Spa will not hang back,' added Alderman Fryer.
While discussions about the membership and operations of the new student body are ongoing, **I can confirm** --> that there will be significant student representation on the new organization.
And **I tell you** --> we had a good laugh out of that; couldn't stop laughing.

Such projecting clauses serve to realize options in various interpersonal systems, including more delicate distinctions within the basic speech functions having to do with force, politeness, and so on. The examples above all involve 'verbal' clauses of projection. 'Mental' clauses of the 'cognitive' subtype serve as markers of explicitly subjective orientation in the system of modality (e.g. Halliday and Matthiessen 2004: 616–25). 'Mental' clauses of the 'emotive' subtype serve as markers of explicitly subjective orientation in attitudinal assessment (see Matthiessen, in press b). 'Mental' clauses of the 'perceptive' subtype and 'verbal' clauses can serve to realize different kinds of evidentiality. And 'relational' clauses can serve to realize objective orientation within a number of these interpersonal systems. In general, such 'mental', 'verbal' and 'relational' clauses may be pressed into interpersonal service and provide the realizational material for expanding interpersonal systems of SPEECH FUNCTION, MODAL ASSESSMENT (modality, evidentiality, attitude, and so on) and MODAL DISTANCE (politeness and honorification) considerably.

The strategies illustrated in reference to English above seem to be quite common around the languages of the world, as in the following Chinese examples of demanding moves (from Hong 1999):

[command:]
Wǒ	mìnglìng	nǐ	líkāi.
I	order	you	leave

I order you to leave.

Wǒ	qǐngqiú	dàjiā	ānjìng.
I	please-ask	everybody	quiet

I kindly request everybody to be quiet.

[question:]
Lǎo	dàyé	qǐng	wèn,	Běihǎi	gōngyuánr	zài	nǎr?
old	grandpa	please	ask	North Sea	park	at	where

Old grandpa, may I ask where is North Sea park, please?

Nǐ	néng	gàosù	wǒ	Běihǎi	gōngyuánr	zài	nǎr	ma?
you	can	tell	me	North Sea	park	at	where	Q

Can you tell me where North Sea park is?

In the evolution of languages, there is an interesting shift from ideational construal to interpersonal enactment in the grammaticalization of interpersonal assessment: historically, languages may develop evidential markers like quotative particles from nexuses with projecting 'verbal' clauses; see, e.g., Harris and Campbell (1995: 168–73).

6.3.3.3 MOOD *systems: common patterns and variants*

When we review the literature on the grammaticalization of speech functional systems as mood systems (see Table 6.7), we can find evidence that 'declarative', 'interrogative', and 'imperative' are mood types that recur in similar systemic contrasts in many, perhaps all, languages of the world. We can tentatively postulate the basic MOOD system represented in Figure 6.5. According to this representation, 'imperative' contrasts with 'indicative', 'declarative' contrasts with 'interrogative', and 'polar interrogative' contrasts with 'elemental interrogative'. This is the systemic or paradigmatic part of the generalized system

Table 6.7 Typological studies of the system of MOOD TYPE

system	terms		studies
mood type	(whole system)		Sadock and Zwicky (1985); Palmer (1986); König and Siemund (2007); Teruya *et al.* (in press)
	indicative	interrogative	Ultan (1978); Chisholm *et al.* (1984); Siemund (2001); Dryer (2005b)
	imperative		Mauck (2005); Mauck *et al.* (2004); van der Auwera, Dobrushina and Goussev (2005); van der Auwera *et al.* (2005); Dobrushina *et al.* (2005)

of mood, and in accordance with systemic functional theory it is kept distinct from realizations of systemic options along the syntagmatic axis.

We have postulated two generalizations about the interpersonal structure of clauses in languages around the world: 'major' clauses are characterized by the presence of a Predicator (distinguishing them from 'minor' ones such as calls, greetings and exclamations);[24] and 'elemental interrogative' clauses are characterized by the presence of a Q-element (the Wh- element in English), although languages vary with respect to the nature of the items serving as the Q-element, some languages having an overlap between interrogative items and relative ones, and other languages having an overlap between interrogative items and indefinite ones. Beyond these two generalizations about Predicator and Q-element, the only fairly certain generalization we can make about realizations along the syntagmatic axis is that they tend to be prosodic in nature (see Matthiessen 2004).

Against the background of the generalized MOOD system in Figure 6.5, we can identify three areas of variation:

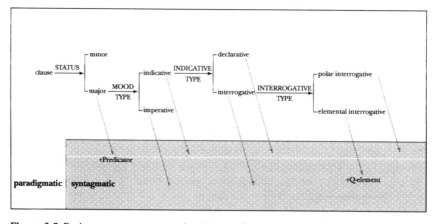

Figure 6.5 Basic MOOD system operating in many languages around the world

- Looking at the MOOD system 'from above', from the point of view of the semantic system of speech function, we find variation in the patterns of realization. In particular, the division of labour between 'imperative' clauses and 'indicative' ones seems to vary across the semantic distinction between 'goods-&-services' (exchanged by proposals) and 'information' (exchanged by propositions).
- Looking at the MOOD system 'from roundabout', from the point of view of its own systemic organization, we find variation in how languages elaborate the basic mood types (see Bateman *et al.* 1991; Bateman *et al.* 1999; Teruya *et al.* in press). We also find variation in the extent to which the mood system interacts with a system of SPEECH LEVEL of the kind found in, e.g., Japanese (e.g. Teruya 2006), Korean (e.g. Martin 1992; Sohn 1999) and Thai (e.g. Iwasaki and Ingkaphirom 2005: Ch. 14; Patpong 2005). As already noted, we also find variation in the presence and nature of the systems of SUBJECT PERSON and DEICTICITY.
- Looking at the MOOD system 'from below', from the point of view of the realization of mood options along the syntagmatic axis, we find variation with respect to the medium of realization – whether a given language tends towards intonational realization, segmental realization (modal particles, modal verbal affixes), sequential realization (relative sequence of Subject and Finite), or some mixture of these media of realization. With languages using segmental realization, there is also variation in rank between free modal particles operating at clause rank and bound verbal affixes at word rank, with modal clitics as an intermediate class of item. We also find variation with respect to the presence of certain elements of inter-personal structure: while Predicator and Q-element seem to be general across languages, certain other elements are more variable – in particular, Subject, Finite, and Negotiator, and also the grouping of Subject and Finite as a Mood element and the complementary grouping of Predicator plus Complements and/or Adjuncts as a Residue element.

We will illustrate variation seen 'from above' after we have illustrated variation seen 'from roundabout' and variation seen 'from below'.

6.3.3.4 Variation in MOOD systems viewed 'from roundabout'

MOOD systems vary with respect (1) to how they are extended in delicacy and (2) to what extent they are simultaneous with a system of SPEECH LEVEL. Common types of variation are shown in Figure 6.6. Congruence and variation within a small 'opportunistic' sample of languages – Chinese, Danish, French, Japanese, Oko and Thai – is represented systemically in a multilingual network in Teruya *et al.* (in press).

(1) The different mood types may all be extended further in delicacy, and there are recurrent types of such systemic elaborations. (a) 'Declarative' clauses may be further differentiated in terms of EVIDENTIALITY (having to do with

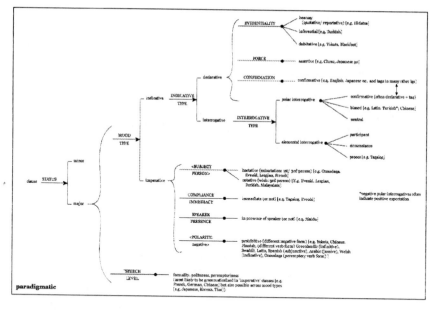

Figure 6.6 Basic MOOD system operating in many languages around the world, with indications of extensions in delicacy for the basic mood types found in languages around the world (represented by bullets followed by one or more possible distinctions)

the source of the information being given), FORCE (having to do with degree of commitment to the information being given), and CONFIRMATION (having to do with request for confirmation by addressee). (b) 'Interrogative' clauses of the 'polar' type may be further differentiated in terms of the speaker's expectation of the polarity of the addressee's answer. For example, in Mandarin Chinese, there is a distinction between 'unbiassed' and 'biassed' polar interrogatives (Halliday and McDonald 2005: 334–5, 343). (c) 'Interrogative' clauses of the 'elemental' type may be further differentiated in terms of what elements can be probed – participants, circumstances and the process. For example, in Tagalog, not only participants and processes can be probed with a Q-element but also the process (see Martin 2004: 287). (d) 'Imperative' clauses may be further differentiated in terms of the immediacy of the compliance expected of the addressee in response to a command and the speaker's presence at the time of the compliance; and also in terms of the (SUBJECT) PERSON, with special 'imperative' types for person categories other than 'interactant: addressee' (the core 'jussive' or 'command' type of 'imperative'), and POLARITY, with distinct 'imperative' forms for 'positive' and 'negative' polarity. For example, in Modern Standard Arabic, in 'positive' 'imperative' clauses, the Predicator is realized by a verb in the imperative form, but in 'negative' ones, the Predicator is realized by a verb in the so-called 'jussive' form.

For 'interrogative' clauses, there is also another source of variation: interaction with the textual systems of THEME and INFORMATION. In 'elemental' interrogatives, languages vary in the textual treatment of the Q-element – it may be unmarked Theme (as in English), or it may be unmarked Focus of New information (as in Sesotho), or it may not be given a special textual status, appearing *in situ* (as in Chinese and Japanese; see Matthiessen 2004: 616–17).

In a sample of 803 languages, Dryer (2005c) found that in 241 languages the Q-element ('interrogative phrase') appears in 'obligatorily initial position' in the clause, while in 542 languages it is 'not obligatorily initial'; and in 20, the situation is mixed in that some Q-elements are obligatorily initial while others are not. It is plausible that 'initial position' means that the Q-element is given a special textual status. This status is likely to be that of Theme (as in English), but it may be that of the Focus of New information, as in Malagasy (Dryer 2005c: 378). In Malagasy, it seems that the Q-element is focused in a 'cleft' construction (optionally if it is an oblique) – placed at the beginning of the clause and followed by the particle *no* (Keenan 1976: 268–70). Here it would seem that the Q-element is in fact given the status of both Theme and Focus of New, the 'cleft' being functionally theme predication. The initial position of the clause is also associated with 'topicalization' (*op cit.*, 271–3). When the Q-element is 'not obligatorily initial', it may appear *in situ*; but it may also be given a special textual status, as in those 'SOV' languages where it is placed in 'pre-verbal' position since this position has often been characterized as the (unmarked) Focus position in SOV languages.

In 'polar' interrogatives, languages that operate with an interrogative particle serving as Negotiator may locate this particle in different positions in the clause. In a sample of 467 languages with polar interrogative particles, Dryer (2005d) found that in 272 languages, it is placed at the end of the clause (as in Chinese and Japanese); in 118 languages, it is placed at the beginning (as in Arabic and French); in 45 languages, it is placed in second position in the clause (as in Tagalog; see Martin 2004); in 8 languages, it is placed in some position other than final, initial or second position; and in 24 languages, it is placed in 'either of two positions' (e.g., either initially or finally). Initial position and final position are, of course, interpersonally significant; they are *juncture prosodies* in the clause as a move in dialogue (see Matthiessen 2004) and second position seems to be favoured for interpersonal elements in a number of languages. Initial position is also textually significant; in languages where the Negotiator appears in initial position, it is very likely that it is given thematic status since it is likely that the beginning of the clause is associated with thematic status. This is certainly the case in (Modern Standard) Arabic.

The placement of the interrogative particle may also be variable, being determined by textual considerations – more specifically by what is the Focus of the interrogative clause (Dryer 2005d: 375), as in Tamil (Krishnamurti 2003: 416) and Quechua. In Huallaga Quechua, the interrogative particle *–chu* appears after the verb in the unmarked case, but when a particular element of the clause is the focus of the question, this particle is placed after it (Weber 1989: 325–7).

(2) A language may have a system of SPEECH LEVEL operating together with the systems of MOOD and (SUBJECT) PERSON. Languages with such a system for enacting what we might call the interpersonal distance between speaker and addressee – distance in terms of some combination of power ('vertical' distance) and familiarity ('horizontal' distance) – vary considerably with respect to how pervasive 'speech level' distinctions are within the system of MOOD. We can postulate a cline from minimal speech level influence on mood to maximal influence. At the 'minimal' pole of the cline, we find examples familiar from languages spoken in western Eurasia and in Europe, where there is typically (with exceptions such as English and Irish) a two-term distinction in person between 'tu' and 'vous' (see Brown and Gilman 1960), a distinction that is most likely to be grammaticalized in the 'imperative' mood, as in German and French. At the 'maximal' pole of the cline, we find examples familiar from languages spoken in eastern Eurasia, and East and South-East Asia, where there is often a multi-term distinction in person and in mood, as in Japanese, Korean and Thai. The intersection of the systems of speech level and mood is set out and illustrated for Korean in Table 6.8 (based on information in Sohn 1999: 269ff; see also S. E. Martin 1992: 306).

6.3.3.5 Variation in MOOD systems viewed 'from below'

MOOD systems also vary with respect to how the terms in these systems – the mood types – are realized along the syntagmatic axis, as shown for a small sample of languages in Teruya *et al.* (2007). As already noted, this variation in realization can be characterized as variation in the medium of realization – intonation, segment or sequence, and (in the case of segmental realization) rank of realization. These possibilities are set out in Table 6.9. Realization by means of intonation often accompanies segmental or sequential realization so it is likely to be very wide-spread as a medium of realization of modal distinctions, but intonation may also serve as the only medium of realization.

Drawing on Dryer (2005b), we can illustrate this variation in media of realization for 'polar interrogative' clauses: see the map in Figure 6.7 (where interrogative clitics are grouped with interrogative particles).[25] Dryer's study is based on a sample of 842 languages. As in the case of the realization of other mood types, intonation may operate together with segmental or sequential realization; but there are a number of languages in which intonation is the only medium of realization. In descending order, the most common forms of realization are as follows:

- Segmental – 687 (82%): interrogative particle (including interrogative clitics) – 520 (62%), interrogative verbal affixes – 155 (18%), mixture of the two – 12 (1.4%);
- Intonational, intonation only – 138 (16%);
- Sequential ('interrogative word order') – 12 (1.4%).

Table 6.8 Intersection of the systems of mood and speech level in Korean (based on information in Sohn 1999: 269)

	free				bound
	indicative		imperative		
	declarative	interrogative	jussive	propositive	
plain	pi ka o-n-ta rain NM come-IN-DC	pi ka o-ni rain NM come-Q pi ka o-(nu)-nya rain NM come-IN-Q	yeki tto w-ala here again come-IM	yeki tto o-ca here again come-PR	
intimate	pi ka w-a rain NM come-INT	pi ka w-a rain NM come-INT	yeki tto w-a here again come-INT	yeki tto w-a here again come-INT	
familiar	pi ka o-ney rain NM come-FML	pi ka o-na rain NM come-Q pi ka o-nu-nka rain NM come-IN-Q	yeki tto o-key here again come-IM	yeki tto o-sey here again come-PR	
blunt	pi ka o-o rain NM come-BLN	pi ka o-o rain NM come-BLN	yeki tto o-o here again come-BLN	yeki tto o-p-si-ta here again come-AH-RQ-PR	
polite	pi ka w-a.yo rain NM come-POL	pi ka w-a.yo rain NM come-POL	yeki tto w-a.yo here again come-POL	yeki tto w-a.yo here again come-POL	
deferential	pi ka o-p-ni-ta rain NM come-AH-IN-DC	pi ka o-p-ni-kka rain NM come-AH-IN-Q	yeki tto o-si-p-si-o here again come-SH-AH-RQ-IM	yeki tto o-si-p-si-ta here again come-SH-AH-RQ-PR	

Table 6.8 *Continued*

	free		imperative		bound
	indicative				
	declarative	**interrogative**	**jussive**	**propositive**	
neutral	pi ka o-n-ta rain NM come-IN-DC	pi ka o-(nu)-hya rain NM come-IN-Q	yeki tto o-la here again come-IM	yeki tto o-ca here again come-PR	pi ka on-nu-nya ko rain NM come-IN-Q QT mut-sup-ni-ta ask-AH-IN-DC

Table 6.9 Types of syntagmatic realizations of terms in systems of MOOD – variation in medium of realization and location of realization in terms of rank

RANK	MEDIUM		
	intonation	**segment**	**sequence**
clause	intonation contour [common – many languages, e.g. Spanish]	modal particle serving as Negotiator [common – many languages, e.g. languages spoken in E and S-E Asia – Mandarin, Cantonese, Japanese, Vietnamese, Thai; languages spoken in West Africa; languages spoken in the Americas]	relative sequence of Subject and Finite [very restricted, certain languages spoken in Europe, mostly Germanic, e.g. English, German, Danish, Swedish, French and Czech; and certain Austronesian languages, e.g. Malay, Palauan; and Warakena, an Arawakan language]
group	–	modal clitics [intermediate between particle and affix; e.g. Tagalog]	–
word	–	modal verbal affixes [fairly common, often on polysynthetic languages, e.g. Inuit; but also, e.g., in Korean; geographically, languages spoken in S Asia, e.g. Kannada, in Central Asia, in the Americas]	–

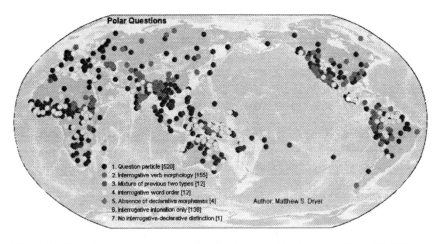

Figure 6.7 Polar interrogative clauses: distribution of realization types (Dryer 2005b)

Intonation is no doubt a very important realizational resource in many – perhaps most – languages; but there are certainly some tone languages in which its role is reduced because pitch is as it were used up locally within syllables to make distinctions of a 'phonemic' kind. This is the case in Cantonese (see, e.g., Matthews and Yip 1994) but not in Mandarin (see Halliday and McDonald 2004: 342).

In languages where segmental realization is the main strategy, the segment is often closely associated with the verbal group serving as Predicator – necessarily so in languages where the segment is a verbal affix, and commonly so in languages where the segment is a 'particle' serving as Negotiator in the interpersonal structure of the clause.

Variation across languages 'from below' – variation in forms of realization of terms in interpersonal systems – is important from the point of view of typology and comparison; but as far as translation is concerned, variation 'from below' should in principle not be an issue. When one translated from one language to another, it does not matter how different mood types are realized – intonationally, segmentally or sequentially, as long as comparable distinctions are maintained in the source language and the target language.

6.3.3.6 *Variation in* MOOD *systems viewed 'from above'*

Let us now turn to variation in mood systems as seen 'from above', from the vantage point of the semantic system of SPEECH FUNCTION. This is the type of variation that is most likely to affect translation: as just noted, variation 'from below' will be dealt with automatically in translation and variation 'from roundabout' will be significant in the first instance in so far as it relates to variation 'from above' (see Matthiessen 2001, on the environments of translation).

We noted above that there is a difference in the grammaticalization of propositions and proposals. In particular, while commands are regularly grammaticalized congruently as the 'imperative' mood, offers rarely if ever have a mood type of their own; and even the imperative mood is 'at best a fringe category' (Halliday 1984: 20). This fringe status is no doubt related to interesting variation in the realization of different types of command that research has revealed within particular registers. In other words, variation 'from above' can be – and has been – observed at the instance pole of the cline of instantiation in sets of comparable texts and in sets of parallel texts, and the source of this variation can be located midway along the cline of instantiation, in the region of registers/text types.

Let us begin with an example of realizations in different languages of a recommendation taken from a software manual: see Figure 6.8. The English and German realizations are quite similar, both being congruent realizations of a recommendation as a subtype of command. In the English text (which is presumably the original), the recommendation is realized as an

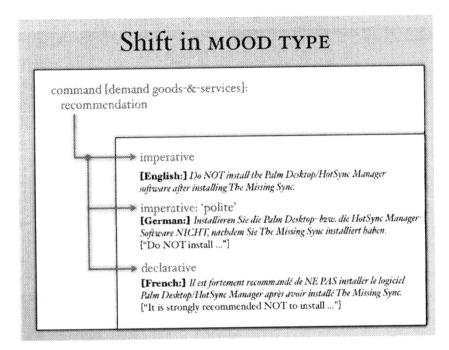

Figure 6.8 Differences in MOOD TYPE in the realization of a recommendation in a software manual in English, German and French

'addressee imperative' clause in 'negative' polarity, and in the German text, the recommendation is similarly realized as an 'addressee imperative' clause in 'negative' polarity. There is one difference in the German version: whereas English does not differentiate 'imperative' clauses according to the tenor of the relationship between speaker and addressee, German does – more specifically, according to power (status) and familiarity (contact); the German clause is of the 'polite' rather than of the 'non-polite' variety (see Steiner and Teich 2004: 147–8). (This is an example of an inevitable in translation between two languages where one is systemically more elaborated than the other with respect to one or more dimensions.) The French realization differs from both the English and German ones; in the French text, the recommendation is realized incongruently (metaphorically) by a 'non-interactant declarative' clause plus a (non-finite) clause representing the action not to be undertaken. This is an explicitly objective form of recommendation: *'it is strongly recommended not to install...'* instead of *'(you) do not install...!'*. (By characterizing the differences in terms of realization in mood type, we do not of course mean to suggest that there are no semantic differences between the French clause on the one hand and the English and German ones on the other.)

By simply examining the MOOD systems (as opposed to the SPEECH FUNCTION systems) of the three languages, we would not be able to predict that the French realization of the recommendation would be different from

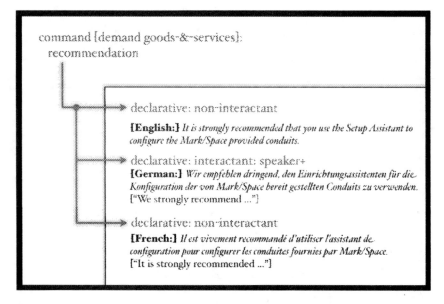

Figure 6.9 Differences in MOOD TYPE in the realization of a recommendation in a software manual in English, German and French

the English and German ones. It is of course perfectly possible that the differences are purely instantial – that is, that it does not reflect a more general pattern of differences among the languages. In the same manual, there are other recommendations; and in the realization of one of them, English and French use fairly similar strategies (though the French version is more impersonal than the English one), the kind of explicitly objective strategy used in the French version in Figure 6.8, whereas German uses an explicitly subjective strategy ('we strongly recommend ...'): Figure 6.9. However, if the differences are not purely instantial, it is very likely to be a property of the register of instructional texts since researchers (see Teich 1999; Murcia-Bielsa 1999, 2000; and Lavid 2000) in the last decade or so have revealed subtle differences of precisely this registerial kind.

Teich (1999) shows that even though the mood systems of English, French and German are comparable in many respects as far as the basic mood types go when we compare them at the potential pole of the cline of instantiation, interesting differences show up when we focus on features of particular registers, as illustrated by the examples from the register of instructional texts in Figure 6.10. Here a 'modulated' 'declarative' clause in German corresponds to 'imperative' clauses in English and French. Teich (*op cit.*: 200) comments on the implications of examples such as those set out in Figure 6.9:

In order to account for translational choices such as the ones illustrated above, a model of cross-linguistic variation must be able to account for

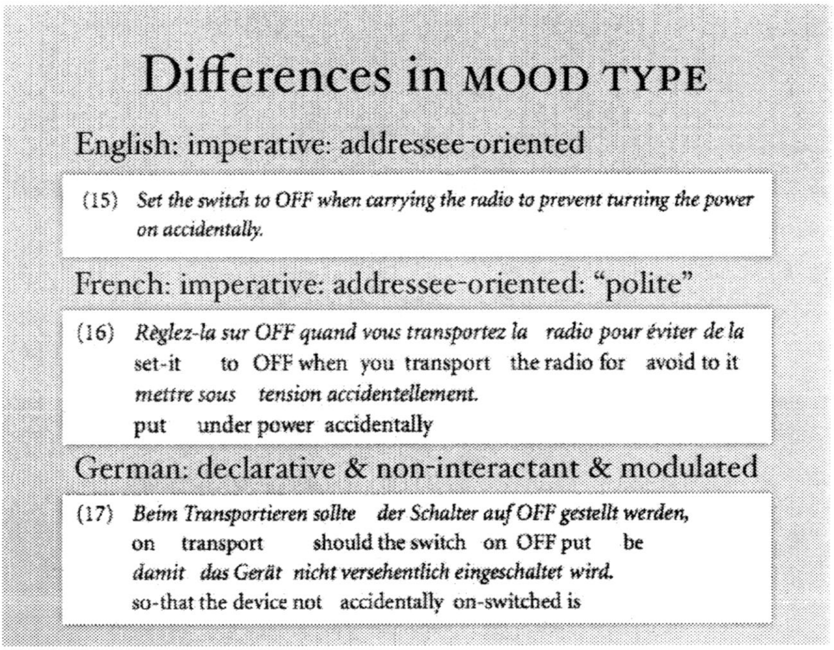

Differences in MOOD TYPE

English: imperative: addressee-oriented

(15) *Set the switch to OFF when carrying the radio to prevent turning the power on accidentally.*

French: imperative: addressee-oriented: "polite"

(16) *Réglez-la sur OFF quand vous transportez la radio pour éviter de la*
      set-it   to OFF when you transport the radio for avoid to it
      mettre sous tension accidentellement.
      put   under power accidentally

German: declarative & non-interactant & modulated

(17) *Beim Transportieren sollte der Schalter auf OFF gestellt werden,*
      on   transport   should the switch on OFF put   be
      damit das Gerät nicht versehentlich eingeschaltet wird.
      so-that the device not accidentally on-switched is

Figure 6.10 Differences in mood type across three languages in the realizations of recommendations in instructional texts (examples from Teich 1999)

cross-linguistic variation in texts, not only in systems. What is important to realize is that this kind of variation is not arbitrary, but functionally motivated variation, i.e., variation according to situational contexts. This is what is commonly called register. In the same way as we find the reflex of cross-linguistic variation in linguistic systems in translation, we find variation across languages in the deployment of those systems according to context. A linguistic mode of translation must therefore take into account cross-linguistic registerial variation as well as cross-linguistic system variation.

In a study of comparable instructional-procedural texts in English and Spanish, Murcia-Bielsa (2000) found interesting similarities and differences between the two languages in the use of commands (what she calls 'directives', following the literature on speech acts). She identifies the different grammatical forms of realization in English and Spanish; we have tabulated these for ease of comparison in Table 6.10 and visualized the relative frequencies of the different forms of modal realization in Figure 6.11. As can be seen from the table and the graph, Murcia-Bielsa's study shows that English and Spanish realize instructional commands by means of the same basic mood types, favouring 'imperative' clauses over 'modulated declarative' ones, and favouring 'modulated declarative' clauses over 'temporal'

Table 6.10 Realizations of instructional commands in English and Spanish instructional-procedural texts (based on Murcia-Bielsa 2000: 122–4)

MOOD			projection of operation	English		Spanish	
				Example	Frequency [n=1087]	Example	Frequency [n=716]
imperative	[jussive]		straight	Lift the handset.	79.30%	*Descuelgue el microteléfono.* 'Lift the handset.'	52.93%
	impersonal: informal [infinitive][26]		straight	–	–	*Limpiar con una esponja o estropajo metálico, utilizando detergentes o jabones ricos en sosa.* 'Clean with a sponge or metallic scourer, using detergent or soda-rich soap.'	21.23%
indicative	declarative	modal: modulated: obligation: high	straight	*This instruction book must be kept handy for reference.*	6.99%	*Siempre debe cubrir los alimentos a freír.* 'You must always cover the food when frying.'	12.43%
		modal: modulated: obligation: median	straight	*The bowl should be washed and dried after use and before storage.*	7.73%	–	–
		temporal: present	straight	*… optimum performance is achieved by preheating the grill for about 1 minute.*	1.29%	*Se abre el Grill y se coloca el alimento a asar.* 'It is opened the grill and it is placed the food to be cooked.'	3.21%

Table 6.10 *Continued*

MOOD		projection of operation	English		Spanish	
			Example	Frequency [n=1087]	Example	Frequency [n=716]
indicative	declarative	temporal: future / straight	*The minimum height of the cooker will be set at 900mm to the top of the hob.*	1.29%	*Una vez conectado el aparato, se seleccionará con el interruptor la temperatura de aire deseada.* 'Once the device is connected, the required temperature will be selected with the knob.'	3.21%
		temporal & verbal ('we recommend') / relational ('it is advisable') ('appeal to reader') / projected	*It is a good idea to clean the inside of your fridge after defrosting.*	4.69%	*Es conveniente limpiar periódicamente los casquetes y quemadores.* 'It is convenient to clean frequently the caps and burners.'	6.98%

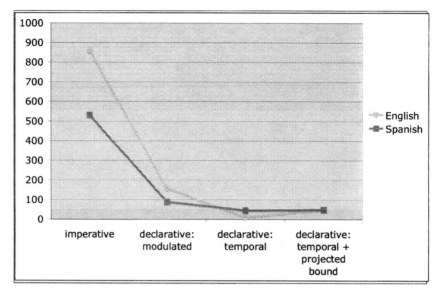

Figure 6.11 Frequency of different forms of realization in instructional commands in English and Spanish instructional-procedural texts (based on counts in Murcia-Bielsa 2000: 122)

ones. However, against the background of these very similar tendencies, there are also interesting differences. For instance, 'imperative' clauses are relatively more common than 'declarative' ones in English than in Spanish; and straight (non-projected) 'temporal' declaratives are considerably less common in English than in Spanish.

In addition to documenting the realizational differences between English and Spanish summarized above, Murcia-Bielsa also develops an account of the meaning of the different forms of realization in the two languages. This account is formulated in terms of the semantics of SPEECH FUNCTION in reference to the context of the kind of instructional-procedural register from which the texts have been taken. She presents two system networks for instructional commands, bringing out similarities and differences between English and Spanish. A key consideration in these two system networks is how essential to the task at hand a given action is: she postulates a 'necessity cline for actions' (p. 130), showing how the different types are distributed along this cline (p. 132).

As part of a trilingual study of administrative forms 'dealing with pension and family benefits, unemployment and disability allowances' in English, German and Italian, Lavid (2000) examined the realization of instructional commands and questions in these three languages. Let us continue to focus on instructional commands. These commands (which she calls 'requests') are concerned with the processing of the form by members of the general public – enabling them to tick boxes, send the forms to the appropriate

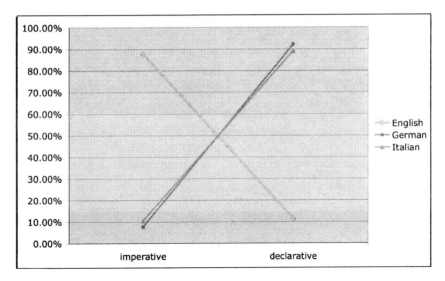

Figure 6.12 Relative frequencies of 'imperative' and 'declarative' realizations of instructional commands in administrative forms in English, German and Italian (based on counts in Lavid 2000)

authority, and so on. The differences in the realizational labour between 'imperative' and 'declarative' clauses in these languages are quite striking: see Figure 6.12. While English strongly favours 'imperative' clauses (with *please*) over 'declarative' ones (approximately 90/10), German and Italian strongly favour 'declarative' clauses over 'imperative' ones (again approximately 90/10). Lavid (*op cit.*: 82) comments:

> As shown by the results of the analysis presented above, there exist statistically significant differences in the realisation strategies selected by different speech communities when requesting action or demanding information from users in administrative forms. While, in general, the English forms favour the use of direct or congruent structures to realise requests and questions, the Italian/German forms opt for the more indirect patterns. Thus, when requesting action from users, the English forms prefer to use the imperative mood structure preceded by the politeness marker '*please*', while the Italian/German forms choose the declarative mood instead. [...]
>
> These linguistic preferences can be interpreted as a reflection of the different socio-cultural contexts where the forms are produced. The English forms reflect a conscious effort on the part of the British administration to achieve a clear, friendly, and polite tone which will reduce the distance with the citizens and increase their audience acceptance. This is achieved, among other devices, through the direct expression of requests and questions, two speech acts which abound in administrative forms. By

contrast, the Italian/German forms are written in a socio-cultural context where the administration has only recently begun to show concern for effective official communication. The choice of indirect, impersonal expressions to realise requests and questions reflects this distant and formal attitude of the administration toward its users.

The English orientation towards the interpersonal has also been contrasted with the German orientation towards the ideational in research by Juliane House and her research team, and they have shown how German is being influenced by English styles of meaning in certain registers (e.g. Baumgarten *et al.* 2002).

6.3.3.7 Commands in a context-based text typology

Let us now locate these studies within a context-based typology/topology of registers (text-types). This typology is originally due to Jean Ure, and has been developed further by us for application to various research contexts (see Matthiessen *et al.* in preparation). Any context-based typology of this kind should include parameters from all three of the fundamental facets of context – field, tenor and mode. We have explored different combinations, but we will present one based on one field parameter (socio-semiotic process) and two mode parameters (medium and turn) here (see Figure 6.13), since in the area of typology we will discuss here, there is a strong association between field and tenor in certain respects. The parameters are:

(1) Field:
• semiotic processes:
• processes of expounding (general knowledge),
• reporting (on sequences of particular events, or description of particular entities),
• recreating various aspects of socio-semiotic life,
• sharing (experiences and values),
• recommending (courses of action),
• enabling (courses of action), and
• exploring (positions and values)
• social processes
• doing (social action, with semiotic processes facilitating)

(2) Mode:
• medium:
• spoken
• written
• turn:
• dialogic
• monologic

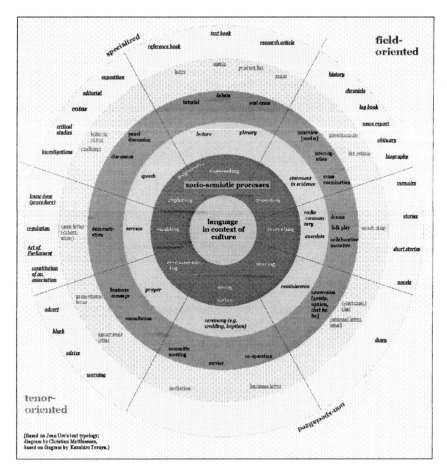

Figure 6.13 Context-based register typology/topology – field values (socio-semiotic process: expounding, reporting, recreating, sharing, doing, recommending, enabling, exploring) represented by different sectors; mode values represented by concentric circles (from inner to outer: spoken and monologic, spoken and dialogic, written and dialogic, written and monologic)

The studies we have drawn examples from above have all been concerned with the same region of our typology/topology – contexts characterized as 'enabling', 'monologic' and 'written': these are the contexts where instructional-procedural texts operate. This is why we have characterized the commands used in these examples 'instructional commands': they are commands but of the special kind issued by speakers (writers) to addressees who can be presumed to be willing to comply because they are hoping to be enabled to perform operations that form part of an activity sequence with an outcome that is desirable to them.

Such instructional commands are characteristic of texts instantiating registers within a region within the enabling sector of Figure 6.13. We can take this further by viewing the exploring – enabling – recommending – doing part of Figure 6.13 from an interpersonal point of view, in terms of interpersonal systems of COMMODITY (cf. Figure 6.3) and of ASSESSMENT, more specifically of assessment in terms of MODALITY. 'Doing' is a social process – a process of performing a service or of exchanging goods. 'Recommending' and 'enabling' are semiotic processes, but they imply contexts of 'doing' – recommending or enabling a course of action (doing); so they are also concerned with goods-&-services in the first instance rather than with information. 'Doing' contexts involve the exchange of goods-&-services, as in teamwork activities, while 'recommending' and 'enabling' contexts can be interpreted from an interpersonal point of view in terms of modality of the modulation subtype, as shown in Figure 6.13. 'Recommending' context and one subtype of 'enabling' context are concerned with modulation of the 'readiness' subtype. 'Recommending' contexts relate to the 'willingness' subtype of readiness. There are two basic subtypes; the addressee can be assumed to be willing to undertake a course of action (as in consultation contexts) and the recommendation is for the addressee's benefit, or else the addressee can be assumed not to be willing to undertake a course of action (as in advertising contexts) and the speaker has to persuade him/her. One type of 'enabling' context relates to the other kind of readiness – ability; the addressee can often be assumed to be willing to undertake some course of action, but not able, so in need of empowerment through instruction. The other type of 'enabling' context relates to the 'obligation' kind of modulation: these are contexts of regulating the addressee's behaviour, as in regulations, laws and constitutions. This is one of the early contexts of socialization, and Halliday's (1973) example of an account of a register-specific semantic system shows what semantic strategies are available to a mother in controlling a young boy's behaviour – more specifically, in preventing him from playing on a construction site again. (This is in a sense on the borderline between enabling of the regulating kind and recommending of the warning kind.)

If we focus on commands – on the combination of 'demand' and 'goods-&-services' (in initiating moves), we can see that they operate in different contexts in 'enabling', 'recommending' and 'doing' contexts and their subtypes, as shown in Figure 6.14 and illustrated in Figure 6.15 in reference to the examples taken from Teich (1999): see Table 6.11. Tenor distinctions

Table 6.11 Type of socio-semiotic process in field and characteristic type of command

socio-semiotic process	subtype	MODULATION		characteristic type of command
enabling	empowering	readiness	ability	instructional command
	regulating	obligation		deontic command
recommending	exhorting	readiness	willingness	exhortative command
	advising	readiness	willingness	consultative command
doing		readiness	willingness	facilitative command

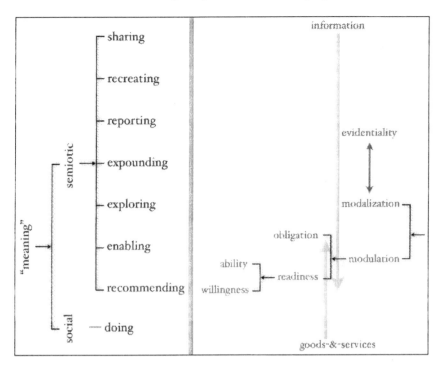

Figure 6.14 Socio-semiotic processes and interpersonal correlates in the systems of SPEECH FUNCTION (commodity) and MODAL ASSESSMENT

having to do with social distance between speaker (writer) and addressee – with power (status, 'vertical relations') and with familiarity (contact, 'horizontal relations') – further differentiate the contexts, of course. The registers that have been investigated by Teich (1999), Lavid (2000) and Murcia-Bielsa (2000) are all in the public sphere as opposed to the private sphere: in terms of familiarity, writer and addressee are strangers, with the writer addressing some segment of the general public. This means among other things that they are subject to policy – institutional policies that may vary from one country to another, or from one institution to another, as Lavid's (2000) comments quoted above point out.

Let us consider some examples from one other register that can be located within the typology/topology in Figure 6.13 and characterized interpersonally in terms of Figure 6.14. This is advertising – the register operating in 'written' 'monologic' 'recommending' contexts of the variety where it can be assumed that the addressee must be persuaded to be willing to undertake the commands being issued by the writers of texts. The register of advertising covers a considerable range of variants; in terms of the types identified by Hermerén (1999: 15–16), we will focus on 'consumer advertising' within 'commercial' advertising – advertising 'directed at a mass audience' (for systemic functional discussions of advertising in relation to translation, see

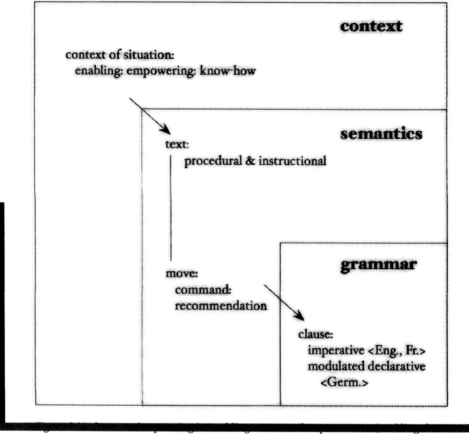

addressee to undertake an activity sequence)

Steiner 2004; Taylor and Baldry 2001). More specifically, we will draw our examples from hard-sell advertising of this kind – advertisements promoting an actual product as opposed to a company image (soft-sell advertising). In this context, advertisements in English typically have a nuclear generic element of Appeal, which is realized semantically by one or more commands. These commands are in turn realized by unmarked 'imperative' clauses:

BOOK NOW [Leadership forum]
Enjoy legendary service on Royal Silk Class. [Airline]
Enjoy our legendary service on THAI. Earn bonus miles with Royal Orchid Plus. [Airline]
Take you super up, up and away. Ask an ANZ Super Hero to help you conquer the new superannuation rules. Call ANZ Financial Planning ... or visit ... [Bank service]
Subscribe to The Bulletin to go in the draw to win. [Magazine subscription]

Subscribe now to Australia's leading magazine for thinkers. [Magazine subscription]

Such commands are often couched in very positive appealing terms, and the action demanded is often represented as one that is beneficial to the addressee (like *Enjoy . . . !*); so the commands characteristic of advertisements sometimes shade into offers. Not surprisingly, meanings of positive appraisal (see, e.g., Martin and White 2005) are 'at high risk' in the Appeal segment of advertisement of the kind we are focusing on, and they are equally at high risk in the Motivation segment that serves to support the Appeal (see Fries 1993, 2002, for an account of the foregrounding as New information of positive features of the product being advertised). For example:

> [Motivation:] Our Korean spirit is moving in the air. It's a spirit of untiring, ceaseless effort and ageless charm that flows from Korean traditions perfected over thousands of years. A spirit of advancing into the future with one of the world's most modern fleets. And a spirit that soars around the globe to 44 cities in 21 countries on 5 continents. *[Appeal:] Fly with us and you'll experience the dedication to excellence that could only be Korean.*

Using the conventions of Rhetorical Structure Theory (e.g., Mann *et al.* 1992), we can analyse this advertisement as a semantic complex organized in terms of rhetorical (logico-semantic) relations of motivation and elaboration: see Figure 6.16. This analysis shows that the text is organized around a nuclear segment, realized by a 'command' move, and that this nuclear segment is

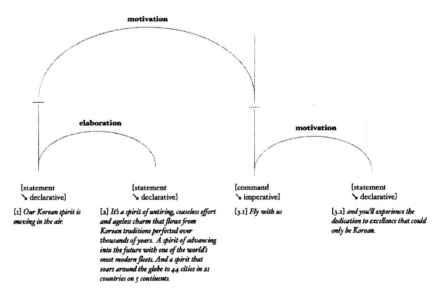

Figure 6.16 Rhetorical-relational analysis of Korean Air advertisement

supported by satellites, realized by 'statement' moves. (The nuclear segment is like the 'head act' in CCSARP studies of requests and apologies.) The nuclear segment of an advertisement of this kind is the Appeal element, which is likely to be realized by one or more commands. This segment is successful if the addressee complies with the command, or at least becomes more willing to do so as a result of reading the advertisement. So the command itself may be supported by a purpose or a motivating consequence that is positively appraised (*to go in the draw to win; and you'll experience the dedication to excellence that could only be Korean*), and the bulk of the advertisement is likely to be taken up by the Motivation element. This element is realized by propositions – predominantly by statements with positive appraisal selections, but also by questions posing problems that the product being advertised is presented as providing a solution to. The presence of the propositions of the Motivation element thus serves to boost the chance of success of the nuclear command(s) of the Appeal element. This speech functional environment is character-istic of commands in 'recommending' contexts where the addressee can be assumed not to be willing to comply with the recommendation at the outset, and it contrasts rather sharply with the speech functional environment of commands in enabling contexts.

In English, the 'exhortative' commands (see Table 6.11) realizing the Appeal element of advertisements are, as we have seen, typically realized by 'imperative' clauses. However, in Chinese, they are not, even though Chinese has been characterized as 'direct' (see Gu 1990; Hong 1999). For example, a Chinese advertisement for the new Toyota Crown has a declarative clause as 'Appeal': *It (the new experience) begins today,* while that for Air China ends with *Air China accompanies you wherever you go.* Exhortative commands are usually left implicit in Chinese to give readers/consumers more thinking space: Don't rush to make a decision; Just think about it. The mindset of the Chinese consumers is like this: if you push them too hard, people will take a step back or totally walk away from the advertised product. In other words, it is fairly uncommon in the Chinese advertisements to explicitly urge consumers to take immediate actions as it is often the case in English.

Similarly, in Japanese, 'exhortative' commands realized by addressee-oriented 'imperative' clauses are uncommon. One fairly common strategy appears to be an appeal realized as a suggestion instead of an 'exhortative' command corresponding to *let's* in English, as illustrated in Table 6.12. Here the inclusiveness of the appeal serves to create a sense of togetherness in doing something attractive.

These brief examples illustrate how the system of SPEECH FUNCTION varies registerially from one context to another within a given language (as suggested by Table 6.11) and how languages vary from one another within comparable registers in how they 'deploy' the resources of the system. Since languages are in a sense nothing more than the aggregate of registers that instantiate them (cf., e.g., Halliday 1978; Matthiessen 1993), one interesting question from a comparative and typological point of view is to the variation

Table 6.12 Examples of Japanese advertisements with suggestions as Appeal

Advertisement	Appeal
	料理の腕をあげるより、このワインをあけよう。 [Goal:] *Ryoori no ude o* [Proc:] *ageru yori,* [Goal:] *kono wain o* [Proc:] *akeyoo.* [27] 'Instead of improving (your) cooking skill, let's open this wine.'
	年齢から自由になろう。 *Nenrei kara jiyuu ni naroo.*[28] 'Let's be liberated from age'.

in registerial repertoires across languages. For example, the general register of advertising is of course a fairly recent development within 'recommending' contexts – and one that will certainly not be common to all languages, since it presupposes a certain kind of socio-economic system. With respect to the speech functional category of 'command', it is interesting to consider the cline of obligation that operates in 'enabling' contexts in particular and which has been identified and explored by Iedema in his work on organizational discourse (e.g. Iedema 1997, 2000). This cline is one that involves what he calls *demodulation*. At one pole of the cline, the addressee is very clearly assigned modal responsibility for complying with a 'command'. However, at the other pole of the cline, the assignment of modal responsibility is totally diffuse. This is achieved through grammatical metaphor – in a move from interpersonal metaphor to the ideational metaphor: instead of being enacted interpersonally, the obligation is construed experientially. Adapting an example from Iedema (2000: 51), we can illustrate the cline as follows: [interpersonal, congruent pole] *Pay the fee! – You must pay the fee! – You are required to pay the fee! – It is required that you pay the fee. – The requirement is that you pay the fee. – The requirement is the payment of the fee. – Fee payment is requirement* [experiential, incongruent pole]. The closer we get to the experiential pole of the cline, the more characteristic the examples of prototypical bureaucratic discourse – the discourse for regulating people's behaviour in modern nation states; and such discourse is characteristic only of certain languages, of standard languages operating in modern nation states.

6.3.3.8 *The systems of* SPEECH FUNCTION *and* MOOD *in cross-cultural pragmatics*

As we have seen, variation in MOOD across languages seen 'from above', from the point of view of the system of SPEECH FUNCTION operating in different registers located in different contexts, has been investigated through the analysis of parallel and comparable texts. This body of research can also be linked to investigations within the tradition of cross-cultural pragmatics, including Blum-Kulka *et al.* (1989) and studies developing this seminal work.

In cross-cultural pragmatics, researchers have investigated variation in the grammatical realization of different speech functions – in particular, of requests and apologies – in a number of different languages around the world (CCSARP, the Cross-Cultural Speech Act Realization Project), starting with seven different languages (Blum-Kulka and Olshtain 1984), including three varieties of English – six Indo-European (Germanic: British, American and Australian English, German, Danish; and Italic: French) and one Afro-Asiatic (Semitic: Hebrew). Typically using a 'discourse completion test', researchers characterize a situation for speakers selected for a given study and ask them to produce the kind of move that they would use in the kind of situation that has been described to them. Recent contributions include Qanbar's (2006) study of requests and apologies in Yemeni Arabic, Hong's (1999) discussion of Chinese, and Aoyama's (n.d.) study of requests between customers and workers and between co-workers in a Japanese coffee shop. These are significant in that they add three languages – two of which are from different families from the original set of languages, Chinese being from the Sino-Tibetan family and Japanese being from the Japanese family, while Yemeni Arabic constitutes another sample of an Afro-Asiatic language from the Semitic branch.

Let us begin by interpreting the characterization in cross-cultural pragmatics of variation of speech act realization. From our point of view,

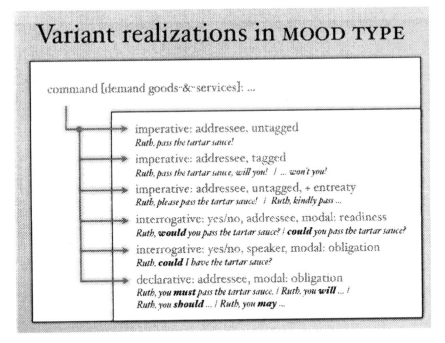

Figure 6.17 Different grammatical realizations of a demand for goods-&-services

requests are demands for goods-&-services (see Figure 6.3), falling within the category of 'command', and the variant realizations of requests that have been studied in cross-cultural pragmatics can be characterized in terms of the interpersonal grammar of MOOD, (SUBJECT) PERSON, DEICTITY (including MODALITY) and metaphorical extensions involving PROJECTION. This spread of variant realizations is illustrated for a demand to 'Ruth' for goods-&-services – more specifically, a demand for tartar sauce – in Figure 6.17.[29] Here the 'imperative' clauses are congruent realizations, while the 'interrogative' and 'declarative' ones are incongruent realizations.

In cross-cultural pragmatics, a number of different kinds are recognized and characterized in terms of how they are realized. We have re-interpreted these different forms of realization in terms of systemic functional descriptions of interpersonal systems in the grammar of English (e.g. Matthiessen 1995; Halliday and Matthiessen 2004), and set them out in Table 6.13. (Note that this account does not include intonation, even though tone – the direction of the major pitch movement – is a central resource in the realization of interpersonal meaning.)

The different grammatical realizations of commands shown in Table 6.13 are not, of course, synonymous; they all represent subtly different kinds of 'command'. In systemic functional descriptions, these realizational alternatives would need to be taken account of when we extend the system of SPEECH FUNCTION set out in Figure 6.3 for each language being investigated, on the

Table 6.13 Grammatical realizations of the 'head act of a request sequence' based on Blum-Kulka *et al.* (1989: 18) and re-interpreted in terms of the systemic functional description of English[50]

congruence	projection	MOOD TYPE		FINITENESS	SUBJECT PERSON	CCSARP term	example
congruent	straight	imperative		–	addressee	'mood derivable'	*Ruth, pass the tartar sauce!*
incongruent	straight	indicative	declarative	modulation: obligation	addressee	'obligation statement'	*Ruth, you must pass the tartar sauce.*
			interrogative: yes/no	modulation: readiness	addressee	'query preparatory'	*Ruth, could you pass the tartar sauce?*
			declarative	(present)	(non-interactant)	'strong hint'	*Ruth, this herring needs some tartar sauce.*
				(modalization: probability)	(non-interactant)	'mild hint'	*Ruth, this herring would be better with some tartar sauce.*
	projected	idea	imperative	–	addressee	'want statement'	*Ruth, I want you to pass the tartar sauce.*
		locution	imperative	–	addressee	'performative'	*Ruth, I am asking you to pass the tartar sauce.*
					addressee	'hedged performative'	*Ruth, I would like to ask you to pass the tartar sauce.*

model provided by Hasan (1996: Chapter 5). Extending the description of the speech functional system in a given language would immediately raise questions about what dimensions are embodied in the more delicate speech functional options that are realized by different grammatical patterns of the kind shown in Table 6.13. The dimensions embodied in more delicate distinctions are likely to operate in the multi-dimensional space of tenor – in particular, in the tenor space of interpersonal relations defined by power (status, 'vertical relations') and familiarity (contact, 'horizontal relations'). This would be consistent with Brown and Gilman's (1960) account of pronouns of 'power' and 'solidarity'. It would also be consistent with accounts of 'speech level' in languages such as Japanese and Korean: the choice of the appropriate 'speech level' is an interpersonal calibration of the tenor of the relationship between speaker and addressee based on considerations of both power and familiarity.

While researchers in cross-cultural pragmatics have not produced descriptions based on detailed networks of speech functions (speech acts), they have been centrally concerned with the factors that differentiate the different realizational patterns. These factors have been explored in terms of generalizations across languages about politeness strategies, relating this work to the account of universals of politeness proposed by Brown and Levinson (1978, 1987).

The extent to which it is possible to make generalizations across languages is of course a central issue not only for cross-cultural pragmatics, but for multilingual studies in general. In a study of requests in Chinese, Hong (1999) comments:

> Concerning requests, one of the most significant findings of the *CCSARP* was that all languages studied overwhelmingly preferred conventionally indirect request strategies (e.g., *Could I borrow your notes?*; *Would you mind moving your car?*).
>
> However, there remains a distinct Western bias in the CCSARP: all of the languages and varieties studied (except Hebrew) are either Germanic or Romance, and all of the cultures are either Western or heavily influenced by Western culture.... On the basis of all the differences discussed in this paper, we can see clear evidence that Chinese does not fit into the universal category of conventionally indirect requests claimed by CCSARP.

After exploring the different types of realization of 'requests' in Chinese, Hong concludes:

> The most distinctive feature of the linguistic realisation of requests in Chinese is the application of basic action verbs that indicate the desired action directly. As a result, Chinese finds imperatives the most proper and efficient way of making a request. On the contrary, imperatives are the least used in English in making a request. Due to this difference, the Chinese

qing 'please' has a stronger sense of politeness and is more often used to achieve the politeness effects than any other modal verbs similar to the English ones such as *would* or *could*. Furthermore, certain common expressions in English such as *Would you mind* are seldom linked with avoidance of imperative in Chinese to show moderate politeness. There are also some other interesting facts found in Chinese which prove that certain linguistic strategies in this particular speech act are either unavailable in or inapplicable to English. On the basis of all the differences discussed in this paper, we can see clear evidence that Chinese does not fit into the universal category of conventionally indirect requests claimed by *CCSARP*.

Other studies of Chinese include Gu (1990), contributions in Kasper (1995), and Domizio (2004). Gu (1990: 241–2) rejects Brown and Levinson's (1987) model of politeness as far as Chinese is concerned.[31]

In his account of politeness principles in Chinese, Gu (1990: 256) is concerned with standard Chinese: 'It is the language taught at schools and universities, and used in mass media. The politeness phenomena this paper captures can be said to be generally prevailing among the (fairly) educated.' This comment is important since it raises the question of variation within a language-culture complex. The original CCSARP involved around 400 college-level students in discourse completion tests, and Qanbar's (2006) study involves Yemeni university students. However, research has shown very clearly that there is significant variation between different social groups, as in Hasan's (1989) report on a large-scale study of speech functional selections in families that can be roughly characterized as middle class vs. working class. This variation is known as *codal variation*, and it also needs to be taken account of in cross-cultural studies: it is important to try to differentiate and control for both variation according to culture and variation according to class-based subcultures.

6.4 Multilingual studies: engagement with the phenomenal realm – reflection and action

In mapping out multilingual studies, we differentiated between the object of study – what we have called the phenomenal realm – and the process of studying this realm, as shown in Figure 6.1 above. This view of multilingual studies is based on field: the phenomenal realm represents the experiential domain aspect of field (the 'subject matter' or 'topic domain'), and the process of engaging with this domain represents the socio-semiotic process aspect of field. (Since the view we have presented of multilingual studies is based on field, it needs to be supplemented by considerations of tenor and mode – considerations of who is taking part in multilingual studies and of what role the studies are playing in the contexts in which they are being conducted. We leave these important aspects for another occasion.)

In exploring the experiential domain of multilingual studies, we have used the major dimensions of the global organization of language in context – the cline of instantiation and the hierarchy of stratification. In exploring the engagement with this domain in multilingual studies – the process of studying itself (see Matthiessen and Nesbitt 1996), we can draw on the basic distinction between *reflection* ('theory') and *action* ('application') (see Halliday 1985): see Figure 6.18.

So far, we have been concerned with multilingual studies in *reflective mode* – that is, with investigations of patterns of similarity and difference we can identify when we compare and contrast different languages. However, multilingual studies also have an *active mode*. In the active mode, we draw on the findings from the reflective mode and develop and implement programmes for action such as machine translation programmes, educational programmes in second/foreign language teaching and in translator and interpreter training, and administrative programmes in language policy and planning. And experiences from implementation in the active mode feed back into the reflective mode.

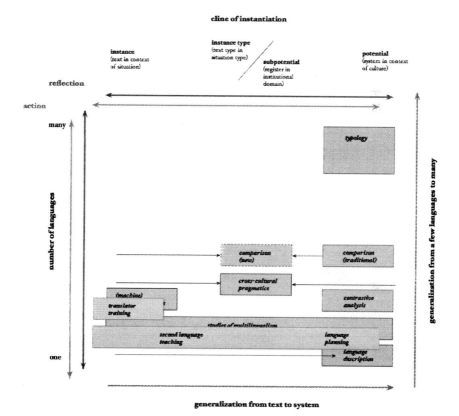

Figure 6.18 The meta-context of multilingual studies in terms of field – phenomenal realm and socio-semiotic process

Within the reflective mode, the tendency has been to focus on *language* as a system–text continuum. Within the active mode, the tendency has been to focus on *people*, ranging from persons (as in second language teaching and translator training) to whole communities (as in language planning and policy). However, the relationship between language and person has, of course, been a focus within systemic functional linguistics since Firth (1950), put it on the pre-systemic research agenda: see, e.g., Halliday 1978; Butt 1991 – and Halliday 1975, for the ontogenetic perspective; and there are cross-over points in multilingual studies between the focus on language and the focus on people; for example, longitudinal studies of persons learning how to mean in a second language (see Ortega and Byrnes forthcoming) shed light on how persons gain access to the collective meaning potential of a language and develop their own personalized meaning potentials.

In systemic functional linguistics, there has always been interaction between the reflective and active modes of different areas of multilingual studies. Examples of systemic functional contributions to the active mode of multilingual studies are set out in Table 6.14.

These contributions to the active mode of multilingual studies cover a wide range of activities within different institutions, but they all have in common the fact that they are theoretically empowered and feed back into the development of theory. For example, Gibbons and Markwick-Smith (1992) demonstrate the power of the system network as a representation of the meaning potential of language. Using the system of MODALITY as an example, they show how the systemic description of this part of the interpersonal meaning potential can be used to diagnose problems in discourse produced by learners of English in comparison with comparable discourse produced by native speakers. Once the problems have been diagnosed, it is then possible to develop tasks that will help students access and master areas of the meaning potential they do not yet control.

Table 6.14 Examples of systemic functional contributions to the active mode of multilingual studies

Activity	Contributions
Second language education	Hasan (1978), Gibbons and Markwick-Smith (1992), Hasan and Perrett (1994), Lock (1995), Schleppegrell and Colombi (2002), Gibbons (2004), Byrnes (2006), Caffarel (2006), Teruya (2006), Rinner and Weigert (2006)
Translator training	Taylor (1998), Taylor and Baldry (2001), Shore (2001), Kim (in press, 2007, in preparation)
Machine translation	Halliday (1956), Bateman (1989), Steiner (1992)
Multilingual text generation	Bateman *et al.* (1991), Bateman (1996) [the KPML system], Matthiessen *et al.* (1998), Bateman *et al.* (1999); many contributions based on KPML[32]

Just as there are many possible dialogues between areas of multilingual studies in the reflective mode, there are also many possible dialogues between areas in the active. For example, the modelling of multilingual systems that was originally developed in the context of text generation (e.g. Bateman *et al.* 1991 and Bateman *et al.* 1999) could serve as a framework for exploring how people learn how to mean in a language other than their mother tongue and how the ability to mean in another language may also include the ability to switch or mix 'codes'. One can imagine a new kind of 'contrastive analysis' emerging at the intersection of the modelling work on multilingual systems and the analysis of texts in the text-based approach to comparative linguistics discussed above.

6.5 Conclusion

In this chapter, we have used interpersonal systems in general and the inter-personal system of MOOD in particular (in its stratal environment) to explore the coherence of multilingual studies as an area of research (reflection) and application (action). We have shown how areas such as typology, cross-cultural pragmatics, comparison, translation studies and second language teaching are all related within a coherent field of multilingual studies – even though they have tended to be pursued in insulation from one another.

Thus we believe that multilingual studies can emerge as a formation of related activities of research and application approaches, findings and resources are shared to a larger extent than they have been so far. Over time it is possible to build up resources that can be shared across these different activities, supporting intelligent applications of the kind targeted by The Halliday Centre at City University of Hong Kong. These resources will include descriptions of the systems of particular languages, profiles of registers within particular languages and analysis of texts within these registers, as well as comparative profiles and typological generalizations that similarly extend along the cline of instantiation from system to instance.

The different areas within multilingual studies relate to one another in a number of ways, but the middle region of the cline of instantiation is likely to define a particularly productive focus for work within the different areas within the next decade or so. For example:

- Typology and comparison: investigation of comparable texts from comparable registers building on the work by Teich (1999), McCabe (1999), Lavid (2000), Murcia-Bielsa (2000) and Rose (2005) mentioned above and linking to the CCSARP experience in cross-cultural pragmatics;
- Translation (studies): investigation of parallel texts from comparable registers (e.g. Steiner 2004), drawing on the experiences with work in machine translation focused on particular registers ('sublanguages'; see, e.g., Kittredge 1987);

- Second language education: development of coherent programmes and curricula based on a progression through different registers (genres); see, e.g., the 'Developing Multiple Literacies' project led by Heidi Byrnes (e.g. 1998) at Georgetown University 1997–2000,[33] Rinner and Weigert (2006), and Martin (2006) on the notion of a 'spiral curriculum' based on genres providing 'learner pathways'.

Focusing on particular registers is also a way of managing the complexity of research and application within multilingual studies in a way that is entirely natural – that is, in a way that derives from the nature of language itself.

As we have indicated throughout our discussion of multilingual studies, we believe that it has great potential as a unified field of reflection and action, and there is clear evidence that part of this potential is already being actualized – this sometimes being a case of returning to the insights from an earlier period. At least two considerations in addition to those we have mentioned strengthen our sense of optimism about the potential of multilingual studies empowered by systemic functional linguistics.

On the one hand, systemic functional work is being published in – and being translated into – an ever-increasing range of languages, including Chinese, Vietnamese, Japanese, Danish, German, Norwegian, Swedish, French, English, Portuguese, and Spanish. This means that researchers have to become increasingly multilingually aware to keep up with the literature in systemic functional linguistics. At the same time, it also means that technical terms in systemic functional linguistics now exist in all the languages mentioned, and scholars are contributing systemic functional glossaries in additional languages – the most recent contribution probably being Holmberg and Karlsson (2006), with a valuable glossary that includes English, Swedish, Danish and Norwegian terms. It also means that the body of work in systemic functional linguistics can itself serve as an interesting 'corpus' for multilingual studies. For example, Halliday's *Introduction to Functional Grammar* has been translated into Japanese and Vietnamese and is being translated into Spanish and Portuguese; and his key paper on computing meaning (Halliday 2002) has been translated into both Chinese (by Wu Canzhong) and Japanese (by Kazuhiro Teruya). There is by now a considerable body of work in a number of different languages that we could have added to our list of references for our overview in this chapter.

On the other hand, an increasing number of systemic functional linguists are becoming involved in two or more areas of multilingual studies. These include scholars working on the description of a particular language and on some other area of multilingual studies such as comparison, translation, translation studies and second language education. Or – to adopt a language-based perspective – more and more languages are being explored in an increasing number of areas within multilingual studies.

Notes

1   See Bateman (1996) and the KPML website: www.fb10.uni-bremen.de/anglistik/langpro/kpml/README.html.

2   For example (from Domizio 2004: 116): 'It is a summer afternoon, and you have parked your bicycle right in front of a grocery store in Xidan shopping center, Beijing. You come out after forty minutes of shopping and find that your bicycle has been taken away because it was blocking traffic. Try to convince the police officer to return your bicycle.'

3   This is of course not a necessary condition; see, e.g., Aoyama (n.d.), who presents a study of request strategies at a Japanese workplace based on naturally occurring examples.

4   The contributions to this book are couched in terms of generative linguistics, more specifically principles and parameters (with references to interpretations within the minimalist programme), and they make no reference to interpersonal systems. However, from a systemic functional point of view, many of the issues raised relate to the modal structure of the clause as a move in dialogic exchange, e.g., the conditions under which the Finite and the Predicator are fused in a language, and the position of modal Adjuncts in relation to the Finite and the Predicator.

5   From *Le retour du mort* ('The dead man's return'), *French Short Stories 2* (Parallel Texts). Penguin, pp. 84–5.

6   From *Une maison Place des Fêtes* ('A house in the Place des Fêtes'), *French Short Stories 2* (Parallel Texts), Penguin, pp. 108–09.

7   From *Une maison Place des Fêtes* ('A house in the Place des Fêtes'), *French Short Stories 2* (Parallel Texts). Penguin, pp. 116–17.

8   From *Trafic de chevaux* ('Traffic in horses'), *French Short Stories 2* (Parallel Texts). Penguin, pp. 208–09.

9   From *Le tabac vert* ('Green tobacco'), *French Short Stories 2* (Parallel Texts). Penguin, pp. 32–3.

10   From *Une maison Place des Fêtes* ('A house in the Place des Fêtes'), *French Short Stories 2* (Parallel Texts), Penguin. pp. 110–11.

11   From *Jimmy* ('Jimmy'), *French Short Stories 2* (Parallel Texts). Penguin, pp. 138–9.

12   From *Les fourmis* ('The ants'), *French Short Stories 2* (Parallel Texts). Penguin, pp. 50–51.

13   From *Les fourmis* ('The ants'), *French Short Stories 2* (Parallel Texts). Penguin, pp. 54–5.

14   From *Le tabac vert* ('Green tobacco'), *French Short Stories 2* (Parallel Texts). Penguin, pp. 40–41.

15   From *Les fourmis* ('The ants'), *French Short Stories 2* (Parallel Texts). Penguin, pp. 74–5.

16   From *Le tabac vert* ('Green tobacco'), *French Short Stories 2* (Parallel Texts). Penguin, pp. 24–5.

17 From *Le tabac vert* ('Green tobacco'), *French Short Stories 2* (Parallel Texts). Penguin, pp. 34–5.

18 From *Les fourmis* ('The ants'), *French Short Stories 2* (Parallel Texts). Penguin, pp. 56–7.

19 From *Le retour du mort* ('The dead man's return'), *French Short Stories 2* (Parallel Texts). Penguin, pp. 84–5.

20 From *Le retour du mort* ('The dead man's return'), *French Short Stories 2* (Parallel Texts). Penguin, pp. 86–7.

21 This is a cline, and the pronominal items of a given language may occupy more than one position, as in French. Finding the location of pronouns along the cline can be difficult; for example, Creissels (2000: 235, 238) comments that subject pronominals in a number of languages spoken in West Africa have traditionally been wrongly analysed as free pronouns when they are in fact bound pronominal affixes.

22 Incidentally, the map represents Swedish as having a binary system. This is true in that there is the traditional distinction between *du* 'tu' and *ni* 'vous' – although there was a campaign for a couple of decades to do away with the 'polite' *ni* form (the so-called 'du reformen') in the interest of equality. However, alongside this binary system, there is also a strategy similar to that found in East and South-East Asia: depending on the tenor of the relationship between the speaker and the addressee (see Ervin-Tripp's, 1972, study of terms of address in American English, showing by means of a flow chart the strategies for determining (in our terms) the tenor of the relationship between speaker and addressee), the 'polite' *ni* form could be rather impolite; to be really polite, one would have to use title (academic, professional or kinship) plus name, given name or surname (depending on the tenor of the relationship). For example, if one wanted to ask one's GP if he had had a pleasant vacation, one would say *Har Dr. Ahrent haft en trevlig semester?* ('Has Dr. Ahrent had a pleasant vacation?') instead of *Har ni haft en trevlig semester?* ('Have you:POLITE had a pleasant vacation?'). Using the 'polite' *ni* form would have been a put-down. As an aside to this comment, subtle distinctions of this kind tend to get lost in typological studies simply because of the challenge of managing the complexity of it all. But this is of course a powerful argument in favour of text-based typology.

23 The term 'mood' has been used in related but different senses in the literature. Here we use 'mood' to refer to the grammatical correlate of the semantic system of SPEECH FUNCTION: the interpersonal system of the clause that is a grammaticalization of the semantic system of SPEECH FUNCTION. This has also been called 'sentence type' in the typological literature. The term 'mood' has also been used traditionally to refer to (interpersonal) forms of the verb such as the 'indicative' vs. the 'subjunctive'. Lower-ranking systems of this kind will be referred to as MODE. (Sometimes the term 'mode' has been used to refer to what we call 'mood'.) Mode distinctions have 'bound' clauses as their domain

in a number of languages, where they are largely conditioned by their grammatical environment, and can be related to modality (see Bybee *et al.* 1994: Ch. 6); but they may also operate in 'free' clauses, as in wishes realized by the 'subjunctive' form of the verb. The term 'indicative' has similarly been used in a few related but different senses. We use 'indicative' in contrast to 'imperative' to refer to the clausal mood category for exchanging information – encompassing 'declarative' and 'interrogative', but the term 'indicative' has also traditionally been used in contrast to 'subjunctive' as a term for a verbal mode.

24 The Predicator may be absent (i) for textual reasons when the clause is 'elliptical' or (ii) for experiential reasons when the clause is 'relational' and the Process is absent in the unmarked 'relational' clause type in a given language.

25 Spanish is indicated as having 'interrogative word order', which seems surprising; it would seem to be more appropriate to characterize it as 'intonation only'.

26 For the interpretation of the infinitive in this context as a realization of the Predicator in informal impersonal imperative clauses, see Teruya *et al.* (2007: section 4.3).

27 From *With,* July 2007. Kodansha, p. 95.

28 From *Orange Page,* 2 June 2007. Tokyo Inshokan, p. 55.

29 The 'imperative' realization *Ruth, pass the tartar sauce!* is the original one; it occurs in a recreated doing context in *Spring and Port Wine,* the filmed version of a play by Bill Naughton.

30 There is one additional category in the CCSARP scheme: 'suggestory formulae'.

31 Brown and Levinson's (1978: 64) original study was based on three languages from three different families – English, Tamil (Dravidian) and Tzeltal (Mayan).

32 For languages, see: www.fb10.uni-bremen.de/anglistik/langpro/kpml/genbank/generation-bank.html.

33 www3.georgetown.edu/departments/german/programs/curriculum/index.html.

References

Abelen, E., Redeker, G. and Thompson, S. A. (1993), 'The rhetorical structure of US-American and Dutch fund-raising letters.' *Text,* 13(1): 323–50.

Anwyl, P., Matsuda, T., Fujita K., and Kameda, M., (1991), 'Target-language driven transfer and generation', in *Proceedings of the 2nd Japan–Australia Joint Symposium on Natural Language Processing* (JAJSNLP 91), 2–5 October 1991, Kyushu Institute of Technology, Iizuka City, Japan.

Aoyama, K. (n.d.), 'Request strategies at a Japanese work place.' Available April 2007 at: www.webpages.acs.ttu.edu/kaoyama/aoyama10.pdf.

van der Auwera, J., Dobrushina, N. and Goussev, V. (2005), 'Imperative-hortative systems', in Haspelmath *et al.* (eds), pp. 294–7.

van der Auwera, J. and Lejeune, L. with P. Umarani and V. Goussev (2005.) 'The morphological imperative', in Haspelmath *et al.* (eds), pp. 286–9.

Bateman, J. A. (1988), 'Aspects of clause politeness in Japanese: an extended inquiry semantics treatment.' *The 26th Annual Meeting of the Association for Computational Linguistics,* 147–54.

Bateman, J. (1989), 'Upper modelling for machine translation: a level of abstraction for preserving meaning.' *Eurotra-D Working Paper* 12.

Bateman, J. A. (1996), *KPML: The KOMET-Penman (Multilingual) Development Environment: Support for Multilingual Linguistic Resource Development and Sentence Generation.* Darmstadt: GMD/Institut für Integrierte Publikations-und Informationssysteme (IPSI) (Release 1.0). {Studie der GMD}, {302}.1996. 276p. (ISBN 3–88457–304–7; ISSN 0170–8120)

Bateman, J. A., Matthiessen, C. M. I. M. Nanri, K. and Zeng, L. (1991), 'The rapid prototyping of natural language generation components: an application of functional typology', in the *Proceedings of IJCAI 91, Sydney.* Volume 2. New York: Morgan Kaufman, pp. 966–71.

Bateman, J. A., Matthiessen, C. M. I. M. and Zeng, L. (1999), 'Multilingual language generation for multilingual software: a functional linguistic approach.' *Applied Artificial Intelligence: An International Journal.* Volume 13.6: 607–39.

Baumgarten, N., House, J. and Probst, J., (2004), 'English as *lingua franca* in covert translational processes.' *The Translator,* 10(1): 83–108.

Biber, D. (1995), *Dimensions of Register Variation: A Cross-linguistic Comparison.* Cambridge: Cambridge University Press.

Blum-Kulka, S. and Olshtain, E. (1984), 'Requests and apologies: a cross-cultural study of speech act realization patterns (CCSARP).' *Applied Linguistics,* 5: 196–213.

Blum-Kulka, S., House, J. and Kasper, G. (eds) (1989), *Cross-cultural Pragmatics: Requests and Apologies.* Norwood, NJ: Ablex.

Bolinger, D. L. (1978), 'Intonation across languages', in J. H. Greenberg, C. A. Ferguson and E. A. Moravcsik (eds), *Universals of Human Language: Volume 2 Phonology.* Stanford: Stanford University Press, pp. 471–524.

Brown, P. and Levinson, S. (1978), 'Universals in language use: politeness phenomena', in E. N. Goody (ed.), *Questions and Politeness: Strategies in Social Interaction.* Cambridge: Cambridge University Press, pp. 56–290, 295–310.

Brown, P. and Levinson, S. (1987), *Politeness: Some Universals in Language Usage.* Cambridge: Cambridge University Press.

Brown, R. and Gilman, A. (1960), 'The pronouns of power and solidarity', in T. A. Sebeok (ed.), *Style in Language.* Cambridge, MA.: MIT Press, pp. 253–76.

Butt, D. G. (1991), 'Some basic tools in a linguistic approach to personality: a Firthian concept of social process', in F. Christie (ed.), *Literacy in Social Processes: Papers from the Inaugural Australian Systemic Functional*

Linguistics Conference, Deakin University, January 1990. Darwin: Centre for Studies of Language in Education, Northern Territory University, pp. 23–44.

Bybee, J., Perkins, R. and Pagliuca, W. (1994), *The Evolution of Grammar: Tense, Aspect, and Modality in the Languages of the World*. Chicago: The University of Chicago Press.

Byrnes, H. (1998), 'Constructing curricula in collegiate foreign language departments', in H. Byrnes (ed.), *Learning Foreign and Second Languages: Perspectives on Research and Scholarship*. New York: MLA, pp. 262–95.

Byrnes, H. (ed.), (2006), *Advanced Instructed Language Learning: The Complementary Contribution of Halliday and Vygotsky*. London and New York: Continuum.

Caffarel, A. (2006), 'Learning advanced French through SFL: learning SFL in French', in H. Byrnes (ed.), *Advanced Instructed Language Learning: The Complementary Contribution of Halliday and Vygotsky*. London and New York: Continuum, pp. 204–24.

Caffarel, A., Martin, J. R. and Matthiessen, C. M. I. M. (eds) (2004), *Language Typology: A Functional Perspective*. Amsterdam: Benjamins.

Calzada Pérez, M. (2007), *Transitivity in Translating: The Interdependence of Texture and Context*. Frankfurt: Peter Lang.

Catford, J. C. (1965), *A Linguistic Theory of Translation*. London: Oxford University Press.

Chafe, W. and Nichols, J. (eds) (1986), *Evidentiality: The Linguistic Coding of Epistemology*. Norwood, NJ: Ablex.

Chang, C. (2004), *English Idioms and Interpersonal Meanings*. Guangzhou: Sun Yat-sen University Press.

Chisholm, W., Milic, M. T. and Greppin, J. A. C. (1984), *Interrogativity: A Colloquium on the Grammar, Typology, and Pragmatics of Questions in Seven Diverse Languages, Cleveland, Ohio, October 5th, 1981*. (Typological Studies in Language.) Amsterdam: Benjamins.

Comrie, B. (1981), *Language Universal and Linguistic Typology*. Oxford: Blackwell.

Connor, U. (1996), *Contrastive Rhetoric: Cross-cultural Aspects of Second-language Writing*. Cambridge: Cambridge University Press.

Creissels, D. (2000), 'Typology', in Heine, B. and D. Nurse (eds), *African Languages: An Introduction*. Cambridge: Cambridge University Press, pp. 231–59

Croft, W. (1990), *Typology and Universals*. Cambridge: Cambridge University Press.

Dobrushina, N., van der Auwera, J. and Goussev, V. (2005), 'The optative', in Haspelmath *et al.* (eds), pp. 298–301.

Domizio, H. L. (2004), 'Initiating, sustaining and concluding social transactions: an analysis of roleplay performance in the Oral Proficiency Interview.' *Journal of Language and Linguistics*, 3(1): 109–38.

Dorr, B. J. (1994), 'Machine translation divergences: a formal description and proposed solution.' *Computational Linguistics*, 20.4: 597–633.

Downing, A. and Lavid, J. (1998), 'Information progression strategies in administrative forms: a cross-linguistic study', in A. Sánchez-Macarro and R. Carter (eds), *Linguistic Choice Across Genres: Variation in Spoken and Written English (Current Issues in Linguistic Theory 158)*. Amsterdam: John Benjamins, 99–115.

Dryer, M. (2005a), 'Negative morphemes', in Haspelmath *et al.*, pp. 454–7.

Dryer, M. (2005b), 'Polar questions', in Haspelmath *et al.*, pp. 470–73.

Dryer, M. (2005c), 'Position of interrogative phrases in content questions', in Haspelmath *et al.*, pp. 378–81.

Dryer, M. (2005d), 'Position of polar question particles', in Haspelmath *et al.*, pp. 374–7.

Ellis, J. (1966), *Towards a General Comparative Linguistics*. The Hague: Mouton.

Ellis, (1987), 'Some "dia-categories"', in R. Steele and T. Threadgold (eds), *Language Topics: Essays in Honour of Michael Halliday*. Volume II. Amsterdam: Benjamins, pp. 81–94.

Ervin-Tripp, S. (1964), 'An analysis of the interaction of language, topic and listener.' *American Anthropologist*, 66(6): 86–102. Reprinted in J. A. Fishman (ed.) (1968), *Readings in the Sociology of Language*. The Hague, Paris and New York: Mouton, pp. 192–211.

Ervin-Tripp, S. (1972), 'On sociolinguistic rules: alternation and co-occurrence', in J. Gumperz and D. Hymes (eds), *Directions in Sociolinguistics: The Ethnography of Communication*. New York: Holt, Rinehart, and Winston, pp. 213–50.

Fries, P. H. (1993), 'Information flow in written advertising', in J. Alatis (ed.), *Language, Communication and Social Meaning*. Washington, DC: Georgetown University Press, pp. 336–52.

Fries, P. H. (2002), 'Theme and New in written advertising', in Huang Guowen and Wang Zongyan (eds), *Discourse and Language Functions*. Shanghai: Foreign Language Teaching and Research Press, pp. 56–72.

Gentzler, E. (1993), *Contemporary Translation Theories*. London and New York: Routledge.

Gibbons, J. and Markwick-Smith, V. (1992), 'Exploring the use of a systemic semantic description.' *International Journal of Applied Linguistics*, 2.1: 36–51.

Gibbons, P. (2004), 'Changing the rules, changing the game: a sociocultural perspective on second language learning in the classroom', in G. Williams and A. Lukin (eds), *The Development of Language: Functional Perspectives on Species and Individuals*. London and New York: Continuum, pp. 196–216.

Givón, T. (1979), *On Understanding Grammar*. New York: Academic Press.

Givón, T. (ed.) (1983), *Topic Continuity in Discourse*. Amsterdam: Benjamins.

Greenberg, J. H., Ferguson, C. and Moravcsik, E. (eds) (1978), *Universals of Human Language. Volume 4. Syntax*. Stanford: Stanford University Press.

Grimes, J. E. (ed.), (1978), *Papers on Discourse*. Dallas: Summer Institute of Linguistics.

Gu, Y. (1990), 'Politeness phenomena in modern Chinese.' *Journal of Pragmatics*, 14: 237–58.

Gussenhoven, C. (2004), *The Phonology of Tone and Intonation*. Cambridge: Cambridge University Press.

de Haan, F. (2005a), 'Semantic distinctions of evidentiality', in Haspelmath *et al.* (eds), pp. 314–17.

de Haan, F. (2005b), 'Coding of evidentiality', in Haspelmath *et al.* (eds), pp. 318–21.

Haegeman, L. (ed.) (1997), *The New Comparative Syntax*. London and New York: Longman.

Halliday, M. A. K. (1956), 'The linguistic basis of a mechanical thesaurus, and its application to English preposition classification.' *Mechanical Translation*, 3.3: 81–8.

Halliday, M. A. K. (1960 [1959]), 'Typology and the exotic', in M. A. K., Halliday and A. McIntosh (1966), *Patterns of Language: Papers in General, Descriptive and Applied Linguistics*. London: Longman.

Halliday, M. A. K. (1975), *Learning How to Mean: Explorations in the Development of Language*. London: Edward Arnold.

Halliday, M. A. K. (1978), *Language as Social Semiotic: The Social Interpretation of Language and Meaning*. London and Baltimore: Edward Arnold and University Park Press.

Halliday, M. A. K. (1984), 'Language as code and language as behaviour: a systemic-functional interpretation of the nature and ontogenesis of dialogue', in M. A. K. Halliday, R. P. Fawcett, S. Lamb and A. Makkai (eds), *The Semiotics of Language and Culture*. Volume 1. London: Frances Pinter, pp. 3–35.

Halliday, M. A. K. (1985), 'Systemic background', in J. D. Benson and W. S. Greaves (eds), *Systemic Perspectives on Discourse*. Norwood, NJ: Ablex, pp. 1–15.

Halliday, M. A. K. (1992), 'The notion of "context" in language education', in T. Le and M. McCausland (eds), *Interaction and Development: Proceedings of the International Conference, Vietnam, 30 March – 1 April 1992*. Tasmania: University of Tasmania Language Education.

Halliday, M. A. K. (2002), 'Computing meanings: some reflections on past experience and present prospects', in Guowen Huang and Zongyan Wang (eds), *Discourse and Language Functions*. Shanghai: Foreign Language Teaching and Research Press, pp. 3–25. (Translation into Japanese by Kazuhiro Teruya in the same volume; translation by Wu Canzhong in a separate volume.)

Halliday, M. A. K. (2003), 'Introduction: on the "architecture" of human language', in M. A. K. Halliday, *On Language and Linguistics. Volume 3 of Collected Works of M. A. K. Halliday*. Edited by Jonathan Webster. London and New York: Continuum, pp. 1–29.

Halliday, M. A. K. and E. McDonald, (2004), 'Metafunctional profile of the grammar of Chinese', in A. Caffarel *et al.* (eds) (qv), pp. 305–396.

Halliday, M. A. K. and Matthiessen, C. M. I. M. (2006), *Construing Experience Through Meaning: A Language-based Approach to Cognition*. Study edition. London: Continuum.

Hansen-Schirra, S. and Neumann, S. (2005), 'The CroCo Project: Cross-linguistic corpora for the investigation of explicitation in translations.' *Proceedings from the Corpus Linguistics Conference Series*, Vol. 1, no. 1, ISSN 1747–9398. www.corpus.bham.ac.uk/PCLC.

Hasan, R. (1978), 'Some sociological considerations in second language teaching', in D. E. Ingram and T. J. Quinn (eds), *Language Learning in Australian Society: Proceedings of the 1976 Congress of the Applied Linguistics Association of Australia*. Melbourne: Australia International Press.

Hasan, R. (1989), 'Semantic variation and sociolinguistics.' *Australian Journal of Linguistics*, 9: 221–75.

Hasan, R. (1996), *Ways of Saying: Ways of Meaning. Selected Papers of Ruqaiya Hasan*. Ed. C. Cloran, D. Butt and G. Williams. Open Linguistics Series. London: Cassell.

Hasan, R. and Perrett, G. (1994), 'Learning to function with the other tongue: a systemic functional perspective on second language teaching'. in T. Odlin (ed.), *Perspectives on Pedagogic Grammars*. Cambridge: Cambridge University Press, pp. 179–226.

Haspelmath, M., Dryer, M. S. Gil, D. and Comrie, B. (eds), (2005), *The World Atlas of Language Structures*. Oxford: Oxford University Press.

Haspelmath, M., König, E., Oesterreicher, W. and Raible, W. (eds) (2001), *Language Typology and Language Universals*. Berlin: Mouton de Gruyter.

Heine, B., Claudi, U. and Hünnemeyer, F. (1991), *Grammaticalization: A Conceptual Framework*. Chicago: The University of Chicago Press.

Heine, B. and Kuteva, T. (2004), *World Lexicon of Grammaticalization*. Cambridge: Cambridge University Press.

Helmbrecht, J. (2005), 'Politeness distinctions in pronouns', in Haspelmath *et al.*, pp. 186–9.

Hermerén, L. (1999), *English For Sale: A Study of the Language of Advertising*. Lund: Lund University Press.

Hirst, D. and Di Cristo, A. (eds) (1998), *Intonation Systems: A Survey of Twenty Languages*. Cambridge: Cambridge University Press.

Holmberg, P. and Karlsson, A.-M. (2006), *Grammatik med betydelse: en introduktion till funktionell grammatik*. Uppsala: Hallgren and Fallgren.

Hong, G. (1999), 'Features of request strategies in Chinese.' Lund University, Department of Linguistics: *Working Papers* 47: 73–86.

Hopper, P. (ed.) (1982), *Tense-aspect: Between Semantics and Pragmatics*. Amsterdam: Benjamins.

Hopper, P. and Thompson, S. A. (1980), 'Transitivity in grammar and discourse.' *Language*, 56: 251–99.

Hopper, P. and Traugott, E. C. (1993), *Grammaticalization*. Cambridge: Cambridge University Press. (Cambridge Textbooks in Linguistics.)

Huang, G. (2006). *Linguistic Explorations in Translation Studies: Analyses of English Translations of Ancient Chinese Poems and Lyrics.* Shanghai: Shanghai Foreign Language Education Press.

Iedema, R. (1997), 'The language of administration: organizing human activity in formal institutions', in F. Christie and J. R. Martin (eds), *Genre and Institutions: Social Processes in the Workplace and School.* London: Cassell, 73–100.

Iedema, R. A. M. (2000), 'Bureaucratic planning and resemiotisation', in E. Ventola (ed.), *Discourse and Community: Doing Functional Linguistics.* Tübingen: Gunter Narr Verlag, pp. 47–69.

Iwasaki, S. and Ingkaphirom, P. (2005), *A Reference Grammar of Thai.* Cambridge: Cambridge University Press.

Johansson, S. (2002/03), 'Viewing languages through multilingual corpora, with special reference to the generic person in English, German, and Norwegian.' *Languages in Contrast,* 4.2: 461–80.

Johnson, A. W. and Earle, T. (2000), *The Evolution of Human Societies: From Foraging Group to Agrarian State.* Stanford: Stanford University Press.

Kasper, G. (ed.) (1995), *Pragmatics of Chinese as Native and as Target Language.* Honolulu: University of Hawaii, Second Language Teaching and Curriculum Center.

Keenan, E. L. (1976). 'Remarkable subjects in Malagasy', in C. N. Li (ed.), *Subject and Topic.* New York: Academic Press, pp. 247–301.

Kim, M. (2007), 'Using systemic functional text analysis for translator education: an illustration with a focus on textual meaning.' *Interpreter and Translator Trainer,* 1.2.

Kim, M. (in press), 'Translation error analysis: a systemic functional approach', in D. Kenny and K. Ryou (eds), *Across Boundaries: International Perspectives on Translation Studies.* Newcastle upon Tyne: Cambridge Scholars Publishing.

Kim, M. (in preparation), 'Application of SFG-based text analysis in translator education: A case study of English/Korean translation'. Macquarie University, PhD thesis.

Kittredge, R., (1987), 'The significance of sublanguage for automatic translation', in S. Nirenburg (ed.), *Machine Translation: Theoretical and Methodological Issues.* Cambridge: Cambridge University Press.

Koller, W. (1979), *Einführung in die Übersetzungswissenschaft.* Heidelberg-Wiesbaden: Quelle und Meyer.

König, E. and Siemund, P. (2007), 'Speech act distinctions in grammar', in T. Shopen (ed.), *Language Typology and Syntactic Description.* Cambridge: Cambridge University Press.

Krishnamurti, B. (2003), *The Dravidian Languages.* Cambridge: Cambridge University Press.

Ladefoged, P. and Maddieson, I. (1996), *The Sounds of the World's Languages.* Oxford: Blackwell.

Lado, R. (1957), *Linguistics Across Cultures: Applied Linguistics for Language Teachers.* Ann Arbor: The University of Michigan Press.

Lavid, J. (2000), 'Cross-cultural variation in multilingual instructions: a study of speech act realisation patterns', in E. Ventola (ed.), pp. 71–85.

Liu, Y. and Yanlong Fan (2007), 'An exploration of interpersonal meanings in advertising discourse from functional grammar perspective'. *Sino-US English Teaching*, 4 (1): 40–44.

Lock, G. (1995), *Functional English Grammar: An Introduction for Second Language Teachers*. Cambridge: Cambridge University Press.

Longacre, R. (1990), *Storyline concerns and word order typology in East and West Africa*. Studies in African Linguistics, Supplement 10.

McCabe, A. (1999). 'Theme and thematic patterns in Spanish and English history texts', PhD Dissertation, Aston University.

Malinowski, B. (1922), *Argonauts of the Western Pacific: An Account of Native Enterprise and Adventure in the Archipelagoes of Melanesian New Guinea*. George Routledge and Sons.

Mallinson, G. and Blake, B. J. (1981), *Language Typology*. Amsterdam: North-Holland.

Mann, W. C., Matthiessen, C. M. I. M. and Thompson, S.A. (1992), 'Rhetorical Structure Theory and Text Analysis.' USC/ISI Report. In W. C. Mann and S. A. Thompson (eds), *Discourse Description: Diverse Linguistic Analyses of a Fund Raising Text*. Amsterdam: Benjamins, pp. 39–78.

Marasigan, E. (1983), *Code-switching and Code-mixing in Multilingual Societies*. Singapore: Singapore University Press.

Martin, J. R. (1983), 'Participant identification in English, Tagalog and Kate.' *Australian Journal of Linguistics*, 3.1, 45–74.

Martin, J. R. (1990), 'Interpersonal grammaticalisation: mood and modality in Tagalog.' *Philippine Journal of Linguistics*, 2–51. (Special Monograph Issue celebrating the 25th Anniversary of the Language Study centre, Philippine Normal College.)

Martin, J. R. (2004), 'Metafunctional profile of the grammar of Tagalog', in A. Caffarel, J. R. Martin and C. M. I. M. Matthiessen (eds), *Language Typology: A Functional Perspective*. Amsterdam: Benjamins, pp. 255–304.

Martin, J. R. (2006), 'Genre and language learning: a social semiotic perspective', MS.

Martin, J. R. and White, P. R. R. (2005), *The Language of Evaluation, Appraisal in English*. London and New York: Palgrave Macmillan.

Martin, S. E. (1992), *A Reference Grammar of Korean: A Complete Guide to the Grammar and History of the Korean Language*. Rutland, VT and Tokyo: Charles E. Tuttle.

Martinec, R. (2003), 'The social semiotics of text and image in Japanese and English software manuals and other procedures.' *Social Semiotics*, 13.1, 43–69.

Mason, I. (2003), 'Text parameters in translation: transitivity and institutional cultures', in E. Hajicova, P. Sgall, Z. Jettmarova, A. Rothkegel, D. Rothfuß-Bastian and H. Gerzymisch-Arbogast (eds), *Textologie und Translation* (Jahrbuch Übersetzen und Dolmetschen 4/2). Tübingen: Narr.

Reprinted in L. Venuti (ed.) (2004), *The Translation Studies Reader* (2nd edn). London: Routledge, pp. 470–81.

Mason, I. (2007), 'Preface', in M. Calzada Pérez (2007), *Transitivity in Translating: The Interdependence of Texture and Context*. Frankfurt: Peter Lang, pp. xv–xix.

Mathesius, V. (1975), *A Functional Analysis of Present Day English on a General Linguistic Basis*. Edited by Josef Vachek. The Hague: Mouton.

Matthews, S. and Yip, V. (1994), *Cantonese: A Comprehensive Grammar*. London: Routledge.

Matthiessen, C. M. I. M. (1993), 'Register in the round: diversity in a unified theory of register analysis', in M. Ghadessy (ed.), *Register Analysis: Theory and Practice*. London: Pinter, pp. 221–92.

Matthiessen, C. M. I. M. (1995), *Lexicogrammatical Cartography: English Systems*. Tokyo, Taipei and Dallas: International Language Sciences Publishers.

Matthiessen, C. M. I. M. (2001), 'The environments of translation', in Steiner and Yallop (eds), pp. 41–124.

Matthiessen, C. M. I. M. (2004), 'Descriptive motifs and generalizations', in A. Caffarel, J. R. Martin and C. M. I. M. Matthiessen (eds), *Language Typology: A Functional Perspective*. Amsterdam: Benjamins, pp. 537–673.

Matthiessen, C. M. I. M. (2006), 'Educating for advanced foreign language capacities: Exploring the meaning-making resources of languages systemic-functionally', in H. Byrnes (ed.), *Advanced Instructed Language Learning: The Complementary Contribution of Halliday and Vygotsky*. London and New York: Continuum.

Matthiessen, C. M. I. M. (in press a), 'The "architecture" of language according to systemic functional theory: developments since the 1970', in R. Hasan, C. M. I. M. Matthiessen and J. Webster (eds), *Continuing Discourse on Language*, Volume 2. London: Equinox.

Matthiessen, C. M. I. M. (in press b), 'The lexicogrammar of emotion and attitude in English'. To be published in a book based on contributions to the Third International Congress on English Grammar (ICEG 3), Sona College, Salem, Tamil Nadu, India, 23–27 January 2006.

Matthiessen, C. M. I. M. and J. Bateman (1991), *Systemic Linguistics and Text Generation: Experiences from Japanese and English*. London: Frances Pinter.

Matthiessen, C. M. I. M. and C. Nesbitt (1996), 'On the idea of theory-neutral descriptions', in R. Hasan, C. Cloran and D. Butt (eds), *Functional Descriptions: Theory in Practice*. Amsterdam: Benjamins, pp. 39–85.

Matthiessen, C. M. I. M., Teruya, K. and Wu Canzhong (in preparation), *Doing Discourse Analysis in Different Languages*. Book manuscript.

Matthiessen, C. M. I. M., Zeng, L., Cross, M., Kobayashi, I., Teruya, K. and Wu, C. (1998), 'The Multex generator and its environment: application and development.' *Proceedings of the International Generation Workshop 98*, August 98, Niagara-on-the-Lake, pp. 228–37.

Mauck, S. (2005), 'Typology paper.' Available April 2007 at: www.georgetown. edu/faculty/portnerp/nsfsite/Mauck_Typology.pdf.

Mauck, S., Pak, M., Portner, P. and Zanuttini, R. (2004), 'Clause Typing in Imperatives: A Cross-linguistic Perspective.' GURT 2004. Available April 2007 at: www.georgetown.edu/faculty/portnerp/nsfsite/GURT04Talk.pdf.

Mauss, M. (1925), *Essai sur le Don*. English translation by W. D. Halls (1990), *The Gift: The Form and Reason for Exchange in Archaic Societies*. London: Routledge.

Mithun, M. (1987), 'Is basic word order universal?', in R. S. Tomlin (ed.), *Coherence and Grounding in Discourse*. Amsterdam: Benjamins, pp. 281–328.

Munday, J. (2001), *Introducing Translation Studies: Theories and Applications*. London and New York: Routledge.

Murcia-Bielsa, S. (1999), 'Instructional texts in English and Spanish: a contrastive study'. Universidad de Córdoba: PhD thesis.

Murcia-Bielsa, S. (2000), 'The choice of directives expressions in English and Spanish instructions: a semantic network', in E. Ventola (ed.) (q.v.), pp. 117–146.

Nesbitt, C. N. (1994), 'Construing linguistic resources: consumer perspectives.' University of Sydney: PhD thesis.

Nettle, D. (1999), *Linguistics Diversity*. Oxford: Oxford University Press.

Nichols, J. (1992), *Linguistic Diversity in Space and Time*. Chicago: Chicago University Press.

Ochs, E., Schegloff, E. A. and Thompson, S. A. (eds) (1996), *Interaction and Grammar*. (Studies in Interactional Sociolinguistics 13.) Cambridge: Cambridge University Press.

Ortega, L. and Byrnes, H. (eds) forthcoming, *The Longitudinal Study of Advanced L2 Capacities*. Hillsdale, NJ: Erlbaum.

Pagano, A. S., Magalhães, C. M. and Fábio, A. (2004), 'Towards the construction of a multilingual, multifunctional corpus: factors in the design and application of CORDIALL.' *Tradterm*, São Paulo, 10: 143–62.

Pagano, A. S. and M. L. Vasconcellos (2005), 'Explorando interfaces: estudos da tradução, lingüística sistêmico-funcional e lingüística de corpus', in A. S. Pagano, F. A. and C. M. (eds). *Competência em tradução: cognição e discurso*. Belo Horizonte: Editora da UFMG. 177–207.

Palmer, F. R. (1986), *Mood and Modality*. Cambridge: Cambridge University Press.

Patpong, P. (2005), 'A systemic functional interpretation of Thai grammar: an exploration of Thai narrative discourse.' Macquarie University, PhD thesis.

Payne, J. R. (1985), 'Negation', in T. Shopen (ed.), *Language Typology and Syntactic Description. Clause Structure*. Cambridge: Cambridge University Press, pp. 197–243.

Payne, T. E. (1997), *Describing Morphosyntax: A Guide for Field Linguistics*. Cambridge: Cambridge University Press.

Portner, P. (2004), 'The semantics of imperatives within a theory of clause types.' MS, Georgetown University. Available April 2007 at: www.semantic-sarchive.net/Archive/mJlZGQ4N/.

Qanbar, N. Y. A. A. (2006), 'Requests and apologies in Yemeni Arabic: a socio-pragmatic study'. Central Institute of English and Foreign Languages, Hyderabad, India, PhD thesis.

Rinner, S. and Weigert, A. (2006), 'From sports to the EU economy: integrating curricula through genre-based content courses', in H. Byrnes, H. D. Weger-Gunthrap and K. A. Sprang (eds), *Educating for Advanced Foreign Language Capacities: Constructs, Curriculum, Instruction, Assessment.* Washington, DC: Georgetown University Press.

Rodrigues, R. R., Alves, D. A. S., Lacerda, P. B. G. (2006), 'A metafunção interpessoal em duas propagandas turísticas institucionais.' *Polissema,* Porto – Portugal, V. 6: 7–39.

Rose, D. (2005), 'Narrative and the origins of discourse: construing experience in stories around the world.' *Australian Review of Applied Linguistics,* 19: 151–73.

Sadock, J. and Zwicky, A. (1985), 'Speech act distinctions in syntax', in T. Shopen (ed.), *Language Typology and Syntactic Description. Volume I: Clause Structure.* Cambridge: Cambridge University Press, pp. 155–97.

Schleppegrell, M. J. and Colombi, M. C. (eds) (2002), *Developing Advanced Literacy in First and Second Languages: Meaning with Power.* Mahwah, NJ: Lawrence Erlbaum.

Shibatani, M. and Bynon, T. (eds) (1995). *Approaches to Language Typology.* Oxford: Oxford University Press.

Shopen, T. (ed.) (1985), *Language Typology and Description.* 3 volumes. Cambridge: Cambridge University Press.

Shopen, T. (ed.) (2007), *Language Typology and Syntactic Description.* 3 volumes. Cambridge: Cambridge University Press.

Shore, S. (2001), 'Teaching translation', in E. Steiner and C. Yallop (eds), *Beyond Content: Exploring Translation and Multilingual Text Production.* Berlin and New York: de Gruyter, pp. 249–76.

Siemund, P. (2001), 'Interrogative constructions', in M. Haspelmath, E. König, W. Oesterreicher and W. Raible (eds) (qv).

Siewierska, A. (2004), *Person.* Cambridge: Cambridge University Press.

Steiner, E. (1992), 'Some remarks on a functional level for machine translation.' *Language Sciences,* 14.4: 623–59.

Steiner, E. (2004), *Translated Texts: Properties, Variants, Evaluations.* Frankfurt am Main: Peter Lang.

Steiner, E. (2005), 'Hallidayan thinking and translation theory – enhancing the options, broadening the range, and keeping the ground', in R. Hasan, C. M. I. M. Matthiessen and J. Webster (eds), *Continuing Discourse on Language: A Functional Perspective. Volume 1.* London: Equinox, pp. 481–500.

Steiner, E. and Yallop, C. (eds) (2001), *Beyond Content: Exploring Translation and Multilingual Text Production.* Berlin and New York: de Gruyter.

Talmy, L. (1985), 'Lexicalisation patterns', in T. Shopen (ed.), *Language Typology and Syntactic Description. Volume III. Grammatical Categories and the Lexicon.* Cambridge: Cambridge University Press, pp. 57–149.

Talmy, L. (2000), *Towards a Cognitive Semantics*. Cambridge, MA: MIT Press.

Taylor, C. (1998), *Language to Language: A Practical and Theoretical Guide for Italian/English Translators*. Cambridge: Cambridge University Press.

Taylor, C. and Baldry, A. (2001), 'Computer assisted text analysis and translation: a functional approach in the analysis and translation of advertising texts', in E. Steiner and C. Yallop (eds) (qv), 277–305.

Teich, E. (1999), 'System-oriented and text-oriented comparative linguistic research: Cross-linguistic variation in translation.' *Languages in Contrast*, 2(2): 187–210.

Teich, E. (2003), *Cross-linguistic Variation in System and Text*. Berlin and New York: Mouton de Gruyter.

Teruya, K. (1998), 'An exploration into the world of experience: a systemic-functional interpretation of the grammar of Japanese'. Macquarie University, PhD thesis.

Teruya, K. (2006), 'Grammar as resource for the construction of language logic for advanced language learning in Japanese', in H. Byrnes (ed.), *Advanced Instructed Language Learning: The Complementary Contribution of Halliday and Vygotsky*. London and New York: Continuum, pp. 109–33.

Teruya, K (2007), *A Systemic Functional Grammar of Japanese*. 2 volumes. London and New York: Continuum.

Teruya, K., Akerejola, E., Andersen, T. H., Caffarel, A., Lavid J., Matthiessen C., Petersen, U. H., Patpong P. and Smedegaard, F. (in press), 'Typology of MOOD: a text-based and system-based functional view', in R. Hasan, C. M. I. M. Matthiessen and J. Webster (eds), *Continuing Discourse on Language: A Functional Perspective*. Volume 2. London: Equinox.

Trubetzkoy, N. (1939), *Grundzüge der Phonologie*. Prague. (Travaux du Cercle Linguistique de Prague 7.)

Ultan, R. (1978), 'Some general characteristics of interrogative systems', in J. H. Greenberg (ed.), *Universals of Human Language. Volume 4: Syntax*. Stanford: Stanford University Press, pp. 211–48.

Ventola, E. (ed.) (2000), *Discourse and Community: Doing Functional Linguistics*. Tübingen: Gunter Narr Verlag.

Wang Peng (2004), ' "Harry Potter" ' and its Chinese translation: an examination of modality system in systemic functional approach'. PhD thesis.

Weber, D. J. (1989), *A Grammar of Huallaga (Huánuco) Quechua*. Berkeley and Los Angeles: University of California Press.

Whaley, L. J. (1997), *Introduction to Typology: the Unity and Diversity of Language*. Thousand Oaks, London and New Delhi: Sage.

Wierzbicka, A. (1996), *Semantics: Primes and Universals*. Oxford and New York: Oxford University Press.

Willett, T. (1988), 'A cross-linguistic survey of the grammaticalization of evidentiality.' *Studies in Language*, 12(1): 51–97.

The Scamseek Project – Using Systemic Functional Grammar for Text Categorization

Jon Patrick
University of Sydney

7.1 Introduction

Text Classification has a tradition of treating documents to be processed as a 'bag-of-words' or n-grams, that is, the words or word groups within a text are treated as independent and uncorrelated with each other. Such a model of language is exceedingly simple but has been proven to satisfy many researchers and commercial installations. A great deal of the research on text classification has been promoted by the public release of the Reuters data, a set of newswire articles with a category scheme composed by that agency. More recently it has been released again with a larger corpus with more precise classifications.

However, the Reuters data set has many characteristics that are idiosyncratic and have led to the development of methods suited more to that data than to the general problem of document classification. Some of these characteristics are: a constrained genre of newswire article, limited scope of the category scheme, and moderately balanced class sizes. All these characteristics have encouraged an uncritical n-gram-based view of text classification which is of itself an impoverished view of the task.

The Scamseek project has sought to separate itself from the bag-of-words tradition of text classification. Rather, the project team preferred to use linguistically principled grounds to make decisions with respect to corpus analysis and feature extraction, hence the linguists played a central role and placed key demands on various other workers in the project team. In particular the model of language used in the project was Systemic Functional Grammar (SFG) (Halliday 1994). This model is a semantically oriented grammar following the traditions of Firth rather than a syntactically oriented grammar of the Chomskyan tradition. It takes the position that language usage is a matter of choice set in a configuration of hierarchically layered strata of graphics, graphology, lexicogrammar, semantics and context. Systemic grammar is a network of 'systems' that interact with each other rather than a set of rules as with generative grammar.

In computing classifications, texts of a given class, apart from a small number of very common topic words, are more closely related by the minute intricacies of a weak network or chains of correlations that persist at low levels across small sub-sets of the class and the persistent meaning they represent, rather than by large persistent clusters of resoundingly dominant word sets that trumpet the presence of their class. Hence we view the task of computing text classification as modelling significant intricacies in the collection rather than the commonplace approach of generalizing the content of classes through coarse collations of the dominant word collections that separate classes. That is, not necessarily the most common words represent the common semantic intentions of the authors. This aspect of text classes is even more true for financial scam texts.

In the general case, the use of SFG states that the social context of the text's composition dictates choices of meaning intentions which in turn influence the shape of the form of the text. For text classification the linguist's task is to make sense of the decision-making process of the author and render a description of it in a manner that might be suitable for computation. The computational linguist then has to convert the linguist's modelling of the putative essentials of the text into a computable representation in the context of the target analytical methods, which in this case is the procedures of machine learning.

Unlike other authors we place the definition of the task of text classification as machine learning in a linguistic envelop of SFG. The accuracy of any text classification system is first and foremost determined by its *span* over the total conceptual, structural and semantic spaces of the whole of the corpus. The span is determined by its ability to reach into every corner of those spaces to capture the detail of the similarities and differences which are embodied in every text that is the same as its classmates and different to its rivals. Hence the system must be comprehensive in description of what is common within family members and likewise for what is different between families. Failure to do so will confuse cousins as siblings and siblings as distant relatives. Span, therefore, has three aspects to it and an agency that gives it integrated coherence. A metaphor of the human body is used below to elucidate the tripartite nature of span. Whilst this is not a linguistically conventional manner in which to present the problem of document categorization, it aims to demonstrate how the complexity of the task is not captured by any of the current computational methods.

Conceptual Span is the description of the range of topic information at a coarse level which amounts to the skin of a classification. It holds together the bones and organs of the class body and is the most visible, masquerading as the whole being, while hiding behind its façade the true depth and complexity of the being. It is typically represented by the unigrams and like all beauty is only skin deep. Conceptual reach is the only aspect computed by current unigram approaches to text classification. In our work we have found unigrams convenient for the coarse modelling of those parts of the corpus not of interest to the client, that is, the non-scam documents.

Structural Span is the skeleton of the classification that forms the backbone of a more elegant creature. It is ubiquitous and imperceptibly variant from body to body but remains forever necessary without ever being consciously recognized, yet its variability contributes secretly to the shape of each class family. It is represented by the syntax of the delivery language and is captured computationally in fragmentary ways by n-gram analyses and feature extraction from parsings. However, this manner of computing structural reach fails to represent the notion of authorial choice between different possible structural representations as demanded by SFG. In our work we model the structure through grammatical networks and the choices of structures by computing proportions of representation between nodes at each level of the networks.

Semantic Span is most representative of the depth of the class. It is the organic part that represents the class entity in its richest complexity. It is made up of many soft and flexible parts, forever omnipresent and controlling the functioning but yet only visible through the lenses of close and detailed linguistic modelling. It is the most complicated part of the body, hidden yet contained by the skin but forever clinging to the form created by the structural skeleton. Its interconnectivity is infinitely richer than its container and its architectural frame but even more hidden than either. Its richness is what makes it the hardest part of the system to perceive, catalogue and compute. It is only identified by deep semantic analysis of the lexico grammar of the texts. We have modelled semantic reach of the corpus by building SFG semantic networks for each register in the scam component of the corpus. The registers have been identified and created from manual analysis by linguists.

Systemic Cohesion is the integration of Conceptual, Structural and Semantic Span. It represents the whole of the animate body in its entire environment and captures the essence of how the body operates as a discrete entity and also how it interacts with the world around it. Systemic Cohesion understands that the complete meaning of the text is represented not only by the components used for each type of reach but by the choices available in each case and the mental decisions made by the speaker/writers to create their representations. Hence the use of language is seen as a living entity in which choices made and the functions of these choices are meant to serve in conveying the meanings of the text. Systemic Cohesion is modelled in our computational system by the integration of the three reaches into a feature set input into a machine learner.

In effect, this modelling has led to a hybrid solution which investigates the intricacies of the particular target classes of the client with SFG analysis, while at the same time using conventional methods, that is n-grams, in part to sluice off the detritus of the classes irrelevant to the client's needs.

7.2 Scamseek project specifications

The Scamseek project was commissioned by the *Australian Securities &*
Investment Commission (ASIC), a Federal government department responsible
for administering the laws controlling the conduct of financial investments
and markets in Australia. The project was classifying webpages and two
other Internet channels.[1] The delivery time was 15 months from project
commencement. The project team consisted of two linguists, two computational linguists, three software engineers and a director. Throughout the
project there were four research assistants providing support roles, three
PhD students making exploratory research contributions and two linguist
advisors. Other part-time staff and consultants also made contributions. For
the webpage material the client provided a manually classified corpus of
about 7,500 documents.

7.3 Project operations

The Scamseek team was set up as an operational model that represented
the task as consisting of four groups with different job functions: the client,
linguists, computational linguists, and software engineers. The client was in
contact with the linguists to deal with the classification of data and in contact
with the software engineers to deal with user interface design and installation
in their operational environment. The linguists had the task of preparing
the semantic models of the data and passing them to the computational
linguists who in turn had to prototype computational methods to compute
the semantic models and devise machine learning experiments to optimize
the classifiers. The computational linguists would pass their prototype code
that algorithmically solved the processing problem to the software engineers
for efficient industrial quality implementation.

   The aim was to keep the linguists and software engineers to minimum
contact and likewise the client and the experimentalists. This configuration
operated effectively throughout the project development with two important
exceptions. As the software engineers became more experienced with the
nature of the task, their role was enhanced in two ways. The linguists from
time to time would request software to be built for investigative functions.
Whereas initially the computational linguists provided this programming
support, it was shifted to the software engineers as the configuration of
integration of data matured and required more expert knowledge to manipu-
late. Secondly, the computational linguists were shaped into producing
code that configured more easily into the existing software hence their
programming decreased as a prototype process and increased as final code,
in principle at least, at the software architectural design level. However, often
the engineers rewrote code details.

7.4 Computational linguistic research topics

7.4.1 Linguistic vs. administrative classes

One of the early problems to emerge with the project requirements was the difference between the classification scheme of the client designed to conform to an administrative perception, that is, that there are three types of scam under the law (unlicensed advisors, unregistered fundraising, and share ramping), and the linguistic manifestation of those three types. After a significant amount of linguistic analysis, a set of 19 registers was created representing subdivisions of the three scam types, that is, a separate semantic model, in terms of an SFG network, was designed for each register. The register configurations were changed a number of times and expanded when the client opted to create different subdivisions in the data. The three scam types were treated as one document class with registers and the remaining part of the corpus was classified by the client into three more classes, Other-Agency-Scams, Scam-like and Irrelevant. These classes were also divided into registers to capture the linguistic variation within the classes. However the semantic networks for the non-scam registers were only weakly developed. In all, over 70 registers were created.

7.4.2 Linguists' compilation procedures

The linguists conducted their work by a two-part strategy. Firstly they read the documents and collated them into registers and at the same time created descriptions in the form of SFG semantic networks. In the early stages the computational linguists produced n-gram feature sets that were fed to the linguists to help them guide their searches for optimal features. It was the aim of the project in principle to ensure that the highest ranking attributes in the classifier were dominated by SFG features rather than n-grams. Hence the linguists needed to create linguistic explanations for the highest ranking words and phrases selected by the n-gram computations. In the latter stages of the work the linguists were able to scrutinize documents that were incorrectly classified and attempt to adjust their SFG networks for both the register of the misclassified document and the register it was computed to belong to.

7.4.3 Specification of linguistic model

From the outset a decision was made to use a strong linguistic model to govern the direction of the work. This position was taken because the problem of identifying specialist content very thinly distributed and written in a particular manner was not believed accessible automatically by any other strategy. The use of SFG for modelling this data was strongly criticized by a referee of the original proposal as unworkable. The experimental work was conducted in a manner to evaluate this criticism and show that our original assessment was correct.

The development of the linguistic model of the registers went hand in hand with the creation of the registers. The linguists read the documents and developed small scale characterizations of them. As the work developed, documents of similar ilk were paired together until all scams were assigned to a register and described for their features of differentiation and 'scaminess'. Once the register scheme was mature, a semantic motif of 'scaminess' was extracted from the register semantic networks and used as a separate 'Persuasion' semantic network in the classifier development program.

At first, the register descriptions were collated into spreadsheets and once the team had an appreciation for the form of this data it was decided to represent it in an ontology-like form rendered by XML. The upper part of these networks conformed to the SFG grammar as generally published, and the lower part is an ever-increasing delicate rendition of the detail of the relevant content in the documents of the register. At no time was there any effort or intention to render the *whole* document in an SFG analysis but rather just those elements of the document that appeared to the linguists to represent what differentiated the register from other registers. This provided an interesting opportunity for the machine learners to assess this judgement and advise the linguists of potential over-representation in their models. An objective of the work that was never achieved was the capacity to view a document and render it with an overlay of a register semantic network and allow the linguists to do their extraction directly from the document image on the screen rather than via laborious hand collation.

Midway through the project the linguists identified that one of the scam-like registers displayed the same linguistic characteristics as documents in some other scam registers. This prompted us to question the client's criteria in the categorization process and pressed them to review their criteria. This in turn triggered a major review of the register descriptions and allocations which resulted in more scam registers and non-scam registers being created. At the same time the linguists, with increasing understanding of the nature of the corpus, advocated that greater amounts of the most structural components of the SFG model needed to be introduced into the assessment. Hence, the SFG networks for modality, interpersonal, polarity and experiential were introduced as separate networks. The resulting configuration gave more than 20 scam register networks divided into four client classes, four SFG grammar networks, and one semantic motif network ('Scaminess').

7.4.4 Small footprints of target classes

The scam class as a whole represented less than 2 per cent of the corpus in phase 1; however, with the development of the register model of the data there became registers with sizes <0.1%. This represented significant problems with underrepresented classes and led to an experimental program to alleviate its effects. Ultimately the small footprint problem was resolved by the development of the SFG networks for registers and structural phenomena. The effort spent on each individual register was related to some degree to the difficulty of separating it from other registers and therefore de facto addressed this problem.

7.4.5 Computational implementation of hybrid language model

The linguistic model can be considered to be designed in two parts. The first part was the SFG register descriptions of the most important subdivisions of the corpus, the scams. The second part was the collection of all the non-scam classes and the irrelevant material, which was the largest class (about 60 per cent) constituting three classes. The task required was to develop classifiers for the four classes (one scam and three non-scam) as well as the scam registers. Another perspective was to see the problem as multi-layered, with the need to separate large classes from each other and smaller registers within the scam class between themselves. The solution was to develop SFG networks for separating registers and use n-grams to separate the classes. This led to multiple lines of experimentation, namely,

- developing language processing functions for the system networks;
- exploring the optimum n-gram feature selection for the classes, independently of the registers;
- bringing the two solutions together to construct a combined classifier.

The SFG networks consisted of words and phrases from the texts organized in an SFG hierarchy, the upper parts reflecting the theory of SFG and the lower parts representing the greater delicacy of the documents under analysis. The leaves of the networks were initially strings chosen from the texts classified in the given register. Over time the networks were developed so that they became rich representations of the total document collection of their respective registers. As the structural shape of the networks formed, we addressed the issue of what elements of the leaves needed to be retained as strings and what elements could be treated more generically, e.g., replacing names and numbers by generic representation. Whilst planning was achieved for upgrading the networks to use more formal generative grammatical constituents as substrata for SFG elements, it was only implemented to a small degree due to lack of time.

7.4.6 Machine learning—classifier development programme

The problem of processing a very large number of irrelevant documents was treated as the unbalanced class problem following traditional Information Retrieval methods. The first strategy was to investigate the usefulness of unigram and bigram models. While using both models was successful with a list of multi-word nominal expressions, using two-grams, three-grams and four-grams, e.g. 'chief executive officer', the bigram model failed to make any statistical contribution to the results and hence was discarded as a line of investigation.

Investigations were conducted into the selection of unigram features from the set of registers and independently from the set of classes. While there was a significant overlap in the features chosen by an Information Gain metric there was still an appreciable improvement by using the feature set chosen from both the registers in the small classes and the classes in the large classes, thus giving a blend of features.

Selection of features from register semantic networks required an extensive series of experiments. The register networks performed well independently of other feature sets once they were developed to a very mature stage. Later the four grammatical networks were added which made various levels of contributions in intriguing ways. For example, the Modality grammatical network performed particularly poorly by itself on some occasions classifying no documents correctly, yet when it was added to other models it consistently improved their scores. This result indicated clearly that there is an interaction effect within the grammatical networks that exploits a weak correlation not recognizable within the individual systems themselves. It is their union and cohesion with other systems that created their strength, that is the span of the networks in unison gives the best performance results. This result is entirely predictable with the SFG model of language and further justifies its use for this task.

7.4.7 Mapping features to attributes

We use the terminology of *feature* for the linguistic phenomon on that is the target of interest, *attribute* for its numerical instantiation, and *mapping* for the computational transformation of the frequency count of the feature into its attribute representation. This distinction is unimportant for n-gram methods as the difference between features and attributes is inconsequential since the mapping transformation is trivial. This position cannot be taken in our work as the mapping transformation is different depending on the theoretical origin of the feature.

Practical implementation of the semantic networks was achieved by rendering them as trees. Raw feature counts for the networks were created by accumulating scores up the tree. SFG in principle argues that the language is choice and therefore the important aspect of understanding the difference between two texts is the choice made by the authors. Hence by this principle the relative proportions of the choice to use one part of the tree over another should be the best differentiating feature. This is the case for the grammar networks but it does not apply to the register networks. The reason is that the register networks represent the most common semantic phenomena of a given register type, rather than choices between competing ways of expression. Hence, the attributes of domain register features are mappings to accumulative scores which are unnormalized, and grammar register features are mapped to proportional scores, whereas the n-gram word tokens are frequency counts normalized by document length. Note that a deliberate decision was made not to normalize n-grams over the corpus but only over document length as the corpus was considered not to be fully representative of the potential collection and therefore would not be optimal for future data.

7.5 Results

7.5.1 Audit corpus

The results of the first evaluation of the webpage classifier for the scam classes as applied to an audit corpus are presented in Table 7.1. This corpus was unseen by the development team and made available by ASIC at the time of delivery of the beta version of the system. The processing was conducted by the ASIC staff and the project team was given one week in which to request revisions to ASIC's manual classifications. The Scamseek classifier in this instance identified four scams that had been manually misclassified by ASIC. An audit report authored and approved by both parties was completed.

Table 7.1 Performance results for an audit corpus of the phase 1 webpage classifier conducted on 21/10/2003 in the ASIC offices

	Computed Class		
ASIC Class	Scam	Non-scam	TOTAL
Scam	18	26	44
Non-scam	6	1525	1,531

The results in Table 7.1 represent performance values of: Precision = 0.75, Recall = 0.41, and F-value = 0.53 and are to be contrasted with the laboratory results of the completed system on the training corpus using ten-fold cross validation of: Precision = 0.74, Recall = 0.35, F = 0.48. A baseline 1,000 single words has F = 0.21. ASIC was entirely satisfied with these results.

7.5.2 System results

The final results of the webpage classifier for the scam classes applied to the corpus are presented in Table 7.2. ASIC did not require that a second audit corpus be assessed. Table 7.2 provides results for three separate corpora, webpages and two other corpora. The Webpages(1) result represents the system delivered to ASIC as of 30 June 2004, and Webpages(2) represents results produced at the close of the project, from investigating further solutions to the problem of a large class of irrelevant documents, but they

Table 7.2 The performance results from webpage classifier and two other classifiers for identifying scams on the Internet as delivered to ASIC

	Webpages(1)	Webpages(2)	Corpus 2	Corpus 3
Precision	.744	.767	.850	.852
Recall	.528	.655	.834	.639
F-value	.618	.707	.844	.730
Scam/non-scam texts	373/6391	373/6391	686/1483	1395/13716

have not been fully explored experimentally. The exact nature of the other corpora cannot be presented due to security obligations. The performance figures are determined by ten-fold cross-validation.

7.5.3 Performance of SFG features

The use of SFG in this project can be analysed from both qualitative and quantitative aspects. The qualitative aspects relate to the role of SFG theory driving the decision-making in terms of choosing what lines of research to follow. The quantitative aspects are indicative of future research directions that need to be pursued.

The pursuit of an SFG description of the scam class led to a number of developments, namely, the identification of the 20 scam registers and the allocation of documents into those registers. The registers are striking for their significant differences: for example, the scam register of Software focuses on the description of software functionality whereas the register of Book concentrates on the descriptions of the contents of the book, which is a very different genre. It is highly unlikely that a non-SFG method would effectively identify these two registers as belonging to the same class. Rather they are likely to create conflicts in a broad-based unigram classifier.

The process of correcting the corpus was also directed by an SFG philosophy. The manual data analysis was supported by a process where feedback from the computational classification came back to the linguists in terms of the documents that were misclassified and the unigrams that made the greatest contribution to the correct classification of each register. Hence the SFG analysis was driven by the need to describe a document in sufficient detail to have it allocated to the correct class at a minimum and hopefully the correct register, and also to claim the contribution of a significant unigram into the SFG model, hence shortcutting its contribution to the unigram model. That is, the contexts of important unigrams had to be explained from an SFG modelling perspective so that they were more contributory to the accuracy of the classification.

The SFG approach also led to the development of the 'scaminess' motif, which in effect was an integration of the commonality of the scam registers. This would not be detectable unless a topic-based computational process was applied to the corpus and these are only just now emerging in the research literature.

The quantitative results using SFG are presented in Table 7.3. The baseline performance is experiment #1437, the four-class-unigram with a result of F = 0.446.[2] against which the other results should be compared. There are six experiments testing the performance of various combinations of the grammar network and the 'scaminess' motif (#1462, #1469, #1470, #1471, #1473 and #1484), they all produce results above the baseline in the range 0.475 to 0.587, the best using only the SFG normalized network plus the 'scaminess' motif. These results show that none of the grammatical features either by themselves or in combination make a worthwhile contribution to the classification. In fact the combination of the SFG features and the 1,764 unigrams (#1454) provides nearly the best results. However, the most successful strategy is experiment #1454U with a more restricted set of unigrams and the addition of the 'scaminess' motif.

While these results may appear disappointing for the support of the value of SFG structural features, it is strong support for the general SFG modelling of the individual scam registers and its cumulative effect on the scam class as a whole. The explanation for the poor performance of the grammar models reveals a deeper issue. The models of the phenomena of Expansion, Determiners, Modality and Polarity are all treated as independent hierarchies in the computation and suffer from identification at little better than the lexical level, that is, we model them in an unsophisticated way without being able to identify variations in usage within the contexts they occur in. This limitation is created more by the lack of computational knowledge on how to reveal the parameters of context that are important and a lack of time for the linguists to do an extensive manual analysis. Hence the conclusion at this stage is that we don't have enough knowledge on how to compute the contexts for these phenomena beyond those that are irrelevant to the task.

Table 7.3 A selection of results from Round 5 of the Scamseek experiments showing the results for word n-grams, combinations of SFG models, and combined SFG and n-gram models. P, R and F are for the scam class of the corpus

Exp. No	Feature Sets	F
1437	Four-class-unigram (1,764 atts)	0.446
1469	SFG-Normalized + Expansion + Determiners + Modality + Scaminess	0.475
1470	SFG-Normalized + Expansion + Determiners + Modality + Polarity + Scaminess	0.476
1471	SFG-Normalized + Expansion + Determiners + Scaminess	0.488
1473	SFG-Normalized + Expansion + Scaminess	0.509
1484	SFG-Normalized + Expansion	0.511
1462	SFG-Normalized + Scaminess	0.587
1454	**SFG-Normalized + 1,764 unigrams**	**0.618**
1454U	**SFG-Normalized + 975 unigrams + Scaminess**	**0.707**

On the other hand, the results show significant support for the SFG features as a model of each scam register, and this is where most of the manual analysis was directed, naturally, with improvements of 0.17 and 0.26 over the unigram baseline. This is not the whole story as a number of processing functions were introduced based on the discoveries made in the manual processing that raised the value of the unigram base to its current value, such as multi-word expression recognition including named entities, targeted stop-lists and admission lists, and testing for optimal ranking for feature selection, particularly to minimize over-training. Hence the improvement created by the SFG features is an under-estimate of its real contribution.

7.6 Conclusions

The Scamseek project is a success for ASIC in that it is operable 24 hours a day, 7 days a week. In its first operational run it discovered an activity that has since been taken to the stage of litigation. The estimate of savings in human effort in its monitoring role is of the order of 100 to 1, as previously ASIC had to read 80 documents to find one of interest whereas they now read five documents to find four of interest. The estimate in savings to the community by bringing speedier detection and intervention of scams cannot be estimated readily but is likely to be of the order of tens of millions of dollars. ASIC is not prepared to release all details about the technology but has released the following summary statement: 'The Scamseek technology is deployed in such a way that any scam proposal on any Internet channel that is generated in Australia or directed at Australians is highly likely to come under scrutiny.'

The research contribution has been significant in that it is the first project that has used Systemic Functional Grammar for automated text classification. Solutions to serious problems in practical text classification, namely unbalanced classes, and the integration of semantic and n-gram language models have also been developed.

Acknowledgements

The following people worked on the Scamseek project and made contributions to the final solutions: Michele Wong, Kathryn Tuckwell, Stephen Anthony, Tim Yeates, Dr. James Farrow, Neil Balgi, Jian Hu, Carlos Aya, Will Radford, Mathew Honnibal, David Smoker. The following doctoral students contributed to the work: Maria Couchman, Casey Whitelaw, David Bell. The following people acted as advisors: Prof. Christian Matthiessen, Prof. Jim Martin and Prof. Vance Gledhill. Participating organizations were Australian Securities & Investment Commission (ASIC), Capital Markets Co-operative Research Centre (CMCRC), University of Sydney, Macquarie University, and the Australian Centre for Advanced Computing and Communications (AC3).

Notes

1   Details about these channels cannot be described due to security restrictions by ASIC.
2   F is the geometric mean of the Precision and Recall values averaged over ten-fold cross validation sampling of the corpus.

References

Halliday, M. (1994), *Introduction to Functional Grammar* (2nd edn). London: Arnold.

Patrick, J. (2004), 'The Scamseek Project—Text Mining for Financial Scams on the Internet'. *Proceedings of the 4th Australasian Data Mining Workshop* (G. Williams, S. Simoff eds).

Explicitation: Towards an Empirical and Corpus-based Methodology[1]

Erich Steiner
Saarland University
Saabruecken, Germany

8.1 Specific properties of translations and 'explicitation' – state of the art

There is a small but significant tradition of work on assumed properties of translations as text, and more recently as 'text-type' or 'register'. The following are to various degrees part of this tradition, without, of course, representing a complete overview:

- Levy (1963) on lexical impoverishment and explicitation;
- Duff (1981) on translationese;
- Berman (2000 [1985]) on rationalization, clarification, expansion, ennoblement, popularization, and other assumed properties of translations;
- Blum-Kulka (1986) on explicitation in translation;
- Sager (1994): 179ff: on translation text types;
- Toury (1995): on growing standardization vs. interference;
- Baker (1996): Laviosa-Braithwaite (1998); Olohan (2001); as well as Kenny (2001) on simplification, normalization, levelling-out, explicitation, sanitization;
- Fabricius-Hansen (1996, 1999); as well as Ramm and Fabricius-Hansen (2005) on changing informational density in translations, and on explicitness of discourse relations;
- Doherty (1991, 1996), as well as (2004a,b) on perfect adequacy through adaptation to the stylistic principles of the target language system;
- House (1997 [1977]): on covert vs. overt translation, and 'cross-cultural pragmatics' (especially informational explicitness vs. implicitness (2002: 200));
- Vinay and Darbelnet (1958: 182ff);
- Johansson (2004, 2005), as well as Hasselgard (2004), on properties of (English–Norwegian) translations;

- Englund-Dimitrova (2005): on level of expertise as one determinant of explicitation in the translation process.

While 'explicitness/explicitation' has been postulated as one possible property of translated texts by most of those just mentioned, some have suggested other phenomena and relationships, as indicated in our list above. Yet even those properties will at least contribute to 'explicitness/explicitation' in the sense assumed here. The very different approaches to translation of Doherty and House have been particularly influential for our work, even though the property of 'explicitation' as such plays a significant role only in the latter's work.

House postulates 'explicitness vs. implicitness' (see House 2002: 200) as properties of texts within her cross-cultural pragmatics, alongside 'directness vs. indirectness; orientation towards self vs. orientation towards other; orientation towards content vs. persons; ad-hoc formulations vs. verbal routines'. This is where our efforts clearly meet, with the difference that we are concentrating more on the micro-structural realizations of what a possible property of 'explicitness' may mean for texts as wholes.

Doherty (e.g. 1991, 1996, 2004a,b) may be seen to represent a sort of 'null-hypothesis', which would be that translations do not have (should not have) specific textual properties. Through her rich and controlled set of theoretically interrelated language-specific parameters of and constraints on information distribution she attempts to describe and explain how an optimal translation is a perfect text in its target language. The work to be undertaken in our project here should lead to a framework for empirically testing such claims: whereas our initial hypothesis is that translated texts may be more explicit and/or dense and/or direct than registerially parallel texts in their target language, it is a hypothesis and may well be disconfirmed. Ultimately, and on a general level, our assumption is that translated texts may indeed be somewhat different from their parallel texts in their target language, though in ways which do not make them inferior, but interestingly different texts, and thus potential catalysts in situations of language contact and language change. However this may be, our main goal is to create possibilities for empirically testing such claims.

After this very brief review of some main lines in the investigation of properties of translated texts, let us add a few remarks about the corpus architecture which the current project is designed to develop.

Earlier exploratory work leading up to the current attempts is published in Baumann *et al.* (2004), Hansen (2003), Neumann (2003), Steiner (2001, 2004a,b, 2005 a,b), Steiner and Teich (2004), Teich (2003), Teich *et al.* (2001). In this strand of work, we have developed different aspects of corpus architecture, and of variables to be investigated. The corpus which we are building up at the moment consists of a background of cross-register reference corpora in English and German, together with both independent and aligned register-specific corpora of originals and their translations, all of these on the basis of representative excerpts from full texts. The corpora are represented as layered XML-data and indexed for correspondences by layer of representation and as originals and translations. This is illustrated in Figures 8.1 to 8.3 below (taken from Neumann and Hansen-Schirra 2005). The question of the operationalization of the property of explicitness (sometimes in interaction with those of density and directness) poses itself independently of any particular corpus design, but is certainly aimed at the type of multi-level annotated electronic corpus of the type exemplified here. The corpus itself is described in more detail in Neumann (2005).

Figure 8.1 shows our corpus architecture, consisting of the cross-register reference corpora (ER, GR), the register-controlled corpora of originals and their translations into German and English (EO/GTrans and GO/ETrans). Note that the corpus itself consists of randomly sampled excerpts, rather than full texts.

Figures 8.2 and 8.3 show multi-layered annotated corpus structures, both in aligned and non-aligned constellations. With this architecture, we are aiming at inclusion and control of our theoretically motivated annotations on various layers in our sub-corpora (for more detail see Neumann and Hansen-Schirra 2005, Hansen-Schirra *et al.* 2006). Note that in the aligned corpora, we align grammatical units. 'Translation units' may emerge as a result of our work, but are at this stage not taken as something established in our annotations.

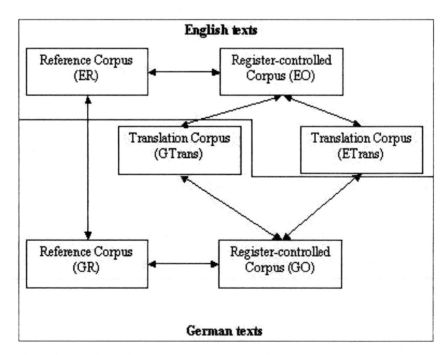

Figure 8.1 The CroCo Corpus design (Neumann and Hansen-Schirra 2005)

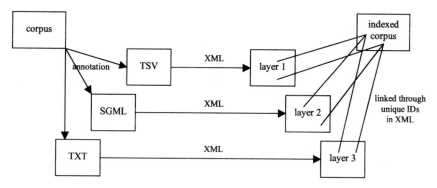

Figure 8.2 Multi-layer annotation in XML stand-off mark-up (Neumann and Hansen-Schirra 2005)

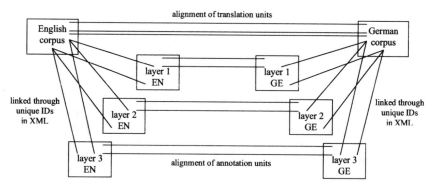

Figure 8.3 Alignment of source and target language annotation (Neumann and Hansen-Schirra 2005)

8.2 'Explicitation' and the notion of 'explicitness'

The notion of 'explicitness', and its counterpart 'implicitness', represents a challenge in several respects. For one thing, they are very general, central to some models of language, especially for a philosophically anchored semantics (see, e.g., Carston 2002; Burton-Roberts 2005), and highly complex in any case. They usually refer to fully interpreted acts of communication in a communicative context of situation. However, a methodologically empirical project will have as data not high-level interpretations of utterances by human interpreters, but text corpora with relatively low-level lexicogrammatical and cohesive categories reflected in multi-level annotations. The data thus yield information about *properties of encoding*, rather than about high-level *interpretations of such data by human interactants*. Precisely the former are the focus of the current project – an attempt to empirically enquire into properties of encoding which have to do with 'explicitness', rather than adding yet another set of example-based discussions of (interpretations of) the data.

While we have developed notions leading up to this discussion in earlier papers (see Steiner 2005a,b,c), 'explicitness/explicitation' deserve further refinement and discussion here. We shall therefore discuss a few relevant general definitions, gradually focusing in on more specific notions of 'explicitness' which are not restricted to, but firmly anchored in, lexicogrammatical realization and thus amenable to empirical investigation.

An initial distinction is suggested here between 'explicitation' and 'explicitness': 'explicitation' is a process, or a relationship, which presupposes that some meaning 'is made explicit' in moving from one text or discourse to some other. It also presupposes that in some sense, whatever is 'explicitated' must have been 'implicit' in the other variant. The two texts/discourses (or their variants) must therefore in some sense share at least some of their meaning. As a result of such 'processes', some textual variant may be more or less 'explicit' than the other, and it is to this term and its definition in relevant other models that we turn next.

Linke and Nussbaumer (2000: 435ff) in 'Concepts of Implicitness: Presuppositions and Implicatures' (my translation) anchor their discussion in the widespread metaphor, or allegory, which conceptualizes texts as 'icebergs': only a smaller part of them is visible, the larger part is hidden from perception. The visible part (of form and meaning) is called 'explicit', the invisible part 'implicit'.

More specifically, they draw a distinction between meanings which are *implicit, non-literal, dependent on use* (the province of pragmatics) on the one hand (B), and those meanings which are *fixed, literal and independent of use* (the province of semantics) (A). Only within the latter do they distinguish between *implicit (non-realized)* and *explicit*.

Staying with the latter category of what they call 'semantics' (A) initially, they sub-classify the semantic, but implicit, meanings into:

(A 1) *presuppositions*: they are constant under negation, presupposed by (wh-)questions, applying to proper names and definite descriptions, but also to grammatical constructions presupposing facticity, such as types of projecting verbs, verbs expressing certain logical relationships such as reciprocity or relational opposites, focus particles and focusing constructions.

(A 2) *implications (entailments)*: they can be inferred from an expression but without remaining constant under negation, e.g. prepositions, again certain lexical relational opposites, certain conjunctions etc. This is NOT the same as 'implicature' (see below).

(A 3) *connotations, affective and deontic meanings*: associated with frequencies, collocations, contexts etc.

(A 4) *Remaining marginal types to do with inferencing*.

Going over to the former category of meanings which are *implicit, non-literal, dependent on use* (the province of pragmatics) (B), the sub-classification is into:

(B 1) Pragmatic presuppositions (*frames, scripts*), but also *intertextuality, pragmatic ellipsis, lexical vagueness and ambiguity, structure of argumentation and rhetorical relations.*

(B 2) Conversational maxims and conversational implicatures.

(B 3) Illocution and perlocution.

In a first attempt at situating our own concept of 'explicitness' here, it appears as if our classification cuts across theirs, even though the two can be related.

First, in our corpus-based research design, we can only investigate meanings which are *explicit* in one of the registerial variants compared to some other, or else can be grammatically or cohesively related *as explicit/implicit variants* to our data. What remains outside of our methodology is simple *adding or dropping* of meanings without any grammatical or cohesive relationships between variants.

Second, the meanings which we investigate do not have to be *literal*, they may, indeed, be (grammatically or lexically) metaphorical, provided they are 'explicit' in one of our variants (registers, translations).

And, finally, the meanings which we investigate are dependent on use in the sense that the data are drawn from linguistic instantiations, i.e. texts. However, our operationalizations in terms of lexicogrammatical or cohesive realization will bias our observations towards whatever is grammaticalized and lexicalized, or at least highly conventionalized (cohesive relations, rhetorical relations), and in that sense we will appear quite system- and grammar-oriented.

The reason why our perspective seems to cut across that of Linke and Nussbaumer is that by being corpus-based, and thus product-based, rather than interpretation-based and process-based, we are methodologically forced to link our investigations to lexicogrammatical realization, so that any meanings which they call 'pragmatic' and which are not linked systematically to realization appear invisible to our perspective – which is not the same as saying they are unimportant. They will feature in hermeneutic example-based interpretations of our data, but only there. Following on from our particular research design, they can, and have, become the object of investigation through psychological testing (for which see Hansen 2003).

Let us furthermore attempt to situate our own methodology relative to a discussion contrasting 'Relevance Theory' with Gricean Pragmatics, this time taken from Burton-Roberts' (2005: 389ff) review of Carston's (2002) *Thoughts and Utterances: The Pragmatics of Explicit Communication.*

We assume, like Burton-Roberts (and Carston), that our 'explicit vs. implicit' distinction cuts across at least several Gricean dichotomies: (A) semantics vs. pragmatics, (B) what is said vs. what is implicated, (C) explicit vs. implicit, (D) linguistically en(/de)coded vs. not linguistically en(/de)coded, (E) context-free vs. context-sensitive, (F) truth-conditional (entailment) vs. non-truth-conditional (non-deductive). Furthermore, and addressing

Carston's (2002: 117) and at this point also Burton-Roberts's (2005: 391) position, we would also claim that variants (1) (a) to (d) below cannot simply be contrasted on a binary 'explicit vs. implicit' dichotomy:

(1) (a) Mary Jones put the book by Chomsky on the table in the downstairs sitting room.
    (b) Mary put the book on the table.
    (c) She put it there.
    (d) On the table.

According to Carston and Burton-Roberts, any of 1 (a–d) above 'could be used, in different contexts, to communicate explicitly one and the same proposition (or thought or assumption)' (Carston 2002: 117). This appears to be true – what we are investigating with our research design, however, is *not a communication (and interpretation)* situated in a specific context, but rather *properties of the encoding* ('explicitness', alongside 'directness' and 'density'). In our terms (see Figure 8.4 below, and its application to the text analysis later on), 1 (a) to (d) are partly identical as far as ideational and interpersonal explicitness are concerned. There is also no difference between them in terms of directness, but there are differences along several dimensions in density, and there are differences in explicitness on the interpersonal and textual dimensions and in terms of some sub-parameters of cohesion.

However, if we regarded 1 (a) to (d) as intralingual translations of each other, we could also investigate 'explicitation', rather than only 'explicitness'. In this case, (b) to (d) would be implicitations of (a), albeit with lexicogrammatical and cohesive markers which would still trigger a fully instantiated interpretation along the lines of (a) (definite articles, phoric elements, ellipsis) in a fully instantiated discourse.

With respect to Relevance Theory, then, the characteristic of our approach is that we measure explicitness as a property of the encoding, not as a property of the communicative act as such. And although the latter is of great significance for any attempt at understanding communication, our own approach focusing on textual encoding provides a necessary prerequisite for investigations of communication.

A distinction which seems somewhat closer to our own modelling is that of Polenz (1988: 24ff, 40ff, 92ff, 202ff). He draws a basic distinction between 'elliptical, compressed/compact, and implicating' modes of expression, and their respective corresponding 'full, expanded and explicating' counterparts. In his classification, what we are investigating through our methodology would be the difference between

- 'compressed/compact' modes of expression and their 'expanded' counterparts,
- plus the difference between 'elliptical' textures which can be related through grammar or cohesion to non-elliptical 'full' counterparts,

– plus the difference between 'implicit' textual configurations and their 'explicit' counterparts.

It has to be said, though, that Polenz frequently uses 'explicit' as an opposite term to all three of 'compressed/compact, elliptical, implicit' (1988: 24ff). Where our methodology is more constrained than Polenz's terms would suggest is in that we would restrict our notion of 'realization' to 'lexicogrammatical and cohesive realization'. We would demand some sort of lexicogrammatical reflex for an assumed 'elliptical, compact/compressed, implicit' meaning, rather than allowing any meaning as potentially 'implicit' which is 'addable' to the piece or discourse in question without violating coherence.

Summarizing our debate here, in comparison to Linke and Nussbaumer, to Carston, to Burton-Roberts, and to a lesser extent to Polenz, our methodology appears restrictive in the sense of being tied to formal realization. However, all of the realizational patterns are considered to be signals only, instructions, to the full (inter-)textual meaning, and in that sense, we are opening the door towards a fuller view, ultimately taking into account the invisible part of the 'iceberg' as well. Methodologically, though, we can only do this in our example-based hermeneutic interpretations of individual examples, not in the empirical part of our investigations. Philosophically, this is, of course, only to be expected if we assume that understanding texts is ultimately not an empirical, but an interpretative hermeneutic exercise.

Methodologically, we are in some respects closer to, for example, Biber (1988: 142ff) on 'explicit vs. situation-dependent reference', but also Biber (1995: 157ff, 161ff), than to the authors above. However, we do believe that it is possible to develop a linguistically richer and theoretically better motivated notion of 'data' than is used by Biber, while building on his achievements in making linguistic enquiry a more empirical discipline than before. The linguistically richer conceptual tools to be outlined below and based on the notions of 'grammatical metaphor' and on metafunctional diversification (Halliday and Matthiessen 1999, 2004; Matthiessen 2004) are intended to narrow the gap between the more conceptual and hermeneutic top-down and the more empirical bottom-up approaches.

8.3 Explicitness, explicitation and linguistic levels

After having clarified the present notions of 'explicitation' and 'explicitness' by relating them to some discussions in the literature, let us now attempt a stratification of the notion of 'explicitness' in terms of the linguistic levels of lexicogrammar and text. There are relevant phenomena intuitively classified under the general notion of 'explicitness' on either level, but they are not of the same degree of abstraction from the data: it is not the case that textual explicitness is simply the sum of the explicitness of clauses, and whereas both are structural phenomena, inside the clause they are grammaticalized (and in a general sense cohesive) phenomena, but outside and beyond it, they are cohesive only.

'Explicitness' on the lexicogrammatical (structural) level is conceptually related to 'density' and 'directness'. These three are properties of (lexico-) grammatical constructions (see Steiner 2004b, 2005a,b). The opposite of 'explicit' here is 'lexicogrammatically not realized', but still part of the construction (unrealized participant roles, unrealized features in non-finite constructions, grammatical ellipsis, projection onto different grammatical categories, grammatical metaphor, transcategorization, etc.).

'Explicitness' on the textual level is conceptually related to properties such as 'lexically impoverished, rationalized, clarified, expanded, ennobled, popularized, standardized, simplified, normalized, levelled-out, sanitized, direct vs. indirect; oriented towards self vs. oriented towards other; oriented towards content vs. persons'; and similar ones in the sense of those referred to in our list in section 8.1. The 'explicitness' of higher-level units such as texts/discourses is not simply the sum total of 'explicitness' features of clauses. It is an 'emergent property' on a higher level in the sense that the properties on text level are perceived as a result of the interaction of clause level features, such as 'explicitness, directness, density', with textual features such as cohesion, markers of genre, or register. All of the latter will, in turn, be realized as lexical and/or grammatical patterns, but their function is not accounted for by lexicogrammar. 'Explicitness' on this level can furthermore be a result of global textual patterns (such as type–token ratio, lexical density, etc.), which are 'epiphenomena' of lexicogrammatical patterns, but not lexicogrammatical themselves. 'Explicitness' – a property of lexicogrammatical or cohesive structures and configurations not requiring any shared meaning between variants – is measured through operationalizations as in our Figure 8.4 below.

'Explicitation', as we have already said at the beginning of the previous section, is a process or a product, not a property. The products resulting from 'explicitation' are more 'explicit' lexicogrammatically and cohesively than their counterparts. In terms of instantiated discourse, the product of an explicitation is, of course, a more explicit discourse. Explicitation is thus defined on instantiated, indexed and aligned pieces of discourse/text, translations in particular, which share all or some of their meaning.

Definition: We assume 'explicitation' if in a translation (or language-internally in a pair of register-related texts) meanings (not only ideational, but including interpersonal and textual) are realized in the more explicit variant which are not realized in the less explicit variant, but which are in some theoretically motivated sense implicit in the latter. The resulting text is more 'explicit' than its counterpart.

Note that the final part of this definition is meant to exclude the indefinitely many possibilities through which meaning can simply be added to some text/discourse, without being in any sense 'implicit' in the source variant. We shall discuss these phenomena more extensively below under 'boundaries of the notion of explicitness'.

It should also be said that the data in our non-aligned corpora will initially only show which texts are more or less explicit, more or less dense, or compact. Whether or not 'explicitation' in our further sense obtains can only be determined through the co-indexation in our aligned translation units, in principle including translation between different variants of a text within a language. 'Explicitness', and even more so 'explicitation', are thus inherently relative terms, presupposing the comparison of two or more variants.

8.4 The metafunctional modularization of language and 'explicitness'

In Figure 8.4, we shall intersect the properties of 'explicitness, density, and directness' with the linguistic metafunctions according to Systemic Functional Linguistics (SFL) (Halliday 1978; Halliday and Matthiessen 1999, 2004; see also Steiner 2005b). Figure 8.4 expresses two key assumptions. The first of these is that languages modularize their lexicogrammar along a small set of functional dimensions (ideational, interpersonal, textual, and their sub-dimensions), and the second is that on each of these levels, the mapping of semantics onto lexicogramnmar will vary in terms of explicitness, directness and density. Our focus here is clearly on 'explicitness', but as this property is closely related to density and directness, we would at least give an operationalization of all of these. It should also be said that, whereas the metafunctional hypothesis is a basic assumption developed and elaborated in *Systemic Functional Grammar*, the further assumption of properties of encoding, or of the mapping between semantics and grammar, is not foregrounded in current formulations of the model. It is, however, in my view directly derivable from SFL.

A discussion of a number of specific questions to do with operationalizations, as well as an application to two sample texts, will be postponed until section 8.7 below. At this point, we shall present the operationalizations without further discussion.

The operationalizations given in Figure 8.4 are meant to constitute a frame for classifying texts, and constructions, in terms of three properties and along all of the SFL-metafunctions as well as in terms of cohesion. Some of these can be directly queried in our tagged corpora, while others will at this stage still have to be computed by human interpreters based on the data in our corpora.

If we apply a scheme as here in Figure 8.4 to aligned pairs (or tuples) of textual variants, e.g. translations, what it measures directly is explicitness, density or directness *of constructions*. Only if we then trace the information in co-indexed (instantiated) matches do we find traces of whether or not any particular quota of meaning is explicitated (or otherwise) in one of the

Erich Steiner

Properties / Metafunctions	Explicitness	Directness	Density
Ideational: Experiential	No. of explicit functions per discourse unit: No. of implicit functions	No. of directly mapped experiential clause functions: No. of indirectly/metaphorically mapped clause functions	No. of functions: Grammatical Unit CC: Cl ranking Cl ranking: Cl embedded Clauses finite: Clauses non-finite Clauses: Clause elements Phrases: Phrase elements Groups: Group elements
Ideational: Logical²	No. of explicit functions: No. of implicit functions	No. of directly mapped logical functions per unit: No. of indirectly/metaphorically mapped functions	No. of functions: Discourse Unit
Interpersonal: Mood	No. of explicit Mood-markers per discourse unit: No. of implicit Mood-markers	No. of directly/congruently marked Mood-options: No. of indirectly marked Mood-options	No. of Mood-markers: Discourse Segment
Interpersonal: Modality	No. of explicit Modality-markers: No. of implicit Modality-markers	No. of directly/congruently marked Modality-options: No. of indirectly marked Modality-options	No. of Modality-markers: Discourse Segment
Textual: Theme	No. of auto-semantic Themes: No. of syn-semantic (phoric) Themes	Not applicable	No. of Themes: Clause Functions

Figure 8.4 Properties of lexicogrammatical encoding across metafunctions

Properties / Metafunctions	Explicitness	Directness	Density
Textual: Information	Not applicable	Not applicable	No. of NEW elements: Discourse Segment No. of marked NEW elements: Discourse Segment
Cohesion: Reference	No. of implicit referents: No. explicit referents; No. of phoric phrases: No. of autosemantic phrases	Not applicable	No. of newly introduced referents per discourse segment
Cohesion: Ellipsis	No. of cohesive ellipses: Discourse Segment	Not applicable	Not applicable
Cohesion: Substitution	No. of cohesive substitutions: Discourse Segment	Not applicable	Not applicable
Cohesion: Lexical	No. of lexical words: No of grammatical words	Not applicable (lexical metaphor is not yet counted here)	Type–token ratio; Lexical words per clause
Cohesion: Conjunction	No. of explicit relations: No. of Figures	No. of cohesively realized relations: No. of non-realized RST realizations	No. of relations

Figure 8.4 *Continued*

variants. The former can be done on the basis of fully or semi-automatic information extraction, whereas the latter is, for the time being, only accessible through human interpretation of the aligned variants.

8.5 Boundaries of the notion of 'explicitness'

So far, a selective overview has been given of relevant investigations of properties of translated texts, and some relevant approaches to 'explicitness' and 'explicitation' in linguistics and adjacent areas have been discussed. This was followed by a stratification of the notion of 'explicitness' into the levels of lexicogrammar and text. In addition to this initial diversification of the notion, a modularization of 'explicitness' has been proposed according to linguistic metafunctions and phenomena have been additionally divided between those which are lexicogrammatical and those that are cohesive. A parallel modularization has been given for the properties of 'directness' and 'density', as these heavily interact with explicitness (see Figure 8.4). 'Experiential Explicitness', however, still seems to present some particular problems: one of these is that much of what is called 'explicitness' in the literature elsewhere is covered by 'logical' and generally interpersonal and textual explicitness in our multifunctional framework. So, explicitness is in no way only explicitness of experiential meaning. Another is that experiential directness and experiential density cover additional aspects of what is often referred to under the phenomenon of explicitness, albeit in an indirect way. However, there is a residual category of truly 'experiential explicitness', appearing in the top left-hand corner of our Figure 8.4, which needs further clarification at this point.

First, it is not the case that any quantum of information 'added' to a given piece of discourse is a form of 'explicitation'. Very often it is simply 'adding information and meaning'. In order for the term of 'explicitation' to make sense, we need to have a notion of 'implicit information'. Most approaches to discourse representation have such a notion, for example in the work of 'discourse representation theory' (Kamp and Reyle 1993; Asher 1993; applied to problems of translation, Fabricius-Hansen 1996). Usually, it means something like 'information which must be added to linguistically explicitly expressed information in order for (the interpretation of) a piece of discourse to become complete and coherent'. I find this notion intuitively appealing (see also Steiner 1991: 80ff), yet difficult to apply in empirical work, unless we tie it down to linguistic clues for implicitness. Where there are no such clues, our methodology will not identify any implicit meaning.

At the other (and very 'grammatical') end of the spectrum, there are notions of lexicogrammatically encoded types of implicitness, for example in non-finite constructions unrealized participant roles, logico-semantic relators (conjunctions, prepositions), tense, aspect, number or in lexico-grammatical 'cryptotypes' in general. Staying more on the word-level, and with English as a specific language, grammarians (e.g. Dixon 1991: 68–71) have noted the optional dropping of complementizers, relative pronouns, copulas from complement clauses. In all of these cases, of course, it can be argued that the (highly generalized) grammatical meaning signalled by the absence of the word is there, at least in the features of the construction, if not in lexicogrammatical functions. It can be brought out by contrasting the construction with its agnates. However, this notion of 'implicitness' is very grammar-oriented and thus also very language specific. It will be visible to our methodology, and will be used as a relevant indicator – although not necessarily of experiential, but often of logical, interpersonal or textual meaning.

Then there are SFL-based notions of 'implicitness/explicitness', as in accounts of modality and modulation (Halliday and Matthiessen 2004: 620ff), or inferred/implicit discourse relations, often triggered by genre or register (Halliday and Matthiessen 2004: 363ff). A further context for the notion of 'implicitness' is cohesive ellipsis (Halliday and Hasan 1976: 142ff). And there is, of course, the important notion that grammatical metaphor, at least the type involving relocation in rank between semantics and grammar, has far-reaching influences on how much and what kinds of information are made explicit (Halliday and Matthiessen 1999: 231ff, 258, 270; Halliday and Martin 1993). These are our starting points for recognizing more and higher-level types of implicit meaning, but operationalizations at the borderlines (i.e. those to do with genre and register) are not far enough advanced to admit reliable quantification in all cases.

In order to make the boundaries of our notion of 'experiential explicitness' clearer, let us give three examples of phenomena, all of which are sometimes discussed under the label of 'explicitness', or 'explicitation'. Our aim here will be to illustrate which types of phenomena are captured by our operationalizations.

The following ((2) and (3)) are two short excerpts from popular scientific prose in English and German (see House 2002: 205). These are meant to illustrate phenomena which, however frequent they may be in real-world translations, and however much they may contribute to the cultural and contextual acceptability of a piece of text, are not subsumed under our notion of 'experiential explicitness':

(2.1) **Groundbreaking** *work that began* **more than a quarter of a century ago** *has led to* **ongoing** *insights about brain organization and consciousness.*

(2.2) *Jahrzehntelange Studien* **an Patienten mit chirurgisch getrennten Großhirnhälften** *haben das Verständnis für den* **funktionellen** *Aufbau des Gehirns und* **das Wesen** *des Bewußtseins vertieft.*
(M. Gazzangia: 'The Split Brain Revisited'. *Scientific American*, July 1998; 'Rechtes und linkes Gehirn: Split-Brain und Bewußtsein'. *Spektrum der Wissenschaft*, Dezember 1998.)

My own word-for-word back-translation of the German:

(2.3) *Decade-long studies on patients with surgically-separate brain-halves have*

> *the understanding for the functional structure of the brain and the essence of*
> *consciousness deepened.*

Cases such as these, not infrequent in translations, have referents and properties added and/or missing in the translation relative to the source text (marked by boldface). This adding of experiential meaning is not explicitation, but simply adding (or in the opposite case dropping) of information – which may or may not be closely triggered by something in the immediate or wider context. If it is so triggered, as in the frequent cases of 'compensation', in which units of information have to be translated non-locally, they are again not cases of explicitation, but simply cases of non-local translations. The classification of 'non-local' depends on our choice of relevant translation unit in each case.

Additionally, and very typically, we find cases of different degrees of 'specificity' and/or 'vagueness' between original and translation, as in the translation '*more than a quarter of a century ago*' by '*jahrzehntelang*'. Increasing specificity of a sign is a case of explicitation, but interestingly one which does not necessitate any addition of structure, but may simply result in choosing the same structure with a more specific feature set.

While we are thus excluding cases such as those above from the notion of 'explicitation' as used here, all the variants involved above do have properties along all the dimensions covered in Figure 8.4. Yet these measure the explicitness, density or directness of a lexicogrammatical or cohesive configuration, rather than textually or discursively instantiated 'explicitation' in principle.

Our second excerpt, again taken from House 2002, shows the same phenomenon:

> (3.1) *Treatment may reduce the chance of contracting HIV infection after a risky*
> *encounter.*
>
> (3.2) *Eine **sofortige** Behandlung nach Kontakt mit einer Ansteckungsquelle ver-*
> *ringert unter Umständen die Gefahr, dass sich das Human-Immunschwäche-*
> *Virus im Körper festsetzt. **Gewähr gibt es keine, zudem erwachsen eigene***
> ***Risiken.***
>
> (S. Buchbinder: 'Avoiding Infection after HIV Exposure'. *Scientific*
> *American*, July 1998; 'Prävention nach HIV-Kontakt'. *Spektrum der*
> *Wissenschaft*, Oktober 1998.)

My own word-for-word back-translation of the German:

> (3.3) *An **immediate** treatment after contact with a source of infection reduces under*
> *circumstances (possibly) the chance, that itself the human-immune-weakness*
> *syndrome in the body implants. **Guarantee there is none, additionally grow***
> ***specific risks.***

In the original and published German translation above, the entire second sentence is added, apparently without any clear trigger in the original. Again, this would not show up as 'explicitation' in our data: in terms of instantiated and indexed discourse entities, there is no match for the added sentence in its original, and therefore explicitation would not apply. In terms of the lexicogrammatical and cohesive constructions, we would of course register different degrees of explicitness, density and directness as specified in Figure 8.4, but these would be outside any translation relation, which would also be shown in our (missing) alignments for the added fragments. The translation of 'risky' by '*Ansteckungsquelle*' would also fall outside of what we are counting, unless we find a generalizable way of handling this as a form of 'specification'. The same might hold for the translation of 'infection' by '*im Körper festsetzt*'.

A different type of example ((4), see Fabricius-Hansen 1996: 522) would seem to fall more easily into our category of 'explicitation':

(4.1)   *Frankreich trauert über den Tod eines sehr bekannten französischen Schauspielers.*
'France mourns the death of a very famous French actor'

(4.2)   *Ein französischer Schauspieler ist gestorben. Er war sehr bekannt. Frankreich trauert über seinen Tod.*
'A French actor has died. He was very famous. France mourns his death.'

In terms of properties of the constructions (Figure 8.4 above), version (4.2) here is more explicit than version (4.1) along several dimensions (although least experientially), and less dense and more direct, as we shall argue below. In addition, in terms of instantiated discourse, and as shown in alignments of translation units, the two variants are close to equal in terms of explicitness, except that the tense selctions in version (2) can be seen as a real explicitation of information implicit in version (1).

A third example, constructed by me from example (2.1), will show a different, though related, type of clear 'explicitation' (see (5) below):

(5.1)   *Groundbreaking work that began more than a quarter of a century ago has led to ongoing insights about brain organization and consciousness.*

(5.2)   *Because they have broken new ground by working for more than a quarter of a century, people have become able to understand increasingly how the brain is organized and what consciousness is.*

(5.3)   *Weil man neues Terrain erforscht hat indem man mehr als ein Viertel Jahrhundert gearbeitet hat, konnten die Leute zunehmend verstehen, wie das Gehirn organisiert ist und was Bewusstsein ist.*

The example in (5) illustrates a deliberately constructed and unambiguous case of both differences in explicitness and instantial explicitation on the constructional and instantiated discourse level: (5.2) would be more explicit, more direct and less dense than (5.1) on the construction level, and it would be an explicitation in instantial terms, as shown by aligned and indexed versions of the two variants (5.1) and (5.2).

8.6 An operationalization of linguistic phenomena in terms of properties of lexicogrammatical constructions – some micro-level operationalizations and hypotheses

The property of 'explicitness', and the process of 'explicitation', have frequently been postulated on a merely intuitive level in hermeneutically-based work, relying on the analysis of individual, and in the best cases, representative examples. In other more empirically-oriented approaches, they have been reduced to low-level criteria, such as words per text, words per sentence, realization of individual conjunctions or pronouns, or individual cohesive devices, lexical density etc. (see for example, Baker 1996; Laviosa-Braithwaite 1998; Olohan 2001). We are attempting a theoretically more motivated operationalization in this paper by defining explicitness and explicitation, by stratifying it in terms of different linguistic levels, by tightening its boundaries, and by modularizing it in a multifunctional perspective. Explicitness and explicitation, however, still need to be directly connected to the data in our electronic corpora. Therefore, we shall move onwards to formulating research hypotheses first in theory-neutral terms, and then in terms of the more SFL-based notions of Figure 8.4. Finally, in order to test such hypotheses, we need a level of annotation at which they can be expressed and checked against data.

The following are relatively theory-neutral operationalizations in terms of which we attempt to investigate 'explicitness':

- The proportionality form : content words
- Average number of words per clause
- Biber's informational : involved production
- The proportions between the following lexical categorical types : conjunction : preposition; verb: noun; adverb; adjective; finite : non-finite[3]
- Proportionalities between ranks (levels of projection): clause complexes : clauses : groups/phrases : words
- Proportionalities between directly verbally governed to directly nominally governed phrases
- Degree of specificity of lexical items
- Number of grammatical units (clauses, phrases/groups, words) per discourse segment,[4] where the number correlates positively with explicitness
- Explicitness of grammatical categories, such as person, number, gender, but also diathesis (including voice), relativization, complementation, etc.
- Explicitness of cohesive relations, especially reference and conjunction
- To these operationalizations, we must add those used in Figure 8.4 above,

although from then on we cease being theoretically neutral. Figure 8.4 is also at a different level of abstraction, constituting an interpretation already of some of the more shallow data formulated in the earlier part of our list. And finally, the operationalizations in Figure 8.4 are for 'explicitness', but also for 'density' and 'directness', which constitute properties of their own, even if they interact with 'explicitness'.

Using these operationalizations, we are comparing the relative 'explicitness' of linguistic encoding in sub-corpora, or individual texts, along the independent variables language, register, translation. And in those cases where we compare aligned texts (translations), we additionally investigate 'explicitation' as a relationship between instantiated pieces of discourse, because in translationally related pairs of texts, both exemplars are assumed to refer to experientially identical (or at least very similar) instances.

The operationalizations suggested here presuppose corpora tagged, annotated and query-able for variables which we shall list in section 8 of this paper.

But let us now, by way of exemplification, illustrate how we can proceed from assumptions about 'explicitness' and its related properties to research hypotheses making reference to the types of information presupposed in our operationalizations above (see Steiner 2005a for an earlier formulation of these).

Globally, our strategy is designed to

a) partly reduce an intuitive notion of 'information distribution' in texts and sentences to more technical and better understood notions of *information structure, informational density* and *grammatical metaphoricity*, and

b) operationalize these latter notions in such a way as to make them empirically testable on electronic corpora, using the 'shallow' concepts of *explicitness, density,* and *directness* as properties of semantics-to-grammar mapping in sentences.

Let us consider a couple of examples, some of them already used above, to make our point clearer (examples under Figure 8.4 are from Fabricius-Hansen 1996, (6) to (16) are slightly altered from original examples by Halliday and Matthiessen 1999: 231ff):

(4.1) *Frankreich trauert über den Tod eines sehr bekannten französischen Schauspielers.*
'France mourns the death of a very famous French actor.'

(4.2) *Ein französischer Schauspieler ist gestorben. Er war sehr bekannt. Frankreich trauert über seinen Tod.*
'A French actor has died. He was very famous. France mourns his death.'

(6) Lung cancer death rates are clearly associated with increased smoking.
(7) (It is clear that) if more people smoke, then more people die of lung cancer.
(8) (It is clear that) some people smoke more, so they die faster of lung cancer.
(9) A rising number of people smoke.
(10) The number of people dying from lung cancer is increasing.
(11) A rising number of people smoke. *As a consequence*, the number of people dying from lung cancer is increasing.
(12) *Because* a rising number of people smoke, the number of people dying from lung cancer is increasing.
(13) *Because of* an increase in the number of smokers, the number of people dying from lung cancer is increasing.
(14) The increase in smoking *leads to* an increase in death rates from lung cancer.
(15) Increasing lung cancer death rates and the *causally related* increase in smoking ...
(16) *The cause of* increasing lung cancer death rates is increased smoking ...

Focusing on 'explicitness' first, we consider the following operationalizations:

– number of grammatical units (clauses, phrases/groups, words) per discourse segment,[5] where the number correlates positively with explicitness;
– explicitness of grammatical categories, such as person, number, gender, but also diathesis (including voice), relativization, complementation, etc. per discourse segment;
– explicitness of cohesive relations, especially reference and conjunction per discourse segment.

The notion of 'explicitness', in the context of this discussion, is restricted to meaning 'lexicogrammatically and/or cohesively realized'. Furthermore, 'realized' may mean 'phorically', rather than fully lexically realized. Formulating two hypotheses now for our three notions of 'information structure', 'informational density' and 'grammatical metaphoricity', we would say that while information structure has to be directly annotated or parsed in a corpus of running text, for informational density and for grammatical metaphoricity we assume that:

(H1) The more informationally dense and the more grammatically metaphorical a stretch of text, the less it will be explicit grammatically (and cohesively).

(H2) The more informationally dense and the more grammatically metaphorical a stretch of text, the more the explicit grammatical and cohesive marking will be of the general nominal, rather than verbal, type.[6]

By way of exemplification, we would like to point to our examples (6) to (16), but also (4.1.), (4.2), all of which positively illustrate our hypotheses (H1) and (H2). In particular, the more highly metaphorical and the informationally denser variants are related to their respective opposites as

- less explicit to more explicit, in terms of absolute number of grammatical units per discourse segment,
- less explicit to more explicit, in terms of absolute number of grammatical features per discourse segment,
- more nominal to more verbal in terms of type (quality) of phrases.

Turning to 'grammatical density' next, as a second operationalization of informational density and of grammatical metaphoricity, let us emphasize that here 'density' is a grammatical notion, not a semantic or discourse notion. Consider sample sentences such as (17) and (18), which illustrate the phenomenon in the area of translation, that is to say, across languages (from Doherty 1991):

(17) The suspicion that volcanic eruptions are the primary source of aerosols in the upper atmosphere has been around for many years.

(18) Seit vielen Jahren vermutet man schon, dass die Aerosole in den höheren Schichten der Atmosphäre vor allem aus Vulkanausbrüchen stammen.
(Lit: 'Since many years suspects one already that the aerosols in the higher layers of the atmosphere above all from volcanic eruptions stem.')

If we align translationally corresponding phrases and then consider the proportions between types of phrase, then we find both quantitative and qualitative effects, predicted by the following hypotheses (H3) and (H4):

(H3) The more informationally dense and the more grammatically metaphorical a stretch of text, the higher the proportion of 'intermediate phrase types' (groups, phrases, rather than words or clauses) per clause.

The resulting figures for examples (17) and (18) are:

((number of groups + phrases) : number of clauses)) : number of clause complexes

English Original: $((10:2):0) = $ infinite[7]
German Translation: $((8:2):1) = 4$

According to the model of grammatical metaphor, we should not simply count the relationships of ranks to each other, giving us a quantitative effect, but rather look at the differences between types of phrases and groups, dependent on the class of their lexical heads, a qualitative effect. This will give us at least one more type of hypothesis:

(H4) The more informationally dense and the more grammatically metaphorical a stretch of text, the higher the proportion of phrases with a nominal head relative to phrases with a verbal head per clause.

The figures for our sample sentences are:

(number of units with a nominal head) : (number of units with a verbal head)
English Original: 9:5
German Translation: 7:7

Similar results are obtained for the same test on our other examples (4) to (16) in this paper. They will again be illustrated in our text analysis in section 7 below under 'experiential density'.

We would also stipulate that:

(H5) The more informationally dense and the more grammatically metaphorical a stretch of text, the higher the number of grammatical features per unit.

Hypothesis (H5) is also borne out by our examples (4) to (18). Note that, in this case, we are not considering the number of grammatical features per discourse segment, which is a measure of explicitness, but the number of features per grammatical unit.

We thus expect that one central type of grammatical metaphoricty, more precisely the one involving relocation in rank between semantics and grammar, seems to be straightforwardly mirrored in grammatical density as we are using the term here. And to the extent that informational density is related to this type of metaphoricity, the same would apply.[8]

One implication of the type of 'density' illustrated above is that for the encoding of a given discourse segment, or part of it, density would increase as we move 'downwards' on the rank scale, i.e. from clause complex into clause, phrase/group, word, and morpheme. We need to be aware of a simplification, though: 'some semantic phenomenon', once it is re-encoded on a different rank, does not simply remain 'the same'. Instead, it gets expanded or reduced, according to the particular systemic options valid at the given rank. A process plus modality plus tense plus phase configuration (verbal group), if it is re-expressed metaphorically as a nominal group, is no longer anchored in temporal deixis, modality and phase, but now through expressions of identifiability, personal deixis etc. – whatever is expressed in the grounding part of the nominal group (see Langacker 1999; Davidse 1998; Taverniers 2005 in press). It should furthermore be clear that, as we have said before, any direct comparison across languages requires the use of comparative figures for languages (and registers) against which to standardize our findings.

Let us finally turn to directness. By this we mean the sense in which (7) and (8) above are more direct than (6), (11) is more direct than any of (12) to (16), (18) is more direct than (17), and even (4.2) is more direct than (4.1), although probably to a lesser extent (for extensive usage of the concept, see, e.g., Hawkins 1986: 53ff; Doherty 1996: 604ff; and Halliday and Matthiessen 2004, Chapter 10; Halliday and Matthiessen 1999: 231ff under the labels of (non-) congruent realization). Directness is a graded property of the semantics-to-grammar mapping, for example between participant (semantic) roles and grammatical functions, between expressions of modality in different lexicogrammatical categories, or between logical relationships, such as causation, and their lexicogrammatical or cohesive expression. In order to be able to use the concept of 'directness vs. indirectness' in the relationship between semantics and lexicogrammar, that is to say *between levels within one language,* we need to further operationalize them. A direct encoding of a given semantic meaning is a 1:1 realization into its corresponding and thus transparent and motivated lexicogrammatical category. Often – though by no means necessarily – the less metaphorical version will be the more explicit lexically, morphologically and/or grammatically. All of this would be an operationalization of 'directness' from within one linguistic system. Because of this, it is also gradable and relative across languages. It has to be said, though, that directness can at this stage only be counted on hand-coded corpora.

The properties of 'explicitness, grammatical density, and directness' are assumed to be relatively shallow evidence of (aspects of) informational density and grammatical metaphor. Note that these are properties of semantics-to-grammar mappings, whereas the realizations of these mappings are syntactic, lexical, and finally phonological and phonetic categories. These properties have to be kept conceptually distinct from each other in their influence on the overall phenomenon of information distribution. In principle, they can be shown to vary independently, even though there is co-variation in naturalistic data. A further methodological issue is their applicability across languages: whereas 'explicitness, density, and directness' can be reasonably well defined as properties of semantics-to-grammar mapping within a language, it requires additional clarification to apply them cross-linguistically.

Finally, information structure as the third realization of information distribution does not become empirically visible through explicitness and grammatical density directly, but through word order, phoricity, definiteness, and intonation, and therefore has to be read off directly from the parsed corpus (see Baumann *et al.* 2004).

8.7 An example: a comparison of two original texts in terms of explicitness, density and directness

In the following, we shall reproduce two texts which are both examples of relatively 'autonomous' discourses, in the sense that they are written by a native language author in each case, are mainly addressed to a native speaking readership, and are also both specimens of well-established registers and genres in their respective communities. Both excerpts are the opening section from the monograph in question, written at approximately the same time and with similar fields, modes and tenors of discourse.

We shall apply the operationalizations of explicitness, directness and density, dispersed

– by metafunction
– by stratum (grammar vs. cohesion)

which were introduced in Figure 8.4 above.

Obviously, the comparison of two single texts, and additionally across languages, does not in itself provide evidence of anything other than of methodological properties and questions. Furthermore, we are contrasting explicitness, density and directness as properties of encodings. We are not investigating either instantial explicitation, as defined in earlier parts of this paper, nor are we in this example using any alignment – which would be impossible because of the lack of a translation- or otherwise register relationship.

We shall reproduce the German sample text first, then give a word-order-preserving 'translation' into English, and then reproduce the English sample text. The comparisons will then be between the German and the English sample texts, using the operationalizations from our Figure 8.4, and some additional ones from our section 8.6 above. In an overall and integrated interpretative framework, we are using

a) the data in the columns of Figure 8.5 below;
b) generalization about textual properties 'explicitness, directness, density';
c) 'explicitness, directness, density' in b) as indicators of (resulting from) information structure, informational density and grammtical metaphoricity of constructions in the texts.

Additionally, we shall raise a number of methodological issues in notes. One of these deserves to be mentioned more globally here: all categories of analysis, starting even from word-class tags, extending through phrasal categories, and certainly categories such as 'Theme' and 'Rheme', are anchored in necessarily language-specific grammars. In our work, in which we necessarily

Properties / M-functions	Explicitness	Directness	Density
Experiential	No. of explicit functions per discourse unit: No. of implicit functions G: 230:6 E: 358:13[9]	No. of directly mapped experiential clause functions: No. of indirectly/metaphorically mapped clause functions G: 66:10 E: 82:13[10]	No of functions: Unit[11] **English:** CC: 8 Cl ranking: 12 Cl embedded: 17 Clauses finite: 7 Clauses non-finite: 10 Clause elements: 95 Phrases: 33 Phrase elements: 66 Groups: 136 Group elements: 197 Words: 248 **German:** CC: 7 Cl ranking: 12 Cl embedded: 6 Clauses finite: 3 Clauses non-finite: 3 Clause elements: 76 Phrases: 25 Phrase elements: 48 Groups: 125 Group elements: 206 Words: 233

Figure 8.5 Properties of lexicogrammatical encoding across metafunctions for two register-parallel texts

Properties / M-functions	Explicitness	Directness	Density
Logical[12]	No. of explicit functions: No. of implicit functions[13] G: 6 (2 conj + 4 preps): 0[14] E: 5 (3 conj + 2):0	No. of directly mapped logical functions per unit: No. of indirectly/metaphorically mapped functions G: 6:0 E: 5:0[15]	No. of Functions: Discourse Unit G: 6:1 E: 5:1
Mood	No. of explicit Mood-markers per discourse unit: No. of implicit Mood-markers E: 0:10 G: 0:9	No. of directly/congruently marked Mood options: No. of indirectly marked Mood-options E: 10: G: 9:0	No. of Mood-markers[16]: Discourse Segment E: 10 G: 9[17]
Modality	No of explicit Modality-markers: No. of implicit Modality-markers E: 1:0 G: 0:1	No. of directly/congruently marked Modality-options: No. of indirectly marked Modality-options[18] E: 0:1 G: 1:0	No. of Modality-markers: Discourse Segment E: 1:0 G: 1:0
Theme	No. of auto-semantic Themes: No. of syn-semantic (phoric) Themes[19] G: 7:0 E: 16:0	Not applicable	No. of Themes: Clause Functions G: 7:76 E: 16:95

Figure 8.5 *Continued*

Properties / M-functions	Explicitness	Directness	Density
Information	Not applicable	Not applicable	No. of NEW elements[20]: Discourse Segment Unavailable at this stage No. of marked NEW elements: Discourse segment G: ca. 8 E: 4–5
Cohesion: Reference	No. implicit referents: No. of explicit referents G: 7:99 E: 16: 97[21] No. phoric phrases: No. autosemantic phrases[22]: G: 86 E: 86 G: 13 phoric (+28 definite articles) E. 11 phoric (+ 8 definite articles)	Not applicable	No. of newly introduced referents[23] per discourse segment E: 55 (per 29 Figures (verbs)) G: 64 (per 20 Figures (verbs))
Cohesion: Ellipsis	Number of cohesive ellipses G: 1 E: 3	Not applicable	Not applicable

Figure 8.5 *Continued*

Properties / M-functions	Explicitness	Directness	Density
Cohesion: Substitution	No. of cohesive substitutions G: hardly applicable (0)[24] E: 0	Not applicable	Not applicable
Cohesion: Lexical	Ratio lexical/grammatical words G: 106 lexical/110 grammatical E: 130/117[25]	Not applicable (lexical metaphor is not yet counted here)	Lexical words per clause: G: 106:18 E: 130:29 Type-token ratio?
Cohesion: Conjunction (cohesive relations only)[26]	No. of explicit relations: No. of Figures G: 13:20 E: 9:29	No. of cohesively realized relations: No. of non-realized RST realizations[27]	No. of relations[28] G: 13 E: 9

Figure 8.5 *Continued*

code data across languages, we hope that categories have a better chance of being interlingual the more general they are, and the closer the languages are typologically. That is to say, a part of speech coding in terms of 'nominal' and 'verbal' is somewhat less problematic than one in terms of 'phrasal verb' vs. 'prepositional verb' across languages, and a grammatical analysis in terms of 'process, participant role, circumstantial role' is less problematic than one in terms of any of their finer sub-classes. And finally, English and German are easier to compare with a cross-linguistic tag-set, than are, say, Chinese and German. However, the problem of interlinguality of analytic categories is one that we share with all attempts at comparing texts in different languages.

Sample Text (1) Siegfried Jäger (1993), *Kritische Diskursanalyse. Eine Einführung.* (p. 9ff)
Einleitung
Es geht mir in dieser Einführung in die kritische Diskursanalyse darum, einen neuen integrierten **sozialwissenschaftlich-linguistischen** (emphasis in original) Ansatz für eine Diskurstheorie und – darauf aufbauend – eine Methode von Diskursanalyse zu entwickeln, der die traditionellen primär strukturalistisch orientierten Ansätze der Sprachwissenschaft, die heute noch bis in die Textlinguistik hinein dominieren, ebenso überwindet wie solche Ansätze, die im Rahmen qualitativer Sozialforschung entwickelt worden sind.
Da beide Disziplinen, ebenso wie die Diskursanalyse, auch den Anspruch stellen, Grundsätzliches über den Zusammenhang von Gesellschaft und Sprache/Kommunikation auszusagen, werde ich mich im ersten Teil dieses Textes exemplarisch kritisch mit einigen Grundannahmen der (Sozio-) Linguistik und der (qualitativen) Sozialforschung auseinandersetzen. Zunächst jedoch einige Vorbemerkungen zur **Linguistik** allgemein:
Aufgefallen ist mir insbesondere, dass linguistische Konzepte aller Art dazu neigen, die mit Hilfe sprachlicher Mittel transportierten **Inhalte** auf der Mikro- und Makroebene zu vernachlässigen bzw. programmatisch aus der Linguistik auszuschließen.
Mit den Inhalten wird aber zugleich alles Gesellschaftliche aus der Linguistik vertrieben....
Diese Position gilt es zu überwinden, auch wenn sie im Selbstverständnis der meisten Linguisten noch zutiefst verankert ist.
So schreibt etwa Bernhard Sowinski in seiner Einführung in die Textlinguistik, dass die Sprachwissenschaft sich in den letzten Jahren zwar verstärkt der Untersuchung von Texten zugewandt habe. Die Behandlung von Inhalten sei jedoch eine Sache anderer, teils benachbarter Disziplinen, etwa der Theologie, der Juristerei, der Literaturwissenschaft, der Geschichte oder auch der Soziologie etc., nicht aber eine Aufgabe der Linguistik.

English (preserving word-order as far as possible):
Introduction:

It concerns me in this introduction to the critical discourse analysis about, a new integrated socialscientific-linguistic approach for a discourse theory and – on that building – a method of discourse analysis to develop, which the traditional primarily structuralistically oriented approaches of the linguistics, which today still into the textlinguistics dominate, supersedes as well as such approaches, which have been developed in the framework of qualitative social science research.

Because both disciplines, in the same way as the discourse analysis, also make the claim to proclaim fundamentals about the relationship between society and language/communication, will I myself in the first part of this text exemplificatorily critically with some basic assumptions of the (socio-) linguistics and the (qualitative) social research engage. At first however some preliminary remarks on the linguistics:

Impressed has me particularly, that linguistic concepts of all kinds tend towards the with help of linguistic means transported contents on the micro- and macro-levels to neglect respectively programmatically from the linguistics to exclude.

With the contents is however at the same time everything social from the linguistics expelled....

This position necessitates it to overcome, even if it in the self-concept of the most linguists still deeply anchored is. Thus writes for example Bernhard Sowinski in his introduction into the textlinguistics that the linguistics may have turned in the last years more forcefully to the examination of texts. The treatment of contents, however, be a task of other, partly neighbouring disciplines, for example of the theology, the law, the literary studies, the history or the sociology etc., not however the task of the linguistics.

Sample Text 2: Norman Fairclough, *Discourse and Social Change* (Fairclough. 1993:1)

Today individuals working in a variety of disciplines are coming to recognize the ways in which changes in language use are linked to wider social and cultural processes, and hence are coming to appreciate the importance of using language analysis as a method for studying social change. But there does not yet exist a method of language analysis which is both theoretically adequate and practically usable. My main objective in this book, therefore, is to develop an approach to language analysis which can contribute to filling this gap – an approach which will be particularly useful for investigating change in language, and will be usable in studies of social and cultural change.

To achieve this, it is necessary to draw together methods for analysing language developed within linguistics and language studies, and social and political thought relevant to developing an adequate social theory of language. Among the former, I include work within various branches of linguistics (vocabulary, semantics, grammar), pragmatics, and above all the 'discourse analysis' that has been developed recently mainly by linguists (the various senses of 'discourse' and 'discourse analysis' are discussed shortly); and I include among the latter the work of Antonio Gramsci, Louis Althusser, Michel Foucault, Jürgen Habermas and Anthony Giddens (see references). Such a synthesis is long overdue, but there are various factors which have militated against it being satisfactorily achieved so far. One is the isolation of language studies from other social sciences, and the domination of linguistics by formalistic and cognitive paradigms.

With a reminder that our analysis undertaken here serves as an illustration only, let us briefly go through our findings, adding a few comments where appropriate.

Experiential: Counting implicitness only in a restricted grammatical sense, we see that the German text has a proportion of 6:230 (roughly 0.026), while the English has one of 13:358 (roughly 0.039). Furthermore, we see that both texts exhibit approximately the same degree of 'directness' as far as their clause functions are concerned. The German text, however, comes out as more dense than the English one, expressed by the proportions of clause elements per clause (G: 4.2 vs. E: 3.29) and the proportion of group elements per group (G: 1.64 vs. E 1.44). It also comes out as more dense than the English one in terms of proportionalities between ranks (levels of projection) suggested in section 8.6. The ratio of

clause complexes : clauses : groups/phrases : words
is for the English text : 8 : 29 : 169 : 248
for the German text: 7 : 18 : 150 : 233.

The German text has a substantially higher proportion of phrases/groups per clause, and of words per clause than the English one. The percentages of words per group/phrase, however, are not so different – and all this in spite of the fact that English, being the more morphologically analytic language, has morphological properties which should bias it generally towards a higher proportion of words per higher unit as compared to German.

On the other hand, the English has many more embedded clauses (both finite and non-finite clauses functioning as group elements), which results in the overall higher number of grammatical functions and clauses in absolute terms. In other words, the information in the English text is much more expressed in clauses than that of the German, which seems to condense the information into clause and group elements.

But let us emphasize at this point again that the figures obtained here are figures for two registerially parallel texts, not for a translation pair. We are thus measuring density (and explicitness and directness) of constructions, not the relative explicitness or explicitaion between two related variants (translations). Figures such as those obtained here will, however, figure as part of the reference profile for English and German for the given register and will then be statistically factored out of any comparisons of translation pairs in order to obtain possible effects of the process of translation and the translation relationship as such.

Logical: The German text is slightly more explicit in its encoding of logical functions, it is also more direct and more dense. If we take these figures together with those under cohesive conjunction below, we can see a picture of a logically much more explicit and denser German text.

Mood: There are hardly any differences here in any of the variables explicitness, directness and density. This is likely to be a consequence of the register of our texts here.

Modality: Again, the numbers are much too small for any conclusions. However, the few instances that we find differentiate the two versions along the dimensions of 'explicitness' and 'directness'.

Theme: For both texts, their Themes are all explicit, in the sense of auto-semantic, which may be partly the consequence of the fact that both passages come from the opening of the books. The English version is more explicit in having more multiple Themes, but this seems typologically motivated. 'Directness' does not apply, but 'density' is again much higher in English because of its obligatory 'SV' properties and the associated frequency of multiple Themes.

Information: In this case, the notions of 'explicitness' and 'directness' may not be applicable, because of the nature of the textual metafunction: either some constituent is encoded as NEW or it isn't, and if it is, there is no immediate sense in which it could be encoded 'indirectly'. One might think of an operationalization of 'explicitness' in terms of lexical vs. word-order and intonational encoding. There may be a valid notion of 'density', operationalized as 'number of NEW elements per discourse unit'. We have not counted this variable here, simply because of time constraints involved in having native speakers produce plausible readings of the texts. What we have tentatively done, though, is count the number of (lexico-grammatically) marked NEW units, which gives a denser picture for the German text.

Reference (Cohesion): Here two operationalizations come to mind: one would be the proportion of implicit to explicit referents. This is for German 7:99 (approx. 0.07), for English 16:97 (0.16). The other is the proportion between phoric and autosemantic referents (G: 13:86; E: 11:86). Along this dimension, the two texts appear relatively similar at first sight. However, we notice a far higher percentage of NPs with definite articles in German (28:86) than in English (8:86). Of course this has to do with the systemic differences between the two languages as far as the expression of 'genericity' with abstract NPs, and of countability and boundedness, are concerned. Furthermore, German often uses NP-attributes where English prefers non-finite ones.[29] There may be additional effects due to a higher percentage of phrases in German being treated as 'recoverable' from co(n)-text, but this remains to be investigated. As far as 'directness' is concerned, we do not see an immediate sense in which it could be used, other than in the sense of 'directness of encoding of experiential meaning', which is covered above. For 'density', though, we are counting the number of newly introduced referents per discourse segment, or rather, per semantic 'Figure' (E: 55:29; G: 64:20). These proportions would classify the German text as substantially more 'dense' than the English one.

Ellipsis (Cohesion): Under this category, a high number of cohesive ellipses would contribute to low 'explicitness'. Absolute numbers are, again, low here, but the English text is less explicit on this dimension than the German one. 'Directness' does not seem to play a role here, nor 'density' – although one could count the number of 'ellipses' relative to clause or phrase functions.

Substitution (Cohesion): Once more, the categories of 'directness' and 'density' do not seem to be applicable. A high number of 'substitutions', especially through general nouns and verbs, would contribute negatively to 'explicitness', but is not given in our present text. One might suspect that general high frequency nouns in the English text (individuals, ways, processes, factors) play a role here, but this will be taken up again under 'lexical cohesion'.

Lexical Cohesion: In an initial step, we have operationalized 'explicitness' here as the proportionality of lexical to grammatical words. Interestingly, this relationship is counter to first expectations (G: 106:110 vs. E: 130:117), but is perhaps less surprising if we remember the role of compounding (16 in our short German text) in the two writing systems. 'Directness' is not applicable, or rather, would require an analysis of lexical metaphor, which we haven't done here. Finally, the number of fully lexical words per clause shows German (106:18) denser than English (130:29) (see Halliday and Martin 1993:69ff). The type–token ratio has not been counted here, because it would be meaningless over such a short stretch of text. However, it can be taken to be a measure of overall lexical density.

Conjunction (Cohesion): The explicitness of the German text is much higher than that of the English (G 13:20 as against E 9:29). This is even strengthened by the fact that the German is also higher in its explicitness in the expression of grammaticalized logical meanings (see above). In terms of 'directness' we do not find any non-realized rhetorical relations. The Figures for 'density' look similar, but the semantic subtypes and the semantic spread of the relations are quite different.

In summary, then, our German text would be

– experientially more explicit and denser
– logically more explicit
– thematically less explicit and less dense
– informationally denser
– referentially more explicit and denser
– lexically denser
– conjunctively more explicit

than its English counterpart. Otherwise, they would be classified as similar. However, and this is of paramount importance, our summary comparison creates the wrong impression, i.e. that there are cross-linguistic properties of explicitness, density and directness which can be compared in their absolute numbers and proportionalities directly. This is not the case: if English and German texts for the register which they exemplify here were different generally – numerically and proportionally – in the way that our two texts are, then the two texts would be of equal (un-)markedness in their registers, and in their cultural communities. Any figures obtained in direct comparisons must therefore be interpreted against the statistical background of their registers and their languages, which is what our corpus design is intended to allow.

8.8 Towards an annotation scheme

In summary, and repeating something we have already said in section 6, we have suggested the following relatively theory-neutral operationalizations, or categories of analysis, in terms of which we shall attempt to investigate 'explicitness':

- The proportionality form : content words
- Average number of words per clause
- Biber's informational : involved production
- The proportions between the following lexical categorical types: conjunction : preposition; verb : noun; adverb : adjective; finite : non-finite[30]
- Proportionalities between ranks (levels of projection): clause complexes : clauses : groups/phrases : words
- Proportionalities between directly verbally governed to directly nominally governed phrases
- Degree of specificity of lexical items
- Number of grammatical units (clauses, phrases/groups, words) per discourse segment,[31] where the number correlates positively with explicitness
- Explicitness of grammatical categories, such as person, number, gender, but also diathesis (including voice), relativization, complementation, etc.
- Explicitness of cohesive relations, especially reference and conjunction
- To these operationalizations, we must add those used in Figure 8.4 above, although from then on we cease being theoretically neutral. Figure 8.4 is also at a different level of abstraction, already constituting an interpretation of some of the more shallow data formulated in the earlier part of our list. And finally, the operationalizations in Figure 8.4 are for 'explicitness', but also for 'density' and 'directness', which constitute properties of their own, even if they interact with 'explicitness'.

In order for the operationalizations above to work, our corpora should be tagged, or otherwise annotated, with the following categories:

- Number of words
- Form words
- Content words
- Lemmatized lexical items
- Morphological items and their grammatical features
- Number of constituents at some level
- Realized constituents at some level
- Non-realized constituents at some level (grammatical)
- Non-realized constituents at some level (cohesive)
- Biber's textual factors and dimensions (1988: 104ff), in particular dimension 1 (informational : involved production) and dimension 3 (explicit vs. situation-dependent). Features for German need to be developed where necessary.
- Part-of-Speech-Tagging (POS)
- A phrase-structure analysis, preferably involving several levels of projection (ranks)
- Tagging of heads for lexical categories
- Topological analysis into something like *Vorfeld-Mittelfeld-Nachfeld*
- Degree of specificity of lexical items (parsed with word-net)
- Functions of grammatical units
- Mood-features of clauses: finiteness, clause-moods
- Modality realizations: (semi-)auxiliaries, other lexical categories
- Realizations for marked NEW: extrapositions, clefts, focusing adverbs and particles
- Indexing for (newly introduced) discourse referents
- Substitution (clausal, nominal, verbal), depending on the language
- Cohesive conjuncts

What is of paramount importance to be observed is the fact that we cannot only retrieve information which is directly covered by our tagging and further annotation, but additionally information which can be queried in our (tagged, enriched, annotated) corpus, so that the information surplus in our corpus, as compared to a raw corpus, derives from enriched data plus theoretically guided querying. A first sorting of the information in our annotations depending on the source of that information is given below.[32]

Corpus processing and querying steps
Raw statistics (no annotation needed)
- Number of words
- Type–token ratio
- Average sentence length
- Part-of-speech-tagging
- TnT-Tagger

Perl-script 'Lexical Density'
- Form words and content words (not segmented into clauses) (builds on POS-Tagging)

MPro[33] (including phrase-chunking)
- Lemmatization and morphological analysis
- Number of constituents at some level
- Realized constituents at some level
- A phrase-structure analysis, preferably involving several levels of projection (ranks)
- Mood-features of clauses: finiteness

Word-net
- Degree of specificity of lexical items (parsed with word-net?)

Topology parser[34]
- Topology (Vorfeld-Mittelfeld-Nachfeld)

Manual analysis
- Non-realized constituents at some level (grammatical) (builds on chunking)
- Non-realized constituents at some level (cohesive) (builds on chunking)
- Tagging of heads for lexical categories (builds on chunking)
- Indexing for (newly introduced) discourse referents (builds on chunking)
- Mood-features of clauses: clause-moods
- Substitution (clausal, nominal, verbal)
- Functions of grammatical units (builds on chunking)

Query building on annotation
- Biber's textual factors and dimensions (1988: 104ff), in particular dimension 1 (informational : involved production) and dimension 3 (explicit vs. situation-dependent). Features for German need to be developed where necessary.
- Realizations for marked NEW: extrapositions, clefts, focusing adverbs and particles
- Modality realizations: (semi-)auxiliaries, markers of other lexical categories
- Cohesive conjuncts (difficult, because open-set)

In an overall and integrated interpretative framework, we are using

   a) the data in the columns of Figure 8.4 (and 8.5), derived from corpus tags, annotations and queries
   b) generalization about textual properties 'explicitness, directness, density' (and others)

c) 'explicitness, directness, density' in b) as indicators of (resulting from) information structure, informational density and grammatical metaphoricity of constructions in the texts.

All of a) to c) are dependent variables, however, on different levels of abstraction from the data. These dependent variables, or their behaviour, then need to be explained in terms of a few independent variables as outlined below.

8.9 Independent and dependent variables

Our overall research architecture is an attempt to link the following independent and dependent variables:
Independent Variables:

(1) **Language:** here we are comparing cross-register corpora in English with cross-register corpora in German (a comparison of the reference corpora as in Figure 8.1).
(2) **Register:** here we are comparing texts of one register A with texts of one register B in English and German, respectively (language-internal comparison of registers).
(3) **Translation:** here we are comparing translations of a constant register A of English and German texts with originals of the same register in the respective language (language-internal comparison of translations and originals).
(4) **Translation:** in interaction with language (and possibly register): here we are comparing source texts in English with their translations into German (direct comparison of source texts and target texts).

In (1), (2) and (3) above, the investigation is one of properties of constructions, i.e., 'explicitness/implicitness' in the sense defined in this chapter. In (4) only, where the investigation will be one of translations and their originals, the object will be aligned and ultimately also referentially indexed texts, investigating 'explicitations' in the sense defined here, alongside 'explicitness' of constructions. Dependent variables will be those operationalized in the previous sections, ultimately interpreted within a framework such as in Figure 8.4 (or some other linguistically-based model). By then comparing the differences found in the comparisons under (1) to (4) above, we hope to pair individual independent and dependent variables.

Notes

1   This chapter is part of the first phase of DFG-project STE 840/5-1 'Linguistic properties of translations – a corpus-based investigation for the language pair English–German' (www.fr46.uni-saarland.de/croco/). Parts of this report were written during a research period with the SPRIK-project of the University of Oslo in September/October 2005, where an earlier version appeared as Steiner 2005c. I am grateful to SPRIK and its members for creating this possibility and for discussions of various aspects of the paper, in particular Cathrine Fabricius-Hansen, Stig Johansson, Bergljot Behrens, Hilde Hasselgard and Wiebke Ramm. I am also very much indebted to colleagues in and around the project's home base in Saarbrücken, where Silvia Hansen-Schirra and Stella Neumann are co-authors of the project proposal, Kerstin Kunz and Mihaela Vela are constant contributors, and Alberto Gil, Hans Haller, David Horton and Andrea Kamm have provided critical comments at several points. It should also be obvious how the work of Elke Teich, now of Darmstadt, has been influential in the genesis of our project, as has been the work of Michael Halliday and Christian Matthiessen in its influence on my linguistic thinking. None of those mentioned, though, should be held responsible for any remaining weaknesses.

2   Grammaticalized/lexicalized expressions only, i.e., not counting here conjunctive cohesive ties.

3   Note that these oppositions are ultimately scalar, rather than binary.

4   This is not the same as the number of intermediate phrase types *per clause*, which we shall use below in our operationalizations of density and metaphoricity in (H3) and (H4).

5   Note: this is not the same as the number of intermediate phrase types *per clause*, which we shall use below in our operationalizations of density and metaphoricity in (H3) and (H4).

6   Cross-linguistically, grammatical explicitness will be directly dependent on the morphological type of language, so that for any comparative work across languages, figures have to be standardized for type of language and for type of register (for some cautionary remarks along these lines, see Steiner 2001).

7   The value 'indefinite' results from the fact that the English original has no clause complex and thus undergoes division by zero. This particular value is not very meaningful if derived from an individual example such as the one here. In general, however, it is obvious that the numerical value of the informationally denser and grammatically more metaphorical variants will be higher because of the higher percentage of groups and phrases per clause and per clause complex than in the case of the less metaphorical and less dense variants.

8   There is another type of grammatical metaphor, though, the type involving re-arrangement of semantics-to-grammar mapping not in

terms of rank, but in terms of class on one rank, which has to be treated separately (see Steiner 2001, 2004a for detailed coverage).

9   Counting only implicit functions resulting from non-finites. Cohesive ellipsis is counted further below.

10   Operationalization of 'congruent/direct' is difficult in many cases. Clause functions only are counted at this point, and only realized Functions. Clauses under clause combining (tactic) relations are also not counted as clause elements.

11   Here we are counting CC, Cl (ranking vs. embedded), all phrases and groups plus their elements (recursively).

12   Grammaticalized/lexicalized expressions only; conjunctive cohesive ties are counted under 'cohesion' below.

13   Non-finite clauses without explicit linkage, certain prepositions.

14   Projection is not counted here, but conjunctions and prepositions encoding logical meaning are (i.e., excluding prepositons with only case assigning function, or such with only locational and temporal meaning). Two instances of '*und*' in the German text are not counted, nor are 14 in English – although the discrepancy there is interesting in itself, yet the functions of '*und*/and' are extremely varied.

15   Difficult notion, because of the wide usage of spatio-temporal prepositions for logical relations.

16   Mood-options/markers are not counted for embedded clauses (i.e., those without choice). Note also that there are ranking (non-finite) clauses without mood selection. Finally, lexicogrammatical encoding of mood counts as 'implicit', vs. the 'explicit' version by 'speech-act verbs'.

17   In two German projecting clauses, I have counted the Mood-option preselected by the verbs (*auffallen, schreiben*).

18   I am not sure about the precise operationalizations here, and about the interactions with 'appraisal'. We could use Halliday's features here (Halliday and Matthiessen 2004: 613ff).

19   We only count realized Themes in finite main clauses; the numerical difference is due to the frequency of multiple Themes in English.

20   We haven't counted NEW elements for lack of a spoken version. As marked NEW, we counted any constituent which was so marked through word-order or lexical means.

21   The number of referents is much lower than the number of phrases, because by no means all phrases refer (they may predicate, for example.). The number of implicit referents here is small, assuming that dropped Subjects in cases of non-finites have already been counted under 'experiential'.

22   Including proper names, i.e., individuals; noun–noun compounds are counted per entity introduced.

23   Here we are counting referents, NOT concepts or lexical items. So, a referent is only counted if newly introduced into the discourse. Nominalizations are also not counted twice, unless they introduce

different referents. The discourse unit here is the 'Figure' (see Halliday and Matthiessen 1999).

24   German has hardly any 'substitution' in the strict sense of Halliday and Hasan 1976.

25   Interesting, because contrary to first expectations deriving from the morphologically analytical nature of English vs. German – although the more extensive compounding of German points in the opposite direction (see Steiner 2001 for remarks on these issues).

26   Grammaticalized expressions are treated under 'logical' above. The proportionalities between grammaticalized and cohesive ways of expression of logical relations are an interesting matter in themselves. This may also be the place to comment on the counting of German 'pronominal adverbs' (*darauf, darum,* etc.): when they are part of the prepositional or otherwise phrasal verb, they are syntactically obligatory and thus are not counted, just like their English counterparts. Where they have a cohesive function, they are counted under reference (due to the demonstrative character of their first part), and additionally as conjunctive relation, where there is one involved (*deswegen, dafür* etc. where they are not part of the verb).

27   Difficult to operationalize.

28   Ultimately counted as a proportion per Figure. The mere numbers hide the fact that in the English version, 5 out of 9 are of the type simple additive or adversative types, whereas this is true of hardly any one of the German. The adversative types in German are not simple, but more marked, specialized.

29   Further systemic differences in English and German NPs relevant to reference can be found in Doherty (2004a,b) and in Königs (2000: 479ff).

30   Note that these oppositions are ultimately scalar, rather than binary.

31   Note: this is not the same as the number of intermediate phrase types *per clause,* which we use in our operationalizations of density and metaphoricity in (H3) and (H4).

32   Thanks to Stella Neumann for suggesting this first classification, which may still be elaborated, extended and modified.

33   MPro has been developed by the IAI in Saarbrücken, the help of which is hereby gratefully acknowledged. For a general description see Maas 2005.

34   See Braun 1999.

References

Aijmer, K. and Hasselgard, H. (eds) (2004), *Translation and Corpora. Selected Papers from the Goteborg-Oslo Symposium.* Goteborg: Acta Universitatis Gothoburgensis, pp. 163–88.

Asher, N. (1993), *Reference to Abstract Objects in Discourse*. Dordrecht: Kluwer.

Baker, M. (1996), 'Corpus-based translation studies: The challenges that lie ahead', in H. Somers (ed.) *Terminology, LSP and Translation: Studies in Language Engineering in Honour of Juan C. Sager.* Amsterdam: John Benjamins.

Baumann, S., Brinckmann, C., Hansen-Schirra, S., Kruiff, G.-J., Kruiff-Korbayova, I., Neumann, S., Steiner, E., Teich, E. and Uszkoreit, H. (2004), 'The MULI Project: annotation and analysis of information structure in German and English', in *Proceedings of LREC 2004*. Lisbon, Portugal.

Berman, A. (2000 [1985]), 'La Traduction comme épreuve de l'étranger', translated by L. Venuti as *Translation and the trials of the foreign* in Venuti, L. (ed.), pp. 284–97.

Biber, D. (1988), *Variation Across Speech and Writing*. Cambridge: Cambridge University Press.

Biber, D. (1995), *Dimensions of Register Variation: A Cross-linguistic Comparison*. Cambridge: Cambridge University Press.

Blum-Kulka, S. (1986), 'Shifts in cohesion and coherence in translation', in: House, J. *et al.* (eds), *Interlingual and Intercultural Communication: Discourse and Cognition in Translation and Second Language Acquisition Studies*. Tübingen: Narr, pp. 17–35.

Braun, C. (1999), 'Flaches und robustes Parsen deutscher Satzgefüge'. Diplomarbeit, Universität des Saarlandes, Saarbrücken.

Burton-Roberts, N. (2005), 'Review article: Robyn Carston on semantics, pragmatics and "encoding"'. *Journal of Linguistics*, 41, 389–407.

Caffarel, A., Martin, J. R. and Matthiessen, C. M. I. M. (eds), (2004), *Functional Typology*. Amsterdam: Benjamins.

Carston, R. (2002), *Thoughts and Utterances: The Pragmatics of Explicit Communication*. Oxford: Blackwell.

Davidse, K. (1998), 'The Dative as participant role versus the Indirect Object. On the need to distinguish two layers of organization', in W. Van Langendonck and W. Van Belle (eds), *The Dative. Vol. 2: Theoretical and Contrastive Studies*. (Case and Grammatical Relations across Languages, 3.) Amsterdam: Benjamins, pp. 143–84.

Dixon, R. M. W. (1991), *A New Approach to English Grammar, On Semantic Principles*. Oxford: Clarendon Press.

Doherty, M. (1991), 'Informationelle Holzwege. Ein Problem der Übersetzungswissenschaft'. *Zeitschrift für Literaturwissenschaft und Linguistik*, 21(84).

Doherty, M. (ed.) (1996), 'Information Structure as a Problem of Translation'. Special Issue of *Linguistics*, 34.

Doherty, M. (2004a), 'Reorganizing Dependencies.' SPRIK Reports of the project *Languages in Contrast* (**Språk i kontrast**). www.hf.uio.no/german/sprik No. 23, October 2004, p. 18.

Doherty, M. (2004b), 'SAP – a strategy of attributive parsimony and its constraints characterizing translations between English and German.'

SPRIK Reports of the project *Languages in Contrast* (**Språk i** kontrast). www.hf.uio.no/german/sprik No. 24, October 2004, p. 22.

Duff, A. (1981), *The Third Language: Recurrent Problems of Translation into English*. Oxford: Pergamon Press.

Englund-Dimitrova, B. (2005), *Expertise and Explicitation in the Translation Process*. Amsterdam: John Benjamins.

Fabricius-Hansen, C. (1996), 'informational density: a problem for translation theory', in M. Doherty (ed.), Information Structure as a Problem of Translation, *Linguistics*, 521–65.

Fabricius-Hansen, C. (1999), 'Information packaging and translation: Aspects of translational sentence splitting (German–English/Norwegian)', in M. Doherty (1999: 175–214).

Fairclough, Norman (1993), *Discourse and Social Change*. London: Polity Press.

Halliday, M. A. K. (1978), *Language as Social Semiotic. The Social Interpretation of Language and Meaning*. London: Edward Arnold.

Halliday, M. A. K. and Hasan, R. (1976), *Cohesion in English*. London: Longman.

Halliday, M. A. K. and Martin, J. (1993), *Writing Science: Literacy and Discursive Power*. London: The Falmer Press.

Halliday, M. A. K. and Matthiessen, C. M. I. M. (1999), *Construing Experience Through Meaning. A Language-Based Approach to Cognition*. London: Cassell.

Halliday, M. A. K. and Matthiessen, C. M. I. M. (2004), *An Introduction to Functional Grammar*. London: Arnold (earlier versions by Halliday in 1994 [1985]).

Hansen, S. (2003), *The Nature of Translated Text. An Interdisciplinary Methodology for the Investigation of the Specific Properties of Translations*. Saarbrücken: Saarbrücken Dissertations in Computational Linguistics and Language Technology, Vol. 13.

Hansen-Schirra, S., Neumann, S. and Vela, M. (2006), *Multi-dimensional Annotation and Alignment in an English–German Translation Corpus. Proceedings of the 5th Workshop on NLP and XML (NLPXML-2006). 11th Conference of the European Chapter of the Association of Computational Linguistics. April 4, 2006, Trento, i*, pp. 35–42.

Hasselgard, H. (2004), 'Spatial linking in English and Norwegian', in K. Aijmer and H. Hasselgard (eds), *Translation and Corpora. Selected Papers from the Goteborg-Oslo Symposium*. Goteborg: Acta Universitatis Gothoburgensis.

Hasselgard, H., Johansson, S., Behrens, B. and Fabricius-Hansen, C. (eds) (2002), *Information Structure in a Cross-Linguistic Perspective*. Amsterdam and New York: Rodopi.

Hawkins, J. (1986), *A Comparative Typology of English and German*. London: Croom Helm.

House, J. (1997 [1977]), *A Model for Translation Quality Assessment. A Model Revisited*. Tübingen: Gunter Narr (revised model of the earlier 1977 version).

House, J. (2002), 'Maintenance and convergence in translation – some methods for corpus-based investigations', in H. Hasselgard *et al.* (eds), *Information Structure in a Cross-Linguistic Perspective*. Amsterdam and New York: Rodopi, pp. 199–212.

Jäger; Siegfried (1993), *Kritische Diskursanalyse. Eine Einführung.* Duisberg: Diss.

Johansson, S. (2004), 'Why change the subject? On changes in subject selection in translation from English into Norwegian.' *Target* 16.1, 29–52.

Johansson, S. (2005), 'Sentence openings in translations from English into Norwegian'. *Norsk Lingvistik Tidsskrift*, 23, 3–35.

Kamp, H. and Reyle, U. (1993), *From Discourse to Logic.* Dordrecht: Kluwer.

Kenny, D. (2001), *Lexis and Creativity in Translation. A Corpus-based Study.* Manchester: St. Jerome.

Königs. K. (2000), *Übersetzen Englisch Deutsch.* Munich and Vienna: Oldenbourg.

Langacker, R. (1999), *Grammar and Conceptualization.* Berlin and New York: Mouton de Gruyter.

Laviosa-Braithwaite, S. (ed.) (1998), *Meta.* Special Issue: 'The Corpus-based Approach', (43)4.

Levy, J. (1969), *Die literarische Übersetzung. Theorie einer Kunstgattung.* Frankfurt: Athenaum.

Linke, A. and Nussbaumer, M. (2000), 'Konzepte des Impliziten: Präsuppositionen und Implikaturen', in K. Brinker, G. Antos, W. Heinemann und S. F. Sager (eds), *Text- und Gesprächslinguistik. Ein internationales Handbuch zeitgenössischer Forschung.* Halbband 1. Berlin and New York: Walter de Gruyter. pp. 435–48.

Maas, D. (2005), 'Multilingualism in MPro'. www.iai.uni-sb.de/docs/mmpro.pdf.

Matthiessen, C. M. I. M. (2004) 'Descriptive motifs and generalizations', in A. Caffarel, J. R. Martin and C. M. I. M. Matthiessen (eds), *Functional Typology.* Amsterdam: Benjamins, pp. 537–674.

Neumann, S. M. (2003), *Die Beschreibung von Textsorten und ihre Nutzung beim Übersetzen. Eine systemisch-funktionale Korpusanalyse englischer und deutscher Reiseführer.* Frankfurt/M. : Peter Lang.

Neumann, S. and Hansen-Schirra, S. (2005), 'The CroCo Project. Cross-linguistic corpora for the investigation of explicitation in translations', in *Proceedings from the Corpus Linguistics Conference Series.* Vol. 1, no. 1, ISSN 1747-9398. www.corpus.bham.ac.uk/PCLC.

Neumann, S. (2005), 'The CroCo Corpus design'. Deliverable No. 1.1. www. fr46.uni-saarland.de/~croco.

Olohan, M. (2001), 'Spelling out the optionals in translation: a corpus study'. UCREL Technical Paper No. 13. Special Issue, *Proceedings of the Corpus Linguistics 2001 Conference. Lancaster. UK. 29 March–2 April 2001,* pp. 423–32.

Polenz, P. (1988), *Deutsche Satzsemantik. Grundbegriffe des Zwischen-den-Zeilen-Lesens.* Berlin: Mouton de Gruyter.

Ramm, W. and Fabricius-Hansen, C. (2005), 'Coordination and discourse structural salience from a cross linguistic perspective'. SPRIK Reports No. 30, University of Oslo. www.hf.uio.no/forskningsprosjekter/sprik /publikasjoner/sprikreports.html. pp.1–11.

Sager, J. C. (1994), *Language Engineering and Translation: Consequences of Automation*. Benjamins Translation Library, Vol.1. Amsterdam: John Benjamins.

Steiner, E. (1991), *A Functional Perspective on Language, Action and Interpretation*. Berlin: Mouton de Gruyter.

Steiner, E. (2001), 'Translations English–German: investigating the relative importance of systemic contrasts and of the text-type "translation". Papers from the 2000 Symposium on Information Structures across languages.' SPRIK-Reports No.7. Reports from the Project 'Languages in Contrast', University of Oslo. www.hf.uio.no/german/sprik/english/reports.shtml pp. 1–48; updated version in Steiner 2004a.

Steiner, E. (2004a), *Translated Texts: Properties, Variants, Evaluations*. Frankfurt/M.: Peter Lang Verlag.

Steiner, E. (2004b), 'Ideational grammatical metaphor: exploring some implications for the overall model. *Languages in Contrast*, Vol. 4:1, 139–66.

Steiner, E. (2005a), 'Some properties of texts in terms of "information distribution" across languages'. *Languages in Contrast*. 5.1., pp. 49–72.

Steiner, E. (2005b), 'Some properties of lexicogrammatical encoding and their implications for situations of language contact and multilinguality', in Franceschini, R. *In einer anderen Sprache. Sondernummer der Zeitschrift für Literaturwissenschaft und Linguistik*. Stuttgart: Metzler Verlag. Jahrgang 35, Heft 139, pp. 54–75

Steiner, E. (2005c), 'Explicitation is lexiocogrammatical realization, and is determining (independent) variables – towards an empirical and corpus-based methodology'. SPRIK-reports No. 36. www.hf.uio.no/forskningsprosjekter/sprik/docs/pdf/Report_36_ESteiner.pdf.

Steiner, E. and Teich, E. (2004), 'Metafunctional profile for the grammar of German', in A. Caffarel, J. R. Martin and C. M. I. M. Matthiessen (eds), *Functional Typology*. Amsterdam: Benjamins, pp. 139–84.

Steiner, E. and Vandenbergen, A. (eds.) (in press), special issue of *Language Sciences* on 'Functional approaches to discourse: perspectives, interactions, and recent developments.'

Steiner, E. and Yallop, C. (eds), (2001), *Exploring Translation and Multilingual Text Production: Beyond Content*. Berlin: Mouton De Gruyter.

Taverniers, M. (2005), 'Subjecthood and the notion of instantiation', in E. Steiner, and A. Vandenbergen (eds.) (2005), special issue of *Language Sciences* on 'Functional approaches to discourse: perspectives, interactions, and recent developments', pp. 651–78

Teich, E. (2003), *Cross-linguistic Variation in System and Text – A Methodology for the Investigation of Translations and Comparable Texts*. Berlin and New York: Mouton De Gruyter (published version of *Habilitationsschrift* of 2001).

Teich, E, Hansen, S. and Fankhauser, P. (2001), 'Representing and querying multi-layer annotated corpora', in *Proceedings of the IRCS Workshop on Linguistic Databases*. Philadelphia, pp. 228–237.

Toury, G. (1995), *Descriptive Translation Studies and Beyond*. Amsterdam and Philadelphia: John Benjamins.

Venuti, L. (ed.) (2000), *The Translation Studies Reader*. London and New York: Routledge.

Vinay, J-P and Darbelnet, J. (1958), *Stylistique comparée du francais et de l'anglais*. Paris: Les Éditions Didier. Page references are to the English translation in. Venuti (ed.) (2000), *The Translation Studies Reader*. London and New York: Routledge, 284–97.

9

Creativity in English Globalized: Signifiers and Their Signifieds

Edwin Thumboo
National University of Singapore

Firstly, what follows is exploratory, a limited incursion to tentatively map a large and complex subject. It has gaps, and is driven by personal interests that, in turn, influence how issues are prioritized and sorted into first- and second-order matters. Secondly, as the framework, the underlying assumptions, the distinction between fact and opinion, why different kinds of knowledge ought to be treated for what they are, should be seen steadily and whole and foreground all discussion. It would not matter if neglecting them had no serious consequences, no compound sin of partiality, marginalization and over-confidence. But when and where there are – and therefore jeopardizing something no less basic, essential and magical than our informing consciousness, our intellection – reminders should not be dismissed but taken seriously. Familiarity breeds not contempt but a self-confidence that is both intolerant and incapable of self-introspection; the greater the familiarity, whether imagined or real, the greater this self-certainty.

Nowhere is this more pronounced than in fields within the Humanities and Social Sciences (HSSs). Nowhere is it less pronounced than in the Hard Sciences (HSs). The reasons are not hard to find. Values, attitudes, assumptions – and other nuclei of thought and action – form, energize and dominate the former. Whatever their character, and whether working alone or in tandem, the bundle of values, attitudes and assumptions are primary. They work up front. In contrast, such nuclei are secondary in the HSs where facts, accepted because indisputable, dominate. What constitutes evidence, and how the intrinsic nature of this evidence affects the way it enters and is managed in discussion, are not only different but contrasting. The grounds for agreement, the relatively clear division between fact – the inherent reality – and opinion and hypotheses – the constructed reality – and what constitutes progress and advancement, are radically different. Processes in the HSs can be demonstrated and replicated. In the HSSs they proliferate. The *one* and the *many*: it is the difference between what constitutes and underpins physical geography and human geography. Or, for instance, between astronomy and astrology; or women's rights in Afghanistan and France; or democracy in

Zaire and India and Fiji and Australia. Once you get down to perception and governance, astrology, woman's rights and democracy are not the same in these three – and other – nations. As labels they are universal; as processes they are not. Taken intrinsically, there is only right or wrong science, but not good or bad science, a judgement that can only arise when that science is applied. There is only good or bad application of science.

The HSs's 'real' world has its own structure and laws. Its key concepts, processes, boundaries, and what are treated as absolutes at any given time, are transformed by discoveries. While we investigate, their nature is fully independent of us. While we can alter their application, we cannot alter their nature to suit our lifestyle as Singaporeans or Maltese in the way we can culture, or custom, or tradition. This 'real' world provides stability through a widely accepted body of knowledge and processes. It changes as each of its constituent disciplines expands. As progress is incremental, that stability is maintained and with it the line between knowledge – and its theorizing – and the hypothesizing which precedes change. There is no 'real' world of comparable scale, complexity and stability in the HSSs to perform similar functions. There are facts but they are secondary. William Wordsworth was born in 1770 and died in 1850. When did World War II start in Europe is far less important than where it did. Moreover, while related to them, both are less important than who started it and why. Such questions lead immediately to the determinants that shape and maintain a people, their identity, society and nation. These determinants include folkways, religion, philosophy, aesthetics, language, history, politics and sociology, and key components of culture such as literature, sculpture, painting, architecture, music and dance.[1] Apart from subsets that elaborate their content, they link and draw upon each other to form multiplying networks of meaning and significance arising from theoretical developments whose substance has a local habitation. Examples include the sociology of religion – an old linkage given a new lease on life – and the sociology of language, the sociology of literature, the sociology of architecture, the sociology of art, and so on. Politics and economics each provide their foci and perspectives, refurbishing old connections and forming fresh ones. Theoretical constructs were fleshed out by the particular inheritance and experience of First, Second and Third World countries and nations. Of the many factors that contributed to the dialectics of intellectual contact and consequence, two are of particular interest: the impact of colonialism and the post-independence response. They provide a context for the examination of various themes including the function of the colonizing language before and after national independence. Colonial languages have the potential to become international languages. Of those at the core of modern colonialism – Spanish and Portuguese, English and Dutch, French, German, then Italian, and Japanese – only Spanish, English, French are true international languages, with English leading the pack. English is so widespread today, and has set down such deep roots, especially in the former British dominions and colonies, that she is *the* international language. In each of its locations, her status is secure as an administrative as well as a major language of creativity. Yet in each instance English had to be domesticated, responding to the dynamics of the linguistic, political, social, economic situation prevailing in the particular colony. I have suggested elsewhere that, as colonies differed, colonialism created different categories, which when the settlements and dominions are included (America, Canada, white South Africa, Australia, and New Zealand) amount to twelve.[2] Therefore, the issues involved in the use of English varied significantly, as revealed by the following.

(1)

As a writer who believes in the utilization of African ideas, African philosophy and African folk-lore and imagery to the fullest extent possible, I am of the opinion the only way to use them effectively is to translate them almost literally from the African language native to the writer into whatever European language he is using as his medium of expression. I have endeavoured in my words to keep as close as possible to the vernacular expressions. For, from a word, a group of words, a sentence and even a name in any African language, one can glean the social norms, attitudes and values of a people.

In order to capture the vivid images of African speech, I had to eschew the habit of expressing my thoughts first in English. It was difficult at first, but I had to learn. I had to study each Ijaw expression I used and to discover the probable situation in which it was used in order to bring out the nearest meaning in English. I found it a fascinating exercise.[3]

(2)

Waiata (a term covering both songs and poems generally) were of many kinds. They can be sorted into five broad groups: waiata aroha are love songs; waiata tangi are songs of lamentation; waiata patere deal with cursing, war, and abuse; waiata oriori are lullabies, formerly sung to the nobly born to teach them their duties and heritage; and waiata tapere are songs of entertainment in general. Some idea of the range of each grouping may be gained by this example: within waiata patere are ngeri – these are songs and chants with actions directed against people. There are at least seven kinds of ngeri: hahani, which shames a person for a wrong they committed; kaioraora, which is a cursing song; manataunga, which is sung to keep a grievance alive; manawa-wera, which is used by relatives of those killed in battle, asking for vengeance; patere, which is an abusive chant with gestures; puha, which is a chant plus war dance; ngarahu, which is a virulent song of revenge for injury or defeat; and tutara, which is used by wronged husband against wife.[4]

(3)

My generation had looked at life with black skins and blue eyes, but only our own painful, strenuous looking, the learning of looking, could find meaning in the life around us, only our own strenuous hearing, the hearing of our hearing, could make sense of the sounds we made. And without comparisons. Without any startling access of 'self-respect'. Yet, most of our literature loitered in the pathos of sociology, self-pitying and patronized. Our writers whined in the voices of twilight, "Look at this people! They may be degraded, but they are as good as you are. Look at what you have done to them." And their poems remained laments, their novels propaganda tracts, as if one general apology on behalf of the past would supplant imagination, would spare them the necessity of great art.[5]

(4)
[...] verse in English is really a matter of courage. At the heart of it must be the anxiety that it is difficult to justify the claims of poems such as these on even the language in which they are written. But these poems need to be written. They are of a time, a place, of a people who find themselves having to live by institutions and folkways which are not of their heritage, having to absorb the manners of languages not their own. Such little knowledge as comes to them of the human predicament is no less knowledge than what comes to other peoples in other times and places.[6]

Consequently, the literature that emerged in writing their separate nations, some nascent and in the process of formation, others immemorial and making a transition from traditional oral to literate societies, yet others recovering and reasserting their classical traditions, as in the case of India, created a varied body of writing in English. Okara, Walcott, and Wong Phui Nam had their distinctive histories of formation. Moreover, what they saw as dominant challenges facing them as a sort to write in English, their English, reshaped and re-orientated to express the distinctiveness of their experience and sensibility, meant meaning-making in distinctive circumstances and ways.

9.1 Explication and assessment

How meaning is created is obviously central to any explication and assessment of literature. What does a particular text, generated in a particular set of circumstances, in each of the circumstances suggested above, mean? How does it go about creating its meaning? One could theorize, and many have, but trying to grasp the literature steadily and whole, mapping its signifi-cances, ultimately rests on reading it closely, attentive to the elements of its articulation. Scrutiny may not be fashionable, but there is no substitute. Yet it is ignored; it is no longer a key component of university programmes. It has requirements in terms of approaches, coverage, methods, and so on, that best engage the literature. The serious study of literature in any language rests on the critical tradition it has developed over the years. This critical tradition is there from the very beginning of the literature, implicit in the act of making. Formal criticism is a subsequent development. That for English Literature is about 500 years old, for the American about 150 and for the other literatures in World Englishes 60.

British and American literatures have been dominated by Critical Theory in the last two to three decades. The field is still thriving; a happy hunting ground for Theory and its practitioners. Not all are satisfied with the labels, concepts, definitions and paradigms employed. There are, after all, sides, and sides – disguised as positions and approaches – to be taken. For instance, calling these literatures 'post-colonial', virtually the first commandment for many, is misleading and hegemonic. How 'post' is 'post'? Well before freedom at midnight, these nations were energetically national. And despite uneven histories in many of them caused by systematic and prolonged corruption of their leaders, nationalism is a powerful force. The colonial condition is what they move away from as they journey towards national independence. And literature has been and remains a deep part of that national spirit and liberating process. That there is reluctance in the former metropolitan centres to accept this as a rich development is understandable. Even the computer program refuses to accept 'Englishes'; it underlines it in red.

As a distinctive enterprise, Critical Theory is on the decline, and the new directions the study of literature will take have emerged. In the case of English, both meaning-making and its study have broadened considerably as she becomes ever more global/international, more deeply entrenched; as she/it turns into Englishes. These developments are manifest in the large body of pre- and post-independence texts in increasingly national varieties of English. Such texts are fact, reality. They have opened up a field; they test the assumptions, the validity of much current critical practice. The old claim that these are either minor literatures or extensions of the literature in English dominated by British and American literature ceased to have sense decades ago. The strategy is to concentrate on cultural studies, themes such as the conflict between generations or the impact of modernization, or on individuals such as Wole Soyinka, Derek Walcott and V. S. Naipaul who won the Nobel for Literature, and Raja Rao and Nuruddin Farah the Neustadt. It is easier to treat major figures in a loose literary confederation than to bring together the literary environment to which they belong; to study them, but not the literature of which they are part. The concern is therefore not with the larger, more systematic scrutiny and explication and assessment of these literatures, which is necessary if we are to see these literatures in Englishes.

The challenge is to see these literatures in World Englishes through representative texts; to see them steadily, to see them whole. It requires reader and critic to be aware of contexts, of the writer's milieu, where he/she and his/her society and nation come from and are going, what dominates his/her life and times, and what of that is crucial in and to the larger meaning generated in and by their work. We did no less for Chaucer, Wyatt, Spenser, Marlow, Shakespeare, Donne, Milton, Dryden, Pope, Blake *et al*. That is how we entered that literature; that is how these literatures should be entered. There is nothing new in this, not even their neglect.

9.2 A way in

The challenge is, as I said, to see each of the literatures steadily and whole, which requires a necessary preparation. A useful way to the nub of what needs addressing would be to use Ferdinand de Saussure's ideas and concepts, namely,

(i)   the 'associative centre of the speaker' (p. 13),
(ii) his linking of *concept* and *sound-image* which 'intimately united, and each recalls the other' (p. 66), i.e., 'by an associative bond' (p. 66), and
(iii) his strategy 'to retain the word *sign* [*signe*] to designate the whole and to replace *concept* and *sound-image* respectively by *signified* [*signifé*] and *signifier* [*signifiant*]' (p. 67) as 'the last two terms have the advantage of indicating the opposition that separates them from each other and from the whole of which they are parts' (p. 67).[7]

Their neatness makes these terms useful despite the fact that there is a fundamental difference between the situation that Saussure was addressing and the one underpinning the basic issues I will be referring to. Saussure was dealing with a homogeneous society in which 'all the individuals that are linked together by speech, some sort of average will be set up: all will reproduce – not exactly of course, but approximately – the same signs united with the same concepts' (p. 13) because 'every means of expression used in society is based, in principle, on collective behaviour – or what amounts to the same thing – on convention' (p. 68). Presumably, the space for creativity is provided by 'not exactly but approximately'.

9.3 Universals/determinants

Saussure's formulations assume a homogeneity, a nation, a singularity in which the parts are shaped by and in sync with one another as mutually supportive universals, and all are directly linked to an over-arching whole. Broadly, these universals are

(i)   belief in God/Christ, Allah, Jehovah, or other religious/spiritual beliefs, and their moral values;
(ii) myths, legends, folklores;
(iii) histories, collective memories;
(iv) constructed, imaginative, spiritual and material worlds;

(v)   political, economic, social, educational and other institutions;
(vi) aesthetic preferences and interests;
(vii) language; and
(viii) orality/texts/discourse ranging from the divinely revealed, through epics, philosophy, art, music to literature and so on.

Through their substance, form and expression, these eight – whose force varies from society to society, from family to family, from individual to individual – generate those determinants that shape nation, community and individual, that construct their crucial interlocking identity. Moreover, the firmer that identity, the longer it will endure to oversee change, while ensuring its parts reflect, if not represent, the whole. First and second level details help to explain why, when they are taken together, *satu bangsa, satu bahasa, satu ugama* link, consolidate, even amalgamate the content, substance of the *signified,* and account for the bonding between a *signified* and its *signifier.* That accounts for the potency of the *sign.*

9.4 Nation

These three *satu*s whose parts continue to evolve, usually in tandem, bind nation and society in a unique over-arching identity that, despite substantial and larger cross-cultural sharing of basic values, ultimately marks it, the nation, off from all others. So we refer to 'the Malay world', Americans and Russians; the British and the French. Or to 'the Chinese Mind' or 'the Indian Mind',[8] discussions of which, inter alia, outline their rich, far-reaching content and practice, spread across a network of universals.

It is worth reminding ourselves that a nation is:

- a country, especially when thought of as a large group of people living in one area with their own government, language, traditions, etc.;
- a large group of people of the same race who share the same language, traditions and history, but who might not all live in the same area;
- an independent country (a *nation state*), especially when thought of as consisting of a single large group of people all sharing the same language, traditions and history (*Cambridge International Dictionary of English,* 1995)
- a people or group of peoples; a political state;
- a large aggregate of communities and individuals united by factors such as common descent, language, culture, history, or occupation of the same territory, so as to form a distinct people. Now also: such a people forming a political state; a political state. (In early use also in *pl.*: a country.);
- a group of people having a single ethnic, tribal, or religious affiliation, but without a separate or politically independent territory. (Frequently used of the Jewish people in the Diaspora.);

- (with *the*): the whole population of a country, freq. in contrast to a smaller or narrower body within it;
- (in *pl.*, in modern use with *the*.) †**a.** [After post-classical Latin *nationes*, Hellenistic Greek τὰ ἔθνη, and Hebrew *gᵊyᵌm*.] In and after Old Testament use: the heathen nations, the Gentiles. *Obs;*
- a group of people representing a nation. †**a.** A group of people belonging to a particular nation, esp. acting or regarded as its representatives. *Obs.* (Source: The Oxford English Dictionary Online, www.oed.com 2003)

This intimacy cannot be overstressed. It is a *satu* situation. The parameters are set by one language, its creative and critical tradition and reach, both powerful and active, as instrument and identity. We should not be surprised that Ben Jonson puts it thus in *Timber, or Discoveries,*

Language most shews a man: Speak, that I may see thee.[9]

Jonson is obviously referring to the individual's idiolect, and its great defining reach. Yet for one's idiolect to carry that much revelation – *Speak* that I may *see* thee – surely requires a considerably deep sharing of language, culture and environment. It is only that encoding which enables this kind of decoding. It implies a tremendous, and a tremendously active, homogeneity. It is in these circumstances that the language develops its totalizing power. There are needs and necessities if we are to sketch this totalizing power which goes beyond the language. It is the absence of this interrelated binding intimacy that underpins Walcott's deep wish for his own dialect.

Nowhere is this desire for an identifying distinctive linguistic creativity greater than in poetry. For all the features that make it distinctive – symbol, image, metaphor; syntax, phonology, morphology, etc. – have their greatest strength when they have a local, communal, national power. It is the poetry that makes the English language great; the poetry in Chinese, in Sanskrit, in Tamil, in Greek, in Latin, in Egyptian hieroglyphics of the 18th Dynasty. It is their poetry which carries their best moments. How these best moments are defined, while challenging in a *satu* situation, becomes even more complex when the language moves out of its original culture and environment, and settles without that culture and environment in areas with their own distinctive culture and environment.

There are three major settings for how language is used creatively. The first is the *satu* situation. The second is where the language has been part of a diaspora, going with its people. An example of this is the spread of Tamil first to Sri Lanka, and then much later to Malaysia and Singapore. Tamil was used to write about the Tamil experience, the experience of Tamils in whatever surroundings they found themselves. No literary works have been created by non-Tamils in Tamil. The same can be said of and for Chinese, whose linguistic commonwealth includes various countries in Southeast Asia. As it is in the case of Tamil, no non-Chinese has contributed to Chinese literature. The same broad generalization can be made of Malay. It is the third of these settings that are of greatest literary and linguistic interest. Its boundaries are marked by the more successful and widespread of modern international languages, namely Spanish, Portuguese, English, and French. But within this, there are divisions based on how each of these languages took root in their new environment. Although the factors are complex, it is possible to generalize. Spanish and Portuguese moved deeply into all levels of their colonial societies because there was a policy – which later turned into a tradition – of interracial marriage, while indigenous languages in Central and South America flourished, especially when they were supported by large, economically viable populations; Spanish was the *lingua franca* that transcended tribal, regional, national boundaries. Catholicism played an important part in this racialization, which was responsible for the rooting of Spanish. And, we might add, Portuguese. In the case of the French, it was a cultural penetration, reflected in their attitude to the treatment of colonies. The policy was driven by a strong desire to 'civilize', reflected in the way they were treated as overseas departments of France. For the British, the main instrument was 'indirect rule', which was formalized in the Treaty of Pankor, Malaya, formalized in 1874. Unlike the Spanish and the Portuguese, there was no tradition of interracial marriage. In fact, there was fairly strict segregation best exemplified in the British clubs that were an important feature of colonial life: the Cricket Club in Singapore, and the Selangor Club in Selangor. Those familiar with E. M. Forster's *A Passage to India* will recall the Chandrapore Club, whose importance as a focal point for British identity, emotion, sentiment, and attitude he spells out in considerable detail. The point here is that English did not become the inevitable language of life, in the way that Spanish and Portuguese did, and French to some extent.

Yet, because of the extensiveness of empire, and the world trade that evolved out of it, to which America contributed a great deal, English became the major global language. Its various functions gave it particular importance in all its former colonies. The language of globalization has always been English, which has left its closest competitor, French, far behind. What literature we have in English, in its major varieties today – now manifested as World Englishes – ensures it a great future.

It is worth reminding ourselves via S. I. Hayakawa's *Choose the Right Word* of what the last two determinants – namely *vii) language; and viii) orality/texts/ discourse ranging from the divinely revealed, through epics, philosophy, art, music to literature and so on* – map,

(i) '*Mean* is the least formal and the most general in embracing every kind of import a sign many have, whether explicit or implicit.' It breaks into other words each marking off a specific area: *denote, connote, imply, indicate, signify, suggest, symbolize.*

These are verbs. Let us look at the nouns.

(ii) '*Meaning* has the widest range of use, embracing everything from specific, concrete denotation to a general suggestiveness. The meaning of a word, sign, or symbol is the idea it expresses, the object it designates, or the concept it conveys'. It breaks into *implication, import, sense, significance* and *signification*.[10]

These are *satu* situations. Diasporas provide the biggest test of such contact and change where identities face each other, when the degree of their retention is the degree of their strength. The Jews and the Goanese to a lesser extent are examples. Through cultural and other contacts, the change today is more rapid and insistent than ever before, leading to a notable order/disorder of things.

The business is meaning-creation. The issues are basic, arising from a collocation of (i) *mean*, (ii) *meaning* and (iii) *meaning creation* in a language, English, taken on the back of trade and colonialism from its habitual home, then left as a legacy in bi- and multilingual communities and nations where its use and status have particular official and private histories. My main concern is with (iii) *meaning creation*, discussed chiefly with reference to my poem 'Uncle Never Knew'.

That homogeneity, that singularity behind the three *satu*s is altered, is dismantled in degrees when civilizations meet. The processes of change set loose depend on the circumstances of contact, whether voluntary or imposed, or a mixture of the variations lying between the two. An example from William Shakespeare – who else? – would be Henry V giving the first TESOL lesson on behalf of the yet unborn British Council. The exchange between King and Princess is emblematic. We have here the beginnings of putting a new sensibility, its needs and its culture, into English, and into French, presumably.

King Henry: Fair Katharine, and most fair,
　Will you vouchsafe to teach a soldier terms
　Such as enter at a lady's ear
　And plead his love-suit to her gentle heart?
Katharine: Your majesty shall mock at me; I cannot speak your England.
King Henry: O fair Katharine, if you will love me soundly with your French heart, I will be glad to hear you confess it brokenly with your English tongue. Do you like me, Kate?
Katharine: Pardonnez-moi, I cannot tell vat is 'like me'.
King Henry: An angel is like you, Kate, and you are like an angel.
Katharine: Que-dit-il? que je suis semblable aux anges? (What does he say? That I am like the angels?)
Alice: Oui, vraiment, sauf votre grâce, anisi dit-il. (Yes, truly, save your grace, he says so.)
King Henry: I said so, dear Katherine; and I must not blush to affirm it.
Katharine: O bon Dieu! Les langues des hommes sont pleines de tromperies. (O good God! the languages of the men are full of deceit.)

King Henry: What says she, fair one? That the tongues of men are full of deceits?

Alice: Oui, dat de tongues of de mans is be full of deceits: dat is the princess.

There are two main processes at work. The focus is on the last two of the universals (vii) language and (viii) orality/texts/discourse, what they were, are and will be. I will be looking at poetry. In a sense, it is in poetry that the signified is at its richest, where the denotative, the arithmetic of meaning, the simplest, the plainest of the signified, becomes connotative, a calculus, and therefore, the most complex of the signified.

9.5 Signifier, signified (1) *satu* situations

That they are written in a variety of English – broadly the *signifier* – should not mislead us unto thinking that they are either extensions of English-or American-Literatures. This is one of the central issues, if not the central one. For the *signified* is radically, tellingly different; non-Anglo-Saxon. It is Asian – Israeli, Pakistani, Indian (Tamil, Marathi, Punjabi, Kannada, Bengali), Sri Lankan (Sinhalese, Tamil, Dutch Burgher), Singapore/Malaysian (Malay, Chinese, Indian, Eurasian), Filipino (Ilocano, Cebuano, Chinese, Mestizo), Hong Kong Chinese, Indian, British, etc.

Try and compute the variety and depth of what the *signified* represents *in toto* in each of these national locations and sub-locations. That is what the *signifier* is to carry for each nation and its peoples, from the acrolectal, through the mesolectal down to the basilectal. The focus is creativity; language stretched and layered beyond the habitual, exploring and making the familiar new and significant. That takes us beyond the main arteries and veins of what a language does, to its most delicate capillaries, to nuances of feeling, thought and perception, that turn the metaphor to this and not that, to what make for uniqueness.

9.6 Global signifiers, national signifieds

What happens when English – or any other language for that matter – is taken out of its habitual/traditional home and (i) first exported as part of colonialism, (ii) then adopted as a post-independence instrument of modernization, and (iii) becomes gradually domiciled and re-orientated to generate enough confidence in its new habitation for its speakers to use it creatively? What is added to English for it to become Indian, Sri Lankan, Malaysian, Singaporean, Nigerian? Furthermore, this topping up, cultural in part, has its source in other indigenous cultures. With time, these cultures weaken with each succeeding English-speaking generation, especially as modernization, globalization and internationalization bite ever deeper. What part does the transference of discourse from Word to Image play in all these processes? What kind of meaning-generating resources are left? What are the implications for writer and critic? If literature is an intrinsic part of culture and should be among the main instruments that maintain that culture, what burden would any diminution impose on other cultures and their languages, especially in the long term? In this process, much that has a powerful local habitation and a name is lost unless it enters and becomes an organic part of the particular discourse, especially where it is poetry. Unless this is done, the global language would be marked by its originating history, sociology, custom, etc. Nor can language remain neutral, as mere denotative instrument. Language cannot be neutral, a free-floating radical. That would leave it without the energy of meaning-making, within the identity of a strong new cultural setting. As Raja Rao reminded us, he could only write as an Indian, we write as what we are. Language must thus acquire a local habitation and a name. Some of the issues will be noted when I conclude with references to 'Uncle Never Knew', a poem that indicates some of the cross-cultural challenges I faced when writing it.

There is a process in this transformation, one that goes through various phases: pre-colonial, colonial, independent, post-independence. This would be the normal progress covering the historical experience of nations that have been part of the British Empire.

9.7 English in different phases of the colonial experience

The pre-colonial profile is more fully a *satu* one, in which cross-cultural contacts are absorbed under the auspices of *satu* determinants, so change is more evolutionary, seldom revolutionary. Identities are more stable, more shared, the connection between signified and signifier firm and the processes that Hayakawa listed in place.

With colonialism, the *satu* situation is radically changed. Depending on the basic colonial style, that is, whether it was one of 'indirect rule', which characterized British colonialism, or as full assimilation that occurred under the Spanish and Portuguese, or cultural assimilation, and political incorporation of the territory into the metropolitan centre, which is what the French generally did, the new profile varied accordingly. There was a second factor; namely, the status of the individual and his family and the extent to which they accepted the colonial language and its culture. In various parts of the British Empire, an English-speaking middle class emerged. They were the first hyphenated individuals. It is members of this class who produced the literatures in English in all the non-Anglo-Saxon areas of the British Commonwealth. Yet this generation, despite having a foot in two worlds, had enough of their pre-colonial inheritance to mark and shape and move their English. In effect, while the signifier remained, the signified altered. While the denotative was the same, the connotative was enriched by the substance of the particular culture. And not merely substance in terms of language and sensibility, but substance in terms of a total political, economic, social and cultural history. In these circumstances, language, even a new language, was identity.

What marks the independence phase is the increasing number of hyphens that undermines the *satu* position whose supporters tend to fight a desperate rearguard action. The most notable among them would be the language chauvinists, who in Singapore were best exemplified by the unyielding, inflexible advocates of 'Chinese for the Chinese, now and forever'. Language preservation is an important part of cultural preservation. And the desire to preserve can only be realistic if the speech community is large as well as politically and economically powerful enough to sustain such linguistic desires, however passionate. A classic example in Asia would be the Chinese, Japanese and Koreans, though in the case of the latter two, the number of serious English users, already significant, is rapidly increasing. Smaller nations do not have much of a choice. The history of study of Chinese in Singapore provides an obvious cautionary tale. Passing Chinese with credit in order to move from Secondary school to Junior College, and as a requirement for obtaining a degree, is no longer compulsory. The demands of modern life as part of globalization require the mastery of a great deal of knowledge and practices and that is done in English, the more sophisticated the better, so the linguistic energies that used to be split half and half between mother tongue and English are now devoted more to English with the result that the mother tongue and access to its culture have declined. Therefore, the correlation between signifier and signified that was there during the colonial period as part of cultural capital is no longer present in strength. This is a development that flattens language. It is understood in general terms, without the meaningful angularities and curves of a particular culture and its environment. Its calculus has been reduced to algebra, to an arithmetic.

While it is obvious, it should be stressed that change within the segments of the process, of the continuity and change outlined here, have enormous variations from individual to individual, accounted for in part by family history and tradition and individual interests.

9.8 Bi-cultural, bilingual: singular signifier, plural signifieds

Of migrants, those who came to Singapore and Malaya/Malaysia are an exception. The Indians from India had a taste of colonialism before arrival. The Malays from various parts of Southeast Asia had either British or Dutch colonial experience, the exceptions being those who came from Southern Thailand. And the Chinese, chiefly from Fujian and Guangdong, had known the ravages of European imperialism, chiefly economic and indirectly. So for us, the pre-colonial and colonial histories differed. The point is of some importance because the depth of the subtle experience depended on these histories. That of my own family on the Indian side – my grandfather came from Madras in the 1880s – included a great deal of English. The kind of hyphenation arising from cross-cultural contact had already begun. He had entered the English language, trained as a civil engineer, become a Christian, and moved to Singapore, then Malaya. English changed their way of life, not merely professionally. My auntie, for instance, believed in Christian Science, had a Goanese cook who made terrific steak, knew how to whip cream, and produced an excellent tea with scones, etc. punctually at 4:30pm using the second best set of silver. My aunties had patent leather boots and dressed accordingly. I remember my family photograph of them in very frilly ankle-length skirts plus parasols and the inevitable hat, trying to look serene in equatorial Muar.

My mother's side was Teochew with a dash of Peranakan. The Swatow roots were very strong. My grand-uncle was relatively illiterate. He knew the importance of learning and also of English, living as he did in the British colony. He sent two of my older uncles to Chinese school, and the others to English school. The ladies of the household were brought up in the traditional way. His brothers and nephews in Swatow had a very strong Chinese education, living as they did in the ancestral home, a family of traders and merchants with a slight anti-establishment strain. Divided into dialect groups, the Chinese community went about their own affairs, including business, with minimum interference from the colonial powers, who were interested in the trade and business they generated. There were clan associations as well as Chambers of Commerce that formed networks within Singapore as well as with other Chinese communities within the region. The rice imported from Thailand by Teochews in Singapore was from Teochew merchants in Thailand who had developed a monopoly based in Bangkok over the years. The rubber trade in Southeast Asia was chiefly in Hokkien hands and the merchants did their banking with establishments founded and run by the Chinese: Overseas Chinese Banking Corporation, Ban Lee Hin, Chun Kiaw, Overseas United Bank, all of which prospered because Chinese merchants relied on them rather than British banks such as Hong Kong and Shanghai, Chartered Bank, and Mercantile Bank. My Chinese relatives, the Lee and Kang families, maintained a strong Chinese family life. The Lees were traders and merchants, and anyone who came from China had to go into the family business.

Such a dual inheritance in terms of culture and language – Teochew and English, as Tamil had no part to play – leads to a series of hyphenations, integrations, contrasts, conflicts and resolutions, all leading to an interesting notion of self, of identity. I had to constantly negotiate between cultures, between languages. As time went on, English dominated, a fact that had strong influence of how my identity evolved. Helen Vendler's *Poems.Poets. Poetry: An Introduction and Anthology* (St Martin's Press, Boston, 1997) provides a number of useful labels and their elaborations which I would like to enlist as a time-saving device. Three are of immediate concern: 'Constructing the Self' (Chapter 6), 'Poetry and Social Identity' (Chapter 7), and 'History and Regionality' (Chapter 8). In addition to what she has to say, the construction of self for a poet brought up in an environment dominated by two languages, in my case both inherited, was the beginning of the formation of a hyphenated, compound, psyche. As I grew older, and as the formal study of English took root, the ability to use English developed at the expense of the Teochew I had acquired. My mother tongue ceased to grow. It had enough to service me for social purposes. It was English that became the language of my mind and a large part of the language of my feeling. Teochew could still move me but less so as time went by. The limits of my personality had more and more English markers. I studied its literature with all the analytical energies that the systematic English honours scores demanded and received. I started to write poems in English. The construction of self meant firstly understanding the most complex possible making of meaning in English, with all the intensity of poetries and will beaten hard, at times frustratingly. This formation of course was ongoing, unending. But I would like to return to Vendler's 'Poetry and Social Identity' –

> The identity of the lyric speaker (by contrast to the speaker of satire or of dramatic monologue, for instance) has historically been 'open-ended', meaning that the words of the speaker could be spoken by any reader within the culture. In the past, in literate cultures, both Western and Eastern, education was preliminary to the (male) professions; and writers, who usually came from the group of those so educated, directed their writings to people who belonged to the same group and possessed the same culture. As we look at the lyrics being produced today, especially in the United States, we can see a marked change in the conception of the lyric speaker. The speaker often is not 'neutral', but is given a defined nationality, race, class, sex, or sexual preference, so that we may say, 'This is a poem spoken by an African American', or 'The speaker is a mother who addresses her sister' or 'This is a gay love poem spoken by one man to another' or 'This is a poem spoken in Hispanic dialect'.
>
> The choice of identity in a poem is up to the writer, for whom identity is never simple. All writers know that besides the forms of identity listed above (which can be combined into such a mixture as 'African American middle-class gay male') there are other important identity components such as religion, generation (elder or younger), family roles, social roles, and so on. (P. 211)

But it is 'History and Regionality' that is finally the most crucial. Vendler writes that:

> Immediate challenges arise for a lyric poet who is writing a poem about (or within or against) history. In the first place, written history is a narrative

genre, and the history of a complex event (the American Revolution, the Civil War in England leading to the execution of Charles I, the Easter Rising) is not only narratively complicated, but always politically disputed.... How does the poet incorporate history within the miniature dimensions of the lyrics? There are several central techniques:

1. Focusing on a problem rather than on incidents;
2. Finding an emblematic scene or scenes;
3. Finding a symbolic or mythological equivalent for a historical episode;
4. Seeing the human inside of the event as corresponding to the historical outside;
5. Finding an epigrammatic summation;
6. Adopting a prophetic or philosophic view larger than that of a mere eyewitness. (p. 238)

So the uncle, who is the subject of the poem, had a very strong Chinese background, as he had been brought up and educated in China. But he could not fit into family life in Singapore, whose mainstay was business. Despite the family's strong merchant background, he was radicalized by Communist ideology, and had developed strong anti-capitalist and anti-Japanese feelings. When he arrived in Singapore, he was expected to join the family business, or at least to apprentice himself. My grand-uncle arranged for him to be attached to his friend's trading house located in Boat Quay,[11] whose Chinese associations are extremely precise and part of Sir Stamford Raffles' original plan for that part of Singapore. Given his lifestyle and propensities, uncle did not want to stay in the extended house of the family in Minto Road. He lived in North Boat Quay which was then a very solid Chinese merchant enclave, many with families. There were of course the great British merchant houses such as Guthrie's and Harrison and Crossfield.

Uncle Never Knew

I

He lived – if you could call it that – two streets off
Boat Quay North. Tranquil as leaves left in a tea cup.
Always alone but never lonely. The daily bustle
Of barge and coolie ferrying rubber, rice and spice,
All energy and profit, for towkays and Guthrie's,
Slipped past without ripple or sound or promise.
No enterprising cleverness to make his brothers
Happy, as nothing drew him to our hot meridian.
Often after rain, he would watch the day dry out.
But if a few fine drops caught the sun and glittered
Against that thinning blue strip of northern sky,
He was back in Swatow. At his table. Preparing

Ink and brush; fingering his father's piece of jade;
Intoning Li Po, Tu Fu, and reading Mao. Sipped tea;
Fed his carps, while waiting for his friends.

II

Great houses are history, clan, essential unity; belief.
A way of life which brooks no breaking of fidelity.
Rooted comforts reaffirm; nothing is extinguished.
Memory is full and whole: he was ensconced; secure.
For a few it's the only pulse. Many need this bedrock,
This island, so little that Cheng Ho barely noticed.

Post-astral, Uncle

Stroked his undernourished beard. Spoke to clouds,
Not people. The moon climbed roofs as he waited
For glow-worms to signify the darkening bamboos.
Communing with self, he was his favorite neighbour.

He could not hear migrant hearts change rivers,
From big to a small, smelly one. Or feel dreams
Gather along Carpenter Street, then roll down Telok
Ayer, up Ang Siang Hill, to answer temple bells.
The world was hard language, felt daily, as heart,
And will, drop into soft releasing opium working
Up hungry lungs, as shadows flickered on the wall.

He never knew our age in full; had no transplanted way
To name its joys, its follies. True exile, he denied our
Home, till life do us part, in '51, leaving companions
Marx, Engels and Mao, Lu Shun, the *Li Sao*, T'ao Ch'ien.

When I am by you, river, I feel Uncle watching me.
I hear much from inside his spirit, his affirmations.
Old Country stories re-surface, tell their tale.
That House I've never seen, tries to sketch itself.

The footnote on North Boat Quay provides information that is essential if we
are to have a sense of the historical geography of Singapore. British colonial
experience within individual colonies and across colonies had made them
realize the wisdom of careful planning to facilitate management. Inevitably,
we had an area for the Malays, Arabs and Indian Muslims, an area for Indian
Hindus, an area for the Chinese. Consequently, modern Singapore has its
Chinatown, Little India, Geylang Serai/Jalan Eunos at one time strongly
Malay areas, and Arab Street. North Boat Quay, which is part of Chinatown,
played in important part an Singapore's economic development, and the

mention of Guthrie's and towkays would invoke a strong sense of time and place, and the economic rhythm of that part of Singapore, at least among the older generation. The name has a special significance that draws on its local history.

I am not going to comment on the whole poem, but only two other points. Uncle's background is sketched in by a series of quick references, 'preparing ink and brush' suggests his interest in calligraphy and literature and painting, all of which have very powerful ongoing traditions. Where he differs from his elders is his interest in Mao, Marx, and Engels, and Lu Shun. That puts him among the modernizing Chinese, those who saw China's problems as rooted in a Confucianism and the feudal structure it sustained. A history of more than two thousand years was something to be cherished. Confucianism was too total a philosophy and value system as a way of governance. The two were interlinked, but Uncle took the view that the philosophy and value system was vital to maintenance of the Chinese identity. That capacity was all the more important if the governance side was to be renovated and modified, as it had to be if China were to be a great nation again. There was no contradiction in him arising from his re-integration of inheritance and hope. The way he loved his father's piece of jade, which he brought with him, and which he handled with essential nostalgia, showed his deep attachment to Chinese culture, his inheritance, and when he talked about his life, it was plainly bourgeois with strong feudal elements based on hierarchy of master, sons of master, and servants. Obviously, his interest in poetry, in drinking tea with friends, admiring his carps, had a long history behind it. That life was the source of much satisfaction, and yet he realized the need for change. It is important, therefore, that *signifier* and *signified* are seen as flourishing and as energizing. This is only possible if you know the history, the culture, and all that made the individual, his life, his society, and its life.

Notes

1 For a discussion, see Edwin Thumboo (1989), 'Self-Images: Contexts for Transformations', in *Management of Success: The Moulding of Modern Singapore*, ed. Kernial Singh Sandhu and Paul Wheatley (Singapore: Institute of Southeast Asian Studies), pp. 749–68.

2 Edwin Thumboo, 'Conditions of Cross-cultural Perceptions: The Other Looks Back'. Forthcoming, in the *Proceedings of Conference on 'Embracing the Other: Addressing Xenophobia in the New Literatures in English'* (Erfurt, Germany).

3 Gabriel Okara (1973), 'African Speech ... English Words', in *African Writers on African Writing*, ed. G. D. Killam (London: Heinemann), p. 137.

4 Keri A. L. Hulme (1981), 'Mauri: An Introduction to Bicultural Poetry in New Zealand', in *Only Connect*, ed. Guy Amirthanayagam and S. C. Harrex (Australia: The Flinders University Relations Unit), pp. 290–91.

5   Derek Walcott (1972), 'What the Twilight Says: An Overture', intro-
     duction to *Dream on Monkey Mountain and Other Plays* (London: J. Cape),
     pp. 9–10.

6   Wong Phui Nam (1968), Foreword to *How the Hills are Distant* (Kuala
     Lumpur: Department of English, University of Malaya, Kuala Lumpur).

7   Ferdinand de Saussure. Charles Bally, Albert Sechehaye and Albert
     Riedlinger, (eds.) (1959), *Course in General Linguistics*, translated with
     introduction and notes by Wade Baskin (United States: McGraw-Hill
     Paperbacks).

8   The title of two volumes edited by Charles A. More and published by
     the University Press of Hawaii (1967), which drew on the proceedings of
     four East–West Philosophers' Conferences held between 1939 and 1964
     at the University.

9   Ben Jonson (1953), *Timber, or Discoveries* (Syracuse, NY: Syracuse
     University Press).

10   S. I. Hayakawa (1968), *Choose the Right Word: A Modern Guide to Synonyms*
     (New York: Funk & Wagnalls), pp. 271–2.

11   Boat Quay (Chinese: 驳船码头) is a historical quay in Singapore which is
     situated upstream from the mouth of the Singapore River on its southern
     bank. It was the busiest part of the old Port of Singapore, handling three
     quarters of all shipping business during the 1860s. Because the south
     bank of the river here resembles the belly of a carp, which according to
     Chinese belief is where wealth and prosperity lie, many shophouses were
     built, crowded into the area.... As early as 1822, Sir Stamford Raffles
     had already designated the area south of the river to be developed
     as a Chinese settlement. Boat Quay was completed in 1842 and the
     Chinese, mostly traders and labourers, settled there in large numbers.
     Conditions were squalid but Boat Quay flourished, rapidly exceeding
     in volume the trade on the north bank where the Europeans had their
     offices, houses and government buildings. (Source: www.en.wikipedia.
     org/wiki/Boat_Quay.)

Nominalization, Verbalization and Grammatical Metaphor

Zhu Yongsheng
Fudan University

10.1 Introduction

Ever since M. A. K. Halliday put forward the notion of grammatical metaphor in his *An Introduction to Functional Grammar* published in 1985, there has been much discussion about its definition, classification, function, realization forms, and working mechanisms, and its relation to ideology, language development, register and genre. Among these publications, we can find comprehensive research such as Halliday (1994 [1985], 1992, 1993a, 1996, 1998a, 1998b), Matthiessen (1988), Matthiessen and Nesbitt (1996), Goatly (1997), Hu (1996) Zhu and Yan (1999, 2001), discussions on the relationship between grammatical metaphor and ideology such as Martin (1992, forthcoming) and Goatly (1993), discussions on the relationship between grammatical metaphor and language development such as Derewianka (1995) and Painter (1993), on ideational metaphor such as Halliday (1994 [1985]), Martin (1992), Matthiessen (1993, 1995a, 1995b, 1998), Ravelli (1988a), and Zhu (1994), on interpersonal metaphor such as Butler (1988, 1996), Martin (1995), Lemke (1998), Matthiessen (1993), Thibault (1995), and Zhu (1994), on textual metaphor such as Martin (1992), and Matthiessen (1992), on the relationship between grammatical metaphor and register such as Goatly (1993), and Ravelli (1985), on grammatical metaphor in technical discourse such as Halliday (1993b, 1997), Halliday and Martin (1993) , Martin and Veel (1997) and Dong (2005), and on grammatical metaphor in art discourse such as Ravelli (1998b).

Although so many achievements have been made, there is still much to be desired. As far as we can see it at this stage, there are at least two weak points to be overcome in our future research work: (i) nominalization, especially taking process as thing, is regarded as the main or the only means of grammatical metaphor; and (ii) little attention has been paid to verbalization and its metaphoric function. This chapter attempts to further the discussion of grammatical metaphor by looking at the following issues: (i) the basic criteria of grammatical metaphor, (ii) the definition and classification of nominalization, (iii) the definition and classification of verbalization and its relation to grammatical metaphor, and (iv) the comparison between nominalization and verbalization in terms of their metaphoric functions.

10.2 Basic criteria of grammatical metaphor

According to systemic linguists, language is a layered social semiotic, which consists of three strata: phonology, lexicogrammar and discourse semantics. Discourse semantics is symbolized or realized by lexicogrammar and lexicogrammar is symbolized or realized by phonology. The lexico-grammatical realization of discourse can appear in the congruent form or in the incongruent form.

By congruent form, we refer to the realization of participants, process, quality, assessment and circumstantial meanings such as place, time, manner and instrument in an unmarked way, i.e. by using nouns to represent participants, verbs to represent processes, adjectives to represent quality, modal words to represent assessment, adverbs and prepositional phrases to represent circumstantial meanings, and connectives to realize logical meanings, as in (1):

(1a) The driver drove the bus too fast down the hill, so the brakes failed.

In this clause complex, the three participants are all realized by nouns (*the driver*, *the bus* and *the brakes* respectively), the two material processes are both realized by verbs (*drove* and *failed* respectively), the circumstantial meaning of manner is realized by an adverbial phrase (*too fast*), the circumstantial meaning of direction is realized by a prepositional phrase (*down the hill*), and the logical meaning of cause and effect is realized by a conjunction (*so*). In this way, its surface meaning at the lexicogrammatical level and its deep meaning at discourse level become identical.

By incongruent form, we refer to the marked realization of discourse meanings at the level of lexicogrammar. More specifically, by taking measures such as treating process as thing and treating quality as thing, the surface meaning at the lexicogrammatical level is different from that at the level of discourse semantics. This discrepancy is called the tension between the different strata of language. And it is the existence and functioning of this tension that leads to the generation of grammatical metaphor. Look at (1b) for illustration:

(1b) The driver's over-rapid downhill driving of the bus caused brake failure.

(1b) is the incongruent form of (1a). The participants in (1a) have become epithets or post-modifiers in nominal groups (*driver's, of the bus, brake*), the logical meaning of cause and effect in (1a) has been turned into a process (*caused*), and the original process has been changed into a participant by way of nominalization (*driving*).

This kind of example tells us that the tension between lexicogrammar and discourse semantics makes grammatical metaphor theoretically possible but two basic criteria must be satisfied before we can take something as grammatical metaphor. First, it must meet the following three sub-criteria: (i) it must involve two meanings; (ii) these two meanings must be layered, one literal at the level of lexicogrammar and the other transferred at the level of discourse meaning, or one surface meaning and the other deep meaning; and (iii) one must resemble the other, i.e., the meaning of lexicogrammar must resemble or symbolize that of discourse semantics. Second, it must be grammatical in the sense that it must involve some grammatical variation other than purely lexical metaphor (see Halliday 1985/1994; Martin forthcoming).

10.3 Nominalization revisited

10.3.1 Definition

According to Quirk *et al.* (1985: 1288), nominalization refers to 'a noun phrase ... which has a systematic correspondence with a clause structure' and 'the noun head of such a phrase is normally related morphologically to a verb'. To some others, nominalization can be paraphrased as the language phenomenon of 'turning a verb or adjective into a noun'. But to us, nominalization simply means taking something that is not a thing as a thing.

10.3.2 Classification of nominalization

In previous studies of nominalization, the focus has been on reconstruing the process as a thing. However, there exist other types that also deserve our attention. In this section, we will take a look at other types of nominalization.

10.3.2.1 Taking process as thing

In the congruent form of realization, a process should be realized by a verb. But in the incongruent form, a process can be represented as a thing, as in (1b) above and (2b), (3b) and (4b) below:

(2a) The police *investigated* the matter.
(2b) The police conducted an *investigation* into the matter.
(3a) The floods considerably *eroded* the land.

(3b) There was considerable *erosion* of the land from the floods.
(4a) First, she *reviewed* how the dorsal fin evolved.
(4b) There was a first *review* of the evolution of the dorsal fin.

This kind of language phenomenon is called ideational metaphor in Hallidayan terminology (Halliday 1994 [1985]) and has received most of the attention of linguists in their studies of nominalization.

This kind of metaphor has three functions. First, it can turn a dynamic process into a static entity through class-shift or recategorization and provides us with a different way of construing the world, as shown in (1b), (2b), (3b) and (4b). Second, it can increase the information load of the nominal group by nominalizing the dynamic process and putting several epithets before the head of the nominal group, and thus succeeds in condensing the information of the clause, as shown by *considerable erosion* in (3b) and *a first review* in (4b). Third, it can blur or cover up the actor by using nominalizations. For example, the actor, *the flood* in (3a) is turned into a circumstantial element in (3b) as a result of the use of the nominalization of *erosion*, and the actor, *she*, in (4a) disappears completely in (4b) as a result of the use of the nominalization of *review*. These functions can make the meaning of the clause more objective and impersonal, which is one of the reasons why nominalization is favoured in technical discourse (Halliday 1993b, 1997, 1998b; Halliday and Martin 1993; Martin and Veel 1997; Dong 2005).

10.3.2.2 *Taking quality as thing*

In the congruent form, quality is realized by adjectives. But in the incongruent form, it can be represented by a noun. That means that the speaker can take quality as thing, as in (5b), (6b) and (7b).

(5a) I was not *hungry* to be free.
(5b) I was not born with a *hunger* to be free.
(6a) They ceased to be *hostile* because they lost personnel.
(6b) They ceased *hostilities* because they lost personnel.
(7a) They were *narrow-minded* and I don't like it.
(7b) I don't like their *narrow-mindedness.*

This kind of language phenomenon also belongs to ideational metaphor in Halliday's functional grammar. The only difference lies in the fact that what is turned into a thing is not a process but a quality. In this type of metaphor, quality can appear in the form of a circumstantial element as *hunger* in (5b), in the form of a participant as *hostilities* in (6b) and *narrow-mindedness* in (7b). In the meantime, the original carrier can become the epithet of a participant as *their* in (7b), and in this way its role in the clause becomes less important.

10.3.2.3 *Taking assessment as thing*

In the congruent form, assessment is expressed by modal verbs or modal adverbs. But in the incongruent form, it can be expressed by a noun, as in (8b), (9b), (10b) and (11b):

(8a)   I achieved what I *could.*
(8b)   I achieved my *potential.*
(9a)   You *can* go now.
(9b)   You have got my *permission* to go now.
(10a)   That's what you *should* do.
(10b)   It is your *obligation* to do that.
(11a)   I *must* do it.
(11b)   It is my *responsibility* to do it.

This kind of metaphor is termed interpersonal metaphor by Halliday (1994 [1985]). Modal adverbs such as *must* and *should* differ not only in meaning, e.g. *could* in (8a) indicates ability, *can* in (9a) expresses permission, *should* in (10a) means obligation, and *must* in (11a) represents responsibility, but also in the attitudes taken by the speaker, with *must* being the strongest and *could* the weakest. However, all these modal verbs are colloquial and informal in style. Comparatively speaking, their corresponding nominalizations sound more formal. This difference can result in different interpersonal meanings, which can influence the establishment and maintenance of the interpersonal relationship between the speaker and the listener and affect the fulfilment of the goal of their verbal interaction.

10.4 Verbalization and grammatical metaphor

10.4.1 Definition of verbalization

By definition, verbalization refers to the language phenomenon that something that is not a process by itself is taken as a process or a non-action is realized by a verb.

10.4.2 Classification of verbalization

In our observation, verbalization can be divided into the following four sub-categories: (i) temporal relation as process, (ii) cause–effect relation as process, (iii) condition as process, and (iv) concession as process. These types share two functions in common: (i) they can express a certain logical meaning, and (ii) they can increase the information load of the incongruent form by turning the original subordinate sentence into a simple sentence and packing the information of two or more than two clauses into one.

10.4.2.1 Taking temporal relation as process

There are roughly two types of temporal relation: same time and different time.

To express two or more-than-two events that happen at different times congruently, connectives such as *before, after, then* and *afterwards* are used. But this kind of temporal relation can also been taken as process and realized by verbs, as in (12b) and (13b):

    (12a) She left *before* I arrived.
    (12b) Her departure *preceded* my arrival.
    (13a) Motorcycles came first. Motorcade appeared *afterwards.*
    (13b) The motorcade *followed* motorcycles.

To express two or more-than-two events that happen at the same time congruently, connectives such as *while, meanwhile, concurrently, simultaneously* and *at the same time* are used. But like the different-time type, this kind of temporal relation can also been taken as process and realized by verbs, as in (14b) and (15b):

    (14a) The strike took place last Monday. The party conference was held *at the same time.*
    (14b) The strike was timed to *coincide* with the party conference.
    (15a) There were strong winds. And *in the meantime* there was a heavy rain.
    (15b) Strong winds *were accompanied* by a heavy rain.

To express the same or different time, the congruent forms tend to take the temporal relation as a logical element outside the transitivity structure of the clause concerned like *before* in (12a), or as a circumstantial element like *afterwards* in (13a), *at the same time* in (14a) and *in the meantime* in (15a). The incongruent forms, however, tend to take this relation as a dynamic process and make it part of the transitivity structure.

10.4.2.2 Taking cause–effect relation as process

To express cause–effect relation in the congruent way, connectives such as *because, so, since, for, therefore* and *for the reason* are used. But this kind of logical meaning can also be taken as process and realized by verbs, as in (16b) and (17b):

    (16a) *Because* he was careless, a traffic accident occurred.
    (16b) His carelessness *caused* a traffic accident.
    (17a) We rushed and *so* became confused.
    (17b) Our rushing *led to* our confusion.

(16a) and (17a) use the conjunctions *because* and *so* respectively to realize the causal relation, but (16b) and (17b) use the verbs *cause* and *lead to* to express the same relation. This transformation turns the causal relation into a dynamic process.

10.4.2.3 *Taking condition as process*

To express the meaning of condition in the congruent way, connectives such as *if* and *unless* are used. But in the incongruent form, this meaning can be realized by verbs as in (18b) and (19b):

(18a) *If* you have good food, exercise and enough sleep, you will have good health.
(18b) Good health *depends on* good food, exercise and enough sleep.
(19a) I sleep with the window open *unless* it's really cold.
(19b) Whether I sleep with the window open *is determined* by the weather condition.

The meaning of condition is realized by the conjunctions *if* and *unless* as in (18a) and (19a) respectively, but by the verbs *depend on* and *determine* as in (18b) and (19b).

10.4.2.4 *Taking concession as process*

To express the meaning of concession in the congruent way, connectives such as *although, even though* and *even so* are used. But in the incongruent form, verbs can be used instead as in (20b), (21b) and (22b):

(20a) I felt he was wrong, *although* I didn't say so at the time.
(20b) My silence *didn't mean* that I felt he was right.
(21a) *Even though* the motor housing was unstable, the research staff completed the field trials.
(21b) The instability of the motor housing *did not preclude* the completion of the field trials.
(22a) She is annoying at times. *Even so*, I like her.
(22b) Her annoyance *does not stop* me from liking her.

In the congruent forms (20a), (21a) and (22a), the meaning of concession is expressed by the conjunctions *even though, even so* and *although* respectively, but by the negative verb forms *did not preclude, does not stop* and *didn't mean* in the incongruent forms. In this way, the implicit negative logical relation becomes an explicit process and the static meaning becomes dynamic.

10.4.3 Verbalization but not grammatical metaphor

We must note that some uses of English verbs can be mistaken as grammatical metaphor, as in the underlined parts in the following examples:

(23) to <u>water</u> the flowers
(24) to <u>stone</u> somebody to death

These verbs can be used as nouns and function as participants of the clause, so it is very likely for some people to mistake them as grammatical metaphor. However, if we look closely at the meanings of these words, we will find what they represent is a process rather than some thing although they are morphologically identical with their corresponding nouns. For instance, *to water* means *to pour water on plants* rather than the liquid called *water*, and *to stone* means *to throw stones* rather than the substance called *stone* in the English language. That is to say, (23) and (24) are not examples of using nouns to realize processes but examples of using verbs to embody processes.

In order to give a further explanation, let us take a comparative approach by looking at the English verb *to water* and its Chinese equivalent *jiao* (浇). In Chinese, the verb *jiao* and the noun *shui* (水) are two different characters. They are different not only morphologically but also functionally. For this reason, nobody will take *jiao* as in *jiao hua* (which means 'to water the flowers') as a verbalization or grammatical metaphor. The English verb *to water*, however, is confusing because it is morphologically the same as the noun *water*. If we fail to see this point, we are very likely to mistake the underlined Chinese character 饭 (meaning 'to eat' and 'food' if taken out of its context) in (25) and 将 (meaning 'to lead' and 'general in the army' if taken out of its context) in (26) as Chinese grammatical metaphor:

(25) 廉 颇 老 矣，尚 能 <u>饭</u> 否?
      Lian Po old particle still can eat no
      Lian Po is old now. Can he still eat a lot?
(26) 韩 信 <u>将</u> 兵，多多 益善。
      Han Xin command soldiers, more better
      The more soldiers Han Xin leads, the better.

Compared with (23–26), the verbs in the following examples are even more confusing:

(27) to <u>baby</u> the car
(28) He <u>dogged</u> my steps all the way.

They are more confusing because the verb *to baby* in (27) is morphologically identical with the noun *baby* and the verb *dog* in (28) is morphologically the same as the noun *dog*. What is more important is that both (27) and (28) contain a metaphor. In (27) the metaphor is 'car is a baby' and in (28) it is 'he is a dog'. But we must point out that the metaphor here only occurs at the lexical level without any syntactic transformation. Therefore they should not be taken as grammatical metaphor.

10.5 Nominalization and verbalization compared

There are both similarities and differences between nominalization and verbalization.

They are similar in three aspects. First, they both result from the tension between lexicogrammar and discourse semantics. Second, they both make it possible for the language user to recategorize the world and construe human experiences and meanings in a new and different way. And third, they are often interwoven. That is to say, the use of nominalization can lead to the occurrence of verbalization and vice versa.

They are different in three aspects. First, information load: the incongruent forms containing nominalization tend to have fewer words than their corresponding congruent forms without fundamental changes of the information load. That is to say, nominalization has the function of condensing information. Second, explicit expression of the actor: nominalization can blur or conceal the actor of a process whereas the use of verbalization requires the explicit expression of the actor. Third, frequency of occurrence: nominalization is more frequently used than verbalization, especially in technical discourse (Halliday 1998b).

10.6 Coda

Twenty years have passed since Halliday put forward the concept of grammatical metaphor. We believe the following three issues deserve our attention in our future research on this topic. First, we need to look at grammatical metaphor from an epistemic perspective and take it as a way of construing the world rather than treat it purely as a syntactic variation. Second, we need to look at it from a systemic perspective and take it as the result of the tension between lexicogrammar and discourse semantics. Third, we need to look at it from a lexicogrammatical perspective and find out how grammatical metaphor is realized by nominalization and verbal-ization. If we ignore the first point, we will fail to see the significance of the research on grammatical metaphor. If we ignore the second point, we will fail to see the source of grammatical metaphor. And if we ignore the third point, we will fail to see the working mechanisms of grammatical metaphor. Only if we bear all these three points in mind can we make our research on grammatical metaphor more comprehensive and more insightful.

Note

This chapter is the English version of a paper with the same title published in Chinese in the second issue of *Waiyu Jiaoxue yu Yanjiu* (*Foreign Language Teaching and Research*) 2006.

References

Publications in English:

Butler, C. S. (1988), 'Politeness and the semantics of modalised directives in English', in J. Benson, M. Cummings and W. S. Greaves (eds), *Linguistics in a Systemic Perspective*. Amsterdam: Benjamins, pp. 119–53.

Butler, C. S. (1996), 'On the concept of an interpersonal metafunction in English', in M. Berry, C. S. Butler and R. P. Fawcett (eds), *Meaning and Choice in Language. Studies for Michael Halliday*. Vol. 2: *Grammatical Structure: A Functional Interpretation*. Norwood, NJ: Ablex.

Derewianka, B. (1995), 'Language Development in the Transition from Childhood to Adolescence: The Role of Grammatical Metaphor'. PhD thesis, Macquarie University.

Goatly, A. (1993), 'Species of metaphor in varieties of English', in M. Ghadessy (ed.), *Register Analysis: Theory and Practice*. London: Pinter, 110–48.

Goatly, A. (1995), 'Congruence and ideology. Or: Language and the myth of power. Or: Metaphors we die by. Or: Annihilating all that's made versus green thought', in *Social Semiotics*, 5.1: 23–63.

Goatly, A. (1997), *The Language of Metaphors*. London: Routledge.

Halliday, M. A. K. (1994 [1985]), *An Introduction to Functional Grammar*. London: Edward Arnold.

Halliday, M. A. K. (1996), 'Things and relations: Regrammaticizing experience as technical knowledge', in J. R. Martin and R. Veel (eds), *Reading Science: Critical and Functional Perspectives on Discourses of Science*. London: Routledge.

Halliday, M. A. K. (1992), 'How do you mean?', in M. Davies and L. Ravelli (eds), *Advances in Systemic Linguistics. Recent Theory and Practice*. New York: Pinter, pp. 21–35.

Halliday, M. A. K. (1993a), 'The act of meaning', in M. A. K. Halliday, *Language in a Changing World*. Toowoomba, Queensand: Applied Linguistics Association of Australia, pp. 42–61.

Halliday, M. A. K. (1993b), *Writing Science: Literacy and Discursive Power*. London: Falmer.

Halliday, M. A. K. (1996), 'On grammar and grammatics', in R. Hasan, C. Cloran and D. G. Butt (eds), *Functional Descriptions. Theory and Practice*. (Current Issues in Linguistic Theory, 121.) Amsterdam: Benjamins, pp. 1–38.

Halliday, M. A. K. (1997), 'The grammatical construction of scientific knowledge: The framing of the English clause', in R. Rossini, G. Sandri and R. Scazzeri (eds), *Incommensurability and Translation*. Cheltenham: Elgar.

Halliday, M. A. K. (1998a), 'Linguistics as metaphor', in A.-M. Simon-Vandenbergen, K. Davidse and D. Noël (eds), *Reconnecting Language. Morphology and Syntax in Functional Perspectives*. Amsterdam: Benjamins pp. 3–27.

Halliday, M. A. K. (1998b), 'Things and relations. Regrammaticising experience as technical knowledge', in J. R. Martin and R. Veel (eds), *Reading Science. Critical and Functional Perspectives on Discourses of Science*. London: Routledge, pp. 185–235.

Halliday, M. A. K. and Martin, J. R. (1993), *Writing Science: Literacy and Discursive Power*. London: Falmer.

Halliday, M. A. K. and Matthiessen, C. (2004), *An Introduction to Functional Grammar* [M]. London: Hodder.

Lemke, J. L. (1998), 'Resources for attitudinal meaning', in *Functions of Language*, 5.1: 33–56.

Martin, J. R. (1992), *English Text: System and Structure*. Amsterdam: Benjamins.

Martin, J. R. (1995), 'Interpersonal meaning, persuasion and public discourse: Packing semiotic punch'. *Australian Journal of Linguistics*. 15: 33–67.

Martin, J. R. (1997), 'Analysing genre: Functional parameters', in F. Christie and J. R. Martin (eds), *Genres and Institutions*. London: Cassell, pp. 3–39.

Martin, J. R. (forthcoming), 'Making meaning: the grammatical politics of symbolic control.'

Martin, J. R. and Matthiessen, C. (1990), 'Systemic typology and topology', in F. Christie (ed.), *Literacy in Social Processes*. Darwin: Centre for Studies of Language in Education, Northern Territory University, pp. 345–83.

Matthiessen, C. (1988), 'Representational issues in systemic functional grammar', in J. D. Benson and W. S. Greaves (eds), *Systemic Functional Approaches to Discourse*. (Advances in Discourse Processes, XXVI.) Norwood, NJ: Ablex, pp. 136–75.

Matthiessen, C. (1992), 'Interpreting the textual metafunction', in M. Davies and L. Ravelli (eds), *Advances in Systemic Linguistics. Recent Theory and Practice*. New York: Pinter, pp. 37–81.

Matthiessen, C. (1993), 'The object of study in cognitive science in relation to its construal and enactment in language', *Cultural Dynamics*, 6.1: 187–242.

Matthiessen, C. (1995a), 'Theme as an enabling resource in ideational "knowledge" construction', in M. Ghadessy (ed.), *Thematic Development in English Text*. (Open Linguistics Series.) London: Pinter, pp. 20–54.

Matthiessen, C. (1995b), *Lexicogrammatical Cartography: English Systems*. (Textbook Series in the Language Sciences.) Tokyo: International Language Sciences Publishers.

Matthiessen, C. (1998), 'Construing processes of consciousness. From the commonsense model to the uncommonsense model of cognitive science', in J. R. Martin and R. Veel (eds.), *Reading Science. Critical and Functional Perspectives on Discourses of Science.* London: Routledge, pp. 327–56.

Matthiessen, C. and Nesbitt, C. (1996), 'On the idea of theory-neutral descriptions', in R. Hasan, C. Cloran and D. G. Butt (eds), *Functional Descriptions. Theory in Practice.* (Current Issues in Linguistic Theory, 121.) Amsterdam: Benjamins.

Painter, C. (1993), 'Learning through Language. A Case Study in the Development of Language as a Resource for Learning from 2.5 to 5 Years'. PhD thesis, University of Sydney.

Quirk, R., Greenbaum, S., Leech, G. and Svartvik, J. (1985), *A Comprehensive Grammar of the English Language* [M]. London: Longman.

Ravelli, L. L. (1985), 'Metaphor, mode, and complexity: An exploration of co-varying patterns'. BA thesis, Department of Linguistics, University of Sydney.

Ravelli, L. L. (1998a), 'Making language accessible: Successful text writing for museum visitors'. *Linguistics and Education*, 8.4: 367–88.

Ravelli, L. L. (1998b), 'The consequences of choice: Discursive positioning in an art institution', in A. Sanchez-Macarro and R. Carter (eds), *Linguistic Choice Across Genres: Variation in Spoken and Written English.* Amsterdam: Benjamins, pp. 137–54.

Thibault, P. J. (1995), 'Mood and the ecosocial dynamics of semiotic exchange', in R. Hasan and P. H. Fries (eds), *On Subject and Theme. A Discourse Functional Perspective.* (Current Issues in Linguistic Theory, 118.) Amsterdam: Benjamins.

Publications in Chinese:

Dong Hongle (2005), *Metaphor in Technical Discourse.* Shanghai: Fudan University Press.

Hu Zhuanglin (1996), 'Grammatical metaphor'. *Foreign Language Teaching and Research*, No. 4.

Hu Zhuanglin *et al.* (2005), *An introduction to Systemic-Functional Linguistics.* Beijing: Beijing University Press.

Yan Shiqing (2000), *Metaphor Metaphorization, and Demetaphorization.* Suzhou: Suzhou University Press.

Zhu Yongsheng (1994), 'Grammatical metaphor in English'. *Foreign Languages*, No.4.

Zhu Yongsheng and Yan Shiqing. (1999), 'Motivation and contribution of the theory of grammatical metaphor'. *Foreign Language Teaching and Research*, No.4.

Zhu Yongsheng and Yan Shiqing (2001), *Reflections on Systemic Functional Linguistics.* Shanghai: Shanghai Foreign Language Education Press.

Index